ULL ITEM BARCODE

19 0685469 7

WITHDRAWN

Articles on Aristotle

Plato and Aristotle in dialectical debate, by Luca della Robbia, from the
Campanile del Duomo, Florence (photo Mansell Alinari)

Articles on Aristotle

3. Metaphysics

edited by

Jonathan Barnes
Malcolm Schofield
Richard Sorabji

Duckworth

SHL
WITHDRAWN

First published in 1979 by
Gerald Duckworth & Company Limited,
The Old Piano Factory
43 Gloucester Crescent, London NW1

© 1960, Studia Graeca et Latina Gothoburgensia; 1960, G. Patzig; 1971,
Martinus Nijhoff, The Hague; 1953 and 1976, The Aristotelian Society;
1970, *Archiv für Geschichte der Philosophie*; 1957, Societas Philosophiae
Fennica; 1966, *The Philosphical Review*; 1976, Ohio State University Press.

Editorial matter and arrangement © 1979
Gerald Duckworth & Company Limited

All rights reserved. No part of this publication may be reproduced, stored in a
retrieval system, or transmitted, in any form or by any means, electronic,
mechanical, photocopying, recording or otherwise, without the prior
permission of the publisher.

ISBN 0 7156 0901 7 cloth
     0 7156 0900 9 paper

British Library Cataloguing in Publication Data

Articles on Aristotle.
   3: Metaphysics.
   1. Aristotle – Addresses, essays, lectures
   I. Barnes, Jonathan   II. Schofield, Malcolm
   III. Sorabji, Richard
   185'.08   B485

   ISBN 0-7156-0901-7
   ISBN 0-7156-0900-9

518 off
D

Photoset by Specialised Offset Services Ltd, Liverpool
and printed in Great Britain by
Redwood Burn Limited, Trowbridge & Esher

SHL
WITHDRAWN

CONTENTS

Preface   vii

Abbreviations   xiii

1   *C.M. Gillespie*   The Aristotelian Categories   1

2   *G.E.L. Owen*   Logic and Metaphysics in Some Earlier Works   13
        of Aristotle

3   *G. Patzig*   Theology and Ontology in Aristotle's *Metaphysics*   33

4   *J. Lukasiewicz*   Aristotle on the Law of Contradiction   50

5   *J.M. LeBlond*   Aristotle on Definition   63

6   *Suzanne Mansion*   The Ontological Composition of Sensible   80
        Substances in Aristotle (*Metaphysics* VII 7-9)

7   *G.E.M. Anscombe*   The Principle of Individuation   88

8   *I. Mueller*   Aristotle on Geometrical Objects   96

9   *Jaakko Hintikka*   Necessity, Universality and Time in   108
        Aristotle

10 *Jaakko Hintikka*   Aristotelian Infinity   125

11 *G.E.L. Owen*   Aristotle on Time   140

12 *Richard Sorabji*   Aristotle on the Instant of Change   159

Bibliography   178

Index of Aristotelian passages   199

General index   211

PREFACE

In his *Metaphysics* Aristotle poses and answers some fundamental questions about what there is: what sorts of things are there? is there a primary kind of being? how are the other sorts related to it? what does its being consist in? These ontological problems have exerted a powerful attraction upon philosophers ever since Aristotle wrote; and his treatise largely determined what were to be reckoned as questions belonging to metaphysics for centuries to come. If nowadays metaphysics seems to cover a multitude of different enquiries, we can see some continuity and coherence among them, and we can get some sense of what the subject is, by going back to the first treatise to receive the name, the *Metaphysics* of Aristotle. However diverse their methods of investigation, and however disparate their proffered solutions, metaphysicians since Aristotle can be seen as answering the same basic questions.

Aristotle's approach does differ markedly from that of a philosopher like Descartes whose thinking is dominated by the question: 'What can I know with absolute certainty?' He is much readier to trust common sense, much keener to attend to distinctions implicit in the language we use to talk about things, as furnishing a guide to their nature. In this respect he has considerable appeal for many contemporary philosophers of the analytic tradition who share his ontological concerns, as well as for those of other traditions – as our third volume of articles on Aristotle testifies in an especially striking way. For in making our selection, we have found ourselves led to include essays from pupils of two great Aristotelian exegetes, Léon Robin and Augustin Mansion, and essays by philosophers from Germany, Poland, Scandinavia, Britain and the United States who see Aristotle through analytical spectacles. All these scholars share an enthusiasm for Aristotle's pre-Cartesian approach to metaphysics and for the subtle and powerful conceptual tools he devised for answering ontological questions. These, and not Aristotle's systematic solutions, are the common focus of this volume. The picture of Aristotle presented in it is in consequence not only a rich and coherent portrait but one very different from those available in the textbooks.

Our first three chapters constitute an introduction to the logical structure of Aristotle's metaphysics. In the *Categories* Aristotle made his first attempt to distinguish a basic entity (substance) from all the other kinds of entity. Chapter 1 considers how Aristotle arrived at the classification of entities given in the treatise. Gillespie stresses the influence which dialectical debate played in alerting Aristotle to the need to make distinctions between things of different sorts or categories, and he proposes a very commonsensical explanation of Aristotle's specific list of categories. In the *Metaphysics* Aristotle advances the thesis that all entities can be studied by means of a study of the basic entity (substance) to which the others are related. Chapter 2 explains how Aristotle, despite his characteristic insight into the ambiguity of the notion of being, was able to argue his thesis by connecting the various senses of 'being' to a single primary sense. Both Chapter 1 and 2 reveal the intimate connexion in Aristotle's philosophising between his thinking about the problems of being and his sensitivity to problems which would nowadays be conceived as belonging to the philosophy of language. At the apex of Aristotle's study of being stands the theology of Book XII of the *Metaphysics*. He seems to have believed that God was the entity which exhibited the characteristics of substance in their purest and most general form. In Chapter 3 Patzig explains this doctrine. He argues that Aristotle thought of other substances as related focally to a primary substance, God, who could consequently be made the subject of a study simultaneously special (theology) and general (the science of being – what Aristotle himself called first philosophy, his editors metaphysics).

Aristotle speaks of first philosophy as a *science* of being and substance. He held that sciences rely upon first principles, notably on axioms and definitions. Chapter 4 discusses the axiom of metaphysics to which Aristotle devotes most attention, viz. the principle of contradiction. It might be expected that Aristotle would present the idea that contradictory propositions cannot be true simultaneously primarily in the *Organon*, in his logic. But Lukasiewicz shows how it is for Aristotle principally an ontological axiom, which is construed as a general truth about all beings, or at least all eternal beings. He finds Aristotle's arguments for the principle invalid; but he suggests that although it is incapable of proof, it is nonetheless a valuable practical assumption. For it supplied Aristotle with a weapon against the scepticism of those who insisted that one and the same thing may be both hot and cold (if I feel the wind hot but you feel it cold). And it is our sole defence against error and falsehood: if it were not accepted, no-one falsely accused of murder could prove his innocence before a court. Chapter 5 presents a thorough survey of Aristotle's treatment of definition. As in Chapter 4, so here a criticism is made of Aristotle's theory. LeBlond judges Aristotle's statements concerning the role of definition in science inconsistent; and he finds his view that definitions express scientific intuitions unclear and unconvincing. LeBlond devotes special attention to the three kinds of definition which Aristotle uses: the statement of essence, definition by genus and differentia, and definition by matter and form.

Chapters 6 and 7 present discussions of Aristotle's most sustained attempt, found in *Metaphysics* VII, to answer the question 'What is substance?' Each concentrates on one of the complementary notions which lie at the heart of his conception of substance, Chapter 6 on form, Chapter 7 on matter. Mansion explains how Aristotle first decides that it is the form or essence of a thing which constitutes its being. She shows how he next turns to consider sensible substances, to explore the notion of form as it applies to them. Aristotle stresses its inseparability from their matter, and so is led naturally to consider whether definitions of such substances must contain reference to matter as well as to form. Anscombe's account of Aristotle's idea of matter shows why he could not allow matter simply to be substance, but nonetheless insisted that matter was what distinguished one sensible substance from another.

Aristotle firmly locates substances in the sensible world or in causal relation to it. He rejects the idea that mathematics studies a realm of objects separate from the sensible world, but he does not treat arithmetic and geometry as mere constructions of the human mind. Chapter 8 explains how Aristotle hopes to reconcile the claims of geometry as a scientific study of real things with his rejection of a separate realm of geometrical objects. Aristotle held that geometry studies sensible substances, but ignores all their properties except those which belong to them simply as geometrical solids. In working out this view he was led to an interesting extension of his idea of matter.

In *Metaphysics* VIII, IX and XII the notions of actuality and potentiality become increasingly important in Aristotle's further explorations of the notion of substance. He held that the idea of an actual substance was in many ways more fundamental than that of a potential substance; and that of all actual substances God was the most fundamental, inasmuch as God is without any potentiality for change whatsoever. Chapter 9 examines Aristotle's understanding of the relation between potentiality and actuality, and argues the controversial opinion that according to Aristotle every possibility is realised at some moment of time. This conception of possibility has been very influential in western philosophy. It still captivates some philosophers afresh, particularly metaphysicians fascinated by the logic of modalities. For such an interpretation of possibility provides an impetus to develop both modal logic and tense logic and to exhibit the links between them. In Chapter 10 Hintikka discusses whether the principle he attributes to Aristotle in Chapter 9 is compatible with Aristotle's theory of infinity in *Physics* III, which on the usual interpretation states that infinity has merely potential existence, but is never actualised. Hintikka offers a thorough reinterpretation, which adds to the analysis of the ontological status of the objects of geometry offered in Chapter 8.

Space and time soon came to be viewed as metaphysical topics in the western philosophical tradition. For they are evidently fundamental aspects of the sensible world. But does this mean that they are themselves primary sorts of being, or are they in some way dependent? Aristotle considered this question, like the analogous question about infinity, in his *Physics*, not his *Metaphysics*. But their metaphysical character has made it natural to include chapters on these topics in this volume. Chapter 11 is concerned principally to state and discuss the paradox of *Physics* IV, that while Aristotle recognised that moments are mere limits to stretches of time, he was simultaneously captive to the idea that identification of a 'now', an extensionless present moment, is the prerequisite of our understanding any talk of a period containing that now. Chapter 12 takes up another theme of Chapter 11, viz. the notion of motion at a moment or instant, with respect to the special case of an instant of change which Aristotle debates in *Physics* VI and VIII. Both articles clarify our appreciation of the relation between mathematical and physical descriptions of time and change.

Throughout our preparation, we have had the needs of students in mind, in particular students of philosophy who have little or no Greek, and little or no facility in French or German. This has led us to translate the continental

articles, and to translate or transliterate all Greek words. For ease of
reference, we have given in the margins the pagination of the books or
periodicals in which the articles originally appeared. As an introduction
and guide to further reading, we have supplied a fairly extensive
Bibliographie raisonnée at the end of the book.

We wish to thank authors and publishers who have so generously allowed
us to include copyright material, and who have cooperated with us so fully.
Acknowledgements are made as follows:

Chapter 1: *The Classical Quarterly*.

Chapter 2: Studia Graeca et Latina Gothoburgensia.

Chapter 3: The author.

Chapter 4: We were unable to trace the holder of the copyright.

Chapter 5: *Gregorianum*.

Chapter 6: Martinus Nijhoff, The Hague.

Chapters 7 and 12: The Editor of the Aristotelian Society.

Chapter 8: *Archiv für Geschichte der Philosophie*.

Chapter 9: Societas Philosophiae Fennica.

Chapter 10: *The Philosophical Review*.

Chapter 11: Ohio State University Press.

The essays were originally published as follows:

Chapter 1   C.M. Gillespie *The Aristotelian Categories*
The Classical Quarterly 19 (1925), pp. 75-84.
Chapter 2   G.E.L. Owen *Logic and Metaphysics in Some Earlier Works of Aristotle*
Originally published in *Aristotle and Plato in the Mid-Fourth Century*, ed. I.
    Düring and G.E.L. Owen, Göteborg 1960 (Studia Graeca et Latina
    Gothoburgensia XI), pp. 163-190.
Chapter 3   G. Patzig *Theology and Ontology in Aristotle's* Metaphysics
Originally published as 'Theologie und Ontologie in der "Metaphysik" des
    Aristoteles', in *Kant-Studien* 52 (1960/61), pp.185-205. It has been
    translated into English for the first time by Jennifer and Jonathan
    Barnes; the author has added a postscript.
Chapter 4   J. Lukasiewicz   *Aristotle on the Law of Contradiction*
Originally published as 'Uber den Satz des Widerspruchs bei Aristotles' in
    Bulletin International de l'Académie des Sciences de Cracovie, Cl. d'histoire et de
    philosophie, 1910. Translated into English by V. Wedin as 'On the
    principle of contradiction in Aristotle' in *The Review of Metaphysics* 24
    (1970/71), pp.485-509; retranslated here by Jonathan Barnes.
Chapter 5   J.M. LeBlond   *Aristotle on Definition*
Originally published as 'La définition chez Aristote', in *Gregorianum* 20
    (1939), pp.351-380. Translated here into English for the first time by
    Jennifer and Jonathan Barnes.
Chapter 6   S. Mansion   *The Ontological Composition of Sensible Substances in
    Aristotle* (Metaphysics *VII 7-9*)
Originally published as 'Sur la composition ontologique des substances
    sensibles chez Aristote (*Métaphysique Z 7-9*)', in *Philomathes: Studies and
    Essays in the Humanities in Memory of Philip Merlan*, ed. R.B. Palmer and R.
    Hamerton Kelly, The Hague 1971, pp.75-87. Translated here into
    English for the first time by Jennifer and Jonathan Barnes.

Chapter 7   G.E.M. Anscombe   *The Principle of Individuation*
Proceedings of the Aristotelian Society, Supplementary Volume 27 (1953), pp.83-96.

Chapter 8   I. Mueller   *Aristotle on Geometrical Objects*
Archiv für Geschichte der Philosophie 52 (1970), pp.156-171.

Chapter 9   J. Hintikka   *Necessity, Universality and Time in Aristotle*
Ajatus 20 (1957), pp.65-90. Some of the material used in the paper has been used in a revised form in the author's book, *Time and Necessity*, Oxford 1973, Chapter V.

Chapter 10   J. Hintikka   *Aristotelian Infinity*
Philosophical Review 75 (1966), pp.197-212; reprinted virtually intact in *Time and Necessity*, Chapter VI.

Chapter 11   G.E.L. Owen   *Aristotle on Time*
Originally published in *Motion and Time, Space and Matter: Interrelations in the History of Philosophy and Science*, ed. Peter Machamer and Robert Turnbull, and copyright © 1976 by the Ohio State University Press. All rights reserved. The essay is reprinted here by permission of the author, the editors, and the publisher.

Chapter 12   R.R.K. Sorabji   *Aristotle on the Instant of Change*
Proceedings of the Aristotelian Society, Supplementary Volume 50 (1976). This essay has been revised, and an appendix added.

ABBREVIATIONS

A.Pr.	*Analytica Priora*
A.Pst.	*Analytica Posteriora*
Ath. Resp.	*Atheniensium Respublica*
Cael.	*De Caelo*
Cat.	*Categoriae*
Col.	*De Coloribus*
De An.	*De Anima*
Div.	*De Divinatione per Somnum*
EE	*Ethica Eudemia*
EN	*Ethica Nicomachea*
Eud.	*Eudemus*
fr.	*Fragmenta*
GA	*De Generatione Animalium*
GC	*De Generatione et Corruptione*
HA	*Historia Animalium*
IA	*De Incessu Animalium*
Id.	*De Ideis*
Insom.	*De Insomniis*
Int.	*De Interpretatione*
Iuv.	*De Iuventute et Senectute,*
	De Vita et Morte
Lin. Insec.	*De Lineis Insecabilibus*
Long.	*De Longitudine et Brevitate Vitae*
MA	*De Motu Animalium*
Mech.	*Mechanica*
Mem.	*De Memoria et Reminiscentia*
Meta.	*Metaphysica*
Meteor.	*Meteorologica*
Mir.	*De Mirabilibus Auscultanionibus*
MM	*Magna Moralia*
MXG	*De Melisso, Xenophane et Gorgia*
Oec.	*Oeconomica*
PA	*De Partibus Animalium*
Phys.	*Physica*
Plant.	*De Plantis*
Poet.	*Poetica*
Pol.	*Politica*
Probl.	*Problemata*
Protr.	*Protrepticus*

Resp.	*De Respiratione*
Rhet.	*Rhetorica*
Rhet.ad	*Rhetorica ad Alexandrum*
Alex.	
S.El. (or	*De Sophisticis Elenchis*
Top. IX)	
Sens.	*De Sensu*
Som.	*De Somno et Vigilia*
Spir.	*De Spiritu*
Top.	*Topica*
Virt.	*De Virtutibus et Vitiis*

We follow the book and chapter numbers used in the Oxford translation of Aristotle. Page, column and line numbers are based on Bekker's edition of 1831.

1

C.M. Gillespie

The Aristotelian Categories

The precise position to be assigned to the Categories in the Aristotelian system has always been somewhat of a puzzle. On the one hand, they seem to be worked into the warp of its texture, as in the classification of change, and Aristotle can argue from the premiss that they constitute an exhaustive division of the kinds of Being (*A.Pst.* I 22, 83b15). On the other hand, both in the completed scheme of his logic and in his constructive metaphysic they retire into the background, giving place to other notions, such as causation, change, actuality and potentiality. Investigation, has, moreover, been hampered, especially in Germany, by attempts to correlate them with the Kantian Categories, with which they have obvious points of contact. But Kant's formal *a priori* concepts by which the mind makes for itself a world, to use Mr Bosanquet's phrase, imply an attitude to knowledge and reality so utterly opposed to the Aristotelian that the comparison has tended to confusion rather than elucidation. Scholars now realise better that the Aristotelian Categories can only be understood in connexion with the problems of Aristotle's own age.

The best general account of the Categories known to me is that given by Maier, who accepts the interpretation of Apelt in its main lines, correcting it in some important points.[1] It is the great merit of Apelt to have firmly grasped the principle that, whatever the applications to which Aristotle put the scheme of the Categories, it is primarily connected with the use of linguistic thought to make assertions about reality and hence with the proposition, the judgment as expressed in language. In details, I think, he is misled by the associations of post-Kantian logic, which prevent him from entering fully into the attitude adopted by the early Greek logic towards the fact of assertion.

In view of the undoubted fact that the scheme of the Categories follows the lines of Socratic-Platonic thought, Gercke's suggestion[2] is tempting that it originated in the Academy. Gercke, whose own view of the Categories is strongly coloured by Kantianism, relies almost entirely on the greater point given to the arguments in the *Ethics* against the Idea of the Good if we suppose them to accuse Plato of inconsistency with his own doctrine of the Categories. Except as supplementing strong independent evidence an argument of this kind carries no weight. The case is certainly weakened if it can be shown that Aristotle uses the Categories to solve a philosophical

---

1. H. Maier [106] II, pp.277 ff.; O. Apelt, *Beiträge zur Geschichte der griechischen Philosophie*, pp.106 ff.
2. A. Gercke, 'Ursprung der aristotelischen Kategorien', *A.G.P.* 4, 1891, pp.424 ff.

t opposition to the solution offered by the Academy. This
nk. In *Meta*. XIV 2, 1088b18 he sets the Categories against
. He is criticising the indefinite dyad, and traces the origin
n to 'their old-fashioned way of setting problems': the
it necessary to attack the Parmenidean dictum and
stence of 'what is not' (cf. Plato, *Sophist* 237A, 256D). But
how will tnis account for the plurality of being (for being means sometimes
substance, sometimes that it is of a certain quality, and at other times the
other categories: 1089a7)? In the corresponding passage of the *Physics* (I 2,
184b15 sqq.) Aristotle solves the Parmenidean difficulty through the
multiplicity of the Categories (186a25), and alludes to the inadequacy of the
Academic solution (187a1).

76   The inference to be drawn from these passages, in conjunction with the
chapter in the *Ethics* on which Gercke relies, is the negative one that Plato
and his successors in the Academy did not apply the scheme of the
Categories to the fundamental philosophical questions of Being and Good.
Positive evidence must be sought in another aspect of the doctrine. Now the
Topics exhibits the Categories in intimate association with dialectical logic.
The work itself purports to codify methods in regular use but not hitherto
systematically treated. That these methods were employed in the Academy
is amply attested by the Platonic dialogues.[3] Further, as the *Topics* and
particularly the *Sophistici Elenchi* show, they were developed in close
connexion with the eristic logic of Antisthenes and the Megarians. This fact
at once establishes a contact with the treatment of the problem 'one thing,
many names' in Plato's *Sophist* (251A). This difficulty was removed by
drawing a distinction between different kinds of being, and Aristotle himself
regards it as finally disposed of by the doctrine of the Categories. That some
of the kinds of being included in the scheme were already recognised in the
Academy is plain. In the *Topics* relatives have a number of their own *topoi*
and the varieties of relatives enumerated in the *Categories* follow closely on
the lines of division in the *Charmides*.[4] Much of the matter of the *Topics* must
have been common to Academy and Lyceum. But this is not to say that the
Categories as a complete and exhaustive scheme belonged to the Academy.
Eudemus tells us that Plato solved the difficulties of Lycophron and others
by a *dual* distinction of being.

I shall accordingly assume in what follows that the scheme of the
Categories was evolved in the course of efforts to establish a doctrine of
judgment which should settle the difficulties raised by Megarian and other
critics; that the application to the solution of the larger metaphysical
problems was a later development; that the foundations of the scheme were
laid in the Socratic tradition of the Academy; that the completed scheme is
probably Aristotle's own; and that the original working out of the scheme
did not contemplate extension beyond the metaphysics implied in
predication to the more fundamental metaphysics of the First Philosophy.
Hence we must look to the analysis of empirical propositions for the origin
of the scheme.

   3. Analysis of the arguments in the *Charmides* shows that nearly all make use of
topoi dealt with by Aristotle in the *Topics*.
   4. Cf. with *Cat*. 6a36 sqq., *Charmides*, 168A. The list in *Rep*. 437B is the same and
in the same order.

Now if we examine the scheme itself, we find three aspects of it to have special significance:

(*a*) The first is the distinction between accidental predication (*kata sumbebêkos*) and essential predication (*kath' hauto*).[5] What is musical may be literate, but only 'in virtue of something else' (*kat' allo*), viz.: *qua* Callias; Callias is literate essentially (*kath' hauton*). This distinction provides the first condition of scientific predication, and is regarded as of fundamental importance by Aristotle, who prefaces his accounts of such notions as unity and being with references to the accidental uses of these terms (*Meta.* V 6, 1015b16; 7, 1017a7).

(*b*) Closely connected with the previous distinction is the doctrine that all the Categories (including substance as predicate) imply a subject (*hupokeimenon*), which is the point of real connexion between the predicates, and provides the basis of their coexistence. The Categories classify the many 'names' which we apply to the individual (e.g. a man, *Sophist* 251A), and give expression to the fact that he does not lose his unity in the process.

(*c*) Furthermore, all direct relations of implication and incompatibility lie   **77** within the Categories severally. They are, so to say, independent variables. The relation of genus to species is everywhere confined within the limits of a category and so is the relation of contrary opposition. This suggests a close connexion with the Platonic division, which, as we know from the *Sophist* and the *Politicus* and from Aristotle, was so prominent in the Platonic conception of scientific method.

The intimate connexion between the Categories and the Predicables provides an invaluable clue to the meaning of the Categories. For in the *Topics* we are told that both of these schemes are the principal instruments in the equipment of the dialectician, and they are used in constant conjunction throughout the detailed discussions of that work.[6] Whether the extant treatise on the *Categories* be the work of Aristotle himself or of a later member of the Lyceum, the close general correspondence between its point of view and that of the *Topics* entitles us to use it as an authority for the official doctrine of the school.[7] Now the *Topics* is a practical manual of

---

5. See the distinction of 'being *kata sumbebêkos*' and 'being *kath' hauto*' (*Meta.* V 7, 1017a7 ff.). Apelt's equation of 'being *kath' hauto*' with 'being said in virtue of no combination' (*op.cit.* 117) is manifestly wrong. *Kath' ho* or *kath' hauto* means that the determination attaches to the subject in respect of the subject itself and not in respect of the determination. See *kath' ho* and *kath' hauto*, *Meta.* V 18, 1022a14 ff.

6. See *Topics* I 4-9, 101b11 ff. The predicables and the categories together constitute 'what the arguments are about and what they derive from', 103b39; the material has to be organised on this basis before it can be used in argument. The close correspondence between *Topics* and *Categories* is illustrated, *inter alia*, by the fact that the commonest *topoi* (those of 'more and less', and of 'opposites') are supplemented in the *Categories* by discussions how far these distinctions are to be recognised in several categories.

7. No satisfactory grounds for the rejection of the *Categories* have been adduced. The discrepancies with other works of the Corpus, e.g. the *Metaphysics*, are explicable on the hypothesis that this is an early work, of the same horizon as the *Topics*. The confusion between thought and verbal expression observable in some passages suggests immaturity of logical development.

Dialectic to be compared with the art of Rhetoric;[8] and internal evidence shows that the dialectical practices there codified are at least predominantly, if not exclusively, those of the Platonic tradition. We may, therefore, see a close connexion between the scheme of the Categories and the technique of the Platonic dialectic. This technique embodies the logic of the Academy in large measure, and was the forerunner of the Aristotelian syllogism, leaving its clearly discernible traces in the scientific syllogism of the *Posterior Analytics*.

If we are to understand the dialectical logic, we must bear in mind that it was developed in connexion with the practice of dialectical discussion, which demanded rules of debate so that it should not lapse into aimless conversation. Some of these rules determined the procedure, such as those which defined the privileges and duties of questioner and answerer.[9] Others were of a more strictly logical nature. But this logic was clothed in the dress appropriate to the occasion, and logical distinctions themselves were drawn in a form close to the untechnical speech of everyday life. Thus in Plato definition is simply the answer to the question 'What is it?', carefully limited; the technical name for the process, *horismos*, seems of later date. The ancient commentators on the *Categories* distinguished three relations as implied in the logical judgment: (1) A relation asserted between things; (2) a relation between the terms as verbal signs; (3) a relation between ideas in the mind of him who forms the judgment. These three relations were in ancient times regarded as parallel. The third is recognised by Aristotle as a 'combination of thoughts', but is treated merely as a 'psychological presupposition'[10] of the logical proposition or judgment as expressed in words, which is the subject of logical analysis. So in Plato thought is described as inner speech (*Sophist* 263A). Moreover, as the relation in thought tends to be merged in the relation in language, so the latter tends to have incorporated in it objective relations between things. The formal analysis of proposition and syllogism in the *Prior Analytics* uses the logical term mainly in its aspect of class-denotation; but we do not hear of logical terms in the *Topics*, which represents a less developed stage of logical analysis. There subjects and predicates are distinguished according to the real relations between things which are classified in the schemes of the Categories and the Predicables. The analysis contained in the *Prior Analytics* presupposes the use of symbols and diagrams; the earlier analysis is one that would develop in the process of dialectical discussion, with a marked emphasis on the vital importance of definition. Its nomenclature starts from the simple distinction between names (*onomata*) and things (*pragmata*). At the outset the proposition seems to have been considered as primarily giving

8. *S.El.* 183b25 alludes to the arts of Tisias and other rhetors, and claims to be doing for Dialectic what they did for Rhetoric.

9. The sixth book of the *Topics* lays down the etiquette for questioner and answerer: the treatment implies a strict separation of these rôles. The complaint of Thrasymachus in *Republic* 337A that Socrates will ask, but not answer, questions may perhaps point to a convention established in the Socratic schools.

10. The phrase is Meinong's. Meinong's *Gegenstandstheorie* is useful in its recurrence to the thoroughly objective and realistic attitude towards knowledge which distinguishes ancient from most modern thought.

two names to one thing.[11]

The development of the complementary schemes of Categories and Predicables seems to have been determined partly by the necessity of overcoming difficulties arising from the application of Eleatic and quasi-Heraclitean principles in the domain of knowledge, partly by the original orientation of the Socratic methodology.

The possibility of rational discussion was challenged in the name of strict logic itself. How can I give more than one name to one thing? A thing *is* itself, and not anything else. So I may rationally say 'man is man' and 'white is white'; but I cannot say 'man is white' without an equivocation in the use of the verb to be (*Soph.* 251A; cf. *Meta.* V 29, 1024b32). This Eleatising objection can only be met by an appeal to experience, like the Parmenidean rejection of the plurality of existence. Experience shows that within certain limits many names may be applied to one and the same thing without destroying its concrete unity. In accordance with this fact another kind of 'being' must be assumed. The systematic development of this point of view results in the scheme of the Categories.

Rational discussion was equally imperilled by the tendency of an infant logic to confuse names with things and grammatical forms with logical meanings, and so justify all sorts of absurd inferences. What the trivially ingenious minds of the Greek eristics could do in this line we know from the *Euthydemus* and the *Sophistici Elenchi*. If the doctrine of Antisthenes reduced the area of significant predication to so small a compass that all contradiction disappeared, so this other tendency removed all criteria of truth and falsehood. To meet a laxity of thinking which allowed (e.g.) the inference that if Socrates is both Socrates and a man, he is other than himself (see *S.El.* 166b32) it was necessary to limit systematically the conditions of mutual implication.

The double scheme of Categories and Predicables as a whole centres round the Socratic question 'What is it?'. According to the Socratic method you can only answer the question 'Can virtue (*aretê*) be taught or not?' when you have defined the term *aretê* (*Meno* 70A). Definition implies the analysis of species into genus and differentia; but being teachable is not related to *aretê* in either of these ways – how then is it related to *aretê*? The answer to **79** this question completes the list of the Predicables. The *Topics*, which embodies the point of view of dialectical logic, is so dominated by the system of the Predicables as to represent organised knowledge in a totally different light from the *Prior Analytics*. That work seems to aim at a progressive series of syllogisms after the manner of Euclid, whereas the *Topics* sets up as its goal the systematisation of all possible predicates of one and the same subject. Both subject and predicate are thought of objectively in terms of the

11. The term *katêgoria* in its specially technical sense of Category goes back to this early way of regarding the judgment. As Maier shows (against Apelt) II, p.304n, it primarily expresses, not the relation of predicate term to subject term in the SP proposition of the *Prior Analytics*, but the relation of the *onoma* to its objects. But Maier himself looks at the matter through modern spectacles; he writes: 'Das Wort ist *katêgoria*, sofern als Prädikat seiner Bedeutung, seines Begriffs.' This is too sophisticated for a primitive logic. Adam gave names to things, not to meanings; these things have natures of their own, signified by the name. It is wise to avoid speaking of concepts and Begriffe in connexion with Plato and Aristotle.

objects signified, not in terms of the signs, as things and their modifications, their qualities and their behaviour.

The *Topics* and the Platonic dialogues point to an early dialectical logic, realistic in its general attitude and terminology, the traces of which will survive in the more highly developed system of Aristotelian logic. This dialectical logic works with four fundamental notions: (1) The *pragma* or thing in its empirical setting, of which (2) the *onoma* is the verbal sign; (3) the *ousia* or essence of the thing, the thing as it is for analytical thought, of which (4) the *logos*, or *logos tês ousias*, the defining formula, is the sign in speech. The quadruple distinction is explicitly stated in Plato's *Laws*, appears again and again in the Platonic dialogues, and is not wholly superseded in the developed logic of Aristotle.[12] Its influence may be traced in Aristotle's doctrine of definition. In modern formal logic the definition would be resolved into a proposition with a convertible predicate attached to the subject by the copula. But Aristotle distinguishes the 'is' of definition from the copula of the ordinary proposition: the latter implies that you predicate one thing of another (*ti kata tinos*); but in 'Man is an animal' or 'Man is a twofooted animal' the 'is' does not imply *ti kata tinos* because *twofooted animal* is really part of the *pragma*, because part of its *ousia*. For the same reason the quality (*poion*) of the differentia of anything in the category of *ousia* is properly treated under *ousia* and not under the category of quality.[13]

The objective and material character of the early dialectical logic and its preoccupation with names is well exhibited in the use made by the *Topics* of inherent relations between terms – e.g. similarity and contrariety. The attention of the early logicians was turned to the mutual relations of implication or incompatibility implied directly or indirectly by certain terms. The abstract investigation of the relations between three terms ABC contained in the *Prior Analytics* belongs to a later stage of logical development. The Aristotelian treatment of opposition is instructive in this regard. Of the four varieties enumerated, three – viz. relation, contrariety, possession and privation – are expressed in terms, and only the fourth, contradiction, deals with propositions as such. Dialectic was a material logic, using certain common notions as science now uses the notions of cause or function (*Cat.* 11b16; *Meta.* V 10, 1018a20).

If we regard it as established that the Categories as a scheme were

12. *Laws* 895D: 'Would you not admit that we can think of three things about each thing (*hekaston*)? ... One is its *ousia*, one the *logos tês ousias*, one the *onoma*.' The fourth term, *pragma*, is given in *hekaston*.

13. There is a curious passage in *Topics* II, 1, 109a10, which seems to retain a vestige of a primitive treatment of predication as giving two names to one thing: 'It is very difficult to convert (*antistrephein*) an appropriate nomenclature (*oikeia onomasia*) derived from an accident. For only in the case of accidents can something be predicated in a certain respect and not universally.' *Antistrephein* here does not mean the convertibility of S and P in extension, as in the *Prior Analytics*. It means the interchangeability of the expressions '*B* belongs to *A*' and '*A* is *B*': in definition they are convertible, for 'Being a twofooted animal belongs to *A*' is equivalent to '*A* is a twofooted animal'; but 'Whiteness belongs to *A*' does not imply '*A* is white', for he may be white only in a certain respect – e.g. in the eyeballs. The phrase *oikeia onomasia* recalls the *oikeios logos* of Antisthenes (*Meta.* V 29, 1024b32).

developed from the motives above indicated, the question awaits us, why precisely these ten Categories?

The omission of motion (*kinêsis*) as a separate category has troubled those critics who, under the influence of Kantian ideas or the position of *stasis* and *kinêsis* in Plato's *Sophist*, sought to find in the scheme a classification of primary cosmogonic concepts. But its omission is no more unintelligible than that of causation. For in change is implied something that changes and has successively opposing predicates attached to it. The representation of becoming requires two propositions about being. In point of fact, the scheme provides for an exhaustive classification of change from its own standpoint.

80

Trendelenburg's suggestion that the grammatical parts of speech had at least a considerable influence in determining the details of the scheme has been unduly depreciated by later writers. The account of the category of relation especially shows that grammatical expression was prominent in the minds of those who invented the scheme; and Aristotle himself has to warn his readers that grammatical form may be a misleading guide in assigning a term to its proper category.[14] The *Cratylus* and the *Topics* supply abundant evidence that the first workers in the field of logic had great difficulty in disentangling logical meaning from verbal expression. The suggestion does not carry us very far; but inasmuch as it connects the scheme with the somewhat pedestrian task of clearing up elementary obscurities in the ordinary use of thought, and not with any ambitious attempt to find a formula for the universe, Trendelenburg was on the right track.

The suggestion thrown out by several writers that the number ten is due to Pythagorising influences appears to me baseless. It is impossible to link up the scheme with the list of ten pairs of contraries attributed by Aristotle to some of the Pythagoreans (*Meta*. I 5, 986a22). Aristotle's own list of opposites lies within the several categories (*GC* I 3, 319a14; *Meta*. IV 2, 1004b27). Moreover, the scheme seems remote from the Pythagorean aspect of the Platonic philosophy, and belongs rather to the Socratic dialectic.

The most promising line of investigation lies in examining the examples of the several categories given in the detailed list of the *Categories*. Further illustration comes from the uses to which the scheme is put in the *Topics*; for if it owes its origin to the logical analysis of predication, its primary meaning is to be sought in such passages rather than in those where it is extended to scientific and philosophical questions.

Now if we take the list of examples given in the *Categories*, we find that the subject of which they are all asserted can only be an individual man, naturally designated by a proper name – Socrates, Callias, Coriscus. *Cat*. 4, 1b27 ff.: 'To give a rough idea, examples of substance are man, horse; of quantity: four-foot, five-foot; of quality: white, literate; of relatives: double, half, larger; of where: in the Lyceum, in the market-place; of when: yesterday, last year; of position: is-lying, is-sitting; of having: has-shoes-on, has-armour-on; of doing: cutting, burning; of being-affected: being-cut, being-burned.' This is the only list of examples extant, and, if it stood alone,

---

14. *S. El.* 166b16: 'E.g. *being-healthy* (*hugiainein*) has the same linguistic form as *cutting* or *building*; yet it signifies a quality or disposition while they signify a producing.'

8   *C.M. Gillespie*

might reasonably be regarded simply as one selected for the purposes of
elementary exposition. But it does not stand alone; there are many passages
which give this fact a deeper significance.

As we have seen, the distinction of *kata sumbebêkos* and *kath' hauto* is
intimately connected with the scheme of the Categories. Aristotle is fond of
prefixing to his accounts of the scientific uses of terms some instances of
their use in an accidental sense. It will be found that these instances are
usually of the same type, implying an individual man as subject. Thus in
Meta. V 2, 1013b34 ff., the accidental use of *aition* ('explanation' or 'cause')
is illustrated by the terms *Polycleitus, sculptor, man, animal, white thing, musical
thing*; at 6, 1015b16 ff., *hen* ('one') is illustrated by *Coriscus, musical thing, just
thing*; at 7, 1017a7 ff., *on* ('being') is illustrated by *man, builder, just thing,
musical thing*. Many other examples might be added.

Similarly it will be found that a favourite type of proposition used to
illustrate fallacies in the *Sophistici Elenchi* is that in which the subject is a
proper name.

If, again, we turn to the passage in Plato's *Sophist* where the question is
raised how one thing can have many names (251A), the example is the
individual man. Later on in the same dialogue, where the simple
proposition is analysed, the examples chosen are 'Theaetetus is sitting',
'Theaetetus is flying' (263A).

These passages furnish a basis on which to build. I put forward the
hypothesis that the scheme was built up by an investigation, gradually
becoming more systematic, into types of predicates which could be attached
to one and the same subject at one and the same time. It was built up in
dialectical discussion, and by a convention (students of Greek methods will
have no difficulty in admitting the probability of a convention in this
connexion) one of the company was chosen as the example (as in *Sophist*
l.c.). Observe that the typical proper names used in logical examples in the
Topics and other Aristotelian works tend to be taken from the Socratic-
Platonic circles – Socrates himself, Callias the art-patron of the *Protagoras*,
Coriscus the Academician.[15] The choice of the individual man as subject is
not to be considered fortuitous. For only in the case of human beings was
the proper name in use, and the proper name as such as a mere label
attached to a 'this' and directly implying no 'what', so that it is normally
subject and not predicate. To refute the critic who denied that many
predicates could be asserted of the same thing it was necessary to develop
the scheme with an identical subject throughout. The *Categories* show that
the official exposition of the scheme in the Lyceum took Socrates or Callias
or Coriscus as subject, and worked through the list on this basis. Moreover,
as the most complete, the most concrete object known, a human being
would be most suitable for developing an exhaustive scheme of predication,
since to him alone could moral and many psychological predicates attach.

If the scheme is considered in reference to such a subject as Callias, we
can see something of a serial order in it; for though Aristotle does not always
enumerate the Categories in the same order, still there is a sort of average

15. Jaeger [28], p.116, suggests that the use of Coriscus' name as a school-example
probably goes back to the time, soon after the death of Plato, when Aristotle,
Coriscus, and other Academicians sojourned at Assus.

order. First we have the predicates describing him as a whole in the category of substance. Then a group describing certain qualitative and quantitative aspects of him as he is in himself. To these have to be added some aspects implying determinate relations to others; thus *father* at first sight might seem a substantive predicate, but if it is so regarded or treated as implying an indeterminate correlative, as in some of the eristic quibbles (e.g., *Euthydemus* 298B), absurdities follow. Then come two variable relations to the world around, in place and time: these have to be added in order to meet such sophistical interpretations of 'The sick man is healthy' as imply that health and illness are not incompatible, for if implicit time-qualifications are inserted, the proposition becomes 'The then sick man is now healthy' and the contradiction disappears. Then, again, Callias as a complex body can vary the position of his limbs relatively to each other and to the outer space. In a certain extended sense Callias includes all that he calls *his*, things that from another standpoint are outside him, his possessions, and specially the clothes he is wearing, and the instruments he is using. Lastly, his relations with determinate things in the environment are those of agent or patient: as surgeon he uses knife or cautery, as patient he has these used upon his body. Thus in connexion with Callias the Categories present in a systematised and exhaustive form our idea of Callias as a concrete being, a going concern in a changing environment.

This hypothesis, that the scheme was originally developed in connexion 82 with an individual name as the typical subject, seems to provide a satisfactory explanation of some of the difficulties and anomalies of the list.

Two of the Categories, position and possession, have always been a great stumbling block in the way of interpretation. They are never explicitly mentioned except in the complete list of the *Categories* and that of the *Topics*, both of which treatises belong to the same plane of thought. The ancient commentators had apparently no information about them beyond what is contained in the *Categories* and book V of the *Metaphysics*. As regards their content, the fundamental difficulty is this: all the other categories can be applied quite intelligibly to other objects than men, and are so far free to be used as universal aspects of being. But these two categories in respect of the examples given in illustration include only states peculiar to men: position in its examples is simply 'posture' (rather like *schêma* in the medical treatises), standing, sitting, reclining; while possession means wearing shoes or carrying armour.

We have no real evidence for the use of these terms *as categories* in a generalised sense. Position is capable of extension to any material object in space: the cup may lie the right way up or on its side or upside down, irrespective of its place as a whole (covered by the category of 'where'). But I know of no evidence that such determinations would be included by Aristotle under the category. The position of the stone relatively to the framework of the door determines whether it is to be called lintel or threshold: they differ in position (*Meta.* VIII 2, 1042b19). Position is part of the idea, just as time forms part of the idea of opportunity: the analogy suggests that Aristotle is here thinking of the category of position. But ultimately these distinctions can be resolved into spatial relations, and in any case they do not carry the implications that standing, sitting, and reclining have for human life.

As regards possessing (*echein*), we have accounts of possession and disposition in book V of the *Metaphysics*. Possession is treated immediately after disposition, and both these terms are recognised in the *Categories* and elsewhere (*Cat.* 8b26) as qualities. But before this common sense of possession (*hexis*), the verbal noun correlative with the intransitive meaning of *echein*, the writer notices a use connected with the transitive meaning of the verb: 'We call a possession in one sense what is as it were a certain functioning of the possessor and possessed, like a certain action or change. For whenever one thing produces and another is produced, there is producing between them; just so, there is possession between the possessor of clothes and the clothes possessed. Evidently, it is not possible to possess this kind of possession; for it will go on *ad infinitum* if it is possible to possess a possession of what is possessed' (*Meta.* V 20, 1022b4 ff.). The last words are added in order to contrast this sort of possession with possession as formed faculty, since you can say 'he possesses virtue'; and as possession in the latter sense comes under quality, the writer may be thinking of the category of *echein*. Now this transitive sense of possession is unusual; Liddell and Scott contains no examples except this one in Aristotle and several from Plato.[16] One of these seems to have some bearing on the present subject. In *Theaetetus* 197B a careful distinction is drawn between acquisition (*ktêsis*) and possession. Knowing has been defined, says Socrates, as 'possession of knowledge', but he prefers 'acquisition of knowledge': 'Now to have acquired and to possess do not seem to me to be the same thing; for example, if someone has bought a cloak and owns it but doesn't wear it, we should say that he doesn't possess it but that he has acquired it.' Possessing is *wearing* clothes in contrast with merely possessing them. So in *Laws* 625C the 'possession of arms' means the *carrying* of arms. When Aristotle describes the active possession as a functioning, has he similarly in mind the actuality of wearing the clothes as contrasted with the potentiality of mere possession?

In V 23, 1023a8 ff., various meanings of the verb *echein* are noted. The first includes the case of dress, and apparently seeks to generalise it: 'in one sense it is directing a thing according to one's own nature or according to one's own inclination – that is why fever is said to possess a man, and tyrants cities, and wearers clothes.' The wording of the definition seems evolved in parallelism with the fourth sense of holding or supporting: 'Again, what prevents something from changing or acting according to its own inclination is said to possess that thing, as columns their overlying weight'. Other meanings enumerated are the containing of the form by the matter or receptacle, as the brass contains the form of the statue and the body contains disease, and the containing of the water by the vessel or the population by the city. The common idea found by Aristotle in the examples under the first head is active possession or, more briefly, use, and there is thus a close connexion between this *echein* and the 'possession' of the *Theaetetus*. Both appear brought into conjunction with the Category through the common examples.

I suggest that this is precisely what was meant by the original Category of

16. Ross [4] I, p.336, gives the following examples: *Meta.* 1055b13; *Resp.* 474a26; *IA* 711a6; Plato, *Rep.* 433E12; *Crat.* 414B9; *Theaet.* 197B1; *Soph.* 247A5; *Laws* 625C.

echein. In running through the various items composing your idea of a man, you find one essential to civilised man and not shared by any other creature – viz. the use of artefacta, clothes, arms, instruments. This forms a unique class of activities or bases of activities. In course of time the scheme was put to new uses. From being a sort of working classification of predicates used in connexion with dialectical propaedeutic it came to be a groundwork of scientific logic and method, as in the classification of changes in terms of the four relevant categories. Hence the two categories position and possession, which were directly applicable only to mankind, were quietly dropped, or at least relegated to the background.

The hypothesis that the scheme originated in connexion with dialectical discussion accounts for another important feature of it, the nomenclature. For it is to be observed that six of the categories, all those that are not normally expressed by verbs, have names *implying answers to questions. How much* (i.e. quantity), *of what sort* (quality), *where* and *when* are obvious. In the category of relatives a predicate only becomes precise when the question 'Double what?' 'Slave of whom?' 'Similar to what?' is answered. The category of substance is frequently denominated 'the what?'[17] This has no connexion with the 'What is it?' of definition (itself another example of the derivation of technical terms from questions), for that requires a universal as subject.[18] It is to be correlated with the common question, 'what is Socrates?' as distinguished from such questions as 'what is he like?' 'how tall is he?' As the names are derived from specific forms of question the inference is irresistible that the scheme originated in dialectical practice. We may compare the change in the technical meaning of *protasis*, which is the name for a dialectical question in the *Topics* and becomes the name of a logical proposition in the *Prior Analytics* (*Top.* I 10, 104a8; *A.Pr.* I 1, 24a16).

If the scheme of the Categories had the origin suggested in this paper, we can see that it had no immediate connexion with the Platonic 'greatest kinds' of same and different, rest and motion. These distinctions cover the whole field of existence and knowledge. Sameness and difference are the fundamental features of things regarded from the standpoint of knowledge; they are worked out in classification; but they cannot be Categories, because these are in the last resort a detailed account of the differences to be recognised within an empirical subject, so that the distinction of sameness and difference is a condition of the scheme as a whole. Rest and motion are factors of the universe on the side of reality: from the standpoint of the Categories they imply successive predications of states and positions of the subject.

Moreover, they have nothing to do with the metaphysical question of the ultimate nature of the universal, though they fully recognise its logical validity. In fact some of Plato's characteristic arguments to prove that the universal is distinct from the particular imply some of the essential features of the analysis worked out in the system of the Categories. For the primary distinction between the particular beautiful things and the beautiful is that the former are beautiful *pragmata*, which as *pragmata* have natures of their own as faces, men, actions, etc., but partake in the beauty which is

17. See the table in Apelt, *op. cit.*, p.140.
18. So Maier, as against Apelt, [106] II, p.309n.

84

empirically realised only as an aspect of them.

As may be seen, my case proceeds from the assumption that no explanation of the origin of the Categories is satisfactory unless it accounts for the inclusion of position and possession in the full list, combined with the total absence of reference to them as Categories in any other passage. Hence the only direct evidence that we have for their meaning is the examples given of them in the *Categories*. In both cases the examples seem to imply highly specialised predicates. Position is applicable only to complex animal bodies, with mobile limbs controlled by voluntary effort: possession is applied only to the highest type of animal, having intelligence to make and use clothes and tools for the convenience of life. No other Category is so specialised: the other two dealing with behaviour, viz.: action and passion, can be generalised, though of course they take special forms in mankind. Hence it is intelligible that when the Categories are mentioned, those applicable only to certain limited classes of subjects should be omitted. Assume that these two Categories are specialised in the sense indicated: bear in mind that the usual subject in illustration is the individual man: observe that the complete list of the *Categories* with the examples given aims at supplying an exhaustive classification of the manifold aspects of man as a concrete going concern: then the conclusion seems natural that the scheme in its original intention was built up round the idea of the individual man. It is no objection to this reading of the scheme that Aristotle treats the list as exhaustive, so that we must find a universal meaning for every Category: if the Categories of Aristotle were the Kantian categories, then each must be applicable to any object whatever: but the Platonic-Aristotelian world is divided into things of an ascending order of completeness, and some kinds of predicates can only be attached to the higher orders of existence. I do not claim that these two Categories were confined entirely to predicates of the types given in the examples of the list in the *Categories*; for in the detailed analysis of, e.g., Relation and Quality, many varieties are dealt with which do not appear in the corresponding accounts in the list. That these two Categories also were generalised so as to apply to other objects than human beings I do not doubt; what I argue is that their fundamental ideas were such that in a general survey of the modifications of things they had little importance, and so fell into the background.

If my general conclusion is established, that Category and Predicable together constitute a joint system of preparing the material for formal dialectical discussion, that this system grew up in the Platonic school as the representative of Socratic methodology and was completed by Aristotle, that systematised dialectical rules were the forerunner of the Aristotelian logic – if this is a correct reading of the historical evidence, it follows that Category and Predicable together may be expected to form the substructure of the logic of Aristotle, especially the scientific logic. Or, to express the same meaning in another metaphor, that in the Aristotelian system the raw material of experience should be given a form through the ideas of predicable and category as a preliminary to the building of the larger structures of scientific knowledge, just as the clay must be made into bricks before it can be used by the builder. At some later opportunity I hope to show that the most characteristic features of Aristotle's logic of science can be accounted for on these lines.

2

G.E.L. Owen

Logic and Metaphysics in Some Earlier Works of Aristotle

Much of Aristotle's early work in logic sprang from the practice and discussions of the Academy in Plato's lifetime. This is a commonplace, but I have tried to illustrate it here by evidence which throws an unfamiliar light on the development of some of Aristotle's most characteristic theories. The commonplace itself is not to be confused with a narrower thesis about the origins of the theory of syllogism: on that well-worn issue I have nothing to say here. I have confined myself to another part of Aristotle's logical studies, namely that part which shaped his views on the nature and possibility of any general science of *to on hêi on* ('being *qua* being'), any inquiry into the general nature of what there is. Here his major issues were problems of ambiguity, particularly the ambiguity that he claimed to find in 'being' or *to on* as that expression is used in the different categories. And his problems were shared by his contemporaries in the Academy. By opposition and by suggestion they helped to form the logic that underlay First Philosophy.

There is a justly famous picture of Aristotle's development to which I must try to relate my argument. According to this picture, Aristotle remained for many years after Plato's death wedded to the project of constructing a 'Platonic' mistress-science of metaphysics. Only later, as this Platonic period fell further behind him, did he turn to concentrate his attention on the departmental sciences. When he wrote *Metaphysics* IV, no less than when he had written the *Protrepticus* and the *Eudemian Ethics*, he could still see himself as the 'Erneuerer der übersinnlichen Philosophie Platons' (although by now he had reformed his inheritance to the extent of discarding the transcendent Forms, and so leaving only God as the object of the study). But – according to this same account – in *Metaphysics* IV a new interest has crept in beside the old. For now Aristotle tries to find room for a second and very different inquiry under the old rubric of 'First Philosophy', an inquiry that is not 'Platonic' but essentially Aristotelian: the general study of being, *tou ontos hêi on*.[1]

The evidence I have to discuss does not wholly square with this account. It seems to show that when Aristotle wrote *Metaphysics* IV he had returned to, or newly arrived at, a belief in the possibility of a general metaphysics after a period in which he had denounced any such project as logically indefensible and castigated Plato and the Academy for pursuing it. It was in this period that for reasons of logic he confined his interest to the special sciences (of which theology was one). It was in this period that he wrote,

---

1. Jaeger [28], chs. viii and xiii: 'reviver of Plato's supersensible philosophy', p. 339.

inter alia, the whole or the most part of the *Organon*, the *Eudemian Ethics*, and the polemic against the Academy; and his attitude at the time to a Platonic mistress-science must surely be gathered from that polemic at least as much as from his continuing interest in the special science of theology. Seen in this perspective the kind of inquiry that is introduced in the fourth book of the *Metaphysics* looks more like a revival of sympathy with Plato's aims (or what Aristotle took to be those aims) than like a new departure from them.

Ambiguity and the attack on metaphysics

'In general', says Aristotle in *Metaphysics* I 9, 'it is fruitless to look for the elements of all the things there are without distinguishing the different senses in which things are said to be' (992b18-24). This interest in ambiguity was shared by others in the Academy. Speusippus as well as Aristotle set up criteria for synonymy and homonymy.[2] And we can hear a general debate behind the remark in the *Sophistici Elenchi* that, while some cases of homonymy deceive no one, some seem to elude even the experts, since they often quarrel over such words as 'one' and 'being': some hold that the words have a single meaning in all their applications, others refute the Eleatics by denying this (182b13-27). Aristotle was one of those who denied this. In his view, *to be* was *to be something or other*: for a threshold, he says, 'to be' means 'to have such and such a position', for ice it means 'to have solidified in such and such a way'.[3] And, at the level of greatest generality, to be is to be either a substance of some sort or a relation or a quality or a member of some other category. There is no general sense to the claim that something exists over and above one of the particular senses.

That this dispute over the ambiguity of 'being' and 'one' took some of its impetus from the *Parmenides* and the *Sophist* can hardly be doubted. That it was more than a lexical diversion is proved by many of Aristotle's major arguments, and particularly by those which, like the objection already quoted, were aimed at the Platonists. One of the most remarkable of these forms part of the polemic against the Academy in the first book of the *Eudemian Ethics*.[4] In it Aristotle argues that, since 'being' and 'good' have

2. Boethus apud Simplic., *Cat.* 38.19-39.9, 36.28-31 (cf. Hambruch, *Logische Regeln der plat. Schule*, pp. 27-9).

3. *Meta.* 1042b25-8, cf. *De An.* 415b12-15. This is not to deny the distinction between *einai ti* and *einai haplôs*. For the essential link see e.g. *Meta.* 1028a29-31, *A.Pst.* 73b5-8 and n.16. To be *haplôs* is to be a substance, for substance is what a thing is *kath' hauto*.

4. I find myself unpersuaded by arguments brought against the substantial authenticity of the *Eudemian Ethics* (e.g. recently by Schaecher, *Studien zu den Ethiken des Corpus Aristotelicum* II, Paderborn 1940). The passages in *EE* where older critics discerned the tidying and supplementing hand of an editor tell the other way. The man who wanted the throat of a crane is given his name and patronymic in *EE* (1231a17) but not in *EN* (1118a32): no editor ferreted out this piece of news – it was dropped between the two works. Similarly though less obviously with the quotation from Heraclitus (*EE* 1223b22-4, *EN* 1105a7-8). And the more schematic treatment of *prohairesis* and *orexis* in *EE* (1223a26-7, 1225b22-4) is not an editor's improvement on the looser account in *EN* (1111b10-12) but the plan presupposed by that account. As will appear, the inferences that I draw from the polemic in *EE* could equally be drawn from texts in the Corpus whose authenticity is beyond quibble. But this too confirms the bona fides of the *Eudemian Ethics*.

different senses in the different categories, there can be no unitary science of **166** either being or the good;[5] and he adds later that a science can study only some *idion agathon*, 'special good' (1218a34-6) – or, by implication, some *idion on*, 'special being'. It is a conclusion to make any reader of the *Metaphysics* or the *Nicomachean Ethics* rub his eyes. True, the *Eudemian Ethics* does not deny all connexion between different types of good, or the sciences that study them: like the *Nicomachean*, it orders the humanly achievable goods in a hierarchy of means and ends (1218b10-25). And it is also true that the *Nicomachean Ethics* still retains the old argument against any general science of the good.[6] But the *Nicomachean Ethics* adds the redeeming afterthought that *all* the uses of 'good' may be connected either by affiliation to some central use or else by analogy,[7] and of this there is no hint in the *Eudemian*. So in the earlier work when Aristotle argues that each thing seeks **167** its own separate good he cites the eye which seeks vision and the body which seeks health (1218a33-6), but in the *Nicomachean Ethics* he uses such examples to point the analogy between different uses of 'good' (1096b28-9). And there is another, related difference whose importance will become clearer as we proceed. The *Eudemian Ethics* prefaces its polemic with a warning: the topics to be discussed belong necessarily to another inquiry, one that is in general more dialectical (*logikôteras*), for it is this (sc. dialectic or 'logic') and no other science that deals with arguments which are both general and destructive.[8] But the *Nicomachean Ethics* softens those general and destructive arguments with its own constructive suggestion about the

5. 1217b25-35. Aristotle does not use the word 'homonymy' here, as he does of 'being' and 'one' in the *Topics* passage quoted above and as he does when he reconsiders the present argument in the *Nicomachean Ethics* and *Metaphysics* (see below). He says that 'being' and 'good' are *pollachôs legomena* (said in many ways), an expression which is also used in the *Topics* passage and which in the early logic comes to the same thing. If a *word* is *pollachôs legomenon* then it is a case of homonymy, requiring different definitions in different uses (*Top.* 106a1-8): the only *pollachôs legomena* which are not cases of homonymy are not words but ambiguous *phrases* (110b16-111a7). Gradually Aristotle came to explore a way in which a word could be *pollachôs legomenon* but avoid mere homonymy, but we shall see that in the present argument he does not consider this possibility. *Homônumia* I have rendered conventionally and for brevity's sake as 'ambiguity': on another occasion it may be shown why this is less apt than the clumsy 'plurality of meanings', and how the distinction throws light on Aristotle's metaphysics, but the point is not relevant here.

6. *EN* 1096a23-9 = *EE* 1217b25-35, *EN* 1096a29-34 = *EE* 1217b35-1218a1.

7. 1096b26-9. 'Relative to one' (*pros hen*) and 'derived from one' (*ap' henos*) are not generally distinguished (cf. *GC* 322b31-2, *EE* 1236b20-1 & 25-6); they must not be confused with the 'adding and subtracting' of *Meta.* 1030a27-b4. Nor must they be confused with the 'by analogy' which Aristotle though not his commentators contrasts with them: see pp. 24-6 infra. It may be noticed that the new concession in the *Nicomachean Ethics* does not in fact affect the shape of Aristotle's ethics. He gives an extra paragraph to reconsidering the possibility that there is a 'universal' sense of good or a good that is capable of separate and independent existence, but concludes that these are irrelevant for his purpose since he is concerned with what is humanly achievable. In *EE* and *EN* the humanly achievable goods are ordered in a hierarchy terminating in *eudaimonia*, happiness, and this is defined, firmly in *EE* and with qualifications in *EN*, by a relation to one good that is not *prakton*, something that can be achieved, namely God.

8. 1217b16-19. For the identification of *logikon* and *dialektikon* see Waitz, *Organon* ii, pp.353-5. *Top.* 105b30-1 seems to divide them if it implies (as perhaps it does not)

senses of 'good', and then comments that precision on this question must be left to *another philosophy* (1096b30-1). Commentators have rightly identified this other philosophy with the type of inquiry introduced in *Metaphysics* IV, a general metaphysics whose first object is to mitigate the ambiguity of words which have different uses in the different categories by showing that all their senses have one focus, one common element.[9] So we can say, tentatively: In the earlier ethics a word such as 'good' which is used in different categories is ambiguous, and the analysis of such ambiguities falls to dialectic. In the later ethics the ambiguity is circumvented, and this circumvention is the work of metaphysics.

168

Still more surprising than the intransigence about 'good' in the *Eudemian Ethics* is the corollary that there can be only departmental sciences of being. This runs flatly counter to the argument of *Metaphysics* IV, VI, XI[10] where Aristotle contends that 'being' is used not homonymously but even, in a way, synonymously (*tropon tina kath' hen*), since all its senses can be explained in terms of substance and of the sense of 'being' that is appropriate to substance. To explain what it is for there to *be* qualities or relations one must explain what it is for there to *be* (in a prior sense) substances having qualities and relations. And from this Aristotle concludes at once that there *is* a single science of being *qua* being, and this is universal in scope and not another departmental inquiry.[11] There is nothing new in the suggestion that at one time Aristotle restricted First Philosophy to a single department of reality; but it would be hard to find better evidence for it than this polemic in the *Eudemian Ethics*, which shows both that the restriction was deliberate and why it was so.[12] True, if this were the sole

---

that 'logical' problems, like 'physical' and 'ethical', can be handled either dialectically, *pros doxan*, or scientifically, *kat' alêtheian*. Here (a) Aristotle may mean that, inasfar as the common principles (which are in virtue of their generality 'logical premisses') are employed in this or that science and take their use from the science (*A.Pst.* 76a37-40), their function is understood *kat' alêtheian* only by the particular scientists. Or (b) we may compare *Top.* 162b31-3 which says that the account of *petitio principii* given there is merely *kata doxan*, but the account *kat' alêtheian* can be found in the *Analytics* – viz. in *A.Pr.* II 16, where the treatment is distinguished from that in the *Topics* merely by using the formal theory of the syllogism. Thus the distinction corresponds to that in *A.Pst.* 84a7-9, b1-2, between *logikôs* and *analutikôs*. On either interpretation, 'logical' problems and 'logical' techniques are wholly general. 'Logical' problems can be but need not be handled by 'logical' techniques. And 'logical' techniques are dialectic.

9. Hence Alexander's mention of good as well as being among *pros hen legomena* in his commentary on *Meta.* IV (242.5-6).

10. Nothing in my argument requires the authenticity of *Meta.* XI. See now A. Mansion, *Rev. Phil. de Louvain* 56 (1958), esp. pp. 209ff.

11. 1003a21-b19, 1026a29-32, cf. 1028a34-6, 1045b29-31, 1060b31-1061a10, 1061b11-12.

12. Jaeger defends the suggestion but ignores this section of the *EE*, which conflicts with his account of Phronesis in that work: there, according to him ([28], p.239), it is still Platonically regarded 'as ruling over all the sciences (*kuria pasôn epistêmôn*, *EE* 1246b9) and as the most valuable knowledge (*timiôtatê epistêmê* [no ref.])', and 'this is clearly opposed to the *Nicomachean Ethics*'. But the sense in which it is *kuria pasôn* is given in *EE* 1218b10-25 (esp. 12-13), with which cf. *EN* 1094a26-7; and the sense in which it is *timiôtaton* is given in 1216b20-5, cf. *EN* 1103b26-9.

evidence it might be suspect. Its singularity might reinforce those doubts about the authenticity of the *Eudemian Ethics* which are noticed elsewhere in this paper.[13] But it is not unique, and we need only take it as a clue in our hands to find other evidence which would by itself compel the same conclusion.

In sum, then, the argument of *Metaphysics* IV, VI seems to record a new departure. It proclaims that 'being' should never have been assimilated to cases of simple ambiguity, and consequently that the old objection to any general metaphysics of being fails. The new treatment of *to on* and other cognate expressions as *pros hen kai mian tina phusin legomena*, 'said relative to one thing and to a single character' – or, as I shall henceforth say, as having *focal meaning* – has enabled Aristotle to convert a special science of substance into the universal science of being, 'universal just inasmuch as it is primary'.[14]

Now it is time for some caveats. I am not saying that when Aristotle wrote the *Eudemian Ethics* he was not yet acquainted with the idea of focal meaning. He was, and his use of that idea persuaded von Arnim that he must already have evolved the whole argument of *Metaphysics* IV.[15] But this is a mistake. Von Arnim overlooked the passage that we have considered. Aristotle does indeed use the idea of focal meaning in the *Eudemian Ethics*: he applies it to his stock example 'medical' and then in detail to 'friendship' (1236a7-33). But he has not seen its application to such wholly general expressions as 'being' or 'good'. When he uses it he takes pains to explain it, and it is characteristic of his earlier work – the work of a young man fond of schematic argument – that the explanation he gives in the *Eudemian Ethics* is far more clearcut than the arguments in the *Nicomachean Ethics* and the *Metaphysics* which rely on the same idea (*EN* 1156b19-21,35-1157a3). A word such as 'medical', he says, is not univocal – it has various definitions answering to its various senses, but one of these senses is primary, in that its definition reappears as a component in each of the other definitions. If to be a medical man is to be XY, to be a medical knife is to be of the sort used by a man who is XY (1236a15-22). This is the pattern of reductive translation that Aristotle later applies to 'being'[16] and to those other expressions, such

---

Margueritte and Léonard have pointed out that *phronêsis* is used in an 'Aristotelian' as well as a 'Platonic' sense in *EE*, and in the latter sense generally in noticing the views of others: it is noteworthy that the former sense seems to occur first in the polemic (1218b13-14, where it is bracketed with *politikê* and *oikonomikê*), and thereafter predominates.

13. Nn. 4 and 17.

14. 1003a23-4, 1026a30-1, cf. 1064b13-14. Obviously I am concerned here only with the device by which A. converts a science of substance into a science of *to on hêi on*, not with the quite different reasons for which he selects theology as the pre-eminent science of substance.

15. *Eudemische Ethik und Metaphysik*, Akad. der Wiss. in Wien (1928), pp. 55-7.

16. In *Meta.* IV 2, but the account raises a small puzzle. Where he might be expected to say that all the subordinate senses of *on*, 'being', must be defined in terms of a primary sense of that expression, what he says is that all senses of *on* must be defined in terms of *ousia*, 'substance', just as all senses of 'healthy' must in terms of 'health': a formulation which makes no provision for the *priority* of one sense of *on*. But he then talks as though he had provided for that priority; and the explanation is plain – *on* in its primary sense *is ousia* (cf. 1028a29-31. The formulation in VII-IX is far clearer: with VII 1 cf. IX 1, 1045b27-32).

170   as 'one' and 'same' and 'opposite', which have a use in all categories but a
      primary use in the first (*Meta.* 1004a22-31, cf. 1018a31-8). But in the earlier
      work that ambitious application is still to seek. What is more, in the analysis
      of friendship we are warned against supposing that if one sense of the word
      is *primary* it is therefore *universal* (*EE* 1236a22-9); and this is another
      warning that the Aristotle of *Metaphysics* IV and VI, anxious to minimise the
      contrast between synonymy and focal meaning, will need to retract or
      reformulate.

Logical priority, natural priority

There is another objection to be met before we can move to other evidence.
So far I have suggested that in its polemic against the Academy the *Eudemian
Ethics* takes no account of the logical analysis of 'being', and the consequent
possibility of a single general science of being, that is proposed in parts of
the *Metaphysics*. But in the same context the *Eudemian Ethics*, like the
Nicomachean, recognises not only a difference in the senses of 'good' as it is
used in the different categories but also a general order of *priority* among
different types of good (*EE* 1218a1-15, *EN* 1096a17-23). Now it is natural to
assume that these types of good correspond to the senses of 'good', and
hence that the priority in question is just the priority of the first category.
And if this assumption is allowed, then surely the *Eudemian Ethics* must be
presupposing the argument of *Metaphysics* IV and VI which professes to
show how the other categories are logically subordinate to the first? Once
grant this, and there is a dilemma which is either way fatal. For either the
inconsistency between these two works on which I have laid such stress is an
illusion, or the *Eudemian Ethics* was written in full awareness of the analysis
proposed in the *Metaphysics* and nevertheless contradicts the inference
drawn from it in that work, namely that there can be a single science of
171   being. On this latter alternative, the *Eudemian Ethics* must be a later
      production and presumably not the work of Aristotle at all.[17]
      We might challenge the first move in this objection. For both in the
Eudemian and in the *Nicomachean Ethics* the argument from priority is quite
distinct from that which alleges an ambiguity and exploits the theory of
categories. It seems doubtful whether the original form of the argument
from priority involved the categories at all; in the Eudemian version they are
not mentioned (1218a1-15), and in the Nicomachean the mention of them is
at once superseded by the older Academic dichotomy of *kath' hauto*, '*per se*',
and *pros ti*, 'relative', to which the categories were a more elaborate rival.[18]
Still, let us suppose that the priority in question is the priority of the first

---

17. Perhaps this alternative can be strengthened. It has been suggested that the
rejection of any universal science was characteristic of the Peripatos in the first
generation after Aristotle, because Theophrastus in his fragment on metaphysics
observes that 'being' has more than one sense and that our knowledge of beings must
be correspondingly departmental (8b10-20, 9a10-11, 23-b1). Generally speaking
(*schedon*), says T., all knowledge is of *idia*, special fields (8b20-4). But here the parallel
to *EE* goes astray. T. is careful to correct his overemphasis on the fragmentation of
knowledge (8b24-7): it is also the task of science to aim at generality, and this may
produce a subject-matter which is identical not in kind but simply by analogy.
    18. 1096a17-23; Simplicius, *Cat.* 63.21-4.

category. This does not in the least entail that Aristotle had already reached his analysis of the *logical* priority of substance, the analysis which is propounded in *Metaphysics* IV and which depends directly upon recognising the focal meaning of 'being'. For logical priority – priority in *logos* or definition – is only one of the kinds of primacy that Aristotle eventually comes to claim for substance (*Meta.* 1028a32-b2). Another kind is 'natural' priority, a more primitive notion which Aristotle evidently took to be the older of the two since he fathers it on Plato and says that in a way the other types of priority were named after it (*Meta.* 1019a1-4). *A* is *naturally* prior to *B* (*proteron kata phusin, kat' ousian*) just in the case that *A* can exist without *B* and not *vice versa*; and it is plain that, just as this simple priority does not entail the more sophisticated kind, neither does the recognition of the first in a given case require recognition of the second. Thus a stock example of natural priority was the sequence points, lines, planes, solids; yet the Academy seems to have regarded this relation as allowing either the defining of the posterior terms by the prior, or the converse, or neither.[19]   **172**

Now the sole type of priority that is expressly invoked in our passage of the *Eudemian Ethics* is natural priority (1218a4-5). At the start of the polemic the Idea of the Good has been said to be prior to other good things just in the sense that its annihilation would involve the annihilation of the rest but not *vice versa*.[20] It is true that the Idea is also said to be that by reference to which other things are *called* good (1217b12-13, cf. *Meta.* 987b7-9); but the striking fact is that neither here nor in his other critiques of the Forms does Aristotle take this formula to imply that the definition of 'good' or any other predicate *differs* when the word is applied to the Idea and when it is applied to the participant.[21] That is to say, at this stage or in this context he does not consider the idea of focal meaning or the associated notion of *logical* priority at all; and it is these ideas, and not any older and vaguer account of the primacy of substance, that later enable him to evade his own polemic and circumvent the ambiguity of 'being'.

So the objection fails and we can get on.

Ambiguity and metaphysics in the Organon

Elsewhere we can see the search for focal meaning, by contrast with the simple detection of homonymy, taking on interest and importance for Aristotle. When he elucidates some cardinal expression by displaying some of its senses as elaborations upon a primary sense, his technique marks a major advance on the Socratic search for definitions. He employs it

19. Posterior defined by prior, *A.Pst.* 73a34-7, *Meta.* 1077a36-b2; prior by posterior, *Top.* 141b19-22 (Plato? cf. *Meta.* 992a21-2; but also Aristotle, *Top.* 158a31-b4, 163b20-1); neither, *Meta.* 992a10-18 (Speusippus? cf. the contrast between *pros hen* (relative to one thing) and *ephexês* (in serial succession), *Meta.* 1005a10-11). At *Meta.* 1077a36-b11 Aristotle insists that logical does not entail natural priority (cf. 1018b34-7).

20. 1217b10-16, a standard paraphrase of the criterion of natural priority; cf. de Strycker [35], p. 89.

21. *EE* 1218a10-15, *EN* 1096a35-b5, *Meta.* 1040b32-4, 1079b3-11; cf. the final section of this paper.

173   occasionally in the physical writings[22] and in the Lexicon, *Metaphysics* V,
sometimes with the air of an afterthought.[23] In a special form it comes to
dominate the psychology. Aristotle is already beyond one pitfall in the
Socratic method when he argues in the *Topics* that, since 'life' is used in
different senses of plants and of animals, it is wrong to attempt a general
definition of the word: what we need is a separate definition for each form of
life (148a23-36). But he is beyond the *Topics* when he says in the *De Anima*
that, while we cannot be content with a general account of soul, neither can
we stop at giving separate definitions of the various types of soul. Our
explanation must show how these types are ordered, the posterior
potentially containing the prior (414b25-415a1). Here there seem to be
quite conscious parallels with the language of the *Metaphysics*: with soul as
with being, it is the primary sense of the word that shows what is common
to all the senses (415a23-5), and it is only what is denoted by the word in its
primary sense that can have 'separate' existence (413a31-b10). But at the
same time there are large differences in the two uses of focal meaning, and
we are not concerned here with the psychology. The example raises other
problems that lie on our way. The *Topics* is a commonplace book whose
compiling and subsequent enlarging may have stretched over a considerable
period. Is it reasonable then to say, as I have said in this instance, that in his
later concern with focal meaning Aristotle is 'beyond the *Topics*'? Or, as I
shall argue, that he is beyond the *Organon* as a whole?

Consider first what signs there are in these works of general interest in
focal meaning, disregarding the special use that Aristotle finds for the idea
in *Metaphysics* IV. In the *Topics* he quotes various examples which will later
serve as standard cases of *pros hen legomena*.[24] But here they seem to be
treated merely as cases of ambiguity ('good', for instance, is bracketed with
oxu, 'sharp', 'acute', which is used in different senses of notes and knives and

174   angles). Robin dismissed this treatment as 'une expression insuffisante et
peu exacte de la doctrine d'Aristote':[25] perhaps he thought its inadequacy a
sign of the negative aims of the *Topics*. But the destructive side of the
dialectic has been very much exaggerated, and it is at least as likely that
Aristotle had not yet evolved the general 'doctrine' for which Robin was
looking. At any rate, whether or not he had already met the notion of focal
meaning (a question we shall face later) and whether or not that notion is
implied or foreshadowed in some other passages of the *Topics*,[26] the work
gives no sign that he attached any importance to it. When he recognises a
third possibility beside bare synonymy and homonymy, the possibility is
'metaphor' (with, as a fourth case, something 'worse than metaphor'), and

---

22. *Phys.* 222a20-1, significantly not in 260b15ff.; *GC* 322b29-32.

23. 1016b6-9, 1018a31-8, 1019b35-1020a6, 1020a14-32 (cf. *Cat.* 5a38-b10),
1022a1-3, 1024b17-1025a13. But for an apparent echo of the later metaphysics cf.
1017a13-22.

24. 'Healthy', 106b33-7, 'good', 107a5-12 (cf. von Arnim, *op.cit.*, pp. 55-6), 'being'
in the different categories, 103b20-39. It is interesting that 'medical', which gave A.
his first illustration of focal meaning in *EE*, does not appear.

25. *Théorie plat. des idées et des nombres*, p.153, n. 171; cf. Alexander, *Meta.* 241.21-4.

26. Materials for it seem to be present but unused in 106a4-8, 106b33-7, 114a29-
31, 117b10-12, 124a31-4, 134a32-6, 145a28-30.

there is no attempt to explain metaphor by focal meaning.[27] And there are revealing passages such as the discussion of a problem in the fifth book. The problem depends on the possibility of assigning a predicate both to a primary subject and to other things which are 'called after' that subject (134a18-25), and it would be solved by calling in focal meaning – that is, by allowing the predicate different but connected definitions in its different uses. But, though he seems at one point on the verge of this solution (134a32-b1, cf. 145a28-30), Aristotle treats the predicate as a simple unit throughout and merely enjoins the speaker to say whether the expression is being applied to its primary subject or not (134b10-13). This simple treatment takes on a special significance in his attacks on the Ideas, for he recognises that the Platonists' use of the prefix *auto* or *ho estin*, 'absolute' or 'what [really] is', is just such an attempt to pick out the Idea as the primary subject of a predicate; yet here too he does not suppose that such a prefix entails any variation in the *logos*, the definition of the predicate (cf. p. 19, n.21 above). For him the Idea is 'first of a synonymous set', naturally but not logically prior to its participants.[28]

Nor does focal meaning find formal recognition in the class of paronyms   **175**
which is introduced in the *Categories* and recognised in the *Topics*, for the definition of paronyms is merely grammatical. It shows, not how subordinate senses of a word may be logically affiliated to a primary sense, but how adjectives can be manufactured from abstract nouns by modifying the word-ending.[29] Plainly the *Categories* does not and could not make any use of this idea to explain how the subordinate categories depend on the first. Nor does it use focal meaning for that purpose (2b4-6). If focal meaning can be seen in the *Categories* it is in the analysis of some category – clearly enough in the definition of quantity (5a38-b10), far more doubtfully in the account of the two uses of 'substance' (2b29-37, 3b18-21) – but not in that logical ordering of different categories and different senses of 'being' which lies at the root of the argument in *Metaphysics* IV.

This point can be strengthened and generalised, and then it is fundamental. Whether or not Aristotle did think at the time of writing the *Topics* (and the *Categories*, if he wrote that work) that focal meaning held some interest for philosophers, neither there nor in the rest of the *Organon* is there any hint of the use to which the idea is put in the fourth book of the *Metaphysics*. There is no room in the picture for a general science of 'being *qua* being'. Rhetoric apart, the sole discipline that Aristotle recognises in these works as dealing with material that is common to all sciences and all

27. 139b32-140a17. (I cannot find that any supporter of a widely accepted reconstruction of the *Protrepticus* has discussed this passage, which denounces as 'worse than metaphor' any attempt to describe law as measure or image of things naturally just.)

28. *Lin. Insec.* 968a9-10, Aristotelian though not by Aristotle.

29. Cf. J. Owens, *The Doctrine of Being in Aristotle's Metaphysics*, pp.51 and 330, nn. 19-21. But the idea was apparently extended, *Phys.* 207b8-10 (and cf. the connexion with *para ti legesthai*, 'being so called by virtue of a relation to something', Ross, *Met.* i p.161). In the *Categories* its function is to provide a simple tie between adjective and abstract noun (corresponding respectively to that which is 'predicated of' and that which is 'present in' a given subject) so that both can be treated in the same category.

fields of discourse is dialectic;[30] and dialectic lays no claim to the title of
First Philosophy. In its relation to the sciences it is a preliminary technique
for clarifying and hardening those ideas in current use which they can take
over and put to more accurate work.[31] The common principles that it
investigates have a different use in the different sciences and the different
categories (*A.Pst.* 76a37-40, 88a36-b3) – here is an inescapable parallel to
the treatment of 'being' and 'good' in the *Eudemian Ethics* – and the uses of
such a principle are connected only by 'analogy' (76a38-9). Certainly, this
analogical connexion is itself an admission that words and formulae which
are shared by all fields of discourse are not for that reason baldly equivocal;
but it does not explain why this is so, and we shall see later how far it is from
implying that systematic connexion of meanings by which *Metaphysics* IV
disarms the same ambiguity. It does nothing to show the possibility of a
general science of 'being and the necessary characteristics of being', which
takes the common axioms of the sciences as part of its subject-matter just
because those axioms hold good of being *qua* being. Once Aristotle thinks he
has established this possibility, he can claim a new importance for
dialectical techniques by embodying them in the new science.[32] But no such
science is in view in the *Organon*.

Yet commentators anxious for the unity of Aristotle's thought have
managed to see the later metaphysics in the logical texts. They have
descried it in the *Sophistici Elenchi* when Aristotle explains that dialectical
argument is not confined to a determinate class of objects, does not prove
anything, and – the critical phrase – is not *hoios ho katholou*, 'like universal
reasoning' (172a11-13). What is this universal reasoning (ask the
interpreters, from pseudo-Alexander to Jean Tricot) but the universal
science of being announced in *Metaphysics* IV? Yet in the very next lines
Aristotle flatly denies that all things can be brought under the same
principles, and a little later he says in the same vein that the common ideas
with which dialectic deals do not form a positive subject-matter: they are
more like negative concepts (*apophaseis*, whose claim to a common genus
Aristotle denied from the *De Ideis* onwards).[33] Waitz saw that in this context

---

30. *Top.* 101a36-b4, cf. *Rhet.* 1358a2-32; and texts discussed in the next paragraph.
Finding no other room for a general metaphysics in the *Organon*, Poste (*Sophistici
Elenchi*, p.212) proposed to regard it as 'more or less completely identical' with
dialectic. His problem was correct: there is no room for it.

31. As in much of the *Physics*, for instance. 'Physicam dialecticae suae mancipavit'
(Bacon).

32. As in the defence of the law of contradiction in IV 4. Cf. VII 4, where dialectic
(*to logikôs zêtein*) is auxiliary to the philosophical argument, the first showing 'how we
should speak' and the second 'how things are' (1030a27-8): but 'it doesn't matter in
which of the two ways one puts it' (1030b3-4), i.e. the tenet that 'be' and therefore
the question *ti esti*, 'what is it?', have their primary use in the category of substance
can be shown either by dialectic ('adding' and 'subtracting', 1030a21-7, pointing out
elliptical uses of 'be' in the subordinate categories) or by the philosophical analysis of
'being' as a *pros hen legomenon* (1030a34-b3). (I cannot comprehend why Cherniss
renders *logikôs* at 1030a25 as 'a mere verbalism', *J.H.S.* lxxvii (1957) p.21; 1029b13 if
nothing else would have shown that the word describes Aristotle's own method in the
chapter.)

33. 172a36-8, cf. Alex. *Meta.* 80.15-81.10; *Top.* 128b8-9, *Meta.* 1022b32-1023a7.

the 'universal' method with which dialectic is contrasted can only be that which is explained in the *Posterior Analytics*, the method of the special sciences whose subject-matter is defined by 'universals that are not equivocal'.[34] Alternatively, if we are to see a reference to general metaphysics in the phrase, it must be glossed by that passage in the *Posterior Analytics* where Aristotle distinguishes the special sciences not only from dialectic but also from 'any science that might try to give universal proofs of the common axioms, such as the law of excluded middle' (77a26-31). Here too the commentators from John Philoponus onwards have caught the scent of *Metaphysics* IV. Yet Aristotle held consistently that the common axioms are *amesa*, 'immediate', and cannot be proved; at best, as in the fourth book of the *Metaphysics* itself, they can be recommended by dialectical methods (*Meta.* 1006a11-18). So the science that Aristotle has in mind here cannot be one of his own making. On the contrary, as Ross saw, it is what he repudiates: 'a metaphysical attempt, conceived after the manner of Plato's dialectic (sc. as that is represented in the central books of the *Republic*), to deduce hypotheses from an unhypothetical first principle'.[35] So too when Aristotle says, a little earlier in the *Posterior Analytics*, that one science cannot prove the theorems of another and (almost in the same breath) that geometry cannot prove the general principle that the knowledge of contraries is a single knowledge (75b12-15): *if* (as interpreters unwarrantably assume) he is thinking here of some other science as professing to prove such general principles, it is the *Republic* and not the *Metaphysics* that gives him his model. And this is a model for philosophy that he rejects as wholly misconceived.

Just as it is a Platonic metaphysics that he has in view when he denies   **178**
that the common axioms can be proved, so it is with this target in mind that he rejects the possibility of deducing the special premisses of any given science (76a16-25). Such a proof, he says, would devolve on a mistress-science, *kuria pantôn*. We need not dwell on the struggles of Zabarella and others who read this as a reference to Aristotle's own general metaphysics and then have to explain away the plain repudiation of any such procedure in the text before them. The inquiry described in *Metaphysics* IV is not mentioned in the *Organon*; nor is it hidden in Aristotle's sleeve. In contexts such as those we have considered it must have been noticed if it had already established itself, and there is no sign of it.

The nature of the texts makes the argument from silence a strong one, but it can be corroborated by comparing these passages that we have just considered with a later echo of their argument. For the straightforward conclusions of the *Analytics* reappear in the *Metaphysics* in quite another guise: they have become problems which must be resolved if any general science of being is to be possible. The *Analytics* had argued against any attempt to prove the common axioms of all the sciences and, on connected grounds, against any attempt to prove the special principles of a given science. Both arguments reappear in *Metaphysics* III, but both have been relegated to the preliminary *aporiai* or puzzles of the subject (997a2-11, 15-

34. Waitz, *Organon* ii p.551-2, *A.Pst.* 73b26-8; cf. 85b15-22 on the need for univocity in the scientific universal.
35. Ross ad loc.: *Analytics*, p.543.

25) – just as the reason which was given in the *Eudemian Ethics* for rejecting a single science of being turns up again in the *Metaphysics* merely as another difficulty to be circumvented (1003a33, 1060b31-5). The conclusion seems inescapable. The arguments against any universal science which are collected and to some extent disarmed in the *Metaphysics* were – at least in some important instances – first formulated when Aristotle thought them conclusive, namely when the polemic against the Academy was at its height and when the sole model of general metaphysics that Aristotle had in view was some form or version of Platonic dialectic. Any such would-be universal science, he then believed, must commit two logical crimes. It must aim at giving wholly general proofs of matters proprietary to particular sciences, and it must ignore the ambiguity of 'being' and all those ubiquitous words **179** with which it tried to define its own subject-matter. Later, when he introduces his own programme for a general metaphysics, he deals differently with these two objections. The first he is ready to accommodate. The new enterprise is not cast in the form of a deductive system and it does not dictate premisses to the special sciences. Instead of general proofs it undertakes general analyses of the use of those same ubiquitous words and formulae; but here it runs against the second objection. And what gives the new departure its impetus and its character is just that Aristotle has now seen, in the concept of focal meaning, a way of defeating that objection.[36]

Analogy and focal meaning

I hope the picture emerges of a fairly clear stage in Aristotle's thought. In his logic he tended at this time to work with the simple dichotomy of synonymy and homonymy; apparently he saw little if any importance in that *tertium quid* for which he was gradually to find such notable uses. In metaphysics this simple scheme enabled him, as part of his critique of Plato and the Academy, to deny the possibility of any universal science of being. This denial was framed without provision for the system he was himself to propose in *Metaphysics* IV, VI and VII. True, he already held a theory of categories in which priority was ascribed to substance, but this priority was of an older Academic vintage which did not involve focal meaning. So it did nothing to mitigate the ambiguity that Aristotle claimed to find in 'being'.

The same polemic against a universal science figures largely in *Metaphysics* I 9. Here too an important weapon is the claim that the Platonists have neglected questions of ambiguity, and here too Aristotle seems to overlook focal meaning. Thus he maintains that if the Platonists had recognised the ambiguity of the expression *ta onta* ('beings') they would have

36. Proved by the place assigned to it at the start of the argument in IV (and cf. VII 4, where it is the focal analysis of 'being' that distinguishes the philosophical from the dialectical treatment of the problem: n. 32). It is this device that enables Aristotle to make the last and most important qualification to the old principle that one science deals with one sort of object (Alex. *Meta*. 79.5-6), a principle qualified first by Socrates' claim that the same science deals with contraries (*Symp.* 223D, *Rep.* 333E-4A); then extended to all opposites, to means and ends, and finally to all *sustoicha*, 'coordinates' (*Top.* 109b17-29, 106a1-8, 110b16-25, 164a1-2, cf. *Phys.* 194a27-8). But none of these previous extensions had infringed Aristotle's thesis that the objects of a science fall inside one *genos* (*A.Pst.* 87a38-b4).

seen the futility of looking for the elements of all the things there are, for **180** only the elements of substances can be discovered (992b18-24). This does not formally contradict the argument of the fourth book, but it is out of tune with the claim that a general inquiry into the elements of the things that are is legitimate and that those who had engaged in such an inquiry were on the right track (1003a28-32). It contrasts too with the argument in *Metaphysics* XII that all things can be said to have the same elements 'by analogy' (XII 4, esp. 1070b10-21). But now it is time to take up an earlier promise and show that these two pronouncements, in IV and XII respectively, are by no means equivalent, despite the immemorial tendency of commentators to describe the theory in IV as 'the analogy of being'.[37]

The claim of IV that 'being' is an expression with focal meaning is a claim that statements about non-substances can be reduced to – translated into – statements about substances; and it seems to be a corollary of this theory that non-substances cannot have matter or form of their own since they are no more than the logical shadows of substance (1044b8-11). The formulation in terms of 'analogy' involves no such reduction and is therefore free to suggest that the distinction of form, privation and matter is not confined to the first category (1070b19-21). To establish a case of focal meaning is to show a particular connexion between the definitions of a polychrestic word. To find an analogy, whether between the uses of such a word or anything else, is not to engage in any such analysis of meanings: it is merely to arrange certain terms in a (supposedly) self-evident scheme of proportion.[38] So when Aristotle says in *Metaphysics* XII that the elements of all things are the same by analogy, the priority that he ascribes to substance is only natural priority (1071a33-5) and he does not recognise any general **181** science of being *qua* being.[39] There is no mention of *pros hen legomena* in XII, and none of analogy in IV. And when he says in the *Analytics* that each axiom has as many uses as there are sciences and kinds of beings, his concession that these uses are connected by analogy is no substitute for the later claim that the axioms hold good of being *qua* being and are therefore to be studied by the single science described in IV. It is IV, not XII, that moves decisively beyond the old polemic, the denunciation of any general inquiry into the 'elements of things' which is still audible in *Metaphysics* I.

That polemic turned on the neglect or suppression of the idea of focal

---

37. Rodier (*Traité de l'Ame* ii. p.218) draws the distinction excellently, but misconstrues Aristotle's definition of the soul as relying on analogy, not focal meaning.

38. See e.g. *Meta*. 1093b18-21, *EN* 1096b28-9. The idea of proportion is central to analogy (*Meta*. 1016b34-5), even when the terms are not fully stated because they are obvious (beings are the same by analogy because as one use of 'being' is to substance so another is to quantity, etc.).

39. 1069a36-b2, cf. Jaeger [28], pp.220-1. I am concerned only with cases in which Aristotle came to think focal meaning a better explanation of some 'systematic ambiguity' than analogy. I do not imply either (a) that he supposed focal meaning would explain every case of analogy or (b) that where he adopted a focal analysis he consequently rejected the weaker description in terms of analogy as false or improper. 'Analogy' would still be the safest general way of characterising the logic of a word whose senses were interconnected but not confined to one genus, as in *Meta*. 1016b31-1017a3, a chapter of V which also uses focal meaning to analyse 'one' (1016b6-9).

meaning at a point where Aristotle later set great store by its use. Neglect or suppression: but which? We cannot take Aristotle's candour here for granted; but what we think of it will depend on what we can make of some earlier traces of the idea in the Academy.

The Academy on focal meaning

There is nothing new in the complaint that when Aristotle attacks the Academy he ignores focal meaning. A familiar example of this omission is the dilemma that he forces on his opponents in *Metaphysics* I 9: either it is a mere equivocation to use the same word of both the Form and its participant, or else they must carry their common name synonymously and so be specifically alike (991a2-8 = 1079a33-b3). Notoriously, the penalty for taking the second option was the regress which the Academy called the 'third man': the Form 'Man' and the individual man can now be treated as a single class whose existence entails that of a further Form 'Man', and so *ad infinitum*. To this dilemma Aristotle's critics retort that if only he had allowed the Platonists the benefit of his own *tertium quid*, focal meaning, the argument would collapse. For suppose Socrates is called 'man' in a sense neither identical with nor merely different from that in which the Form is so called, but derivative from that sense: then the regress cannot get started. If the existence of a class of X-dependent things entails that of an X-thing, this by no means shows that the existence of a class of X-dependent things and one X-thing entails that of another thing that is X.

This neglect of focal meaning is aggravated by an argument that appears only in the version of the polemic that is preserved in *Metaphysics* XIII. There Aristotle suggests, as he does nowhere else, that the Platonists may wish to vary the definition of the predicate so as to distinguish its use when it names the Idea from its use in other contexts (1079b3-11). But the variation he has in mind is merely the incorporation of *ho esti*, 'what [really] is', when the predicate is used of the Idea;[40] and this does not touch hands with focal meaning. It is no more than the warning-index which the *Topics* recommended in such cases (134b10-13, cf. p. 21 above). The absurdities that Aristotle wrings from it here could not have been wrung from the analysis that he is accused of suppressing.

But now perhaps we have the material for a defence. Aristotle, we may argue, was not suppressing that analysis: it is just that his criticisms of the Academy were framed in that earlier period when he habitually worked with the bare dichotomy of synonymy and homonymy. It was not until later, when the heat of the debate was past, that he came to recognise the third possibility and explore it on his own account. And there perhaps the defence might rest – if only there were not evidence that the Academy was already familiar with focal meaning, and that Aristotle must have known this.

We need not turn to the *Lysis* for this counter-evidence. Since Grote's chapter on that dialogue, scholars have hailed its argument for a *prôton philon*, 'primary dear thing', as the source of Aristotle's analysis of friendship

---

40. Reading with Shorey *ho esti* in 1079b6 for the *hou esti* of MSS (so too Ross, Jaeger).

in the *Eudemian* and *Nicomachean Ethics*,[41] and the Eudemian version is probably the first and clearest exposition of focal meaning in the Corpus. No doubt Aristotle wrote it with the *Lysis* in mind; but the logical device **183** which is the nerve of the Eudemian argument is not to be found in Plato's dialogue. What Plato says is that things which are loved for the sake of something else are merely *called* dear, and only that for whose sake they are loved is really dear (220A6-B3). But the relationship between these orders of dear things, which Plato expresses by saying that the first are *phila heneka philou*, 'dear on account of something dear', is not logical but psychological; he is concerned, not with a nexus of meanings, but with the valuing of means to an end.[42] Far more damaging to Aristotle, at first sight, are two other texts. The first seems to show that he himself had already made use of focal meaning in developing a substantially Platonic theory; the second implies that the use of that idea in expounding the theory of Forms was common doctrine in the Academy. This is the evidence that makes his neglect of the idea elsewhere look like a piece of eristic, and the stage of logical puritanism that I have pictured seem the result not of innocence but of malice.

The first evidence occurs in Jaeger's reconstruction of the *Protrepticus*.[43] Not only do the familiar extracts from Iamblichus make use of the old notion of natural priority current in the Academy;[44] they are equally at home with the suggestion that a word may have two senses (*dittôs legomenon*) of which one is primary (*kuriôs, alêthôs, proteron*) and the other is defined in terms of the first.[45] And the author bases a major argument on this latter kind of priority. He contends that, even when a word is used in its primary sense of A and in its derivative sense of B, still a comparison can be made **184** between A and B in the very respect that is marked by the ambiguous word. For *mâllon* can signify 'in a stricter sense' as well as 'to a greater degree'; and thus what is good in an absolute sense can be called *more* good than what is so in a relative sense, and what is actually alive (this being the primary sense of the word) more alive than what is potentially so (57, 6-23). Now this claim is contradicted by the more rigorous doctrine of other seemingly early works of Aristotle. More than once he insists that, if one thing can be

41. *Lysis* 218D-220B. Grote, *Plato*³ vol. i p.525 note *a*, followed by Joachim, Jaeger et al.

42. Esp. 218D-219B. The essential word *heneka*, 'on account of', takes on another sense at 220E4 still further removed from the notion of focal meaning.

43. It is not necessary to find Platonic Ideas in the texts Jaeger reclaims from Iamblichus (as I, for one, cannot) in order to feel that the mid-fourth century would be a natural date for the *Protrepticus*. The identity of the recipient and the apparent connexion with the *Antidosis* suggest that the work was a pamphlet designed to invade Isocrates' field of patronage in Cyprus, and a particularly promising time for this would be when Isocrates was embarrassed by the medising of the Evagorids shortly before or during the mid-century anti-Persian revolt in the island (after which Pnytagoras, an Evagorid with a better record than Evagoras II, seems to have kept the throne of Salamis). If Themison represented a pro-Macedonian reaction this would explain the claim of the later Cypriot Themison to the friendship of Antiochus II and the title 'Macedonian' (Athen. VII 35). It would also, of course, explain Aristotle's connexion with him.

44. Iamblichus, *Protrepticus* 38.10-14 Pistelli (= Aristotle, fr. 5 W & R).

45. *op.cit.* 56.15-57.6 (= Aristotle, fr. 14 W & R).

called more X than another, the predicate must apply to them both in exactly the same sense.[46] And in this contrast the *Protrepticus* seems to show its background, for the convention that what is *really* X is also *superlatively* X is characteristic of Plato.[47] Plato had ignored or exploited the ambiguity in *mâllon*, and when the author of the *Protrepticus* propounds a Platonic *argumentum ex gradibus*, he accordingly seeks to safeguard his argument by recognising the ambiguity but treating it as harmless. Only by minimising it can he go on to argue that the man who is superlatively alive knows that which is superlatively exact and intelligible; for the first superlative and the second correspond to different senses of *malista*. Admittedly, this is an ambiguity which Aristotle himself takes no pains to clear up in some important passages of the *Topics*,[48] and with which he seems to struggle awkwardly at one point in the *Categories* (3b33-4a9). But later in that work, and in the other texts I have just cited, he seems to see its dangers and so to reach his own standards of logical rigour; whereas in the argument preserved by Iamblichus, Aristotle – if he is its author – is still occupied in constructing a logic for theories that were part of his inheritance.[49]

185   So, without querying Jaeger's reconstruction of the text, we could claim that it does nothing to discredit Aristotle. If this were all, his subsequent silence on focal meaning could be excused: its interest for him would be cancelled by second thoughts about the argument he had constructed with it. If a word has a primary and a derivative use then it is ambiguous, and the *Protrepticus* had tried to blink this plain fact. And later, if his analysis of the meaning of such words had been an original contribution to the logic of an old theory, he would surely have the right to file it away with other promising but non-performing ideas, and ignore it in his debate with the Platonists.

But this defence is spoilt by other evidence. The idea was not his to file away. It had already been introduced in defence of the theory of Forms, and his opponents' use of it had been recorded by Aristotle himself. For it is to be found, I think, fully-formed, in the most complex and remarkable of those arguments for the Ideas that Alexander of Aphrodisias has preserved from Aristotle's lost essay on the theory.[50] The argument, according to

46. *Phys.* 249a3-8 (the early seventh book), *Cat.* 11a12-13, cf. *Pol.* 1259b36-8.

47. Cf. *Top.* 162a26-32. Familiar instances are the equivalence of *ontôs onta*, 'really real', and *mâllon* or *malista onta*, 'more' or 'most real', and such arguments as that in *Republic* IX which proves that the philosophically just man has a life which not only is 729 times more pleasant than that of the unjust man but also contains the only real or most real pleasure (587D12-E4).

48. Esp. the treatment of topics of 'more and less' in II 10, V 8, and of the comparison of goods in II 1.

49. But one difficulty deserves notice. It might be suggested (though to my knowledge it has not been) that the baffling reference which Stewart wanted to excise from *EN* VIII 2 ('for [friendship] admits of the more and the less, as do things different in species. We have discussed these matters previously', 1155b14-16) relates to and agrees with the argument in the *Protrepticus*. But Aristotle's 'previously', *emprosthen*, seems always to refer to an earlier context in the same work (cf. Bz. *Index*, 244a5-8). It seems impossible to find a wholly apt context in *EN*, though A. may have in mind the general treatment of vices and virtues as constituted by degrees of some feeling or behaviour (so now Dirlmeier).

50. Alexander, *Meta.* 82.11-83.17. For a fuller discussion of this argument I must refer to *Journal of Hellenic Studies* lxxvii (1957), pp.103-11.

Alexander, is a sample of those which Aristotle describes in the *Metaphysics* as producing Ideas of *ta pros ti*, relatives (*Meta.* 990b16 = 1079a12). It begins by distinguishing different uses of a predicate such as 'man'. We may say 'That is a man' when pointing to a creature of flesh and blood, or we may say it when pointing to a painting of one. The uses are different, but the difference does not amount to homonymy: for in both cases we are referring to the same *phusis*, 'character' – only in the second case the reference is indirect, and what we now mean by 'a man' is '*a likeness of* a man' (where 'man' in its first sense reappears as one element in the meaning). And then it is argued that whenever we call anything in the physical world 'equal' our use of 'equal' bears the same relation to some primary use of the word as the second use of 'man' bore to the first. The definition of 'equal' in its primary sense (*ison auto*, 'absolutely equal', *ison kuriôs*, 'strictly equal') does not fit any mundane case of equality *akribôs*, without modification: like the **186** definition of 'man' in the portrait-case, it must be supplemented in such secondary uses. (The argument seems to show that, for 'equal', the supplement required is the specification of something *to which* or *in respect of which* the particular mundane equality obtains – a supplement which will vary from case to case, and which is not required in the primary use of the word when, as the argument concludes, it stands for a Form.) In all this there are striking parallels of thought and language with Aristotle's own accounts of focal meaning, particularly that which is given in the *Eudemian Ethics*.[51] And, if this is so, it seems to be the damning evidence against him. After this, his insistence that the Idea and its participant are either partners to an ambiguity or parents of an infinite regress must rest on an indefensible suppression of the third possibility propounded by his opponents.

But this picture in turn, I think, is false.

In the first place, we have no evidence whatever to show that focal meaning had been invoked at any stage as a *general* answer to the 'third man'. The academic proof in which we have just found it does not apply to all the types of predicate for which at one time or another the Academy set up Ideas. It neither says nor implies that when any predicate whatever is used of things in this world its use must be analysed in the way in which the proof analyses that of 'equal'; on the contrary, it says that 'man' is used of physical things in its primary as well as its secondary sense, and its reason for denying this of 'equal' is precisely the point in which 'equal' differs from 'man', namely its *relativity*: in the everyday use of the words, nothing on earth can be unqualifiedly equal in the way that Socrates is unqualifiedly a man. This is why in the *Metaphysics* Aristotle distinguishes the sort of proof which produces Ideas of relatives from those which involve the 'third man' (990b15-17 = 1079a11-13). If predicates such as 'man' are to have Ideas, they at least cannot shelter from the regress behind a proof which finds focal meaning in *every* mundane use of the predicate: for no such proof has been given. Accordingly focal meaning plays no part in the other, more general arguments for Ideas that are retailed by Alexander. Aristotle could treat the 'arguments from the sciences', for instance, as proving, not as much as their authors hoped, but at least the existence of universals (*koina*) in his sense **187** (Alexander, *Meta.* 79.15-19); and certainly he did not believe that 'man' is to be defined differently when it is used of Socrates and when it names the universal, i.e. the species (*Cat.* 2a19-27, 3a33-b9, *Top.* 122b7-11, 154a15-20). The same considerations explain why, before launching his simple dichotomy of synonymy-or-homonymy against the Ideas, Aristotle takes care to eliminate by an independent (and provokingly obscure) argument all Ideas other than those answering to substance-words, such as 'man' (990b22-991a8). If focal meaning had not been and could not consistently be used as a general asylum from the regress, he can be excused for not casting it in that role.

This explanation of his silence goes some way, but not far enough. For the fact remains that the author of the Academic proof had illustrated focal meaning by analysing a description which applied both to an original and to a portrait; and the relation between original and portrait (or a more generic relation of which this is one species) had been used quite generally by Plato to illustrate the connexion between any Idea and its participant. So the possibility of extending the focal analysis to all predicates and all Ideas must surely have occured to the Academy, and accordingly should have figured in Aristotle's polemic. Moreover, if his silence in that context can be explained, how to account for his apparent failure at this time to see any value in the device for his own work? One reason for his refusal to allow the Platonists this general refuge seems clear. He did not think that any commensurately general argument had been given (any argument, that is, that embraced all predicates and not merely relatives) for the proposition that the contents of this world are portraits or copies of other, transcendent entities. Taken in this unrestricted form the theory of Paradigms and Copies seemed to him to rest on the assumption that something worked as a copyist in making the world; and this was not argument, merely metaphor (991a20-3).

But there seems to be another reason why Aristotle's polemic does not take more notice of the device on which his opponents' proof depends; and it is also, and more importantly, a reason why he did not yet see its value for his own work. It is that, to all appearance, he thought the analysis by which **188** the Academic author had introduced and illustrated focal meaning a sheer mistake. The example preoccupied him: over and again in his writings he cites the case of a predicate which is applied both to an original and to a picture or statue; but always – even in works which elsewhere make good use of focal meaning – he cites it simply to illustrate homonymy.[52] His reason for doing so is clear and unvarying. An eye or a doctor, a hand or a flute, is defined by what it does; but an eye or a doctor in a painting cannot see or heal, a stone hand or flute cannot grasp or play. So when they are used in the latter way, 'eye' and the other nouns must be used homonymously. And Aristotle, who allows that ambiguity is a matter of degree (*Phys.* 249a23-5, *EN* 1129a26-31), nowhere suggests that *this* homonymy is redeemed and brought nearer to synonymy by the sensible resemblance which, in his view, forms the sole connexion between the eye or doctor in the painting and its fleshly counterpart. That resemblance, be it

52. *PA* 640b29-641a6, *De An.* 412b20-2, *Meteor.* 390a10-13, *GA* 726b22-4, *Pol.* 1253a20-5, and on the conventional interpretation *Cat.* 1a1-6 (but for *zôion gegrammenon*, 'painted animal' cf. *Mem.* 450b21 & 32, *Pol.* 1284b9).

noted, is not only the result of conscious imitation but is expressly invoked to define one sense of the predicate on trial: yet that Aristotle meant to reject the Academy's example of focal meaning seems to be confirmed by his own examples. After citing 'healthy' and 'medical', he adds merely that other words which behave in this way could be found (*Meta*. 1003a33-b5); but if he had allowed his opponents' claim he could have referred to an inexhaustible class of predicates – all those, namely, which can be applied to things both in and out of pictures.[53]

Now on the general point at issue Aristotle seems to be right. If focal meaning is to count as a convincing extension of synonymy – if, from his later point of view, it is to carry the weight of argument he lays on it – then it is not a strong enough condition of focal meaning that the bearers of a predicate should exhibit some physical resemblance and that this resemblance should be used to define one sense of the predicate. (Consider the word 'collar'. Among its meanings, according to the Pocket Oxford **189** Dictionary, is 'collar-shaped piece in machines'. But there is no substantial connexion between this and its more familiar meaning. It would be absurd, for instance, to claim that no one could understand the engineer's use of the word without understanding the more familiar use; yet it is a claim analogous to this that Aristotle wants to make in *Metaphysics* IV in respect of 'being' and 'one' and other *pros hen legomena*.[54] Without this the notion of focal meaning would be of small use to him.) But if such resemblance is not a strong enough condition, what is? When Aristotle himself comes to specify the criteria of focal meaning he is at once too narrowly scholastic and too hospitable. He calls for precise definitions which exhibit a particular formal connexion – *logoi ek tôn logôn*,[55] one definition contained in the rest; yet his criterion would admit the Academic example that elsewhere he seems to reject. But this is not, I am sure, the inconsistency of a controversialist. Aristotle has not solved the problem of defining focal meaning fully and exactly so as to give that idea all the philosophical power that he comes to claim for it: he has given only the necessary, not the sufficient, conditions for its use. But there is no reason to think that this problem can have a general answer. Aristotle's evasion of it may come from the conviction that any answer would be artificial, setting boundaries that must be endlessly too wide or too narrow for his changing purposes. The concept of a word as having many senses pointing in many ways to a central sense is a major

53. No such claim is implied by *GC* 322b29-32 even if this is read (as e.g. by Fr. J. Owens) as saying that *any* word has a number of senses and is used either homonymously or focally; but Joachim's version is surely correct (*Aristotle on Coming-to-be and Passing Away*, p.141).

54. To say this is not to confuse priority *tôi logôi*, in definition, with priority *têi gnôsei*, for knowledge. As Ross remarks (*Metaphysics* ii p.161) the first is one form of the second in *Meta*. 1018b30-2 and entails it in 1049b16-17. In *Meta*. IV Aristotle plainly assumes that his focal analysis of 'being' shows that understanding the primary sense of the word is indispensable to understanding the rest. When in VII 1 he distinguishes the two kinds of priority he is not contradicting this but making quite another point (1028a31-b2): substance is said to be 'prior for knowledge' in the sense that the *ti esti* (what is it?) question, *in any category*, is the most informative; when he wants to show that this question has its primary use in the first category he falls back once again on the focal analysis of 'being' (1030a34-b7).

55. *Meta*. 1077b3-4: on this crabbed text see Ross's note.

philosophical achievement; but its scope and power are to be understood by use and not by definition.

To conclude. On the evidence, Aristotle seems to have been unlucky in his early brushes with focal meaning. If the contexts in which we have just seen it are to be assigned to his years in the Academy, he would regard it as an ill-defined device for which false claims had been made in some Academic arguments, his own and other people's, which on other grounds he had come to reject. The general disregard of it in his criticism of the Platonists was not forensic guile, and the neglect of it in some of his own earlier philosophising was not the price of guile. Perhaps the attack on the Ideas and on any general metaphysics of being encouraged him to treat ambiguity as a matter of black and white. Yet it seems to have been this same debate which gave him the method of analysis that finally freed him from his own objections. It was by suggestion, then, as well as by opposition, that the Academy helped to form the logic of those different inquiries which at different times took on the title of First Philosophy.

3

G. Patzig

Theology and Ontology in Aristotle's Metaphysics*

I

Unlike Aristotle's other treatises, the collection of writing that has come
down to us under the name *ta meta ta phusika* makes a leisurely approach to
its objective and the problems it sets out to attack. Of its fourteen books, six
– or, if we disregard books II and V as not strictly parts of the collection,
four – only touch on these problems and offer a preliminary, if positive,
discussion. In the course of these books (I, III, IV and VI) Aristotle tackles
from various viewpoints the fundamental philosophical science which he
calls first the 'sought-for science' (*hê zêtoumenê epistêmê*) and then '*first
philosophy*' (*prôtê philosophia*). In this introduction, Aristotle follows out a
consistent train of thought, but one which it is not easy to keep constantly in
mind; it is interrupted by long digressions, and Aristotle's shifting points of
view are also confusing. The essential elements in the 'sought-for science',
whose antecedents Aristotle sketches in I 1, often seem strange or even
incompatible bedfellows.

One of the most difficult problems of interpretation set by the *Metaphysics*
lies in the fact that in book IV the 'sought-for science' is characterised very
precisely as the science of 'being *qua* being' (*on hêi on*).[1] Unlike the particular
sciences, it does not deal with a particular *area* of being, but rather
investigates everything that is, in its most general structural elements and
principles. This description fulfils the expectations the reader has derived
from books I and III, which repeatedly aim at insights of the highest
generality. But, on the other hand, and startlingly, we *also* discover that in
Metaphysics VI 1 – only a few pages further on, if we exclude book V as not
part of the collection – Aristotle seems first to accept this opinion and then,
immediately afterwards, to embrace its exact opposite. For in VI 1 we again
find an analysis of the sciences designed to establish the proper place of 'first
philosophy'. Here, however, Aristotle does not, as he did in book IV,

---

* This paper is a revised version of a lecture I gave at a meeting of the 'Inner Circle' of
the Deutsche Gesellschaft für Philosophie on 29 October 1959 in Hamburg. The
lecture developed ideas that were, in all essentials, already presented in my
(unpublished) Göttingen dissertation of 1950. A comparison with recent literature,
especially with Owens' book [111], and with the relevant portions of Moser's
Metaphysik einst und jetzt (see Wagner's review [142]) has revealed some holes in the
framework of my lecture; I hope soon to be able to patch these up in a suitable place.

1. *Meta.* IV 1, 1003a21; 24; 31.

distinguish the 'sought-for science' from all other sciences by its greater generality. First he divides philosophy into three parts: theoretical, practical, and productive; and then he splits theoretical philosophy into three disciplines. To each of these disciplines he entrusts well-defined areas as objects of research. The 'sought-for science', referred to in IV as the 'science of being *qua* being', he now calls 'first philosophy', and defines it as the science of what is 'changeless and self-subsistent (*akinêton kai chôriston*)'. He explicitly gives it the title of 'theology'. Physics and mathematics stand beside it as the two neighbouring disciplines in the field of theoretical philosophy.

Such an unexpected conclusion to so extended an introduction to 'first philosophy' must seem strange to the reader. It is understandable that an author should see the fundamental philosophical science as universal ontology. We can also accept that a philosopher should elevate theology above all other sciences because of the importance of its object. But that Aristotle should attempt to undertake *both* enterprises in a *single* work surely violates 'the greatest duty of a philosopher', which, according to Kant, consists in 'being consistent'.[2]

That Aristotle here contradicts himself has been the dominant view in textbooks and commentaries since the middle of the last century. When faced by such difficulties of interpretation, it is customary to seek help from philology. It seemed necessary to saddle Aristotle with an internal inconsistency; and yet scholars were unwilling to credit him with one. Might not philology show that Aristotle's text did not, after all, contain such an inconsistency? In this way, the problem has submitted to what might be called therapeutic surgery at the hands first of Paul Natorp [115] and then, more recently, of Werner Jaeger ([28], pp.214-21). Natorp resorted to the classical remedy of the nineteenth century, the obelus. Jaeger replaced this by its modern and more lenient counterpart, stratification. The two attempts are, curiously, almost mirror images of each other: Natorp saw the 'theologising tendency' of VI 1 as the result of interpolations by a later hand into Aristotle's text. By making excisions in the text and by giving a somewhat violent interpretation to what was left, he attempted to obliterate this tendency. Jaeger, on the other hand, regards the problematical line of thought which culminates in the description of 'first philosophy' as theology not as the amateurish addition of anonymous epigoni but as the remains of an earlier theologising stage in Aristotle's own development.

187

The following discussion attempts to prove three points:

1. Both Natorp's and Jaeger's solutions, which may be seen as the two end points of a whole spectrum of related solutions,[3] are contradicted by the text of the *Metaphysics* itself.

2. *Critique of Practical Reason* (1787), p.44.
3. Thus Reidemeister in his important article 'Das System des Aristoteles' (now in K. Reidemeister, *Das exakte Denken der Griechen*, 1949, pp.67-87) speaks of a certain 'refractoriness' which 'appears in Aristotle's thought as a double inclination that he could not overcome but is explicitly aware of' (p. 70). Reidemeister rejects, on good grounds, both the separate ascription of these inclinations to Aristotle's youth and to his maturity, and the early dating of books I-VI. And he has informed me by word of mouth that he does not regard the 'refractoriness' as a contradiction.

2. As opposed to these radical solutions, we find that a conservative treatment, based on a detailed analysis of the text, is possible.

3. This interpretation, which defuses the supposed contradiction, reveals a characteristically Aristotelian mode of thought and argument – a mode which can be discovered in other parts of the *corpus* too, and which merits the attention of anyone concerned to give an accurate portrayal of Aristotle's intellectual 'development'.

II

I begin with a criticism of the two solutions sketched above. Natorp removes the supposed contradiction in the account of 'first philosophy' by exercising as interpolations those sentences which characterise 'first philosophy' as theology. The following facts tell against this: Book XI of the *Metaphysics* contains in its first eight chapters a summary of the line of thought in books III, IV, and VI: in the passage answering to VI 1 (7, 1064a33-b14), it contains sentences identical in sense to those in VI 1 that Natorp sees as interpolations. The need to declare the whole of book XI spurious is in itself a distinct drawback to Natorp's solution. Moreover, the rejected passages in VI 1, apart from the fact that, as I shall shortly show, their context requires them, and apart from the parallels in XI 7, find further independent support in I 2. There, the 'sought-for science' is called 'divine among sciences', because it must be ascribed to God and also because it deals with things divine.[4] Finally, Natorp's obelisation is completely excluded by a remark in VI 1, which will prove important to my subsequent argument and which even Natorp allows to be genuine, though he gives it a highly unorthodox interpretation. Aristotle says: 'For physics deals with things which exist separately but are not changeless, and some parts of mathematics deal with things which are changeless but presumably do not exist separately but as embodied in matter; while the first science deals with things which both exist separately and are changeless' (1026a13-16). The plain sense of this passage is unmistakable: first philosophy deals with those beings which *unite* in themselves the two positive characteristics which belong separately to the objects of physics and of mathematics – independent existence and immutability. For, according to Aristotle's theory (*Meta.* XIII 2-3), mathematical objects are only real in the sense that they belong to 'properly real' things, like animals, plants, and stones as their quantitative determinations or forms. Being produced by abstraction, mathematical objects are removed from all change; but they pay for their incorruptibility by a loss in reality. Natural objects, on the other hand, are supremely 'real'; but since, by definition, they can also be described as 'material' objects, and Aristotle links matter (*hulê*) with the possibility of change, we can say correspondingly of natural beings that they have bought their 'reality' at the price of corruptibility.

Natorp would have Aristotle say here that while physics deals with what is independent but not with what is immutable, and mathematics deals with

188

---

4. 'For the most divine science is also the most honourable; and this science alone must be, in two ways, most divine; for the science which it would be most meet for God to have is a divine science, and so is any science that deals with divine objects' (*Meta.* I 2, 983a5-9). Cf. *Phys.* II 2, 194b14-15: 'The mode of existence and the essence of the separable it is the business of first philosophy to determine.'

what is immutable but not with what is independent and immaterial, the 'fundamental science' also deals with what is immutable and immaterial – for in fact it deals with *everything*. From a purely linguistic point of view, this interpretation is not consistent with the text; for example, the phrase *hê men gar phusikê peri chôrista men all' ouk akinêta* cannot mean 'physics deals with independent but not with immutable things'; rather, the words *all' ouk akinêta* define the *chôrista* that are the object of physics. To justify his reading, Natorp would have had to add at least a second *peri* before *akinêta* in the text. Correctly interpreted, our sentence leads logically to the threefold division of theoretical philosophy into physics, mathematics, and theology which follows it in Aristotle's text (1026a18-19) and which Natorp wanted to excise. Natorp's athetising is thus impossible; it remains to show that it is also unnecessary.

189

Jaeger's theory, expounded and defended in detail in his brilliant book of 1923, is liable to very considerable and in part insurmountable objections. As I indicated briefly above (p.34), Jaeger considers the characterisation of 'first philosophy' as theology to be the fossilised remains of an earlier stage in Aristotle's development – a stage which is outgrown in the rest of books I-VI, and whose 'theological and Platonic' principle of investigation found its purest expression, according to Jaeger, in book XII of the *Metaphysics* (Jaeger [28], p.218). For XII represents the period when Aristotle's metaphysics 'was still purely Platonic and did not recognise the doctrine of sensible substance as an integral part of first philosophy' (p.221).

In VI 1, the early 'theological and platonic' conception of first philosophy and the later – in Jaeger's words (p.218) 'more Aristotelian' – view of first philosophy as universal ontology, appear together in 'sharp contrast' (p.217) and indeed in contradiction with one another (p.218). 'These two accounts of the nature of metaphysics certainly did not arise out of one and the same act of reflection. Two fundamentally different trains of thought are here interwoven' (p.218).

We naturally wonder how a writer of Aristotle's calibre could allow two fundamental positions, which belong to very different periods of his development and furthermore contradict each other, to stand side by side in a single chapter of his treatise on 'first philosophy'. But let us not argue over such psychological matters; it is rather on philosophical grounds that Jaeger's interpretation loses its credibility. Even supposing that Jaeger's view of the young and the old Aristotle, meeting in VI 1 as the young and the old Schopenhauer meet in the preface to the second edition of the *Vierfachen Wurzel*[5] – even supposing this view were correct, we could still not understand how the pure theology that Jaeger ascribes to the young Aristotle could ever have come to bear the name of 'first philosophy', a name that Aristotle expressly attributes to it in the chapter under discussion. For how could a man give a judgment on *everything* if his knowledge were limited to the existence and essence of God? The 'sought-for science', which is called first philosophy here in VI 1, has already been defined in I 2, on the basis of common opinions about the 'wise man' or

5. *Die vierfachen Wurzel des Satzes vom zureichenden Grunde*, in Schopenhauer's *Sämtliche Werke* II (ed. M. Braun, Leipzig 1908), pp.11-13.

sophos, as the science whose possessor 'in a certain sense knows everything'.[6] **190**
It is Aristotle's custom – a custom highly characteristic of his manner of
philosophising – to begin a train of argument by tying it loosely to current
opinions and ordinary linguistic usage. Anyone familiar with this custom
will find it impossible to believe that Aristotle had already constructed as it
were a 'first first philosophy' before arriving at the views expressed in book
I. Nor can book XII of the Metaphysics be construed, as Jaeger claims, as
the 'priceless source' for a 'pure' theology which then served as a
preliminary to universal ontology ([28], p. 219). For XII devotes five of its
chapters to an analysis of perishable substances (i.e. natural objects), and
only its latter half to a description of the essence of the prime mover and his
intellectual activity. I shall return to the problem of the connexion between
the two halves of book XII; but now, having become acquainted with
Natorp's and with Jaeger's attempts to solve the puzzle I sketched, and
having for various reasons found them wanting, we must turn our attention
to the text of VI 1 itself.

III

Immediately after the controversial identification of theology with 'first
philosophy', we find in the text a remarkable, not to say astonishing,
passage. As though Aristotle has been listening in to our discussion so far,
he goes straight to the problem with which we are concerned and attempts
to clear up a possible misunderstanding of his doctrine which suggests itself
to him:

> For one might raise the question whether first philosophy is
> universal, or deals with one genus, i.e. some one kind of being;[7] for
> not even the mathematical sciences are all alike in this respect –
> geometry and astronomy deal with a certain particular kind of thing,
> while universal mathematics applies alike to all.[8] We answer that if
> there is no substance other than those which are formed by nature, **191**
> natural science will be the first science; but if there is a changeless

6. 'We suppose first, then, that the wise man knows all things as far as possible,
though he has not knowledge of each of them individually ... The property of
knowing all things must belong to him who has in the highest degree universal
knowledge; for he knows in a sense all the cases which fall under the universal' (*Meta.*
I 2, 982a8-10; 21-3).

7. Here, as often, *phusis* means the same as *ousia*; cf. e.g. *PA* I 1, 639a10.

8. Natorp treated this sentence and the comparison between 'first philosophy'
and 'universal mathematics' or the general theory of magnitudes as a proof of his
claim that the basic philosophical science is simply general ontology: geometry and
astronomy are related, like physics and mathematics, to determinate objects; but the
theory of magnitudes is common to all the mathematical sciences in just the way in
which 'first philosophy' is *general* ontology and thus includes in its domain the objects
of physics and mathematics (p.53). Natorp forgets that elsewhere (*Meta.* XII 8,
1073b3-8) Aristotle describes as the mathematical science most closely related to
philosophy not the theory of magnitudes, but astronomy. For astronomy deals with
objects that are strikingly similar to the 'first mover' and the divine. Thus the analogy
between first philosophy and universal mathematics holds only to the extent that, in
contrast to the other sciences, both are *general*; the peculiarity of 'first philosophy'
remains – it is *at the same time both special and general*.

substance, the science of this must be prior and must be first philosophy, and universal in this way, because it is first. And it will belong to this to consider being *qua* being – both what it is and the attributes which belong to it *qua* being (*Meta.* VI 1, 1026a23-32).

It is clear from these remarks that the embarrassing contradiction between a 'first philosophy' which is universal ontology and a 'first philosophy' which, as theology, investigates only the substance of God simply did not exist for Aristotle. First philosophy is more philosophically reflective than either of these simplifications; it is theology of so special a kind that it is *as such at the same time* ontology. Aristotle is envisaging here a philosophical discipline that is both a first and a general philosophy, and a substance that is so superior to all other substances that it can at the same time be called in a certain sense substance in general. The thought that underlies this conception finds expression in the quasi-formulaic words *kai katholou houtôs hoti prôtê* ('and universal in this way, because it is first': 1026a30). This is not very easy to grasp, but this much at least is apparent: if we are to understand Aristotle correctly, we should not oppose the two apparently contradictory definitions of 'first philosophy' and attempt to decide in favour of one or the other, but should rather try to understand the assertion that these two definitions essentially belong together and that only their conjunction adequately characterises Aristotle's 'first philosophy'. Our understanding of this basic thesis naturally depends in turn on our success in comprehending that metaphysical relationship in virtue of which what is true of the 'first' is true universally, or – to phrase it in a less Aristotelian way – in virtue of which reasoned judgments about the whole domain of being can be provided by a science that deals with a determinate part of that domain.

IV

As we have just seen, Aristotle appears to recognise a very peculiar relationship of part to whole, by which the part supplies in a way the content and principle of the whole. The question arises whether there are examples of this metaphysical relationship between favoured part and whole in addition to the relationship of first philosophy to the other philosophical disciplines. Such examples might of course throw some light on the relationship that concerns us. In fact, Aristotle provides us with a whole array of such cases; and we shall see that this metaphysical structure, under the name of 'paronomy' or of *pros hen legesthai* ('be so called in relation to some one thing'), has a not inconsiderable standing among Aristotle's modes of argument.[9]

192

9. It should be noted that paronymy is construed by Aristotle at *Cat.* 1, 1a12 ff. (cf. 8, 10a32 ff.) as a special case of homonymy, alongside synonymy and 'mere' homonymy, and that this does not *precisely* coincide with what he describes as *pros hen legesthai*. Paronymy holds between *words* like 'wood' and 'wooden', 'courage' and 'courageous'. For discussion see Ross [4] I, p.256; [5] pp.559 ff. Ross too treats the *pros hen* relation as a special case of paronymy, and I adopt this convenient convention in my own discussion. Through the kindness of the author I have had access to Hintikka's important paper ([101], ch.1); and I should like to draw attention to its conclusions which are highly pertinent to the subject of this article. See also E.K. Specht, *Kantstudien* 51, 1959, pp.102-13.

The simplest example appears in book II of the *Metaphysics*. At the end of the first chapter (993b23-6) fire is described as being 'most hot' (*malista thermon*) in the sense that everything else that is called hot only possesses this quality by virtue of the fire contained in or working on it. In this way, fire has a special position in the class of hot things; it is both itself a hot thing and the cause and principle of heat in other things.

In *Metaphysics* IV 2, 1003a33-b1, Aristotle produces a better example of this special relationship: we call many things 'healthy', for example clothes, medicine, a man's complexion or an invalid's constitution. Clothing is called, and is, healthy if it preserves health; medicine if it restores it; healthy complexions merely indicate health, while a healthy constitution gives hope of an early return to health should it be upset. The things that are, and are called, healthy stand in differing relationships to health itself. Health, Aristotle argues, is the source of healthiness in everything else: it is both healthy itself and the cause and principle of being healthy – it is the 'first healthy thing', the *prôton hugieinon*. In both cases, Aristotle only adduces these concrete examples as graphic models for abstract relationships; the case of fire is supposed to illuminate the dependence of everything true on what is 'truest by nature'; the example of health – and the example of the 'medical' that immediately follows it in the text (1003b1-4) – are supposed to clarify the special relation between substance (*ousia*) and the beings in the other categories. *Ousia* (for which I shall hereafter use, wherever possible, **193** the standard translation 'substance', even though this is notoriously misleading) is both itself a being among others *and* a principle and cause of being for all the beings in the other categories – qualities, quantities, relations, etc. Aristotle's doctrine that qualities, quantities, and relations do indeed exist, but only in so far as they are seen and grasped in substances, the true realities, we may assume to be familiar. This doctrine is connected with a characteristic refinement of Aristotle's conception of being, which holds that 'reality' is constituted by the world of forms open to our perception.[10] For our purposes it is important to observe that it is at precisely this point that the logical principle of paronomy becomes indispensable; it is the clamp that prevents ontology from disintegrating. Aristotle had already proved, against Plato, that being (*to on*) cannot be an ultimate genus because it is in itself differentiated from the outset according to the categories:[11] 'being divides directly into kinds' (*Meta.* IV 2, 1004a4). Qualities, for example, and substances, processes and relations are fundamentally different from each other *as* beings. Must we not then abandon all hope of a unified science of 'being *qua* being'? Does not this reduce the word 'being' to a '*merely* homonymous' (i.e. equivocal) concept? Aristotle gives the answer to these and related questions by way of the notion of paronomy: paronomy guarantees the unity of ontology as a science. For, as Aristotle says 'not only in the case of things which have one common nature does the investigation belong to one science, but also in the case of things which are related to one common nature; for even these have in a sense one common nature' (*Meta.* IV 2, 1003b12-15). For Aristotle,

10. Cf. my paper [197].
11. Aristotle uses this argument more than once: e.g. *Top.* IV 1, 121a10 ff.; *Meta.* III 3, 998b14 ff.; XI 1, 1059b24 ff.

then, zoology is 'a single' science of living creatures in a *different sense* from
that in which ontology is 'a single' science of being. For all living creatures
are living creatures in the same way: *as* living creatures they are
synonymous. We can, in principle at least, give a *definition* of 'living creature'
that holds good for all individual cases alike; and 'living creature' becomes a
generic concept. On the other hand, births and deaths, properties and
relations etc. are 'beings' only *paronymously*. Friendship, for example, only
exists in so far as there are men who reveal this particular trait in their
relationships; friendship, and relations in general, only 'are' in so far as
there are substances – men, perhaps – who stand in such a relationship to
one another. In short, *ousia* is, according to Aristotle, the *cause of existence* for
all other beings.

We have seen that paronymy, synonymy, and 'mere' homonymy are in
Aristotle's view relationships between *objects* (this word should be taken in
194 its widest sense of *entia*). Paronymy, so far as concerns the intimacy of the
relationship it establishes, stands between synonymy and 'mere'
homonymy. Synonyms have the same names and the same definitions (thus,
fish and birds are synonyms *qua* living creatures); homonyms (e.g. in
English, a mole: a furry animal, a jetty, or a spot)[12] have only their name in
common and enjoy quite different definitions. Paronyms, on the other hand,
or at least *ta pros hen legomena* (see note 9), have not only the same name but
also one definition by virtue of their different relationships to some identical
thing. This one thing, which serves as the reference point of such
paronymous definitions, is called 'first' by Aristotle; thus *ousia* is the 'first
being' and, in my second example, health is the 'first healthy thing'.

Aristotle now advances the very natural suggestion that the science of a
domain in which such a paronymous unity reigns, is concerned essentially
and primarily with 'the first thing in each category' (*Meta.* IV 2, 1004a29):
'But everywhere science deals chiefly with that which is primary, and on
which the other things depend, and in virtue of which they get their names'
(*Meta.* IV 2, 1003b16). Thus ontology, although it is the science of being *qua*
being and unrestricted in its domain, is nevertheless as a paronymous
science primarily and properly the science of substance, the 'first being',
and hence at the same time the science of beings in the other categories.

V

Guided by Aristotle's examples of fire, health, and substance, we have
attempted to think ourselves into his underlying train of thought and as it
were to agree that there are domains within which we can grasp the whole
in some one favoured part, and only in that. These examples now shed new
light on some of Aristotle's celebrated *mots*. Thus he describes the hand as
the 'tool of tools'.[13] We do not treat this phrase with proper philosophical
respect if we simply read into it a reference to the *superiority* of the hand as
opposed to other tools. This is the sense in which we sometimes speak of a
favourite town as the 'town of towns'; it is a manner of speech that strikes us

12. Aristotle's Greek example – *kleis*, meaning 'key' *and* 'collar bone' (*EN* V 1,
1129a30) – is not a very happy choice.
13. *De An.* III 8, 432a1-2: 'as the hand is the tool of tools, so reason is the form of
forms and perception the form of sensible things.'

as traditional and ceremonial when the Bible is referred to as the 'book of books', and as banal when the daily press refers to a sportsman as the 'ace of aces'. We can, however, see that if Aristotle *does* mean it in this way, he does not *only* mean it in this way; for in our passage from the *De Anima* the example of the human hand is only an illuminating *image* for the obscure   **195** relationship that holds between the human *nous* and the other forms or *eidê*: the hand is a tool among other tools and yet it is also true that these latter tools are only as it were raised to their status as tools through the activity of the hand.[14] Without a hand to use them, all other tools would no longer properly be called tools. Tools are dependent for their status as tools upon the human hand – the hand is, as Aristotle would put it, their 'principle'. This analogy can perhaps give us a better understanding of the famously controversial words that follow in Aristotle's text – words that nonetheless remain enigmatic enough: *nous*, human reason, is the '*eidos* of *eidê*', the 'form of forms' (*De An.* III 8, 432a2). Guided by the tool analogy, we can say, in a purely formal way, that the cognitive faculty is both an *eidos* among other *eidê and* in a certain sense the intrinsic content and principle of the other *eidê*. Closely linked to this paronymous use of *nous* as the *eidos* of *eidê* is Aristotle's celebrated doctrine that 'the soul is in a certain sense everything that is',[15] and also the bold statement in the introduction to the theology of book XII of the *Metaphysics*: 'And thought thinks on itself because it shares the nature of the object of thought' (1072b20).

Here, however, I cannot go further into an explanation of the relationships between divine and human *nous*, and between *nous* as such and the multiplicity of the *eidê*; it is enough to say, on the basis of the examples we have described, that the relation of paronymy, although it seems at first sight to be purely formal and grammatical, nevertheless comes to metaphysical life at certain key points of Aristotle's philosophising. These examples also show that Aristotle is referring to a *single* determinate idea when he calls first philosophy 'universal, because it is first'. There is no question here, as Jaeger supposes, of Aristotle helplessly contemplating a yawning chasm between two conceptions of first philosophy that date from two different stages of his development. The idea in VI 1 is so very much a *single* philosophical idea that we can immediately predict the further assertions to which the remarks in VI 1 commit Aristotle: he must plainly be able to say that theology, properly and rigorously understood, is at the same time nothing but the study of being *qua* being, or ontology. And 'the only possible basis of demonstration' for such an assertion must, according   **196** to our previous reflections, lie in the proof that God is the *first* substance among substances, the genuine substance, the *ousia ousiôn*, on which all other substances rely for their being and which preserves their being – just as substance itself is the 'first being',[16] on which all other beings that are not substances depend as the basis of their being. We should therefore postulate a relation of paronymy on *two levels* as far as being is concerned: first, the

14. Cf. the fine passage at *PA* IV 10, 687b2-5: 'Take the hand: this is as good as a talon or a claw or a horn, or again a spear or sword, or any other weapon or tool: it can be all of these because it can seize and hold them all.'

15. 'Let us now summarise our remarks about the soul, and repeat that the soul is in a way all existing things' (*De An.* III 8, 431b20-1).

16. *Meta.* IV 2, 1003b16-19; VII 1, 1028a13-16; etc.

relation of substance to the other beings (qualities, relations, etc.), which rest upon it, and secondly the relation of the unmoved and independent substance of God to other substances. Ontology is therefore a doubly paronymous science.

VI

I now ask whether Aristotle actually maintained that such a paronymous relation holds between substances other than the substance of God – in particular 'natural beings' – and that single and special substance. If we assume that the substance of God, the most sublime object of 'first philosophy', is identical with the 'first mover',[17] we can put the question more precisely: in what sense, according to Aristotle, is the 'first mover' so much a 'first' among all substances that the substantial character of all other substances derives from it as their cause and principle? Phrased in this way the question is open to solution; the key lies buried in the ground we have already cleared, provided only we remember that Aristotle saw the essence of *ousia* in a very special way. The *ousia* of a thing is its *eidos* or its *ti ên einai*. But a thing's *eidos* is conceived by Aristotle as a cause of its being, that which allows the thing whose *eidos* it is to become what it is.[18] 'Plainly we are seeking the cause. And this is the essence' – Aristotle twice says this in as many words in chapter 17 of *Metaphysics* VII. The 'what' of a thing is for Aristotle in a way the same as the 'why' – the *ti* coincides with the *dia ti*; and Aristotle can say this because he believes that the *eidos* has a certain *efficacy*. If we could prove that, for Aristotle, the 'first mover' is in fact the *cause* of the being of other substances, it would follow that a rigorous account of the being of natural things requires a reference to their relationship to this divine substance. For the being of a thing is the statement of its causes, and one of the causes of every natural being is the 'first mover'. Put more formally, the concept of an *ousia* other than the *ousia* of the first mover logically presupposes the concept of the 'first mover'; and it is plain that we only put this same fact in a different way if we say with Aristotle that ontology precisely *as* ontology must essentially and primarily be *theology*.

In the midst of all these formulae that hover around Aristotle's basic ideas, we should not forget that we have as yet no *proof* that Aristotle in fact saw his 'first mover' in this extended sense as the *cause* of existence of all other beings. Of course, we conjecture that this is so; and our conjecture is justified because in the light of everything else we know about Aristotle, this thesis alone can provide the intrinsic link between ontology and theology, which Aristotle expressly asserts in the passage in VI 1 from which we started. Detailed elucidation of the programme he suggests there must, then, primarily consist in a detailed substantiation of this thesis. I have already mentioned above, in connection with my criticism of Jaeger's solution, that all the evidence suggests that book XII of the *Metaphysics* is a brief sketch of Aristotle's detailed account of first philosophy, otherwise lost, to which books I-VI provide the introduction. We must therefore look to

197

17. The passages are collected and discussed by Zeller, *Philosophie der Griechen*,[2] IIb, pp.270-85.

18. Apart from the passages mentioned in the text (*Meta*. VII 17, 1041a27; b7-9) see especially: *A. Pst.* II 2, 90a6, 14, 31; *Meta*. II 1, 993b23; *De An*. II 2, 413a13-15.

book XII for a discussion of our main question. If we find it, it will strengthen our frail construction, which thus far is made of interpretation, conjecture, and criticism – the interpretation of VI 1; the conjecture that Aristotle's first philosophy was the paronymous science of the causes of beings, and *therefore* theology; and our criticism of Jaeger's interpretation. It would then be evident that XII does not, as Jaeger argues, present a purely theological 'Urmetaphysik', chronologically earlier than books I-VI, – and indeed that Aristotle never asserted to anything as philosophically flabby as Jaeger's 'Platonic-theological *Urmetaphysik*'. At all events, even if XII should turn out to be an early text, this supposition would lose its most important prop.

VII

Let us then turn to book XII of the *Metaphysics*. It contains, as is usually – and up to a point rightly – said, a synoptic account of the three types of substance: the two natural substances, of which one is transitory, the other eternal; and the unmoving and immaterial substance that is God.[19] Aristotle introduces these three types at the very beginning of his account, and adds that while the investigation of the first two types of substance is the task of *natural philosophy*, unmoving substance must be the object of a 'different' science (1, 1069a36-b2). This concise statement of Aristotle's, it must be admitted, seems at first blush to favour the view we are opposing, according to which 'first philosophy' *only* investigates the imperceptible and unmoving substance of God; and thus Prächter, for example, in the last edition of Ueberweg-Heinze, says briefly and confidently that 'imperceptible substances fall under a special science (metaphysics)' (p. 367). But this would make it all the more difficult to understand why, in a treatise exclusively devoted to 'first philosophy', Aristotle should analyse into their elements and principles those substances which he refers to natural philosophy – and devote half of book XII to the analysis.[20] The interpretation which has been dominant since Jaeger's work and which treats book XII as a document of Aristotle's 'pure theology' is seriously weakened by the fact that so much space is given over to physical substances in chapters 1-5. On the other hand, the very construction of the book gives rise to equally grave objections against any attempt to follow Natorp and use it in precisely the opposite sense as evidence that Aristotle's 'first philosophy' was not a specialised theology but a general ontology which investigates with impartial enthusiasm and without prejudice everything that exists, seeking out its elements and principles '*qua* being'. For this interpretation could not explain why a single substance, that of the prime mover, should receive a longer treatment than all other substances *put together*. Alexander of Aphrodisias found, as so often, a felicitous expression for this plain fact: in a passage of his commentary on book III of the *Metaphysics* that bears on our problem, he says that in his ontology Aristotle treats the substance of the prime mover *proêgoumenôs* – 'with special

198

---

19. The opposites 'mutable'/'immutable' are replaced by the pair 'perceptible'/'immutable'. For only material things are perceptible, all material things are as such natural beings, and every natural being is mutable.

20. I omit chapter 8 as an excursus added at a later date.

preference' (171.11). This accurately represents the matter; and if we recall the principle stated in IV 2, which has already been quoted – every science that has a paronymous unity should treat primarily of 'the first, on which the rest depend' (1003b16) – it becomes probable that Alexander too thought that Aristotle saw the prime mover as a paronymous 'first' of this type. These hints would lead us to expect that in XII 1-5 natural substances will be not so much described and investigated as *reduced*, step by step, to the substance of the prime mover. The main line of Aristotle's argument should consist in a proof that other substances are attached to the first mover in their being. The question really calls for a thorough scrutiny of the text, which would be out of place here; but it is pleasing to observe, in this somewhat embarrassing situation, that a commentator as eminent as Ross – who on this issue is not *parti pris* – comes to the same conclusion as I have done in his analysis of chapters 1-5, even if he does not draw all the inferences from it that I have just done. It will suffice here to quote the relevant sentences from the Introduction to Ross' celebrated edition of the

199   *Metaphysics*: 'Its first five chapters discuss the fundamental nature of sensible substance, thus covering the same ground as VII-VIII ... It is to be noted too that while VII-VIII are occupied mainly with the logical analysis of sensible substance into form and matter, XII is concerned rather with the causal explanation of the existence of sensible things, and therefore brings in at an early stage and constantly insists on the necessity of a motive cause as well. It thus prepares the way for the proof of the necessity of a single motive cause of the universe' ([4], I, p.xxviii).

These remarks of Ross' express exactly what would otherwise have had to be proved more elaborately from the text itself. Consequently, it will be enough to quote a few particularly important passages from XII 6-7.[21] 'Since there were three kinds of substance, two of them natural and one unchanging, with regard to the latter we must say that it is necessary that there should be an eternal unchanging substance' (1071b3-5). 'For substances are first among existing things, and if they were all perishable then everything might perish' (b5-6). 'There must, then, be such a principle whose being is actuality' (b19-20). 'For how will anything be put into motion if there is no motive cause?' (b28-9). 'But since there is something which moves while itself unmoved and which is in actuality, this cannot be otherwise than it is. For locomotion is the first of all changes, and again circular motion is the first among types of locomotion; and this the first mover produces. It therefore exists of necessity; and in so far as its existence is necessary, it is at the same time good and in this sense a principle' (1072b7-11). 'On such a principle, then, depend the heavens, and nature' (*ek toiautês ara archês êrtêtai ho ouranos kai hê phusis*: b13-15). These sentences have often been described as the climax of Aristotle's philosophy, not in the sense that we see here the Aristotelian elements in Aristotle in their purest form, but in that the journey to the highest principles and causes, which Aristotle has so energetically pursued from the beginning of the *Metaphysics*, is here at last completed in a few giant strides. Aristotle's extraordinary brevity at this point may be attributed to aesthetic motives – he wants to

---

21. On the formal structure of this argument see now Oehler's valuable article [247].

provide us with a concise account of his theory of first principles. Plato, in a **200** similar passage at the end of the sixth book of the *Republic* where he is dealing with the ascent to the Form of the Good, likewise becomes curt, formulaic, and almost incomprehensible. The weight of thought is too great for words, and Plato resorts to the simile of the Cave. Where direct expression is bound to run aground on the distracting imagery of language, that very imagery is pressed into service by the use of an indirect, 'mythical', language which shows its audience the direction to turn their gaze if they are to glimpse those high objects they cannot directly apprehend. Aristotle does not allow himself the luxury of myth; but at the climax his language too alters and becomes, as it were, granular. The discursive embroidery of ideas is replaced by a severer style; certain central words stand out as linking threads in the web of thought. In our text the most important of these words is 'first', *prôton*: substances are 'first' among beings; locomotion is 'first' of changes; and among types of locomotion circular motion is again 'first': and thus the 'first mover' is what it is – the 'first substance' (XII 8, 1074b9). Paronymy piles on paronymy: if we regard the conclusion that something is 'first' as expressing a chronological succession or an evaluation, the line of Aristotle's thought loses its tension and we easily forget that the final sentence of the passage forms the bridge between XII and IV 2, where Aristotle developed the idea of a paronymous science: 'On such a principle, then, depend the heavens and nature'. The word *êrtêtai* is found in the *Metaphysics* only here and in a passage we have already quoted from IV 2 – in the very assertion that such a science deals principally (*kuriôs*) with that (paronymous) 'first' on which the other things depend (*ex hou ta alla êrtêtai*: 1003b17).[22] This completes Aristotle's proof of his claim in VI 1 that 'first philosophy' *as* theology is at the same time general ontology. For the substance of the first mover is paronymously first among substances: it is the 'substance of substances', as we might phrase it on analogy with the hand as tool of tools or with reason as *eidos* of *eidê*. For all other substances depend for their substantial nature on the prime mover, the 'first substance'. Aristotle is only consistent when, immediately after this proof (XII 7, 1072b14), he turns to an exposition of the intellectual activity and the happiness of the divine substance. We can now say that this exposition is the kernel of his ontology; for theology and ontology are paronymously interrelated in just the way in which their objects, the prime mover and being as such, are. The very name of '*first* philosophy' gives us an indication of how closely it is related to that high object: it is not 'first' philosophy **201** because it was invented first (from this point of view it is rather last);[23] nor is it 'first' philosophy because, as theology, its object entitles it to special respect and precedence (a precedence still shown today in the traditional order of precedence among the academic disciplines). When Aristotle gives the word *prôton* a special importance, he is generally examining some paronymous structure, which has its objective basis in the particular relation that one favoured part bears to the whole. In such places Aristotle's

22. Cf. *Cael.* I 9, 279a28-30: 'From it derive (*exêrtêtai*) the being and life which other things, some more strongly, others feebly, enjoy.'

23. Here one thinks, of course, of the distinction between what is 'prior relative to us' and what is 'prior by nature' (*Phys.* I 1); on this see part II of Wieland's paper (vol I, ch.8).

true meaning will escape us unless we are careful; and they are not confined to the _Metaphysics_. Another important example occurs in the _Analytics_. Aristotle draws a well-known distinction between three syllogistic figures based on the position of the middle term in their premises. Now the figure to which e.g. the mood _Barbara_ belongs ('If _A_ belongs to all _B_ and _B_ belongs to all _C_, then _A_ necessarily belongs to all _C_') – this figure Aristotle calls the 'first'. In his syllogistic he singles out this first figure in many ways: for example, by the fact that its moods (with characteristic exceptions in modal logic) are all called 'perfect syllogisms'. There have been many attempts to explain this preference for the first figure: that Aristotle is dependent on Plato, that this figure is the 'most natural', the most important or the most useful from a scientific point of view, and so forth. All this misses the point;[24] Aristotle calls this figure the first because in his view the logical _validity_ of the moods of the two other figures can _only_ be made _evident_ by their 'reduction' (_anagôgê_) to the moods of the first figure. Hence, the first figure is the part of syllogistic singled out from the rest, and the other two figures can and must be referred and reduced to it – just as the 'prime mover' is the being to which all other substances, and so all other beings, can step by step be reduced. Thus the first figure is for Aristotle not a _figura prima inter pares_, but the principle and cause of syllogistic. Perhaps this one example is enough to show what I mean when I say that we shall understand Aristotle better, in his other works, as well as in the _Metaphysics_, if we take into account the systematic importance of these words he used so often: _prôton, kuriôs, malista, proteron_, – 'first', 'properly', 'especially', 'prior'.

VIII

These remarks mark the end of my attempt to answer my opening question, which was provoked by the dual definition of first philosophy, both as theology _and_ as general ontology, in the introductory books of the _Metaphysics_. I asked whether this dual definition could be understood in such a way as to escape the accusation of self-contradiction. If my interpretation holds water, I have exposed a basic line of argument that binds together books I, III, IV and VI and book XII into a coherent train of reasoning. Such an interpretation clearly is – to use the categories of modern Homeric research – 'unitarian'. Nevertheless, it remains a fact, unaffected by what has been said so far, that the three so-called 'books on substance' of the _Metaphysics_ (VII-IX) cannot be fitted into the account of a doubly paronymous ontology that I have outlined. It is true that in these books beings in the other categories are still related to substance as the 'first being'; but there is no trace of an essential reference in the analysis of natural substances to the doctrine of the 'prime mover'. The artificial unity of theology and ontology appears to be ruptured; at any rate we see no more of it. This fact is, of course, open to various interpretations. We might incline to the view that VII-IX, which are, as a literary whole, linked closely with each other and scarcely at all with the other books of the _Metaphysics_,[25] are also distinct in content from the rest of the _Metaphysics_: as an analysis of natural substance, they really belong to the _Physics_. There is, however, much

24. I discuss all this in greater detail in my book [108A], ch. III.
25. Thus e.g. IX 1, 1045b32 refers to book VII as 'the beginning of our account'.

to oppose this view, and I believe that it is refuted by the considerations Ross advances in his great edition of the *Metaphysics* ([4], I, pp.xviii-xxi). Another interpretation is possible; perhaps books VII-IX of the *Metaphysics* were written later than books I-VI, at a period when Aristotle had *abandoned* the paronymous relationship of theology and ontology. There seems to be a number of arguments in support of this idea; none of them can be called conclusive, but in this area of Aristotelian scholarship we must be content for most of the time with probabilities. I should now like to consider those arguments which tie in most closely to my previous discussion.

1. Firstly, it is plain that the name of 'first philosophy' for the study of 'being *qua* being' lost its point and became unacceptable once the connection between theology and ontology was abandoned; and in fact it appears that Aristotle made a conscious effort to *avoid* the phrase 'first philosophy' in the period when VII-IX were already written. This is indicated by the following fact, which otherwise is not easily explained: in all the places listed in Bonitz's *Index* where Aristotle refers to the *Metaphysics* by the phrase 'first philosophy', his reference is to book XII; books VII-IX, on the other hand, are referred to by such phrases as 'it has been said elsewhere' or 'it is the subject of another type of investigation'.[26] We may well ask whether this fact, which might of course be mere coincidence, is connected with the much discussed fact that our collection of writings only acquired their title '*ta meta ta phusika*' in about 60 B.C., when Andronikos of Rhodes prepared his edition of the collected works of Aristotle.[27] Did Aristotle leave this, alone of his treatises, without a title because the earlier title *peri prôtês philosophias* ('on first philosophy') become questionable and no longer seemed appropriate?

2. The thesis we have to establish rests on the assumption that Aristotle always held fast to the view that *ousia*, the concrete perceptible individual, is the basis of existence for all other beings. In fact, Aristotle explicitly repeats this doctrine at the very beginning of book VII (1, 1028a10-b7). On the other hand, it must also be shown that Aristotle later abandoned the further doubly paronymous reduction of all beings to 'first substance'. Now in Aristotle's other writings there are parallels for such a 'deparonymisation' of the doctrine of principles. It seems probable from our texts that such a 'deparonymisation' holds in the cases of '*hulê*' (matter), '*agathon*' (good), and '*philia*' (friendship), as well as in the case of substance. For the sake of brevity I shall confine myself to the case of *philia* (friendship),[28] because a comparison between the twin accounts in the *Eudemian* and the *Nicomachean Ethics* makes the change that took place here especially easy to grasp.[29] In the two parallel passages, three types of friendship are distinguished according to their essential motives – the moral worth of the friend, the advantage expected from friendship, or simply pleasure. In the *Eudemian Ethics*, Aristotle reduces the other two types of friendship to the one which

203

---

26. *Int.* 17a14; *Phys.* I 8, 191b29; cf. *EN* I 6, 1096a30.

27. I cannot accept Reiner's argument in [117] that the title is an old peripatetic one.

28. There is a corresponding examination of the two other concepts in my Göttingen dissertation, *Die Entwicklung des Begriffs der Usia in der 'Metaphysik' des Aristoteles* (1950, typescript), pp.139-51.

29. The passages are *EE* VII 2, 1236a15-b3; *EN* VIII 3, 1156a6-b6.

has a moral foundation, and he calls this type, in so many words, the 'first *philia*' (VII 2, 1236b2): only through this type do the other two types become capable of participating in the *logos* or definition of *philia*. In order to illustrate the paronymous relation of 'first friendship' to the others, Aristotle adduces the example of the 'medical' which is already known to us from *Meta*. IV 2, 1003b1-4. This example is no longer found in the *Nicomachean Ethics*; neither is the structure it illustrates. In the *Nicomachean Ethics* Aristotle treats the three types of friendship as equally primitive and independent of each other, even if friendship that has as its motive the moral superiority of the friend is called 'perfect friendship', and is praised because it brings with it both utility and pleasure, though on a higher level. Von Arnim drew attention to these changes in his work on Aristotle's ethics,[30] and he took them as an argument for his own early dating of the *Eudemian Ethics*. It is, of course, a further argument in favour of the *authenticity* of the *Eudemian Ethics*, which is still disputed, that they exhibit the paronymous form of argument which was so important to Aristotle, and which, as far as we can tell, none of his pupils adopted.

IX

In place of paronymy, we find in *Metaphysics* VII-IX another methodological tool which Aristotle borrowed from Plato but developed in his biological studies to a greater degree of conceptual precision.[31] This is the method of *analogy*. The basic ontological concepts, such as *eidos* and *hulê, dunamis* and *energeia*, are no longer defined by reference to a 'first' *eidos*, a 'first' *hulê*, a 'first' *dunamis* or *energeia*; rather, in the case of such basic concepts, we must be content, Aristotle says, 'to grasp the analogy' (*Meta*. IX 6, 1048a35-7). A *dunamis* is an x that is related to a y in the same way that a sleeper is to a waker, a block of marble to a statue, and so on. Similarly, an *eidos* is an x which is related to a y as soul is to man, or a constitution to the commonwealth that is a *single* state in virtue of its constitution. The analogical method no longer singles out a special case, which sometimes, as with the 'prime mover', lies beyond the bounds of possible experience. It is still true that everything, or, more precisely, every natural being, has its *hulê*, but it is no longer true that there is something that is the *hulê* of everything. (Compare the fact that for every number there is a number greater than it, but there is no number that is greater than every other number). Now, as before, it is true that every being has its *ousia*, but it is no longer true that there is a being which is the *ousia* of everything.

Thus the analogical method does not look for a special case that forms the basis for a whole class: it limits itself to grasping and making intelligble the common element in the relationships between observable pairs of things. Strangely enough, analogy can also be seen as a formal reflection of paronymy. Between the two of them there is a relationship that reminds the logician of the relationship of *duality* in propositional logic: paronymy, as I have said (above, p. 40), is a relation between objects that holds when the objects (*a*) are described by the same words and (*b*) are defined by their

30. H. von Arnim, *Eudemische Ethik und Metaphysik*, Sitzb. d. Wien. Akad., 207, 1928, pp.6f.
31. See Zeller, *op.cit.*, pp.389 ff.

different relationship to some *one* thing, the 'first in each category'. On the other hand, Aristotle thought that analogy holds between objects when (*a*) they are described by the same words and (*b*) they can be defined by their *identical* relationship to something *different*. Thus the unity of science is still possible; but while in a paronymous science unity is guaranteed by the identity of one pole of a relation, in an analogical science it is guaranteed by the identity of the relation itself.

If the difference that we have established between books VII-IX and the books we discussed earlier indicates a 'development' in Aristotle's thought, we now have a way of *describing* this development: we may call it the passage from a paronymous ontology to an analogical ontology. This will satisfy a requirement that can easily be derived from my criticism of Jaeger's solution: the idea of a development in Aristotle's thought will only be philosophically fruitful if it is construed in terms of the development of certain specific Aristotelian ideas. If the transition of thought we have discussed is characterised as the passage from paronymous to analogical ontology, the fundamental characteristic of Aristotle's 'development' – if indeed there is one at all – is much more pregnantly expressed than if we speak of a contrast between pure theology and general ontology. For no passable road seems to lead from theology to ontology, and we should have to resort to biographical and psychological speculation in order to explain this metamorphosis in Aristotle's notion of 'first philosophy'. On the other hand, the difference between paronymous and analogical ontology is a methodological distinction that falls wholly within the sphere of philosophy; and perhaps we may, without superficiality, compare this distinction with the distinction between Kant's precritical and critical writings.

Note (1973)

This article of 1960, based on the results of my Göttingen dissertation of 1950, has in the meantime received, in the recent literature on the subject, the usual share of agreement and criticism. The critics have been almost unanimous in rejecting the tentative proposal of a new version of Jaeger's development hypothesis, put forward in the last two sections of the paper. I have now abandoned these ideas and regard my development scheme as just another case of a tradition exerting its power even on those who are most eager to get away from it. The main part of my article, the analysis of the theology-ontology paradox, I still regard as basically sound.

My extended use of the terms 'paronymy', 'paronymous' ('paronymisch' in German) for what in Aristotle is referred to as *pros hen legesthai* (see the reservations in note 9), I now regard as a rather unfortunate piece of terminology. Owen's 'focal meaning' is of course much better. It was rendered by von Savigny, in his German translation of Owen's important paper in F.P. Hager (ed.) *Metaphysik und Theologie des Aristoteles* (Darmstadt 1969), p. 406, as 'Brennpunktbedeutung'. I kept to my terminology, however, since I could not easily find an adjective for 'paronymisch', which often occurs in the German text.

SHL
WITHDRAWN

4

J. Lukasiewicz

Aristotle on the Law of Contradiction

15   In my monograph, *O zasadzie sprzeczności u Arystotelesa*, I attempted to provide a thoroughgoing criticism of the remarks which Aristotle makes, principally in *Metaphysics* IV, on the subject of the Law of Contradiction. The vast progress made in the science of symbolic logic, begun by Boole and prosecuted by de Morgan, Peirce, Schröder, Frege, Peano, Russell and others, seems to demand a fresh consideration of the Law of Contradiction. We cannot ignore the fact that modern symbolic logic stands to traditional logic, and in particular to the logic of Aristotle, in the same relation as modern geometry stands to Euclid's *Elements*: in the course of the nineteenth century, a nice examination of Euclid's parallel postulate led to the development of new, non-Euclidean geometries; we cannot rule out of court the possibility that a thorough review of the fundamental principles of Aristotelian logic might perhaps lead to the development of new, non-Aristotelian logics. And even if the principles of Aristotle's logic should hold good for all time, they nevertheless provide the modern student with a mass of unsolved problems. In particular, we may ask how the highest logical principles, whose number has been substantially increased since Aristotle's time, should be formulated; in what relationship they stand to one another, and in particular whether they are all mutually indpendent or in some way derivable from an ultimate principle; whether their range of application is unrestricted or rather allows of certain exceptions; how, finally, we are warranted in holding these principles to be incontrovertibly true. These are all genuine questions; they have occasionally been raised and discussed before, but with the help of symbolic logic they can be more sharply posed and set in a new light.

16   In my monograph I tried to prepare the way for such a treatment of the Law of Contradiction. It seemed to me to be worthwhile, for more than one reason, to relate my critical remarks to Aristotle's discussion of the topic: every critique must be directed against a real opponent if it is not to become an idle bout of shadow-boxing between the critic and the creatures of his own imagination. Aristotle's views on the Law of Contradiction have, by and large, been generally accepted from his time until today; and there is a better collection of arguments for and against the Law in Aristotle than in any modern textbook on logic. My investigations therefore proceeded with Aristotle's text in one hand and the results of modern symbolic logic in the other. This paper gives a brief sketch of my main conclusions.

1. Aristotle formulates the Law of Contradiction in three ways, as an

ontological, a logical, and a psychological law; he does not make explicit the differences between them.

(a) Ontological formulation: 'It is impossible that the same thing should both belong and not belong to the same thing at the same time and in the same respect' (*Meta.* IV 3, 1005b19-20).

(b) Logical formulation: 'The most certain of all <principles> is that contradictory sentences are not true at the same time' (*Meta.* IV 6, 1011b13-14).

(c) Psychological formulation: 'No-one can believe that the same thing can <at the same time> be and not be' (*Meta.* IV 3, 1005b23-4).

2. We might express these laws more precisely as follows:

(a) Ontological formulation: *The same property cannot belong and not belong to a single object at the same time.* By 'object' I understand, with Meinong, anything that is 'something' and not 'nothing'; by 'property' I mean anything that can be predicated of an object.

(b) Logical formulation: *Two contradictory sentences cannot be true at the same*   **17**
time. By 'sentence' I mean a sequence of words or other perceptible symbols which has a meaning insofar as it predicates or denies some property of some object.

(c) Psychological formulation: *Two beliefs which answer to two contradictory sentences cannot exist at the same time in a single consciousness.* By 'belief' I mean a mental act which is *sui generis*: it is also designated by the terms 'conviction', 'recognition' etc; it cannot be more closely analysed but has to be experienced.

3. These formulations agree with those of Aristotle to the extent that he too often distinguishes, in comparable fashion, between the ontological *meaning* of a sentence and the mental act of *belief* which answers to a sentence. Thus:-

(a) Sentences (*apophanseis* – i.e. *kataphasis*, affirmation, or *apophasis*, negation) according to Aristotle signify the fact that something is or is not, i.e. the being or not being (*to einai ê mê einai*), and also the being thus and so and the not being thus and so, of objects. Such facts have recently been called 'objectives' by Meinong. (Stumpf calls them 'states of affairs'.) Thus in general, sentences signify the fact that an object has or has not some property (being, or being thus and so).

(b) Sentences according to Aristotle are perceptible symbols of mental acts of belief (*hupolêpsis*, sometimes *doxa*).

On (a):- The passages in the *De Interpretatione* where Aristotle explains the notion of a sentence show that sentences signify objectives: 'Every utterance (*logos*) is significant ... but not every <utterance> is a sentence (*apophantikos*) but only those which contain truth or falsity' (4, 17a1-3). 'For even "goatstag" signifies something, but not yet anything true or false – *unless being or not being is added*' (1, 16a16-18).

On (b):- That sentences are symbols of beliefs is shown clearly enough by   **18**
the following passage: 'Hence if this is the case with belief [i.e. if a positive belief is contrary to a negative belief], and if *spoken affirmations and negations are symbols of mental ones,* then it is clear that a <spoken> negation ... is contrary to an affirmation' (*De Int.* 14, 24b1-3).

4. None of the three formulations of the Law of Contradiction is *synonymous* with either of the others; for each contains expressions signifying essentially

different objects ('object' and 'property', 'sentence' and 'true', 'belief' and 'consciousness', etc.). But Aristotle thinks that the logical and ontological formulations are logically *equivalent*; for he treats sentences as representations of objectives, with which he puts them in a one-one correlation.[1] The old and inaccurate tag, *veritas est adaequatio rei et intellectus*, received a far more precise statement from Aristotle: 'To say of what is that it is and of what is not that it is not, is true' (*Meta.* IV 7, 1011b26-7). This one-one correlation between sentences and objectives entails the equivalence of the ontological and the logical Laws of Contradiction.

5. Aristotle attempts to *prove* the psychological Law of Contradiction on the basis of the logical Law. His proof falls into two parts.

    (a) 'If it is impossible for contrary properties to belong at the same time to the same thing ... and if beliefs corresponding to contradictory sentences are contrary to one another, it is evident that the same man cannot at the same time believe the same thing to be and not be. For if a man were mistaken on this point he would hold contrary beliefs at the same time' (*Meta.* IV 3, 1005b26-32). Here I interpret the difficult sentence *enantia esti doxa doxêi hê tês antiphaseôs* ('beliefs answering to contradictory sentences are contrary to one another') by reference to the parallel passage in the last chapter of the *De Interpretatione: doxa hê tês antiphaseôs* or *doxa tou enantiou = hê to enantion einai doxazousa* ('the <belief> holding that the contrary is the case' – *De Int.* 14, 23a27-39).

    (b) 'Since it is impossible for contradictories to be true at the same time of the same thing, it is evident that contraries cannot belong to the same thing at the same time. For of contraries, one is no less a privation <than the other>, viz. a privation of being; and a privation is a negation in a determinate genus. If, then, it is impossible to affirm and deny truly at the same time, it is also impossible for contraries to belong at the same time ...' (*Meta.* IV 6, 1011b15-21).

Precisely formulated, Aristotle's proof of the psychological Law of Contradiction runs as follows: If two beliefs answering to contradictory sentences could exist at the same time in a single consciousness, then contrary properties would hold of that consciousness at the same time. But by the logical Law of Contradiction it is impossible for contrary properties to hold of a single object at the same time. Hence two beliefs answering to contradictory sentences cannot exist in a single consciousness at the same time.[2]

6. Aristotle's proof of the psychological Law of Contradiction is *inadequate* because he has not proved that beliefs answering to contradictory sentences are contraries. The last chapter of the *De Interpretatione* contains remarks bearing on this issue;[3] but they fall short of proof, for two reasons.

---

1. Cf. *A.Pr.* I 46, 52a32: 'For "true" and "is" are similarly ordered (*homoiôs tattetai*)'.

2. In the interpretation of these passages I am in full agreement with Maier (cf. [106] I, p.45 n.2). In general I owe many points of historical scholarship to Maier's fundamental and invaluable book.

3. This was already pointed out by Alexander of Aphrodisias: 'That the beliefs in the contradictories are contrary has been proved by several arguments at the end of the *De Interpretatione*' (*Scholia in Arist.* ed. Brandis, p.652) [= *In Meta.* (CIAG I) 270.24-5].

(a) In Aristotle's view, contrary properties are properties which lie at opposite ends of a scale (e.g. black and white on the scale of 'colourless' colours). Every scale must be constructed by an *ordering relation*. Aristotle takes as the ordering relation for the scale of beliefs difference in degree of truth and falsity, and he speaks, accordingly, of 'truer' and 'falser' beliefs (*De Int*. 14, 23b17; 20). *But there cannot be differences in degree of truth and falsity.*

(b) In his psychological investigation of belief (*De Int*. 14), Aristotle falls into the common error of 'logicism in psychology' – the converse of 'psychologism in logic'. Instead of investigating mental acts, Aristotle considers the sentences answering to such acts, and the *logical* relations holding between such sentences. This emerges in two ways:

(i) Aristotle characterises beliefs as true or false; but beliefs, considered as mental acts, can no more be true or false in the primary sense than can sensations, feelings, and the like. 'True' and 'false' are relational properties which belong to *sentences*, considered as representations of objectives.

(ii) Further, Aristotle confuses logical consequence with psychological causation. The following passage is typical: 'The belief <in the contradictory> is intertwined with the belief that the good is bad; for presumably the same man <who believes that the good is bad> must also believe that <the good is> not good' (*De Int*. 14, 23b25-7). He must indeed, provided only that he *thinks* about it – and that is something he should not do, even if it were actually possible to hold such confused 'beliefs'.

7. If we disregard Aristotle's argument, we can say the following things about the psychological Law of Contradiction. (a) The psychological Law cannot be proved *a priori*; it can at best be established by induction as an *empirical law*. (b) The Law has not yet been *empirically* established.[4] (c) It is doubtful whether it can be established at all: there have been enough cases in the history of philosophy where people have consciously and deliberately asserted contradictory sentences at the same time.[5] In order to save the Law   **21**

4. There is no harm in recalling once again Husserl's trenchant remarks: '... in the same individual, or rather in the same consciousness, contradictory acts of belief are incapable of lasting for any time, however short. But is this really a *law*? Can we really utter it with such boundless generality? What are the psychological inductions which justify its acceptance? May there not have been people, and may there not still be people who, deceived by fallacies, contrive at times to believe contradictories together? Has the occurrence of contradictions, even quite obvious ones, been scientifically investigated in the case of the insane? What happens in hypnotic states, in delirium tremens, etc.? Does this law also hold for animals?' (*Logische Untersuchungen* I (Halle 1900), p.82) [= *Logical Investigations*, trans. J.N. Findlay (London 1970), I, p.114].

5. The following passage from Hegel provides a good example of what I mean: 'Something moves, not because it is here at one point of time and there at another, but because at one and the same time it is here and not here, and in this here both is and is not. We must grant the old dialecticians the contradictions which they prove in motion; but what follows is not that there is no motion, but rather that motion is *existent* contradiction itself' (*Wissenschaft der Logik*, in *Werke* IV (Berlin, 1834), p.69) [= *Science of Logic*, trans. W.H. Johnston and L.G. Struthers (London 1929), II, p.67].

from such a refutation one would have to invoke *subsidiary hypotheses* – to which Aristotle himself occasionally has recourse. ('For a man need not actually believe what he says': *Meta.* IV 3, 1005b25-6). But subsidiary hypotheses decrease the probability of the main thesis.

Thus we shall pay no further attention to the psychological Law of Contradiction: it is a thesis of doubtful truth; it is not yet established; it could only be established by empirical means.

22 8. Aristotle regards the logico-ontological Law of Contradiction as an ultimate, unprovable principle. *He does not*, however, *prove that this is so*; instead he merely remarks that 'if there are things of which one could not seek proof, one could not find a better candidate than <the Law of Contradiction>' (*Meta.* IV 4, 1006a10-11).

9. Here we must first stress that there are simpler and 'more evident' principles which might be treated in preference to the Law of Contradiction as ultimate and unprovable laws. In particular, there is the *Principle of Identity*: A property belongs to that object to which it belongs.

(a) The Principle of Identity is *distinct* from the Law of Contradiction. The Law cannot be formulated without using the concepts of *negation* and logical *conjunction* (expressed in the words 'and at the same time'), while the Principle does not require these concepts.

(b) Symbolic logic brings a new clarity to this issue. The old 'philosophical' logic is from this point of view a thicket of confusing verbiage: by *principium identitatis* it sometimes means the Principle of Identity and sometimes the Law of Contradiction;[6] it confuses the Law of Contradiction with the ill-formed *Principle of Double Negation*, 'A is not *not-A*'; it regularly expresses the Principle of Identity by means of the ambiguous or at least imprecise formula 'A is A' (is divisibility by two divisible by two?); it treats the Principle as the 'positive counterpart'[7] of the Law of Contradiction, and thus identifies it with the Law; and so on. 'Philosophical' logic had no feeling for the finer conceptual distinctions; for it did not work with sharply defined concepts and unequivocal symbols, but floundered in the shifting and treacherous quagmire of ordinary language.

23 10. But not even the Principle of Identity is an ultimate law; for it can be proved on the basis of the definition of truth. We might attempt to set down the following axioms:

(a) All *a priori* principles can and must be proved.

(b) There is only *one* principle which cannot be proved on the basis of other principles but is true and proved 'through itself'; that is the sentence: 'I call an affirmative sentence true if it ascribes to an object a property which belongs to it.' This sentence is affirmative, and ascribes a property to *me* – a property which certainly does belong to me, viz. the property of calling sentences of such and such a sort true. That I do do this is established by my very utterance of the sentence in question. The explanation of what I mean by a true sentence is thus true and proved 'through itself'.

(c) Every other *a priori* principle, including the Law of Contradiction, must be derived from previously proved principles if it is to be accounted true.

6. See Trendelenburg, *Logische Untersuchungen*, I (Leipzig 1862²), p.31; Sigwart, *Logik* (Freiburg 1889²), I, p.186.

7. Cf. Sigwart, *loc.cit.*

11. Although Aristotle asserts the unprovability of the Law of Contradiction, he nevertheless attempts to provide proofs for it. 'But we can prove negatively (*elenktikôs*) even in this case that it is impossible <for contradictory sentences to be true at the same time> provided only that our opponent says something' (*Meta.* IV 4, 1006a11-13). But there is a *contradiction* here: it is disguised by the word 'negatively', but it cannot be interpreted away.

(a) By *elenchos* Aristotle means a syllogism whose conclusion is the contradictory of some given thesis (*A.Pr.* II 20, 66b11). Thus if someone asserted that the Law of Contradiction did not hold (thesis), and was then forced to admit premises from which the truth of this Law (and hence the contradictory of his thesis) syllogistically follows, then such a syllogism or proof is called 'negative' (*elenktikôs*). Thus according to Aristotle an *elenchos* **24** is *an ordinary syllogism* differing from a proper proof only in the extrinsic fact that it is used as a means of refutation.[8]

(b) The distinction drawn in *Meta.* IV 4 between a proper and a negative proof of the Law of Contradiction thus seems to me to be entirely empty: 'Negative demonstration I distinguish from demonstration proper, because a demonstrator might seem to beg the question – but if someone else is responsible for this [sc. the *petitio*] there will be an *elenchos* and not a demonstration' (1006a15-18). The sense of the passage seems to be this: 'Anyone who tries to prove the Law of Contradiction commits the fallacy of *petitio principii*, and his proof is unsound; but if someone else is responsible for the fallacy, an *elenchos* is possible – and everything is all right'. What that is supposed to mean I do not know.

(c) Aristotle's first two proofs of the Law of Contradiction do indeed agree, at least in their author's intention, with the definition of *elenchos* given in the *Prior Analytics*. Aristotle concludes his proofs with these words: 'But if this is so, then *it has been proved* that it is impossible to predicate contradictories at the same time' (*Meta.* IV 4,1007b17-18).

(d) Aristotle proves the Law of Contradiction not only by *elenchos* but also by *reductio ad impossibile*. But *reductio* proofs presuppose the Law and thus contain a *petitio* if they are used to prove it.

From what I have said it emerges clearly that Aristotle contradicts himself when on the one hand he says that the Law of Contradiction is unprovable, and on the other hand he attempts to prove the Law both by *elenchos* and by *reductio*.

12. Aristotle's Proofs of the Law of Contradiction.   **25**

The premiss of the negative proof which has to be wrung from the opponent reads thus: Let there be granted a word which signifies something essentially unitary; e.g. grant the word 'man', and let it signify a two-footed animal.

(a) First negative proof:- 'It is necessary that, if it is true to say of anything that it is a man, it is a two-footed animal; for that was what "man" signified. But if that is necessary, it is not possible for the same thing not to be a two-footed animal; for that is what "it is necessary for it to be" signifies – "it is impossible for it not to be". Hence it is not possible to say

---

8. Cf. Maier [106] IIa, p.359: 'Considered as an inference, it [sc. *elenchos*] is identical with the demonstrative syllogism'.

truly at the same time that the same thing is a man and is not a man [or a two-footed animal]' (*Meta*. IV 4, 1006b28-34).

This proof, formally and schematically stated, runs thus: By the word *A* I denote something which is essentially *B*. Hence the object *A* is necessarily *B*. But if *A* is necessarily *B*, then – by the meaning of the word 'necessarily' – it is impossible for it not to be *B*. Hence no *A* can at the same time be and not be *B*.

(b)   The second negative proof:- 'Let it be granted then ... that the word signifies something and signifies one thing. Then it is not possible for being a man to signify the same as not being a man, if "man" signifies ... one thing ... And it will not be possible for the same thing to be and not be, except by virtue of an homonymy – as when what we call man others should call not man. But the question is not whether it is possible for the same thing at the same time to be and not be *called* a man *in name*, but <whether it can be and not be a man> *in fact*' (*Meta*. IV 4, 1006b11-22).

26   This proof, formally and schematically stated, runs thus: By the word *A* I denote something which is essentially unitary. Hence the object *A*, which is essentially *B*, cannot at the same time not be essentially B; for then it would not be essentially unitary. Hence *A* cannot at the same time be and not be *B* essentially.

Of the *reductio* proofs I cite only the *three* most important:-

(c)   The first *reductio* proof:- 'Again, if all contradictory sentences are true of the same thing at the same time, it is clear that everything will be one. For a trireme and a wall and a man will be the same thing ...' (*Meta*. IV 4, 1007b18-21).

(d)   The second *reductio* proof:- 'In addition, it follows that everyone would speak truly and everyone would speak falsely, and <our opponent> himself has to agree that he speaks falsely' (*Meta*. IV 4, 1008a28-30).

(e)   The third *reductio* proof:- 'Hence it is particularly evident that neither any of those who advance this view nor anyone else is actually in this position. For why does he walk to Megara rather than sit at home thinking he is walking there? Why does he not set out early in the morning and fall into a well or over a precipice, as it may be, but evidently takes good care, as though he did not think that falling is alike good and not good? Thus it is clear that he believes that one thing is good and another not good' (*Meta*. IV 4, 1008b12-19).

13.   Criticism of Aristotle's Proofs of the Law of Contradiction:-

On (a): The first negative proof is inadequate because it proves not the

27   Law of Contradiction but at best the *Principle of Double Negation*: If something is *B* it cannot be not *B*. But (i) the Principle of Double Negation is *distinct* from the Law of Contradiction, since – as symbolic logic has shown – the Principle can be perfectly well formulated without the concept of logical *conjunction*, while the Law cannot exist without this concept.

(ii)   There are objects – *contradictory* objects, such as the highest prime number – of which the Principle but not the Law holds. Hence we cannot validly infer the Law from the Principle.

On (b): The second negative proof is inadequate because (i) it would at best establish the Law of Contradiction for a very *restricted* range of objects, viz. for the 'essences' of things or for their *substance*. Its validity for accidents would still be an open question. That in this proof Aristotle does only justify the Law for substance is clear from, e.g., the following passage: 'Even so, then, there will be something signifying *substance (ousia)*. And if that is so, it has been proved that it is impossible for contradictories to be predicated at the same time' (*Meta.* IV 4, 1007b16-18).

(ii) The existence of substance is only *probable*; hence the Law of Contradiction, in so far as it relates to substance, can only hold *with probability*.

(iii) The proof contains a *formal* fallacy, for it uses a premiss which can only be proved by *reductio*: If an object could at the same time be and not be *B* essentially, then it would not be unitary; for *B* is something different from not-*B*. But *reductio* proofs presuppose the Law of Contradiction.

On (c), (d), (e): All the *reductio* proofs are inadequate because they contain the following two *formal* errors. (i) They all commit a *petitio principii*. *Reductio* argument depends on the Principle of Contraposition which – as symbolic logic has shown – presupposes the Law of Contradiction. The point can be made without the aid of symbols: A *reductio* proof runs thus:- If **a** were the case, **b** would have to be the case; but **b** is not the case; therefore **a** cannot be the case. Why not? Because if **a** were the case, then there would be a contradiction – for **b** too would be the case, and it is not the case.   **28**

(ii) All Aristotle's *reductio* arguments commit the fallacy of *ignoratio elenchi*. Aristotle does not prove that the simple *negation* of the Law of Contradiction leads to absurd consequences, but tries to establish the impossibility of the assumption that *everything* is contradictory. This emerges quite clearly from the remark I quoted in §12 (c): 'if *all* contradictory sentences are true ...'. But a man who denies the Law of Contradiction, or asks for a proof of it, is not committed to the assumption that *everything* is contradictory, and in particular that those occurrences and states of affairs that determine practical life are contradictory.

These considerations show clearly that, for all his efforts, Aristotle has not proved the Law of Contradiction.

14. The object of Aristotle's proofs, as I have just pointed out, undergoes a *transformation*; this deserves particular attention. In addition to the passage already adduced (*Meta.* IV 4, 1007b19), the following lines bear on the question: 1006a29-31; 1008a8-16; 1008b31-1009a5 (the final passage in IV 4). The last passage is typical: 'Again, *however much everything may be both so and not so*, still there is a more and a less in the nature of things; for we should not say that two and three are equally even, nor is a man who thinks that four things are five as wrong as one who thinks that they are a thousand. If, therefore, they are not equally wrong, it is clear that one of   **29** them is less wrong and hence says something truer. Thus, if what is more <so and so> is nearer <to being so and so>, there must be an <absolute> truth which the truer is nearer to. And even if there is not, still there is at least something <relatively> more certain and truer, and we shall have got rid of the unqualified view which forbids us to determine anything in our thought'.

This shows as clearly as one could wish that by the end of his argument Aristotle is no longer concerned to prove the Law of Contradiction in all its generality, but only to discover *some* absolute and non-contradictory truth which will show the falsity of the *contrary* of the Law of Contradiction – the thesis that 'the same property at the same time belongs and does not belong to every object'.

15. This *transformation* of the object of Aristotle's proofs is remarkable, and its historical significance has not yet been appreciated: it is founded on certain positive convictions of Aristotle's.

(a) On a point of crucial relevance to the Law of Contradiction, Aristotle seems not wholly to have rejected the views of the sensationalists: 'Those who feel a genuine puzzlement have arrived at their belief that contradictories and contraries may belong to an object at the same time on the basis of observation, seeing that contraries come into being from the same thing ... To those whose belief rests on these grounds, we shall say that in a way they are correct and in a way they are wrong. For what is is so called in two ways, so that in a way it is possible for something to come into being from what is not, and in a way it is not; and the same thing may at the same time be both something that is and something that is not, but not in the same way. *For potentially contraries may belong to the same thing at the same time, but not actually*' (*Meta.* IV 5, 1009a22-36).

First, it is important to establish that Aristotle restricts the validity of the Law of Contradiction to *actual* existents. Compare the previous passage with the following one: 'The reason for their [i.e. the sensationalists'] belief [sc. that things can at the same time both be and not be so and so – 1009b32-3] is that, though they were inquiring into the truth about what is, they supposed that what is is the perceptible world only; but *here there is largely present the nature of the indeterminate and of that which is* in the way we have described [i.e. *potentially*]. Thus they speak plausibly, but they do not speak truly' (*Meta.* IV 5, 1010a1-5).

Thus according to Aristotle, the perceptible world, the world of generation and decay, may, since it has merely potential being, contain contradictions. It is true that Aristotle did not have the nerve to say so openly, and only refers, circumspectly, to an earlier passage; nevertheless, the sense of his assertion is quite unequivocal, and it is confirmed by the fact that he elsewhere identifies the indeterminate with the potential. (Cf. *Meta.* IV 4, 1007b28-9: 'For what is potentially and not actually is the indeterminate'.)

(b) This sheds new light not only on the transformation in the object of Aristotle's proofs, but also on the second, and most important, of the negative proofs. The changing world of sense perception may contain as many contradictions as it pleases; but beyond it there lies another, eternal and immutable, world of *substantial essences*, intact and safe from the ravages of contradiction. The sensationalists are right, but they do not possess the *whole* truth. And that is why Aristotle demands that they should 'believe that there is also another kind of substance among existing things, to which neither change nor destruction nor generation in any way belongs' (*Meta.* IV 5, 1009a36-8; cf. 1010a32-5).

Thus we must conclude that, in Aristotle's view, the Law of Contradiction is to be construed not as a universal ontological law, but as a metaphysical truth which holds primarily of substances and whose application to the world of appearances is at least dubious.[9]

9. My interpretation of Aristotle's Law of Contradiction is thus essentially different from Maier's ([106] I, p.101). But Aristotle is sometimes inconsistent; and on this question, which is far more difficult than is customarily supposed and which

16. Aristotle treats the Law of Contradiction not only as the ultimate but also as the *highest* principle: 'That is why anyone who offers a proof goes back to this opinion in the end; for this is in the nature of things the principle of all the other axioms too' (*Meta.* IV 3, 1005b32-4).

Now in Aristotle's view the Law of Contradiction is not the *highest* principle in the sense that *it states a necessary presupposition of all other logical axioms*. In particular, the *Principle of the Syllogism* is independent of the Law of Contradiction. That emerges from a passage in the *Posterior Analytics* which **31** has for a long time been ignored or misunderstood:[10]

No demonstration [syllogism] assumes that it is not possible at the same time to affirm and deny something, unless the conclusion to be proved must also be of that form. Then it is proved by assuming that it is true to affirm the first term of the middle, and not true to deny it. As for the middle term, it makes no difference if you assume that it is and is not; and the same goes for the third term.* For if some object <e.g. Callias> is given of which it is true to say that it is a man, and provided that a man is an animal and not not an animal, then it is true to say that, even if a man is not a man and Callias not Callias, nevertheless Callias is an animal and not also not an animal.* The reason is that the first term is said not only of the middle but also of other terms, since it holds of more things <than the middle term>; so that it makes no difference to the conclusion if the middle term is both the same and not the same. (*A.Pst.* I 11, 77a10-22).   **32**

Thus according to Aristotle the following syllogism is valid (A = animal; B = man; C = Callias):

B is A (and not also not A)
C, which is not C, is B and not B
C is A (and not also not A)

Now if a syllogism is valid even if the Law of Contradiction fails to hold, the Principle of the Syllogism (and with it the *dictum de omni et nullo*) is independent of the Law of Contradiction.

17. This conclusion is fully confirmed by modern symbolic logic. Symbolic logic further shows that many other logical principles and theorems are independent of the Law of Contradiction. The Principle of Identity, the basic laws of Simplification and Composition, the Principle of Distribution,

---

Aristotle is posing for the first time in history, he is not always very clear in his own mind: these two facts to a certain degree justify different and mutually incompatible interpretations of his train of thought.

10. On this passage see Maier [106] IIb, p.238 n3.; Husik [154].

.... [*Translator's note.* At 77a15-19 I have translated Lukasiewicz' German rather than Aristotle's Greek; Lukasiewicz' interpretation depends on his translation. The Clarendon edition of the *A.Pst.* renders the lines thus: '... For if it is granted that that of which it is true to say man, even if not-man is also true of it – but provided only that <it is true to say> that every man is an animal and not not an animal – for it will be true to say that Callias, even if not Callias, is nevertheless an animal and not not an animal.']

the laws of Tautology and Absorption, and many others would still stand
33 even if the Law of Contradiction failed to hold.[11] Moreover, it would not be
difficult to prove, even without the aid of symbols, that the basic principles
of deduction – and of induction too – do not, by and large, presuppose the
Law of Contradiction. There are innumerable deductions and inductions all
of whose steps are *affirmative* sentences: to these the Law of Contradiction
has no application, since it always makes use of an affirmative sentence and
its contradictory *negation*.

In the end we must, in my opinion, *reject the false but widespread view that the
Law of Contradiction is the highest principle of every proof.* The view is true only for
indirect proofs; it is not true for *direct* proofs.

18. That brings me to the end of my historical and critical remarks. In the
remaining, positive, part of my paper I shall try to answer the question of
why we are warranted in holding the Law of Contradiction to be true.

(a) The Law of Contradiction cannot be proved by being shown to be
immediately evident. For (i) evidence is not a legitimate criterion of truth – it
happens that false sentences are held to be evident (cf. Descartes' proof of
the existence of God). (ii) The Law of Contradiction appears not to be
evident to all eyes – in all probability it was not evident to the eristic
thinkers of the old Megarian school, nor to Hegel.

(b) The Law of Contradiction cannot be proved by being exhibited as a
law of nature contingent on *human psychology.* For (i) false sentences may be
contingent on human psychology (cf. e.g. many sensory illusions); and (ii)
it is doubtful whether the Law of Contradiction does hold as a law
contingent on human psychology (cf. my remarks in §7 on the psychological
Law of Contradiction).

(c) The Law of Contradiction cannot be proved from the definitions of
34 falsity and of negation. This method was proposed by Sigwart,[12] but it is
already present in Aristotle. He says: 'Again, if, whenever the affirmation is
true the negation is false and whenever this is true the affirmation is false,
then it will not be possible at the same time to affirm and deny the same
thing truly' (*Meta.* IV 4, 1008a34-b1). Aristotle, however, at once rejects
this argument because he thinks that 'one might say that it involves a *petitio
principii*' (1008b1-2). It does not involve a *petitio*; but it is nonetheless
inadequate. For (i) even if we assume that the negation '*A* is not *B*' implies
the falsity of the affirmation '*A* is *B*', still the Law of Contradiction cannot
be inferred. The definitions of negation and of falsity do not contain the
notion of logical *conjunction*; but it is precisely this notion that gives the Law
of Contradiction its particular character. Two contradictory sentences
cannot be true *at the same time*; affirmation and negation, truth and falsity,
are *mutually exclusive*; they cannot *together* be properties of the same object. As
far as the definitions of negation and of falsity go, however, it would still be
possible to suppose that the sentences '*A* is *B*' and '*A* is not *B*' both hold at
the same time in that both are true and false at the same time.

(ii) If you prefer to avoid calling one and the same sentence true and
false, you may set up a different definition of falsity which, being more

11. The best introduction to symbolic logic is the lucid and rigorous little book by
Couturat, *L'Algèbre de la Logique*, Scientia, phys.-math. 24 (Paris 1905).

12. *op.cit.* I, pp.182 ff.

carefully formulated, does more justice to the basic content of the concept than the normal definition does. The basic content of the concept of falsity is this: *False sentences are not representations of objectives*; or, in different words: *False sentences do not correspond to any objective.* If the Law of Contradiction does not hold, then there are cases in which *A* at the same time is and is not *B*. **35** The sentence '*A* is *B*' will only be false in *these* conditions if *A* is not *B* and *also contains no contradiction.* From this definition of falsity, then, the Law of Contradiction can in no way be deduced.

19. Any proof of the Law of Contradiction must reckon with the fact that there are *contradictory objects* (e.g. the highest prime number). In its *most general* formulation –'The same property cannot at the same time belong and not belong to a single object' – *the Law of Contradiction is thus indubitably false.*[13] It would only be true, and could only be *formally* proved, if the word 'object' were used to designate only *non-contradictory* objects. But that raises the question of whether there are any such objects at all, whether what is possible and what is real contain no contradictions.

(a) *'Constructive'* concepts – existence-free objects, in Meinong's terminology – such as numbers, geometrical figures, logical and ontological notions, etc., have often proved contradictory on closer inspection. (I call such concepts 'constructive' in contrast to 'reconstructive' or empirical concepts which are intended as representations of reality.) One thinks, e.g., of the squaring of the circle, of the trisection of any given angle, of the difficulties in transfinite set theory. Thus we cannot exclude the possibility that constructions which appear non-contradictory today may nevertheless contain a deeply hidden contradiction which we have not yet been able to uncover. And even if it is true that all constructions are 'free creations of the human mind',[14] and that it is within our power to ascribe any properties we **36** like to existence-free objects, nevertheless we cannot prove their freedom from contradiction; for though we 'create' them, innumerable *relations* between them are, as it were, spontaneously generated in a way which is no longer dependent upon our will. Russell's recent discovery of a contradiction that touches on the logical foundations of mathematics proves that we may come upon completely unexpected and inexplicable contradictions in this area.[15]

(b) Real objects, and reconstructive concepts in so far as they correspond to reality, appear to be raised above all contradiction. *In fact we do not know of a single example of a contradiction existing in reality.* It is in general impossible to

13. Meinong, so far as I know, was the first to advance this view. Commenting on certain critical remarks of Russell's, Meinong writes as follows: 'Russell lays greatest emphasis on the fact that recognition of such {sc. impossible] objects would deprive the Law of Contradiction of its unrestricted validity. Of course, I cannot possibly avoid this consequence ... The Law of Contradiction is applied by everyone only to what is real and what is possible' (*Ueber die Stellung der Gegendstandstheorie im System der Wissenschaften* (Leipzig 1907), p.16).

14. The phrase is taken from the Preface to Dedekind's *Was sind und was sollen die Zahlen?*

15. See Russell, *The Principles of Mathematics* (Cambridge 1903). Ch. X; Frege, *Grundgesetze der Arithmetik* II (Jena 1903), postscript, p.253; also Grelling and Nelson, *Bemerkungen zu den Paradoxien von Russell und Burali-Forti*, Abh.d.Freis'schen Schule, N.F. II, 1908.

suppose that we might meet with a contradiction in *perception*; for negation, which is part of any contradiction, is not perceptible. Really existing contradictions could only be *inferred*. We should not forget, however, that a long tradition has claimed to find contradictions in the *continuous change* to which the whole world is incessantly subject – in the never-ending processes of generation and corruption. It seems improbable that these claims can be justified; we can always find ways and means of rejecting any contradictions that may be inferred. *Nonetheless, we can never say with complete certainty that real objects contain no contradictions.* Man did not create the world, and he cannot penetrate all its mysteries; he is not even master of his own conceptual creations.

It follows from (a) and (b) that *we cannot produce a real proof* of the Law of Contradiction, i.e. a proof which rests on a nice investigation of what is actual and what is possible.

20. The Law of Contradiction has no *logical* value, since it only has the status of an assumption; but it does have a *practical and ethical* value, which is all the more important for that. *The Law of Contradiction is our only weapon against error and falsehood.* If we refused to recognise this Law, and held joint affirmation and negation to be possible, we could not defend ourselves against the false and lying assertions of others. A man falsely accused of murder would have no way of proving his innocence in court. At best he could prove that he had committed *no* murder; but this negative truth will not drive its positive contradictory out of the world unless the Law of Contradiction holds. Thus if there is a single witness who, not shrinking from perjury, charges the defendent with the crime, his false assertion cannot be refuted and the defendant is irretrievably lost.

We see from this that the need to recognise the Law of Contradiction is *a sign of the intellectual and moral imperfection of man.* This fact, more than any other, should serve to awaken and justify our suspicion of the *logical* value of the law.

It appears that Aristotle too at least felt, if he did not clearly acknowledge, the practical and ethical value of the Law of Contradiction. At a time when Greece was in a political decline, Aristotle founded and developed the systematic scientific study of man and the world. Perhaps he saw in that some comfort for the future, and some pledge of the future greatness of his nation. He must have been anxious to stress the value of scientific and philosophical studies. The denial of the Law of Contradiction would have opened the door to every falsity, and have smothered those infant and growing studies in their cradle. In powerful prose, beneath the surface of which we can discern an inner passion, Aristotle attacked the opponents of the Law – the Megarian eristics, the Cynics from Antisthenes' school, the followers of Heraclitus, the partisans of Protagoras – and against them he fought for a theoretical principle with all the ardour of a man fighting for his personal possessions. He may himself have felt the weakness of his arguments; and that may have led him to present his Law as an ultimate *axiom* – an unassailable *dogma*.

5

J.M. Le Blond

Aristotle on Definition

Aristotle is perplexed when he discusses the methods of finding a definition, **351** and he has doubts about the very nature of definition and about the position it holds in science. These facts have often been noticed,[1] and Aristotle himself makes no secret of them – neither in the *Analytics* (where he considers methods of definition and attempts to ascertain the connection between definition and demonstration), nor in the thorny chapters of Book VII of the *Metaphysics* (where he scrutinises, more closely than anywhere else, the nature of definition), nor yet in the famous introduction to the *De Anima* (where he openly admits how difficult it is to find any method of definition).[2]

I do not intend to make a separate analysis of these different texts;[3] **352** rather, I have tried to group the evidence that they provide under three headings: first, the *nature* of definition; secondly, the *method* of arriving at a definition; thirdly, the *role* that definition plays in the sciences. This task might appear to have an empty and formal character: in fact, it leads us to meditate on the nature and value of knowledge, and to put to the test some of the central doctrines of Aristotle's philosophy.

I. *The nature of definition*

1. Let me say at the outset that in Aristotle's view a definition of something is not just another *name* for it – a verbal equivalent is not necessarily a definition. Thus, using a favourite example of Aristotle's, identifying Homer's poem as the *Iliad* is not defining it (*Meta.* VII 4, 1030a9, b10; VIII 6, 1045a13). A verbal equivalent is only a definition if certain further

1. See for example Hamelin, *Le Système d'Aristote*; Roland Gosselin [178]; Festugière [179]; also Zeller, *Philosophie der Griechen* II 2, pp.251-6. I have been greatly helped in this article by the papers of Robin [281], and Festugière, 'Antisthenica', *Revue des sciences philosophiques et théologiques*, 1932. See also Kühn, *De notionis definitione* (Halle, 1834); Rassow, *Aristotelis de notione definitionis doctrina*.

2. The principal sources for any study of definition in Aristotle are: the *Topics* (esp. Book VI, which gives special consideration to definition, and Book I *passim*); the *Posterior Analytics* (Book II, chs. 3-8 on the methods of definition and on its relation to demonstration; ch. 13 on the methods of definition); *Meta.* VII-VIII; *De. An.* I 7; *Phys.* I 9; IV 4. See also *PA* I; and compare, more generally, Aristotle's practice in his scientific treatises.

3. This has already been done for *A.Pst.* and the *De An.* by Roland Gosselin [178]. I do not think, however, that Gosselin draws all the conclusions that his analysis warrants.

conditions are satisfied: for example, the *Topics* lay down that the verbal equivalent must fit all the *definienda*, that it must state the true or proximate genus of the *definiendum*, that it must fit the *definiendum* alone, that it must reveal the essence of the *definiendum*, that it must be 'good' and contain no superfluous elements, and above all that it should be clearer than the phrase whose equivalent it is (*Top.* VI, 1 and 4).

All this is no doubt a matter of common sense. But it includes within itself a metaphysical doctrine. For those thinkers who hold that to define something is merely to give it a new name are in effect denying the importance of abstract concepts. Antisthenes did just that:[4] in his eyes there
353 is no intermediary between an object of sense perception and its name; there are men and there is the name 'man', but there is no such thing as humanity.[5] And since it is impossible to define an individual object of sense perception, Antisthenes concludes that definitions can do no more than designate sensible objects, either by a single word or else by a circumlocution.[6] From this point of view, no definition can make the *definiendum* any 'clearer'; for nothing can be clearer than sense perception. Aristotle agrees that individual objects can only be perceived and named; but, opposing Antisthenes, he holds that there are essences – conceptual entities – which can be defined; and the statement that definitions are more than verbal equivalents thus involves a commitment to the reality of essences – of entities which are not individuals but universal concepts. A definition is the mental representation of such an essence.

2. But this formula remains too vague: to grasp humanity, or to form a mental representation of it, is not to define humanity; defining is not a
354 matter of grasping an essence but of analysing it. It is in this sense that we may say with Hamelin that a definition is not, strictly speaking, merely a *concept*.[7] In Aristotle's view, to be sure, we do possess an intuitive capacity for abstraction by which we may obtain an immediate understanding of what a thing is, penetrating at once to its essence and disregarding its

---

4. Aristotle adverts to Antisthenes' difficulty in *Meta.* VIII: 'therefore the difficulty which used to be raised by the school of Antisthenes and other such uneducated people has a certain timeliness. They said that the "what" cannot be defined (for the definition so-called is a long rigmarole), but of what *sort* of thing, e.g. silver, is, they thought it possible actually to explain, not saying what it is, but that it is like tin' (3, 1043b23-8).

5. Cf. Ammonius *In Porph. Isag.* (CIAG IV 3), 40.6: 'Antisthenes said that kinds and species exist only in the imagination; "I see a horse," he said, "but not equinity"; and again: "I see a man, but not humanity." He spoke thus because he lived by perception alone and was unable to elevate himself, through reason, to higher studies.'

6. On this see Festugière's 'Antisthenica', p.370: 'Is this [Antisthenes' assertion] not to say that every object, simple or compound, is only knowable as an object of apprehension? I know it only as a *pragma*, by my senses; it is an *aisthêton*. I grasp it, I give it a name, and this name expresses the characteristic by which I recognise it. It therefore expresses the nature which is identical with the object itself, the concrete object. Here, then, we have a logic that rejects *ousia*, essence or concept. Now there can be no definition unless we accept *ousia*.'

7. Cf. Hamelin, *Le Système d'Aristote*, pp.116-17: 'The concept is an *intuition* in the strongest sense of the word. There is nothing discursive in it.'

individual and accidental characteristics.[8] But this process yields a grasp and not a definition of the thing; it is the work of *nous*; it is not performed by *dianoia*, the faculty of that discursive thought which is characteristic of scientific knowledge.[9]

3. Definition, on the other hand, is a function of *dianoia*; it is essentially *discursive*, and its form is a *logos* or formula which is necessarily composed of parts.[10] To define is thus to break down a unitary concept into a multiplicity; to move from an intuitive to a discursive understanding. I perceive Socrates, and I may grasp his humanity by intuitive abstraction; but I shall only possess the definition of humanity if I give a discursive analysis of my unitary representation of humanity and distinguish within it the elements of rationality and animality. It is this analysis which makes the definition 'clearer'; for it resolves into its constitutive *principles* an essence which before was grasped as a whole.[11] That is why the most important task of the natural philosopher is to elicit the principles of those essences which he originally grasped as whole by way of intuition.[12]

Defining, however, is not only analysis; for clearly a definition is not a **355** mere multiplicity, but a unified multiplicity. To define something is not to disintegrate it into atomic parts; for even as he analyses, the definer is aware that he is dealing with a unitary thing, a single concept. Aristotle emphasises that the parts of a definition are not just any old parts;[13] they are connected parts which form not an agglomeration but an intelligible

8. In *De An*. III 5 Aristotle states that abstraction is the work of the *active intellect*; nowhere else is he so explicit – *A.Pst*. II 19 seems to explain the elimination of individual characteristics from a universal concept in terms of the accumulation and neutralisation of perceptual images.

9. Aristotle insists more than once that the procedure by which we acquire knowledge of the principles is *prior* to science and not a part of it.

10. Cf. *Meta*. VII 10, 1034b20: 'Definition (*horismos*) being a formula (*logos*), and every formula having parts ...'

11. 'In all disciplines in which there is knowledge of things with principles, causes or elements, it arises from a grasp of those ...' (*Phys*. I 1, 184a10).

12. Cf. *Phys*. I 1, 184a14 ff.: 'Plainly, therefore, in the science of nature, as in other branches of study, our first task will be to try to determine what relates to its principles. The natural way of doing this is to start from the things which are more knowable and obvious to us and proceed towards those which are clearer and more knowable by nature; for the same things are not knowable relatively to us and knowable without qualification. So in the present enquiry we must follow this method and advance from what is more obscure by nature, but clearer to us, towards what is more clear and more knowable by nature. Now what is to us plain and obvious at first is rather confused masses, the elements and principles of which become known to us later by analysis. Thus we must advance from generalities to particulars; for it is a whole that is best known to sense-perception, and a generality is a kind of whole, comprehending many things within it, like parts.' Note that this text suggests that in scientific research we start not from an *intellectual* intuition, but from a confused sense impression. This does not seem quite consistent with what I have just said about the nature of scientific principles; but in Aristotle there is a perceptible vacillation between a rationalist and an empiricist approach to science.

13. Cf. *Meta*. VII 10, 1034b33: 'Perhaps we should rather say that 'part' is used in several senses. One of these is 'that which measures another thing in respect of quantity'. But let this sense be set aside; let us inquire about the parts of which *substance* consists' (Cf. 11, 1036b29 ff.). VIII 3, 1043b5: 'If we examine we find that the

whole. A definition is characterised both by the distinction of its parts and by their intelligible unity. We do not define a man by listing the different parts of his body – finger, foot, head, and so on; nor do we define a house by its bricks, joists, and doors.[14] 'In the case of all things which have several parts and in which the totality is not, as it were, a mere heap, but the whole is something besides the parts, there is a cause' (*Meta.* VIII 6, 1045a8). Definition should reveal this cause of unity: 'A definition is a set of words which is one not by being connected together, like the *Iliad*, but by dealing with one object' (*ib.* 1045a13). We can sum this up by saying that a definition is genuinely *discursive.*

356

4. Definition is thus both analytic and synthetic, its two aspects precisely correlated. Aristotle considers first one then the other of these aspects; but it is evident that the two approaches are inseparable.

Now and then Aristotle makes a point of the *unified* character of definition; I have just quoted a text from the *Metaphysics* which refers to it, and I shall reconsider the matter when I turn to the methods of definition. Here I will just remark that in the *Topics* Aristotle stresses the importance of investigating similarities, in order to help us track down the chief element in any definition, the genus (*Top.* I 18, 108b9-29; cf. *A.Pst.* II 13). Where Aristotle is concerned to explain how a unitary intuition becomes articulated into a definition, the *analytical* procedure, which leads to the distinction of the various parts, naturally enjoys the limelight; even so, this analysis is so different from a mere disintegration that it at once implies a unity in the object analysed.

357

Analysis takes three main forms in Aristotle's investigations. First, and perhaps most importantly, there is analysis into *matter and form.* Festugière correctly summarises Aristotle's numerous remarks when he says that 'every definition takes for granted the alliance of matter and form, the duty of form being to differentiate and distinguish the matter in any given case, e.g. the bricks that compose the house ...' (*op.cit.*, p. 370). This is why Aristotle reiterates that there can, properly speaking, be no definition except of substances which consist of matter and form.[15] From this point of view, then, defining consists in separating matter from form while

---

syllable does not consist of the letters and juxtaposition, nor is the house bricks and juxtaposition. And this is right; for the juxtaposition or mixing does not consist of those things of which it is the juxtaposition or mixing.'

14. Aristotle does in fact accept definitions of this sort; but they are 'material' definitions (Cf. *Meta.* VIII 2, 1043a14) not definitions in the true sense (Cf. *Meta.* VIII 3, 1043b5; VII 10, 1035b20; 11, 1037a24: 'And we have stated that in the formula of the substance the material parts will not be present (for they are not even parts of the substance in that sense, but of the concrete substance)').

15. Cf. *Meta.* VIII 3, 1043b31: '... a definitory formula predicates something of something, and one part of the definition must play the part of matter and the other that of form' (see VII 13, 1039a14; 10, 1035a1). Admittedly, Aristotle mentions definitions which only take account of matter: 'Of the people who go in for defining, those who define a house as stones, bricks and wood are speaking of the potential house, since all these are matter' (*Meta.* VIII 2, 1043a14). Aristotle also mentions definitions which only consider form: 'Those who propose 'a receptacle to shelter chattels and living beings', or something of the sort, speak of the actuality' (1043a16). The complete definition, however, consists in a combination of the two: 'Those who combine both of these speak of the third type of substance, namely the combination of

simultaneously grasping their necessary unity; in picking out, in the house, the materials (bricks, rubble, and planks) from the form (the shelter that is produced by combining these materials).[16]

From another point of view, often misleadingly confused with the first in Aristotle's work, defining consists in the analysis into *cause and effect*. This procedure is instanced in the examples in the *Posterior Analytics* by which Aristotle illustrates the *syllogism of essence* or of definition. Thus, you might define an eclipse as 'the absence of light on the moon effected by the interposition of the earth', thunder as 'the noise in the clouds resulting from the extinction of the heavenly fire' (*A.Pst.* II 8, 93a30 ff.; cf. II 10). Definitions of this sort are, as Aristotle sometimes admits, more suitable to *events*, while analysis into matter and form is better applied to *substances*.[17]   **358**

Finally, there is a third form of analysis that may be used for definition: analysis by *genus and difference*. This is a more abstract type of analysis than the first two. It singles out, first, the element an object has in common with other objects (thus in humanity, animality is common to man and to other creatures), and secondly, the characteristic that the object alone possesses (in humanity, rationality is the *specific difference*). This procedure is not Aristotle's invention: it is close to Socratic definition and to the Platonic method of division. In the *Topics* this is the only type of definition that Aristotle discusses,[18] and it is ubiquitous in the rest of the *corpus*.   **359**

5. What these three types of definition have in common is their analytical procedure; this is not, as I have said, a matter of disintegration and it is not achieved by listing the physical or material parts of a thing, which are posterior to the whole (*Meta.* VII 10, 1035b11; 11, 1037a33). In each of the three types of analysis – matter and form, cause and effect, genus and difference – the parts that definition singles out stand in the relation of *potentiality* to *actuality*, of determinable to determinate.[19] And it is this fact

---

matter and form' (1043a18). When, in *A. Pst.*, Aristotle explains the syllogism of essence, he makes it perfectly clear that he regarded neither definition by matter nor definition by form as genuine definitions; thus, his definition of an eclipse is neither 'the absence of light on the moon' (material definition) nor 'the interposition of the earth' (formal – or, to be precise, causal – definition), but 'absence of light due to the interposition of the earth' (cf. *A.Pst.* II 8, 93a30 ff.; II 10).

16. Note that in the example of the house (which is Aristotle's own: *Meta.* VIII 2, 1043a14), the *formal* cause looks very like a *final* cause; nor is it uncommon for Aristotle to identify formal and final causes. Sometimes, however, he does distinguish between them; and he actually remarks, *à propos* the definition of house, that the final cause must not be neglected: 'If we are to define a house, we say that the bricks and beams are arranged in a certain manner (and sometimes we also add a final cause)' (*Meta.* VIII 2, 1043a8).

17. In these chapters of the *A.Pst.* that I have just referred to, Aristotle appears to treat eclipses and thunder as substances. He is more precise in certain parts of *Meta.* (cf. VIII 4, 1044b8, where he recognises that an eclipse is not a substance).

18. Cf. *Top.* VI *passim; A.Pst.* II 13; *Meta.* VII 12, 1037b12; 1038a1 ff. See also *PA* I 1.

19. Cf. *Meta.* VIII 6, 1045a14: 'What then is it that makes man one? why is he one and not many, e.g. animal and biped, especially is there are, as some say, an animal-itself and a biped-itself? ... Clearly, then, if people proceed thus in their usual manner of definition and speech, they cannot explain and solve the difficulty. But if, as we say, one element is matter and another is form, and one is potentially and the other actually, the question will no longer be thought a difficulty.'

which allows the unity of a substance to be represented in its definition; for it permits us to assert that, despite the analysis, the substance is *incomposite* (*asuntheton*). At the same time, it permits us to *define* it – or clarify it by expounding its parts. For the elements into which the *definiendum* is analysed are not beings 'in actuality'; and the analysis does not shatter the actual unity of the substance under definition.[20]

360   The parts isolated in definition are thus complementary – each depends upon the other and is unintelligible without it. This fact explains the internal necessity of definition. Aristotle often says that the first principles of a science must be necessary – more necessary, indeed, or at least having a 'nobler' necessity than their consequences.[21] It may at first sight seem odd to speak of the *necessity* of a concept, because necessity presupposes *two* things – it is an iron link that chains one thing to another, and it cannot be the property of a genuinely *simple* object. But a definition is not simple; for it involves an inseparable duality. Thus we are able to *understand* the necessity in a definition; for while an indivisible unity can only be '*posited*', the unity of an inseparable duality in which both factors entail each other may be understood and known in the strict sense, i.e. may be recognised as possessing an internal necessity.[22]

        It is this unity in duality – this mutual linking of two factors – that makes definition a rational procedure. And it is this which ensures that a definition

361   is genuinely explanatory, and hence 'clearer' than mere perception.

        6. The three types of analysis used in definition all produce terms which are linked by necessity – otherwise the definition would not be an object of understanding. But there are *striking differences* among the three types, even though Aristotle interchanges them promiscuously.

        In analysis by *genus and difference* the notion of extension has a part to play, although it is absent from the other types of division. Under this aspect, defining is 'classifying'; and the classification enables us to think of the object, and to explain it by its connection with other objects. In truth, classification gives a means of recognising the *definiendum* rather than an understanding of its intrinsic nature and powers. Granted, classification cannot proceed without an analysis of the object that picks out the common element (the genus) and the specific element (the difference); but this analysis is not based on a consideration of the object itself: it is based, as

20. Cf. *Meta.* VII 13, 1039a4: 'A substance cannot consist of substances present in it in complete reality; for things that are thus in complete reality two are never in complete reality one.'

21. See e.g. *A.Pst.* I 2, 72a32. Aristotle says that induction cannot provide knowledge of essences on the grounds that it cannot provide knowledge of what is necessary; it follows that essences contain an internal necessity (*A.Pst.* II 7, 92b37). See also II 19.

22. In *Phys.* IV, when he is defining *place* (*topos*), Aristotle seems to suggest that unless a set of properties is centred about a single point and forms a unitary notion, those properties are only apparent and not real; only if we unify them can we pass from *dokei* ('it appears tò be so') to *huparchei* ('it is so'). Cf. *Phys.* IV 4, 211a6: 'Having laid these foundations [i.e. having assembled the apparent properties] we must complete the theory. We ought to try to make our investigation such as will render an account of place, and will not only solve the difficulties connected with it, but will also show that its apparent properties are real properties.'

Aristotle readily admits, on comparisons and *analogies* (*Top*. I 18, 108b9; 28).

The notion of classification is foreign to the two other types of analysis – cause and effect, and matter and form. In these two cases there is no attempt to set the object in a classification system and compare it with its neighbours; rather the aim is to explain and express the intrinsic nature of the object. Indeed, as Aristotle stresses in the last chapter of Book VII of the *Metaphysics*, the question *ti esti* (What is it?) conceals the question *dia ti* (Why is it?): when I ask what a man or a house is, i.e. when I try to define them, I already know that they exist and hence have sufficient knowledge to distinguish them from other things. I do not ask what a man is in the sense in which someone who had never read the *Arabian Nights* would ask what the Roc was: I am not looking for a way to *recognise* a man or a house. Rather, being acquainted with men and houses, I ask what they are in order to learn what their determinate and what their determinable elements are. In the same way, when I ask what an eclipse is, I am not wondering whether an eclipse is or is not the absence of light from the moon (if I had not spotted this phenomenon, I should not be asking the question); rather, I am investigating the *why and wherefore* of this lack of light. 'Since we must know the existence of the thing as something given, clearly the question is *why* the matter is some definite thing. E.g. why are these materials a house? Because that which was the essence of a house is present. And why is this individual thing, or this body having form, a man?' (*Meta*. VII 17, 1041b3 ff.). In a sense, of course, analysis by genus and difference answers the question *why*; but it answers the question 'Why the name?' rather than 'Why the nature?'; it justifies a classification, and warrants our distinguishing between men and other animals. Only the analyses into matter and form, and into cause and effect, provide an intrinsic explanation of the object and allow us to understand it as it is in itself.

362

7. Between these two types of analysis, there is, as Aristotle sometimes concedes, an important difference: definition by cause and effect should not, strictly speaking, be used of substances or *beings in the primary sense*; such definition is for facts or events, as in the example of the eclipse. Here we find a distinction between the efficient cause (the interposition of the earth) and the effect (the absence of light on the moon); and an eclipse is not a substance.[24] Definition by matter and form is properly applied to *substances*; and since only substances are open to genuine definition, this is the ideal form of definition (*Meta*. VII 4, 1030a21-30). This sort of definition does not

363

---

23. Cf. *Meta*. VII 17, 1041a15: If we are to ask *ti esti*, What is it?, 'the fact of the existence of the thing must already be known – e.g. that the moon is undergoing an eclipse'. Evidently knowledge of existence presupposes some idea of *what* exists: we must know that something definite, distinct from other objects, exists.

24. In *A.Pst*. II 8 Aristotle certainly seems to treat the eclipse as a substance; for he introduces it into an illustration of the *syllogism of the essence*. He is more precise at various points in *Meta*. (e.g. VIII 4, 1044b8; 'Nor does matter belong to those things which exist by nature but are not substances; their substratum is the *substance*. E.g. what is the cause of eclipse? What is its matter? There is none; the *moon* is that which suffers eclipse. What is the moving cause which extinguished the light? The earth. The final cause does not exist. The formal principle is the definitory formula, but this is obscure if it does not include the cause.')

reveal the *antecedent cause*, but rather the *intrinsic 'reason'* of the object. Thus we might say that causal definition is, fundamentally, nothing more than a proof rearranged into a connected sentence, and that definition in terms of form, being distinct from demonstration, is the only genuine sort of definition.[25] Nevertheless, although Aristotle describes, frequently and in central texts, the distinction between formal and efficient causes, he is often tempted to confuse the two. A detailed study of Aristotle's notion of cause would be out of place here – I simply draw attention to the remarks in *Meta.* VII 17 quoted above, where Aristotle fails to discriminate between the efficient and the formal cause in answering the question *Why*.[26]

364

8. I shall now concentrate on definition by *matter and form*, because that applies to substances and is the ideal definition. First of all, we must realise that this sort of definition is not entirely clear or satisfactory, except when applied to *artifacts*; Aristotle's choice of examples, and the recurring case of the house, suggest this; and on reflection we can understand it. For it is only artificial objects, the products of human skill, that possess a prefigured and definable matter (a 'secondary' matter, as the Scholastics were to call it). In natural objects, the form directly determines prime matter: properly speaking, a man is not put together from a soul and a body; rather, the organisation of the body is carried out by the soul. If that were not so, we should have to accept a whole hierarchy of forms inside the human composite, and that, despite some ambiguous remarks, is certainly not what Aristotle intended.[27] It follows that definition by form and matter is very little help in understanding natural substances; for prime matter, being totally indeterminate (*Meta.* VII 3, 1029a20), cannot make any contribution to a definition. It is this fact, in all probability, that induces Aristotle to wonder if true definition does not proceed from *the parts of the form*.[28] Since individuals cannot be defined, the concrete matter which individuates them cannot appear in any definition. It is only 'matter taken universally' that can occur in a definition; for I define humanity and not Socrates, and humanity plainly does not contain any concrete matter, but only the abstract notion of 'matter taken universally' (*Meta.* VII 10, 1035b29).

365

We are defining humanity, and humanity is the *form* of the man Socrates.[29] Moreover in the definition of humanity even 'matter taken universally' only appears by virtue of a *confusion* between two types of analysis, and of an *analogy* that is not clearly drawn. What Aristotle really means by matter here is the *genus*; the 'matter' in the definition of man is

25. We should not overlook the difficulties that beset Aristotle when he attempts to determine the relations between definition and demonstration (cf. *A.Pst.* II 8 ff.). Though he says that the *syllogism of essence* is '*logical*' or artificial, his example of the eclipse syllogism is no more artificial than most of his scientific arguments.

26. On this point see Robin's definitive work [281]; see also Le Blond [120], pp. 149 ff.

27. Aristotle often speaks as though there were a real distinction between body and soul, the body being matter for the soul (see e.g. *Meta.* VII 11, 1036b11); however, he is more careful when he deals with the question *ex professo*.

28. *Meta.* VII 10, 1035b33: 'Only the parts of the form are among the parts of definition, and definition is of the universal.'

29. Hence Aristotle says that form is substance (*Meta.* VII 11, 1037a27; 17, 1041b8), and that only universals or forms can be defined (11, 1036a28).

animality. Thus analysis by genus and difference is constantly confused with analysis into matter and form; but the genus is not really matter at all, neither concrete nor abstract – it is not the matter of the *object*, but at best the 'matter' of the *definition*. Thus a definition which construes the genus as matter does not, *pace* Aristotle,[30] articulate the real parts of the object or its intrinsic nature: its articulation is simply that of the definer's own mind.

The fact is that the only objects that exactly suit definition by matter and form are products of human skill, which assume a predetermined matter. A bronze statue is really composed of bronze and the form of the statue. Here the formal part of the definition answers to the form of the statue and the material part to the real matter (which here of course is not concrete matter, e.g. a particular bit of bronze, but matter taken universally, e.g. bronze). By analogy, and a somewhat stretched analogy at that, this form of definition is extended to natural objects; defining them in this way amounts to treating them as man-made objects, to reconstructing them in our own way which is not the same as nature's. This brings out the importance of Aristotle's treatment of artifacts, which provides the framework of analysis into matter and form. We can also sense that Aristotle is brought up short, as Hamelin puts it, by the 'duality of being and knowing' (op. cit., p.127) – the chasm that yawns between the notions that we formulate and the reality they strive to express.

9. My final remark on the nature of Aristotelian definition concerns its *object*. The objects of definition are, strictly speaking, *substances*. Definition, expressing the being (*ousia*) of something, is *analogical* in the way that being itself is. You cannot ask the question *ti esti* (What is it?), in the primary sense of *esti*, except of substances, i.e. of things that have being in the primary sense (*Meta.* VII 4, 1030a21-30; 5, 1030b26, 1031a1 ff.). *Suntheta* (complexes formed by an accident and a substance)[31] and events can only be defined in virtue of a relation to some substance.[32] According to this doctrine, causal definition is not genuine definition, because it properly applies to events. And that is an intriguing thought; for it is in terms of causal definition that Aristotle, in Book II of the *Posterior Analytics*, expounds his whole theory of definition, taking as his examples eclipses and thunder which are events and not substances. It seems that, at bottom, Aristotle makes no clear distinction between genuine knowledge of what something is and a judgment made in terms of the formula 'what is it?'. Thus I may ask what some accident is; and when I ask this question I treat an accident as a substance. Equally, I can treat a substance as an event, by asking what its cause is and what brought it about. But in these cases our thought assumes a form to which it is not properly entitled.

What *conclusion* may we draw from these notes on the nature of definition? Undeniably, Aristotle throws light on some questions. I have in mind the assertion that a definition contains a unity and a multiplicity inseparably

30. 'The formula is related to the thing in the same way as the part of the formula is to the part of the thing' (*Meta.* VII 10, 1034b21).

31. That is what *suntheton* means; cf. Bonitz, *Metaphysica* II p.409, who says that by this word Aristotle means not 'quae ex pluribus elementis coaluerunt' but 'in quibus substantia conjungitur cum accidente aliquo, veluti homo albus, homo sedens, diagonalis irrationalis et similia'.

32. See *Meta.* VII 4, 1030a21, a medical analogy.

conjoined, and that definitions, as first principles of scientific knowledge, are *relations* that express the intrinsic powers and necessity of the object. Aristotle is very far from mental atomism or the Cartesian idea of *simple natures*. If we posit simple natures as the principles of a science, we shall be hard pressed to explain how those principles can develop and give birth to theorems. Aristotle's definitions are *facts*; what is more, they are necessary facts – and as such they are, on the one hand, suitable objects of understanding and, on the other, pregnant principles teeming with scientific theorems.

It must also be admitted, however, that Aristotle's theories of definition are in places distressingly obscure. First, take the relation of definition to the non-discursive thought upon which it depends: is it an *intellectual* intuition that definition breaks down and articulates? or is it rather a confused *perceptual* datum which definition intellectualizes and introduces into the domain of reason? Aristotle makes statements that support each of these interpretations. On the one hand, the theory of 'active' intellect invites us to believe that definition is both posterior and inferior to these sublime intellectual intutions. On the other hand, Aristotle's practice in his scientific treatises and in certain methodological texts of capital importance[33] appears to suggest that we work from perceptual data of a very inferior intellectual kind: these data are intellectualised by an analysis which replaces simple ideas (which we merely *grasp*) by relations (which we may *understand*). In this way, *intellectual* intuition is not our starting point; rather it is an ideal – an ideal which the unity of definition hints at and towards which the philosopher will strive.

Again, we should not forget the way in which Aristotle muddles together the different types of analysis which play a part in definition. This confusion is so pervasive that Aristotle's arguments are often difficult to follow – Book VII of the *Metaphysics* is certainly most thoroughly entangled.

Finally, we must remember the difficulties Aristotle encounters in his attempt to decide whether the parts of a definition are parts of the *definiendum*; and we should not forget the inconsistencies of his solution. We shall return to this question when dealing with the methods of definition.

II. *The method of definition*

Definition involves the *passage* from intuition (whether intellectual or perceptual) to discursive thought: how are we to achieve this passage? How can we perform the analysis, or *diairesis*,[34] that will make our definitions 'clearer' than our first notions? This is the main question to be raised under the head of *method*; and it is a question that obviously bothered Aristotle; he worries at it in the *Topics*, in the second Book of the *Posterior Analytics*, and in the first Book of the *De Anima*; and he never really gives a satisfactory answer to it.

33. See *Phys.* I 1, cited above, n. 12.
34. Aristotle generally uses the word *diairesis* as a technical term for Platonic division as described in e.g. the *Sophist*. But the verb *diairein* at least often has a wider meaning that makes it eminently applicable to the definition of things by analysis into parts (see e.g. *Physics* I 1).

1. At the risk of stating the obvious, I shall begin by establishing those **369** points on which there is no shadow of doubt. First, it is plain that we cannot reach a definition by way of *intuition*: intuition is simple, individual, unarticulated; definition is complex, abstract, discursive. Defining is not simply a matter of recording or observing: it is a matter of labour.[35] Definition does not arise from intuition. Intuition works unaided, either by accumulating images,[36] or by the unconscious action of the active intellect;[37] it forms universal concepts by observing the essences of things stripped of their individual characteristics. Intuition may form the concept of humanity; but it cannot produce an *articulated definition* of humanity. Moreover, if *induction* is sometimes close to intuition, as Hamelin and Lachelier stress,[38] then we cannot say that induction leads us to definition either.[39] Here and there, it is true, Aristotle speaks as though there were hardly any difference between the answer to the question *ti esti* ('What is it?') and knowledge of *ousia* (*essence*), even though the latter is not necessarily the fruit of definition but may be won by a perception of the essence. But this is an inexactitude which only makes it the more important to heed Aristotle's perfectly explicit theoretical views, and to distinguish between definition and the intuition of essence.

We must also distinguish between the statement that knowledge of *ousia* is a principle of science and the statement that definition is such a principle. Definition and perception of essence are indeed both indemonstrable, and **370** as such they are principles. But they are not principles in the same sense. Perception of essence occurs automatically, either by the good offices of the active intellect, or as a result of the accumulation of sense-images; and it precedes all conscious mental labour and all scientific effort – for it provides the starting-point and the material for that effort. A definition, on the other hand, is the result of thoughtful and methodical research and of hard mental work; it is not a principle in the sense of *preceding* all such work. But it is a principle in as far as it can be the premise of a genuine demonstration, and thus the starting-point of the activity which Aristotle in the *Analytics* calls *science* (*epistêmê*) and whose tool is the demonstrative syllogism.

2. As definition is not perceived intuitively, so it is not *demonstrated* apodeictically. The fact needs no stressing: Aristotle labours it, with a superabundant flow of reasoning, in Book II of the *Posterior Analytics* (esp. chs. 3-8); it is enough to say that all demonstration presupposes a definition in its premisses, and that it leads to knowledge not of essence but of existence, not of what something is but of the fact that something is.

Neither intuition nor demonstration: we may well wonder, with Aristotle, what remains.[40] If we reflect upon definition we are obliged to abandon the simplistic account of knowledge which is occasionally hinted at in the

35. See *De An.* I 1 402a10, on the difficulty of definition and in particular on the difficulties of analysis (402b10).

36. As the beginning of *A.Pst.* II 19 seems to indicate.

37. As is indicated in *De An.* III 5.

38. See Hamelin, *Le Système d'Aristote*, p.258; Lachelier, *Fondement de l'induction*, p.7.

39. That, it seems, is why Aristotle says that induction helps us to recognise not the *ti esti* (what a thing is) but the *hoti esti* (that a thing is); and that it does not provide us with knowledge of what is *necessary* (see *A.Pst.* II 7, 92b37).

40. See *A.Pst.* II 7, 92a34: 'Then what other method is left?'

Analytics: it will not do simply to say that knowledge starts from infallible intuition and proceeds by necessary demonstrations; for in reality there is a gap between intuition and demonstration, and the first principles of demonstration are not intuitions but definitions – the articulated analyses of intuitions. This explains why definition poses so pungently the question of method; for it involves a process different both from intuition and from demonstration – it involves the *passage* or transition from non-scientific to scientific knowledge.

371

3. In an attempt to explain this transition, Aristotle invokes 'a certain kind of demonstration', Platonic division, and 'some other kind of process'. (*De An.* I 1, 402a19 ff.). This is a brief summary of the different methods of definition which he has had occasion to describe at various points in the *corpus*, especially in the logical writings.

It seems that the 'other kinds of process' include principally (despite Aristotle's explicit denials) *induction*, or at least some sort of induction. It is plain that induction has a part to play in the search for definitions: not the intuitive, unconscious induction described in *Posterior Analytics* II 19, but a conscious and controlled induction – the process which Socrates employed in definition, as Aristotle himself remarks.[41] Such induction consists primarily in the search for an element common to the different sorts or manifestations of the thing we are attempting to define. (This common element should not be crudely conceived: Aristotle appeals to the delicate conception of *analogy*, according to which the common element may consist in a similarity of function or relationship (*Top.* I 18, 108b22 ff.).) This process amounts to the third method suggested in *Posterior Analytics* II 13, which recommends the search for 'the same', *t'auton* (97b7 ff.): you should look first for the elements common to a group of things; then for the elements common to a smaller group, and so on.

372

4. The Platonic method of *division* is another important aid to definition, and it is a natural complement to the inductive method. I may refer to the pleasant example of the angler in Plato's *Sophist*. To make a 'division' we first take the highest genus of the *definiendum*; then we pose and answer a series of questions of the form 'Is the *definiendum X* or not?'; and thus we eventually reach the ultimate species by a methodical descent which does not simply list the *differentiae* but arranges them in a hierarchy.[42] Thus induction leads to knowledge of the genus and division to knowledge of differentiae.

My use of the term 'genus' and 'difference' here is enough to show that the method of induction and division will yield a classification of objects rather than a knowledge of their intrinsic nature; the method does not lead to those definitions which analyse into cause and effect or into form and matter.[43] If we wish to find a method for these more important types of

41. See *Meta.* XIII 4, 1078b28: 'For two things may be fairly ascribed to Socrates – inductive arguments and universal definition, both of which are concerned with the starting point of science'.

42. See *A.Pst.* II 13, 96b35: 'Again, division is the only possible method of avoiding the omission of any element of the essential nature'. – The second of the methods suggested in *A.Pst.* II 13 seems to be the method of division.

43. Except in as far as division into genus and difference is confused with division by matter and form.

definition, we must move on to what Aristotle calls 'the logical syllogism of essence'.

5. The logical syllogism of essence is examined in Posterior Analytics II 8. It consists in treating a substance as though it were an event – in treating man, say, in the fashion appropriate to eclipse. In the case of an eclipse there is an obvious duality to be found in cause and effect: the effect (absence of light on the moon) and the cause (interposition of the earth) are not only distinct but actually separate in space; there is a single phenomenon, but two different and separate things. Let us therefore handle man as if he were an event, and treat soul and body as if they were two separate things; then we shall be able to form a syllogism giving the essence of man, just as we can form a syllogism for the essence of the eclipse.[44] But this syllogism will be 'logical' i.e. artificial, and at least in part a fiction.[45]

373

This 'logical' syllogism is the definitory demonstration that Aristotle mentions in the Topics (153a6), names in the De Anima (I 1, 402b19), and expounds in the Posterior Analytics. It is essentially a matter of applying to an individual substance a mode of division which was forged for another task. This method of definition thus relies on an analogy between the dynamic structure of cause and effect and the intrinsic structure of a substance. And Aristotle took note of the analogical character of such definitions in so far as he characterised the syllogism of the essence as logical or artificial.

374

6. Definition by matter and form is, as we have already indicated, inspired more directly by a different analogy. As among events cause and effect are spatially separated, so among artifacts matter and form are temporarily separated. Before the casting and pouring of the statue there is a lump of bronze and a mould; afterwards, form and matter compose a single object – a statue of bronze. Before building there are planks, bricks and rubble; afterwards there is a house. The distinction between matter and form is objective and real; for it is chronologically determined. Let us now try to apply it to natural objects, whose matter is not predetermined and pre-existent in this way. The distinction does not fit properly; for Aristotle does not hold that the matter of a natural object pre-exists it, already endowed with definite qualities – the soul does not supervene on a body that is already constituted; animality is not added to a living creature in order to make an animal in the same way as a shape is added to bronze in order to make a statue. This should lead us to conclude that the distinction between

---

44. It is interesting to note that Aristotle does not formulate the syllogism for the case of man. He gives four illustrations of the syllogism of essence: two are events (the eclipse and thunder), two are substances (man and soul). It is striking that he fails to work out the syllogism in the two latter cases (see A.Pst. II 8).

45. The syllogism is 'logical', according to Robin, because it is only formed 'by a kind of artificial or dialectical decomposition which breaks the true unity of the definition. In this way we can contemplate separately the formal part and the material part of the essence; and by reasoning from the former to the latter we can give a demonstration of the essence' ([281], p.28). According to Festugière, the syllogism of essence is 'a mere artifice; for it has been obtained by separating indissoluble elements and cannot therefore express an essence' ([179], p.86). But we must remember that the adjective 'logical' only really fits the syllogisms that Aristotle does not formulate – those of man and of soul. It does not fit the syllogisms of the eclipse and of thunder, which do reveal a real distinction between cause and effect. See Le Blond [120], pp.157 ff.

the matter and the form of a natural object is another 'logical' distinction: it
is an artificial construction, formed by analogy. Aristotle does not stress this
point and sometimes seems rather vague about it. But it is nonetheless true
that his actual procedure in definition and the mainspring of his method
consist in the use of *familiar* schemes of division in order to break down a
complex datum; the value of any definition reached in this way will
obviously depend on the strength of the analogy – we are reconstructing
natural objects in our own way, which is not the way of nature.

375   This fact has important consequences for epistemology. Knowledge no
longer seems to be the totally objective analysis of intuitive data; it appears
rather to be an attempt to imitate or to reconstruct in our own fashion those
objects which we are unable to understand in themselves: in this case, to
know is to make. Here again, then, we discover the chasm between being
and knowing: inasmuch as Aristotle took a stand against Platonic realism
and refused to hypostatise genus and species, animality and two-footed-ness
(*Meta.* VIII 6, 1045a15), he showed himself aware of that chasm; but it is a
chasm of which, given his conception of knowledge, he was usually
oblivious.

It is unnecessary to stress how awkward and groping – Aristotle would
have said 'dialectical' – the character of these different methods is.[46] Roland
Gosselin has made a faithful summary of them and has emphasised their
non-demonstrative nature. 'If,' he adds, 'we are reluctant to admit that the
methods which Aristotle suggested were unsatisfactory, or that he himself
thought poorly of them, we have only to open the *De Anima*, and read the
first chapter of the first Book' ([178], p.669).

When he introduces his study of the methods of definition in the *Posterior
Analytics*, Aristotle refers to the '*hunt*' on which we must set out (*thēreuein*):
the word points clearly to the speculative nature of the study; in any event,
as Aristotle himself says in the *De Anima*, these methods of definition cannot
produce certain knowledge and will at best instil only belief (*pistis*) (I 1,
402a11).

376   III. *The role of definition*

Aristotle finds it difficult to decide what part definition plays in the
development of the sciences. The studies we have just made will help us to
understand and to assess his difficulty.

1. We must first *recognise* the difficulty. In the *Posterior Analytics* (to look no
further) Aristotle hesitates between several different views of the role
definition plays in science. In the first book he seems to suggest that *nominal*
definitions (*ti sēmainei*: 'what does it signify?') are principles of
demonstration,[47] and that demonstrations aim to prove the objectivity or
truth – Aristotle says, more forcefully, the *existence* – of these definitions. He
is, however, only talking of the definition of *attributes* or properties; the

46. Note too that the methods described in *A.Pst.* II are no more than a
refurbishing of the dialectical methods of definition which are more fully (if less
systematically) explained in the *Topics*.
47. See *A.Pst.* I 1, 71a11-17; 2, 72a23; 10, 76b35: 'Definitions are not hypotheses
... they only need to be understood.'

'existence' of such a definition is proved by establishing a relationship between it and some 'primitive' definition, in which 'existence' and essence are grasped simultaneously.[48] In addition to nominal definitions, then, we must admit as principles of science certain primitive or *real* definitions, whose truth is perceived as soon as their meaning is grasped.

Elsewhere, however, Aristotle seems to say that we must start from an affirmation of existence, and proceed from that to a definition; for it is impossible to define a thing if you do not know that it exists.[49] In this way a definition is no longer regarded as something hypothetical whose 'existence' must be proved (it is no longer a *thesis*, in Aristotle's technical sense); rather definition is a goal of research: instead of passing from meaning (*sêmainein*) to existence (*einai*), we are moving in the opposite direction.

2. We can thus echo Aristotle and say both that definitions are principles and that they are not. A definition is a principle in the sense that it cannot be demonstrated apodeictically and that it is presupposed in any demonstration. It is not a principle in the sense that it is only to be won by mental labour. This labour, different from the labour of apodeictic demonstration but no less taxing, is what the philosopher performs when he tries to pass from a confused concept to a clear or articulated one. More than anything else in Aristotle, this process reveals the characteristic method of definition, which is the passage from the unscientific to the scientific; and it exhibits the difference between definition and demonstration, which by advancing to certainty from certainty never leaves the territory of science. Thus definitions, although they are strictly indemonstrable, may yet figure as the goal of science; for one of the aims of science is to move from an unarticulated apprehension of existence to a rational knowledge of essence (*De An.* I 1, 402a1-16).

If, on the other hand, we look at Aristotle's ideal of a completed science, which moves, demonstration by demonstration, from one certainty to another, then it is clear that definitions can only function as principles of a science. For it is they, and not the simple and non-discursive intuitions whose rational structure they exhibit, that form the first links of any demonstration.

3. We may say, then, both that definition is the result of scientific labour and that it is the principle of scientific labour − but 'science' must be understood differently in these two propositions. We might even assert, with Hamelin, that definition is science itself, considered as a finished product (*op. cit.*, p.248). But in that case, just as we must allow that Aristotle hesitates between science as research and science as demonstration, so we must accept a duality in his scientific ideal: on the one side, the ideal science

48. 'And, he says, in the case of what is given (*to dedomenon*) we must know in advance both that it is and what it signifies or what it is; but in the case of what is sought (*to zêtoumenon*) <we must know in advance> not that it is but what it signifies or what it is. E.g. if a finite straight line is given, we must know in advance both that the straight line is finite and what the word signifies; but in the case of what is sought − i.e. the equilateral triangle − only what it signifies. For here one must not know in advance that it is − for in that case it would not be being sought' (Philoponus, *In A.Pst.* (CIAG XIII 3), 10.7-13).

49. See *A.Pst.* II 1, 89b34: 'It is only when we have discovered that a thing exists that we seek to know what it is.'

is conceived as a chain of *facts*, on the other the ideal science is conceived as a hierarchy of *ideas*; on the one side an ideal of *demonstration*, on the other an ideal of *definition*. This duality is linked to the ambivalent notion of 'cause' (*aitia*), which Aristotle sometimes construes as an *antecedent* that explains the existence of something, and sometimes as an *intrinsic reason* that manifests the essence of something. And this in its turn is linked, in the last analysis, to a fundamental ambiguity in the meaning of the verb *to be*. Aristotle, it is true, makes a clearcut distinction between the existential and the copulative senses of the verb, between its synthetic and its analytic functions (see esp. *A.Pst.* II 1).[50] But in practice he often forgets the distinction. We have already come across one example of this in the *syllogism of essence*: it is because he forgets that in the case of the eclipse this syllogism answers the question *dia ti* ('Why?'), that Aristotle calls it logical – as if it artificially broke up a unitary being and as if it used the verb *to be* to mark a relation between two different things.

Conclusion

1. Our inquiries into the nature, the method, and the role of definition show that definitions, as Aristotle conceives them, are not completely indubitable: they are structures in which we can never have complete confidence; we noted that Aristotle himself says, in connection with the definition of soul, that we can only hope for belief, *pistis* (*De An.* I 1, 402a11). This conclusion assumes some importance when we recall the part which definitions play in Aristotelian science. One of the fundamental laws laid down in the *Prior Analytics* is that the conclusion of a syllogism cannot improve upon the quality of its premisses: then if the definitions which form the principles of science are uncertain, everything which follows from them is equally uncertain. And that blurs the distinction between dialectic and science upon which Aristotle placed so much stress.

2. Moreover, despite his subtle analyses and his penetrating methodological comments, Aristotle appears to have misconceived the true nature of the scientific enterprise. Concerned to found science upon infallible intuitions, he did not fully realise that it was necessary to explain the passage from these intuitions to articulated judgments, and to establish the validity of those judgments which express and analyse the intuitions.

Aristotle should perhaps have located genuine intuition not at the starting point of the enterprise but at its conclusion, and have treated it as an ideal and transcendent goal that will guarantee knowledge 'from above'. Thus, instead of intuiting intelligible essences, the scientist would begin with the humdrum objects of sense perception. He is confident that the world can be understood in universal terms (for that indeed is the very source of his scientific drive); and thus he is bound to impose an intellectual interpretation on the data of perception, and to find in them some unifying

---

50. On the one hand, *ei estin* ('if it is') and *hoti estin* ('that it is') bear upon existence, while *ti estin* ('what is it?') and *dia ti estin* ('why is it?') point to an examination into the content or essence of what exists. On the other hand, *ei estin* and *ti estin* are asked of a single being, while *hoti estin* and *dia ti estin* bear on the relationship between two beings. See Le Blond [120], pp. 168 ff.

necessity which will allow him not merely to *grasp* them but to *understand* them. In this way he will progress towards that genuinely intellectual intuition of essences which forms the transcendent and yet fertile ideal of his 'discourse'. There are passages in Aristotle which point to this approach. In the methodological preface to *Physics* I, he cites as an example the definition of a circle: every ignoramus can perceive a circle (he has only to open his eyes); but only the scientist understands that a circle is and can define it by comprehending the necessary relation between the centre, the radius, and the circumference (I 1, 184b2). We find here the movement from the perception of a simple universal to a definition which conceptualises and analyses it. But these are not the lines along which Aristotle constructed his official theory of definition.

380

6

Suzanne Mansion

*The Ontological Composition of Sensible Substances in Aristotle (*Metaphysics *VII, 7-9)*

75 Book VII of the *Metaphysics*, which is devoted to the study of substance and in particular of sensible substance, is one of the most obscure of Aristotle's works. Its structure is unclear; certain chapters do not appear to fit readily into the general line of argument. Ross, having rehearsed the fragmentation in which Natorp indulged, attempted to re-establish as far as possible the unity of the book, but was forced to confess that chapters 7-9 interrupt the flow of thought that is apparent in chapters 1-6 and 10-12. He observes that the summaries at VII 11, 1037a21-b7 and VIII 1, 1042a4-22 make no mention of VII 7-9, but he adds that Aristotle does nonetheless refer to these chapters at VII 15, 1039b26 ([4] II, p.181).

It is obvious to any careful reader that the 17 chapters of VII, as they appear in modern editions, do not form a logical sequence. Yet this very lack of cohesion, combined with the fact that reminders of previous discussions occur unexpectedly and are missing from the systematic summaries, seems to invalidate the hypothesis of an extensive reworking of Aristotle's notes by some unknown editor. As Jaeger was clearly aware, we have here a text that has been worked on by its author – a thinker who advances slowly, who changes his mind, who, perhaps, inserts into old discussions ideas that till then had only existed separately. This might well be the case with chapters 7-9, which deal with becoming and form a whole.

76 However, I have no intention of investigating further the problem of literary criticism set by the insertion of these chapters into the middle of book VII. Working on the hypothesis that it is neither chance nor a later editor that accounts for their position, I shall try to discover how, even if only as a digression, they help to clarify the central theme of book VII.

The bare outlines of this theme are as follows: We are, says Aristotle, trying to discover what substance is; not only what has a right to be called substance, but also what is as it were the substantiality of substance.[1] Four principal senses of the word *ousia* are mentioned as possible answers. *Ousia* can be understood as quiddity (*to ti ên einai*), as universal, as genus, and finally as subject (VII 3, 1028b33-6). A rapid examination of substance as subject, in ch. 3, comes to a conclusion that seems to Aristotle to be

---

1. Boehm, in his recent work *Das Grundlegende und das Wesentliche. Zu Aristoteles Abhandlung 'Uber das Sein und das Seiende' (Metaphysik Z)* (La Haye 1965), has explained cleary this double sense of the question 'What is *ousia*?' in VII 1, 1028b4; see pp.55 ff.

inadmissible: that substance is matter without determination (1029a26-8). The study of subject is abandoned, at least provisionally.[2] The study of substance as universal occupies chs. 13 and 14. As for genus, its claims to subtsantiality do not appear to be examined separately from the substantiality of universals (cf. Ross [4] II, p.164). All that remains is quiddity or essence. Aristotle devotes all his talents to explaining this meaning of substance. Three chapters, among the most difficult in the book (4-6), doggedly unravel the notion of quiddity and come to two principal conclusions: substances alone have quiddity in the true sense (VII 5, 1031a12-14); and this quiddity, even in the case of sensible substances, is one with their being (VII 6, esp. 1031b18-20; 31-2).

Although chs. 10-12 do not directly continue the argument of chs. 4-6, it is easy to see that they deal with matters that are connected with quiddity. **77** They are, in fact, concerned with definition, the expression of essence, and with its parts, in their relationship with the *definiendum* and *its* parts (matter, form, and their combination). This is the framework of the digression on becoming in chs. 7-9.

Their content is difficult to summarise. They consist of a series of remarks whose apparent connection seems to be that they are all linked to becoming and to its principles, matter and form, concepts with which the reader is assumed to be familiar. The account is clearly influenced by the one in *Physics* Book I. The classic distinction is drawn between natural, artificial, and chance becoming; but our attention is first drawn to the first two: until ch. 9, Aristotle makes no attempt to compare chance becoming to the two other types. The chief points that he wants to clarify in these chapters as a whole are: the identity in natural productions between the generator and what is engenders;[3] the fact that the principles of becoming, form as well as matter, are ungenerable (VII 8, 1033a24-b19; 9, 1034b7-19); and finally the active or efficient character of the form of sensible substances and hence the pointlessness of postulating separate Platonic Forms to explain becoming.[4]

Do these conclusions have any connection with the examination of substance as quiddity and, more generally, do they illuminate the notion of substance with which Aristotle wrestles in the rest of book VII? It seems to me that they do, in as much as they give us a deeper understanding of the connection between matter and form.

In order to see this, we must go back to the beginning of the book and try to dig deeper into Aristotle's puzzle. As we have seen, in ch. 3 he rejects a theory according to which *ousia* would draw all its substantiality from **78** matter. For the ultimate substrate, which is the ontological support of form, cannot be a 'separable' being, capable of independent existence; nor can it

2. In fact Aristotle will only return to this in passing in book VII: see 13, 1038b2-6. See also the summary of VII in VIII 1, 1042a26-31.

3. VII 7, 1032a24-5; 8, 1033b29-32. The principle is universal for the generation of natural substances, in spite of certain apparent exceptions (the mule): 1033b33-1034a2. It may also be applied to a certain extent to artificial productions: VII 9, 1034a21-4, but is invalid for natural becoming in categories other than substance (1034b16-19).

4. VII 7, 1032a24-5; 8, 1033b20-1034a5; 9, 1034a31-2, where *ousia* is taken in the sense of formal substance.

be a determinate object.[5] These two characteristics belong, we might think, more to the forms and to the composites, so that these have a better claim to the name of substance. But since the composite is posterior to its parts, we must examine the substantiality of the latter. Not the substantiality of matter – we have already seen that it is only as a substrate that it has any claims (and those inadequate) to substantiality – but that of form; for form, Aristotle says, is what presents the greatest difficulty. Our examination will begin with the form of sensible substances, he continues, because these are substances recognised by everybody.[6]

Once he has posed this question, it is only natural that his investigation should continue as it does, taking as its theme the notion of essence (*ti ên einai*). For if Plato asserted that true beings (and hence true substances) are intelligible Forms, it was because they are things in themselves, essences; sublunary things only participate in them, drawing from them the characteristics that give them their names and make them recognisable. Is substantiality then 'essentiality', the fact of being a form in itself? As we know, Aristotle's answer is to accept this idea while rejecting the Platonic separation of forms. He allows that substances are substances in virtue of their form, or at least that the possession of an essential form distinguishes substance from every other type of secondary being (quality, quantity, etc.). Yet he believes that this identity between a thing and its quiddity, which is characteristic of subsistent subjects, can be realised in our sublunary world, and that it is useless to postulate, separate from sensible substances, essences that are really only carbon copies of them.[7] The problem of substance is, however, not completely unravelled by this solution, however important it may be. Substances which exist in the sensible world are essentially composite. If we put substantiality down to form, even to form immanent in sensible substance, we are in danger of overlooking the part matter plays in the constitution of substance. For what need is there for the form of sensible substance to inhabit matter? How should we see the formal principle in order to understand that it does not subsist by itself, but must inform some matter in order to become a substance? If we are unable to solve this new problem, the refutation of Platonism will have been in vain and we shall continue to vacillate between a 'formalist' conception of substance (*ousia* is essence) and a materialist approach (*ousia* is the concrete substrate) – both equally unsatisfactory.

5. Literally 'a "this"' (*tode ti*) – not an individual but a substance possessing a determination. On the meaning of the expression *tode ti* see Smith [205]; Tugendhat [173], p.25 n. 22; and my own paper [71], p.194 n. 3.

6. VII 3, 1029a26-34. The restriction that this sentence contains shows that Aristotle is approaching the problem of the substantiality of form in its most general sense and is thinking of possible immaterial substances, which would be pure form. I cannot discuss here Boehm's presentation of the problems stated at the beginning of Book VII (*op.cit.* n. 1). Though his conclusions often seem hard to accept, his penetrating analyses frequently illuminate ancient and complicated problems.

7. The long and subtle analysis that begins in VII 4 culminates in ch. 6, where Aristotle turns back on Plato the argument used to establish the Ideas: if it is necessary in the case of the Forms themselves, because they are pure essence, that their being should be identical with their quiddity, at the risk of seeing the process of separation continuing into infinity, why not admit that even on earth this identity exists for beings 'in themselves and first'? See in particular 1031b31-1032a11.

Without providing a straightforward answer to this question, chapters 7-9 seem to me to shed some light on it, as I will now try to explain.

Aristotle thought up his notions of form and matter in the first book of the *Physics* in order to solve the problems of becoming. It is hardly surprising if a more extensive analysis of the role these principles play in becoming should illuminate more clearly their mutual relationships.

Using a method he is fond of, Aristotle here compares natural becoming to artificial becoming; the comparison is legitimate since 'art imitates nature', and it has the advantage of explaining nature to us through a readily comprehensible model.[8] If my interpretation of ch. 7 is correct, the extended description of an artificial production (a doctor restoring a sick man to health) helps us to understand what part the various factors of becoming play in the generation of substances.

Aristotle first asserts that all production, natural, artificial, or chance, works in response to a cause, starting from a certain subject and culminating in something determinate (VII 7, 1032a12-14). He then remarks that in the generation of a substance, the efficient cause is nature — like the matter and the end product — but nature in the sense of form; and that it is formally identical with the engendered being: man engenders man (1032a16-25). He then moves on to artificial products and shows that there too the efficient principle is of the same kind as the product. If the doctor is capable of producing health in a sick body, it is because he has in mind the form or essence of health, from which he can judge what is defective in his patient's state of health and find the concrete remedy for this defect. Let us suppose, for example, that health lies in a balance of heat and cold and that, as a result of the illness, the sick man's temperature is too low. We must warm the patient's body, which can be done by rubbing. Having reached this conclusion, the doctor has only to put his remedy into practice in order to effect a cure. Analysis reveals two stages in this process: the *conception* of the desired end and of the means to achieve it, and their *realisation*, the last stage in conception being the first in realisation.[9]

Our present concerns draw our attention to the precise part that form plays here. Let us first note the identity drawn between form and essence. It is indeed the essence of health that is under discussion, because it is the essence of health that we assume the doctor knows. Now this essence is

---

8. Similarly in the *De Anima*, to explain what he means when he says that the soul is the form of the body, Aristotle resorts to a comparison with an artifact, an axe. As an axe is a tool intended to fulfil a certain function, it is easy to know what it is, and to see that it is its adaptation to its function that makes it, formally, an axe (II 1, 412b10-17). Cf. *PA* I 5, 645b14-20.

9. 1032a32-b30. For the difficulties that arise in this passage, see Ross' commentary, pp.184-5, and n. 4 p.383 in the Tricot translation. After explaining that in artificial production it is the form (health) which is the efficient cause, Aristotle is somewhat embarrassed by the cases in which the same result is produced by chance. His solution to the problem is that the starting-point of fortuitous production is identical to the first term of the executive phase in artificial production (the warming that the doctor decided to instigate). Thus we can say that this starting-point, linked to the result it has, is of the same sort as the latter: warming is a part of health, the part to be produced in the case under consideration. But, as Ross comments, Aristotle is wrong to compare the heat/health connection to the stones/house connection (1032b29-30).

expressly identified with form (1031b1-2). This is not unusual, for Aristotle
regularly defines the formal cause as the quiddity.[10] However, his
phraseology here is to say the least ambiguous: the health which is in the
doctor's mind (like the house that is in the architect's mind) is health (or a
house) *without matter*. 'Therefore it follows that in a sense health comes from
health and house from house, that with matter from that without matter; for
the medical art and the building art are the form of health and of the house,
and when I speak of substances without matter I mean the essence'
(1032b11-14, Ross's translation). How should we take this? It is obvious
that health and houses do not really exist in the minds of people who are
thinking about them, and that they only have an idea of them. But if
Aristotle wants only to say this, we have a crude muddle between the order
of thought and the order of reality – an improper identification of form, the
real principle of the thing, with the idea that represents it. Without claiming
that Aristotle's mind is entirely free from this confusion, I think we can
safely say that there is another meaning to be read into his words. What he
is analysing is the transition from the conscious act of setting up a goal to
the realising of this objective. It seems to me that what he wants to
emphasise is that this act is dynamic (since it directs a realisation), and that
it is so because, being related to the process it controls, it has the character
of a plan or a form that will be fulfilled by matter. This dual nature,
dynamic and formal, is apparent at both stages of production (conception
and execution), as we shall see.

Let us take the aim to be the restoration to health of a certain invalid.
This aim, Aristotle notes, requires of the doctor a certain amount of.
intellectual labour in his attempt to establish how he should achieve it. He
doubtless knows from the start what his aim is, but not in such a way as to
be immediately aware of the means to attain it: he will have to discover
what these are. It is, however, clear that it is the knowledge of the aim that is
the standard for discovering these means. In stating the aim, he imposes
requirements on his search for the means, and this implies that the
knowledge of the aim is dynamic *because it is schematic and formal*. When the
doctor has at last determined which in the series of means is the first term he
is capable of realising, the executive stage can begin. It will have the same
characteristics as the previous one: it will be dominated by the final aim,
and the dynamism of the aim will be due to the exigency of creating
something that does not yet exist. Taken as a scheme that shapes this
process, the aim could be called a form, and execution would then be the
imposition of this form on some already existing matter.

An analysis of the intellectual activity of the doctor brings us to see that
artificial production is totally dominated by a mental blueprint of what is to
be produced. Both because this blueprint is a *schematic* representation of the
essence of the thing, and because it is the desire of an aim *to be reached*, we
can say that what controls both the conception and the execution of an
action is a form.[11]

10. See *Meta.* I 3, 983a27-8; V 2, 1013a26-7; 1013b22-3; 8, 1017b21-6; VII 10,
1035b32; VIII 4, 1044a36.
11. Strictly speaking, this form is mental, the object thought of and desired. But
since for Aristotle the idea is modelled after a real essence, it would seem none the less

To what extent can the analysis of artificial production be applied to natural production? Aristotle does not say, although he almost certainly did intend to apply it. He was content to begin by asserting the similarity between the two kinds of production: for both, the starting-line and the finishing-post have the same essence; man engenders man as health engenders health. The difference is that in art the essence is represented in thought,[12] while this is not the case as far as natural generation is concerned.[13] Bearing this difference in mind, however, the artificial scheme remains most illuminating in the question of natural processes. **83**

The mysterious transition of form from the generator to the generated can be seen, on the model of what happens in the realm of artificial skills, as the arrangement of a series of means towards a single end. The dynamism of form lies in its ability to organise materials in such a way that a certain result takes place. And if this result can be the coming into existence of a being similar to its generator, that is precisely because the character that is to be reproduced already exists in a certain way in the latter.[14]

Having established this, let us see what new light chapter 8 sheds on the relationship between matter and form. There are two theories relevant to our discussion.

The first states that neither matter nor form are engendered in becoming. As far as the first goes, this is obvious. Matter is the substrate which must exist before becoming can take place. But where form is concerned, things are not as clear; the reason Aristotle gives is that if form were engendered, it too would need a pre-existent substrate, and so on ad infinitum.[15] Besides, it **84** is plain that the craftsman who makes a brass sphere does not make either the brass or the sphere, but simply imposes a spherical form on a given matter.

But then, asks Aristotle, if the form or essence of the sphere is not subject to generation, should we not assume that there exists 'a sphere apart from the individual spheres or a house apart from the bricks' (1033b20-1)? His answer, in the negative, is the second theory that demands our attention. He justifies this in an unusually dense paragraph, whose content is as follows.

---

right to say that, in the last analysis, this essence exerts a causality – also real – on the whole process. It is, however, plain that Aristotle does not make a clear distinction between these two levels.

12. 'A form in the mind': 1032b1.

13. Aristotle draws a parallel between art and nature in which *nous* is opposed to *phusis*: 'For just as intelligence (*nous*) acts for the sake of something, in the same way nature (*phusis*) also <acts for the sake of something> and that is its end' (*De An.* II 4, 415b16-17).

14. In order to be able to state that the result of generation has the character of an end, or good, unconsciously sought by nature, other considerations are necessary that Aristotle here ignores. In the *De An.* he explains the reproductive function of living beings by their desire to participate in the divine and the eternal as far as possible (II 4, 415a26-b2). This justification is, however, not relevant to the problem dealt with in *Meta.* VII, where only the 'how' of generation, and its relationship to form, are examined.

15. VII 8, 1033a24-b19. His example is once again borrowed from art, for the same reasons as before: the domain of human activity is clearer to us, and it is easy to pass from it to the domain of nature.

All generation consists in imposing a qualification on a given substrate (1033b21-4). Now: 'The whole "this", Callias or Socrates, is analogous to "this brazen sphere", but man and animal to "brazen sphere" in general. Obviously, then, the cause which consists of the Forms (taken in the sense in which some maintain the existence of the Forms, i.e. if they are something apart from the individuals), is useless, at least with regard to comings-to-be and to substances' (1033b24-8, Ross's translation). It seems to me that these remarks, obscure in their conciseness, should be understood in this way: what is passed on by generation is not complete substantiality, but only its formal aspect. Now this aspect cannot be isolated from matter; whatever adherents to the Ideas may think, for Platonic Forms, taken as the essences of sensible objects, correspond to what is meant by the concept of these sensible objects: man or animal. Yet the general concept of man is, to the individual, as the concept of brass sphere is to one particular brass sphere; it is the concept of an essentially material being, of a form in matter. A Platonic Form, if it is truly the essence of

85   sensible objects, is not the formal principle, set apart from those objects, nor can it play the rôle in becoming that is demanded of it. A *substance that is only form* cannot be the activating principle in the generation of sensible substances; that rôle belongs to a being whose physical action transforms matter in a determinate sense.

Where can we find such a being, if not in the sensible order itself, in a substance composed of matter and form, capable of reproducing in other matter the arrangement which is its own constitution? This is the conclusion Aristotle reaches, suggesting as the cause of the production of natural substances a concrete generator of the same species as the object generated.[16]

Let us now cast a look backwards and summarise our results. Our examination of the matter-form relationship in generation has shown in a new light the inseparability of these principles in sensible substances. The only complete substance in the sensible world is matter determined by form; for these two principles are correlative and thus neither is capable of forming a basis for substantiality by itself (though for different reasons). Form is the essential determination *of* something; matter is the *something* that has to be determined and organised. Form, the essential determination, can in a sense be described as substance without matter. The comparison between natural becoming and art reveals in what sense the form of the generator is a kind of master-plan of action, organising matter according to its own determination and stamping its mark on a new individual.

Aristotle was well aware that this view of things limits generation to the production of composite substances as such, and denies it to their components. He also realised that this excludes any separate existence of form, which can no more exist without matter than the order or composition of elements can exist without ordered or compound wholes, or than an end can come about without the means of attaining it.

86   There is, however, one extremely important consequence that Aristotle apparently failed to draw from his own doctrines: the form of sensible

16. VII 8, 1033b29-32; 1034a2-8. Ch. 9 examines the apparent and real restrictions we should impose on the principle of generation of like by like. It does not introduce any new theory relevant to this discussion.

substances can no longer be simply identified with their quiddity.[17] What a sensible substance is in itself (its quiddity), is not only its determination: it is its determination in as far as it informs matter; for we have just seen that a sensible substance is essentially an incarnate form. In one sense, then, matter penetrates the essence of sensible substances and must be expressed in the concept that describes this essence. Aristotle saw this when he said that the concept of man is comparable to the concept of the brass sphere; but he did not draw the logical conclusion from this, that form is not the *essence* but the *principle* which endows an object with its essential determination.

A second consequence of this theory did not, however, elude him: if matter enters the essence of sensible substances, it does not do so by becoming something formal; quite the contrary, it must remain implacably opposed to form in order to confer on substance what form cannot, namely, numerical unity.[18]

Thus we see that the analysis of becoming in VII 7-9 is far from unimportant as far as the metaphysical conception of sensible substance is concerned. A study of the rest of book VII shows that Aristotle made good use of it, particularly in chs. 10-12. To conclude, however, I should like to emphasise its theoretical relevance. Not only do these conclusions reveal the respective roles of matter and form in the substantiality of sensible substances, they also pave the way for an answer to the ultimate question of Aristotle's *Metaphysics*: are there substances beyond the sensible? (cf. VII 11, 1037a10-16; 17, 1041a6-9). For, once we realise that it is impossible to separate the form of sensible substances from their matter, we are near to understanding that the difference between the latter and any immaterial substances has no connection with the ontological status of form – separate or inseparable – but rather with its very nature.

87

17. However, Aristotle continues to do so both in these chapters and further on. Cf. VII 7, 1032b1-2; 1032b14; 8, 1033b5-7; 10, 1035b32; VIII 4, 1044a36.
18. VII 8, 1034a5-8: 'And when we have the whole, such and such a form in this flesh and in these bones, this is Callias or Socrates, and they are different [sc. from their generator] in virtue of their matter (for that is different), but the same in form; for their form is indivisible' (Ross's translation).

PAS Supp Vol. 27.

7

G.E.M. Anscombe

The Principle of Individuation

83 1. I wish to express grateful admiration for the extreme clarity with which Professor Lukasiewicz has written.

He follows Aristotle in first taking:–

matter = material or stuff (e.g. bronze)
form = shape,

but his example of the same shape in different matter is a statue of bronze and a statue of stone. For Aristotle two bronze statues would also, and in just the same sense, be the same shape in different matter, and Professor Lukasiewicz's example is misleading because it naturally suggests that in calling bronze matter Aristotle is saying: 'At this stage think of "matter" as if it meant "kind of stuff".'. Aristotle says 'This ... individual, Callias or Socrates, is like *this* bronze ball, while "man" and "animal" are like "bronze ball" in general',[1] and soon after comes the passage that Professor. Lukasiewicz quotes: 'The whole thing, such-and-such a form in this flesh and these bones, is Callias or Socrates; and they are different owing to their matter (for this is different), but the same in form (for the form is indivisible).' These passages show that two bronze balls would be a suitable example of the same shape in different material. Of course, both the concept of 'material' suggested by Professor Lukasiewicz's example, and the concept that Aristotle is here concerned with, are familiar ones; both occur in Aristotle.

2. *The absurdity of the idea of matter.* The hypothesis that things contain something which isn't anything and has no properties is certainly a senseless one, which, as Professor Lukasiewicz says, could not serve to explain anything. A book on logic by a philosopher Joseph, who used to be **84** well-known, expounds an argument that there must be an ultimate subject of predication which itself has no predicates. This parallels the Neo-Scholastics! The idea that what changes must be something that doesn't change precisely because it is what changes, is very like the idea that what has predicates must be something without predicates just because it is what has the predicates: both being based on inadequate reading of Aristotle.

3. I am always uncertain what it means to call a concept 'metaphysical'. But the concept of matter which Aristotle works on is at least an everyday one. If you show me a lump of stuff and tell me that it can be moulded into various shapes, that if you heat it it will turn into a gas, and if you electrify it it will turn into something else, I understand very well what you mean. Let

---

1. *Meta.* VII, 1033b24.

me suppose that you show me a bottle of wine; you heat it, and it expands, you leave it, and after a while it has turned into vinegar. Now someone asks 'But what is it *all* the time?' Some Greek philosophers would have wanted to say it was water or air or fire or something in between. '[They think that] there *must* be some nature, whether one or more than one, out of which the rest come to be while it remains constant.'[2] Aristotle however wants to say: 'There isn't anything which it is all the time. It *was* wine, and *is* vinegar, and there isn't some third thing that it is all the time.' He says in the *Physics*, in the course of arguing against such philosophers: 'Water and air aren't, and don't come, out of one another in the same way as bricks out of a house and a house out of bricks.'[3] (One gets the point of this only by assuming with him that water and air (mist?) do in fact turn into one another.)

(It may be that we have a theory of chemical elements, so that if – to make the case simple – we identify something as a pure sample of an element, we go on saying that it is that element whatever happens to it. But any such theory – whatever its validity – is beside the point in our discussion, for it is necessarily based on the possibility of identifying the same bit of matter in our initial experiments: on our having the idea of 'nothing added and nothing taken away'.) **85**

4. We can see now why this matter (e.g. the stuff I have got in this bottle) is not as such a given kind of stuff (*ti*): for the same stuff was wine and is vinegar. Nor can we say that it is as such *not* a certain kind of stuff – for that would mean that it could not be e.g. wine, and of course, when it is wine, it *is* wine. Similarly there are not any properties, either qualities or dimensions, which you can say it has – or lacks – *qua* this bit of matter. E.g. if you told me that the process of change from wine to vinegar involved expansion or contraction, I should understand you. Just as I understand the information I have about the expansion and contraction of water at different temperatures. So that not even the volume determines the bit of water we are talking about. This is what I understand Aristotle to be referring to when he says that matter is not as such (*kath' hautên*) *so* much (*poson*).[4] Not that matter is: not even extended! – but that I cannot define the stuff (the bit of water, e.g., that I am talking about) as e.g. 'a pint hereabouts'. It will perhaps be more than a pint if I cool it or less if I heat it. And the point about negation is clear here too: I cannot say that this stuff is as such *not* a pint; for perhaps it is a pint, or I can make it a pint without addition or subtraction of matter.

That last word was being used in a completely familiar sense; and it is what Aristotle means by '*hulê*'. (Only he tries to use it by analogy in all sorts of contexts, to extend its application away from where it is so to speak indigenous. I do not know or understand enough to have a general opinion **86** whether the concept, in these extended applications, is so useful an instrument as Aristotle clearly thought it was. Certainly I feel only impatient when he considers calling units the matter of numbers. Nor, for instance, can I make anything of such an idea as 'place-matter'.)

2. *Meta*. I, 983b19.
3. *Phys*. I 4, 188a15.
4. To be precise: not characterised by a particular answer to the question 'How much?'

I have approached Aristotle's idea of matter by way of '*this* matter'. He himself approaches it, in the first book of the *Physics*, in the context of discussions which are not alive for us and of most of which it would not be possible to give more than an external account. '*This* matter' is, however, Aristotelian. – Aristotle says that matter cannot very well be substance (*ousia*), because what specially belongs to substance is being separate and being a 'this something' (*tode ti*)[5]: e.g. 'this man', 'this cabbage'. Now 'this matter' is *tode*, but not *ti*: that is, it is designatable, identifiable, but is not as such of any specific kind or necessarily possessed of this or that property or dimensions, as I have explained. And it is of course not separable: that is, you could not entertain producing a specimen of it, which contrived to be of no kind (to be not *ti*). It is important to understand that this is a *conceptual* statement. That is, if I tell you that the stuff in this apparatus has changed from being water to being hydrogen and oxygen, you show that you are quite at sea about the sense I am using the word 'stuff' in, if you ask me to show you the stuff itself as it really is itself, apart from being the various things it can be.

5. I feel doubtful about Professor Lukasiewicz's comments on 'matter in itself'. For 'matter in itself' does not seem to be used as a name or description by Aristotle, as I gather that '*Ding an sich*' may have been by Kant. You have to take the whole sentence in which '*hulê kath' hautên*' occurs. Professor Lukasiewicz's comments strike me a little as if I were to say 'A chair as such isn't upholstered or not upholstered', and were to be laughed at, not for the pedantic style, but for inventing such a strange object as 'a chair as such', with such extraordinary properties, whereby it defeated the law of excluded middle.

6. Thus I do not think it reasonable to take exception to such statements as that matter is in itself indefinite and unknowable: it 'has to be understood in what changes.'[6] The change in question is substantial change: 'For the rest (of the predicates) are predicated of the substance, while *it* is predicated of the matter.'[7] That is, we say that milk e.g. is white and liquid, and this stuff is milk. But this stuff may be changed from milk into junket; nor apart from such changes should we have any such concept as 'this stuff', *as opposed to* 'this milk'. 'In all changes between opposed characteristics the subject of change is something: e.g. with change of place it is what is now here now there, with change of size what is now so much, now bigger or smaller, with change of quality what is now healthy, now sickly. Similarly with substantial change it is what is now in process of generation, now in process of destruction, now the subject as a "this something" and now the subject in the way of privation.'[8]

The last phrase is obscure. In order to explain what I think Aristotle means by it, I will consider a passage in Professor Lukasiewicz's paper. 'It seems to be evident that all these things (bronze statues, stone balls etc.) are individuals owing to their matter, as every bit of matter has at any time its own proper place and is different from all the other material things in the

---

5. *Meta.* VII, 1029a26-30.
6. *Meta.* II, 994b26.
7. *Meta.* VII, 1029a22.
8. *Meta.* VIII, 1042a32-b3.

world.' This leaves it open whether a given bit of matter, which at a given time has its own proper place and is different from all the other material things in the world, must be supposed always to have had, and always to be going to have, its own proper place and distinctness. If, that is, a given bit of matter is mixed and fused with, or absorbed by, another mass of matter, must we *a priori* suppose it to consist of particles retaining their identity? Aristotle's view of matter is a rejection and criticism of any such belief. Matter only has identity in so far as it is designate, earmarked; in itself it is indefinite (*aoristos*). Suppose I throw a cupful of milk into the sea. It is no longer this milk; and if I ask where and what the stuff that I threw into the sea is, there is no need for there to be an answer beyond that it became part of the sea. And if in such cases there is an answer, this is because the particles continue to be identified by some property. For, if they are not marked out by anything, we cannot mark them out: if we do, they *are* marked out. And yet no one wishes to say that the stuff itself has been destroyed. We know no application for the idea of annihilation: by which I mean, not that we do not know of any case of it, but that we have – even side by side with a strong feeling of meaning for the word – hardly the vaguest notion what we should call a case of it. (Perhaps the total disappearance of a solid object, without a ripple in the surroundings except the inrush of air to take its place.)

Matter only exists as *somehow* designate; but that is not enough to secure the permanent identifiability of a once designate bit of it. And '*this* matter' is matter *thus* designate. (The usual criteria for speaking of the same stuff.) But when this matter loses its identity we do not speak of its being destroyed; and we say that *it* has lost its identity. This is what I take Aristotle to mean when he calls matter 'now the subject as a "this something", now the subject in the way of privation.'

It is always, and especially here, important to notice that Aristotle's 'matter' is not a *hypothesis*.

7. One may easily be puzzled by the expression 'this matter, taken universally', which occurs for example in one of the passages quoted by Professor Lukasiewicz. What could be the point of, say, 'this spot of light, taken universally'? The 'this' seems to war with the 'universally'.

'This matter' contrasts with undesignate matter, not with a general notion under which it falls as an instance. Hence when Aristotle wishes to generalise it, he says 'this matter, taken universally'.

8. *On the analogy between bronze and its shape, and matter and form.* Aristotle's prime examples of 'substance' are: *a* man (*ho tis anthrôpos*[9]), *a* horse, or, I might add, *a* cabbage. There is a contrast between a concept like 'cabbage' and a concept like 'gold'. Cabbage is not just a kind of stuff, but a cabbage is a particular thing; whereas the concept 'gold' does not determine an individual thing in this way. Had Aristotle written in English he would certainly have seized on certain peculiarities of English to make his point: we do speak of bronzes, marbles, irons, steels, woods (in bowls e.g.), glasses etc. Bronze is to *a* bronze as flesh and bones etc. are to a man.

9. 'In a way, matter is obvious.'[10]

9. *Cat.*, 2a13.
10. *Meta.* VII, 1029a32.

10. 'Matter is in a way obvious, but ... (form) is frightfully difficult.'[11] Ross, for whom matter is most difficult, thinks that it is a concept reached by mentally stripping away all forms until you get to a characterless substrate. Aristotle regarded it rather the other way round: 'by form I mean substance without matter':[12] that is, you get at it if you succeed in thinking matter away from substance. And he fell into frightful difficulties here, because he thought that form was the 'what' of substances: but of course the names of sensible substances and their definitions (e.g. 'man', 'two-footed animal') carry a reference to matter in their sense.

I do not understand Aristotle's 'form', and I do not yet know whether he got clear about it himself. Luckily I need not present my half-formed ideas about it here. (I wish Greek grammarians could determine something about the expressions '*to ti ên einai, to ti ên einai A, to einai A, to A einai*' (*A* being a *dative*!), with which the *Metaphysics* is strewn. These queer constructions have escaped their notice.)

The difficulties that Aristotle gets into come out most clearly if we consider the following:

(1) a thing and its *to ti ên einai* are the same[13] (Anti-Platonic).

(2) *to ti ên einai anthrôpôi, to anthrôpôi einai* are clearly equivalent expressions.[13]

(3) *anthrôpos* and *anthrôpôi einai* are *not* the same unless you make *anthrôpos = psuchê*; which is right in one way, wrong in another.[14] It is clearly something special about 'soul' and 'circle' that they are the *same* as *psuchêi einai* and *kuklôi einai*.[15]

All this is supposed to be resolved[16] by the consideration that the form and the matter are the same, but one potentially and the other actually. But this is still Greek to me.

To translate '*to ti ên einai*': 'the essence' produces gibberish – e.g. 'Callias is of himself Callias and the essence of Callias.'[17] It is clear that the correct gloss on *to ti ên einai Kalliâi* in this passage is 'man': 'Callias is of himself Callias and a man'. I.e. Callias is of himself that, to be which *is* being for Callias. Proper names do not, as some philosophers have said, 'have denotation but no connotation'; the criterion of identity for Callias is the criterion for there being the *same man*.

I have mentioned so much about form, only because I want to consider the 'grave inconsistency' which Professor Lukasiewicz ascribes to Aristotle. The inconsistency was this: Aristotle says that individuals are indefinable, but he also says that they consist of matter and form and that whatever has form has a definition. I do not think that Aristotle is in fact at all inconsistent at this point. The individual – say Callias – is indefinable, in the sense that there is no definition of him as opposed to another individual

11. *Meta.* VII, 1029a32.
12. *Meta.* VII, 1032b15. cf. supra, 1032b2.
13. *Meta.* VII, 1031a17-21.
14. *Meta.* VIII, 1043b2.
15. *Meta.* VII, 1036a1.
16. *Meta.* VIII, *ad fin.*
17. *Meta.* V, 1022a26.

of the same species; his definition is the definition of the form. 'Of the concrete substance in one sense there is an explanation (*logos*), in another not. For together with the matter there is none (for it is indefinite), but there is one according to first substance: e.g. the explanation (*logos*) of man is that of the soul.'[18] But this passage and its context are thick with the difficulty that I have described, of which I do not understand the resolution. Hence the defence against Professor Lukasiewicz's particular charge is not worth much.

11. I have the impression that Professor Lukasiewicz equates 'this matter, taken universally', and 'intelligible matter'. This seems to be a mistake. 'Intelligible matter' has to do merely with mathematical objects: on the analogy of sensible matter Aristotle invents 'intelligible matter' to account for the plurality of geometers' circles (e.g.); for when a geometer speaks of two intersecting circles he is not talking about, say, wooden rings. 'Intelligible matter' is an absurd and useless device, of no importance for Aristotle's account of material substance; and it is not 'intelligible matter' but 'this matter taken universally' that is said, together with the definition, to form universals like 'man' and 'horse'.

12. Luckily it is possible to understand what is meant by calling matter the principle of individuation, without understanding about form.

It is not off-hand clear that there has to be a principle of individuation. If X and Y are different, the difference may be made clear by appropriate elucidation of the meaning of 'X' and 'Y'.

Consider:

(*a*) 'X and Y are numbers.' – 'Which numbers?'
(*b*) 'X and Y are men.' – 'Which men?'

Both might be answered by giving a 'definite description'. E.g. 'the even prime'; 'the smallest integer, greater than one, that is both a square and a cube'; 'the philosopher who drank hemlock'; 'the philosopher who wrote the Republic'. Before we accept the definite description we have to be satisfied that it applies, and in only one case. But for (*a*), what satisfies us shows that a man will be contradicting himself, or talking nonsense, if he says 'but still there might be another …'. For (*b*) this is not so.

But isn't there pointing? – if, at least, the man is there to be pointed to? But pointing does not define unless you can say what you are pointing at. If I point, and say 'That is X', and point again saying 'That is Y', nothing in this situation shows that X and Y are not the same. It is of no use to say 'But suppose I point to something different…' – for that is just what is in question: what is something different?

It is also of no use to appeal to definition by means of place and time; for this you require points of origin and for points of origin you have to mention actual objects and events: individuals. No individual is pre-eminent. If I define an individual X by describing its spatial and temporal relation to another individual Y, and Y has no definition, then my definition of X is infected by the lack of definition of Y.

An individual can be defined by pointing and saying what (e.g. a man) you are pointing at. But this means that there is no difference between the

18. *Meta.* VII, 1037a26.

definition of two individuals of the same species. You cannot say it lies in the difference between two acts of pointing, for nothing prevents one from pointing twice at the same thing; and you cannot say: but the difference is that you were pointing at *different* things; the different is not first merely a different *thing*, and then, in virtue of this, a different X.

Thus there is no definition of individuals except the definition of their kind. What, then, is the difference between two individuals of the same kind? It is difference of matter; and if I am asked to explain that, all I can do is, e.g., to cut something up and show you the bits. That is what is called material difference. This is what is meant by calling matter the principle of individuation. To me its truth seems clear and evident.

13. The statement that matter is the principle of individuation does not mean that the identity of an individual consists in the identity of its matter. Thus it is not an objection against it that the matter of a man's body changes in the course of his life.[19]

I don't think that 'principle of individuation' is an expression any counterpart of which is in Aristotle. So far as I know, the statement that according to Aristotle matter is the principle of individuation is based only on his saying that Callias and Socrates are 'different in matter, for it is different' (sc. in each of them).

Clearly what is in question here is contemporaries. There is no question of saying that Professor Popper and Socrates differ materially. But Professor Popper and I, for example, differ in matter.

If I say this, I am not saying that Professor Popper is who he is because of *the* matter of which he is composed; so it is not a difficulty for me that he is materially in a state of flux. But of course if by 'What is the principle of individuation?' you mean, or include, the question 'What makes a man the same man at different times?' – then the answer 'matter' is an absurd one. But as we are talking about Aristotle we have no right to take the question in that second sense at all. And I should say there were two quite different questions here which we ought not to mix up.

Aristotle writes very interestingly about nourishment and growth in the *De Generatione et Corruptione* I 5. 'Someone may wonder what it is that grows? Is it that to which something is added? E.g., if someone grows in the leg, this gets bigger, but not that by means of which he grows, i.e. the food. Well, why don't *both* grow?'[20]

He goes on to say, isn't it because the substance of the one remains, and of the other not?[21] i.e. the food turns into the man. Further: '... flesh and bone and the rest are twofold, as is everything that has form in matter. For both the matter and the form are called flesh and bone. Thus it can be taken that every part grows – and grows by the accession of something – in respect of its form, but not in respect of its matter.'[22] That is, we say that the *hand* grows, or the *flesh* or the *bone*. (Think of the ambiguity of the question 'Is this the clay you were using last week?' – Aristotle would say that when we

19. This paper originally ended here. Professor Popper asked me to elaborate this section; but what follows reached him after he had completed his paper.

20. *GC* I 5, 321a29.

21. *ibid.*, 34.

22. *ibid.*, b19.

speak of 'this (bit of) clay' the word 'clay' refers both to the form and to the matter.) Now matter can be added or taken away, but cannot be said to grow, for growth is *by* addition of matter. Thus it is that we use the term designating the *kind* of thing, to stand for the subject of growth. And then he adds: 'It should be thought of like measuring water by the same measure. For something else keeps on becoming [the thing].'[23] That is, Aristotle compares the form to, say, the mile that we speak of when we say 'This mile of river',[24] into which and out of which different water is constantly flowing. I find this a very illuminating comparison. It suggests the following picture to me: let us suppose that we could tag (as medical researchers speak of tagging) every particle of matter that went into Professor Popper – say by making everything that might go into him radio-active. After a few years had gone by wouldn't he be a reach of a stream of radio-active particles? I think of it literally quite pictorially: a stream of silvery particles with Professor Popper's outline drawn somewhere in the middle of it. – Of course we mark 'this mile of river' by landmarks, as water does not change on entering and leaving it. But food and so on change substantially when they get into Professor Popper, so his form (the flesh and bone of a living man, to put it roughly) does the marking off; and corresponds to the mile of river.

I think this demonstrates quite clearly that if you mean anything Aristotelian by calling matter the principle of individuation, you do not mean that the identity of a person is the identity of the matter of which he is composed.

23. *ibid.*, 24.

24. I am indebted for this interpretation to Mr P. Geach, who threw it out almost as a joke in casual conversation: but I think it is obviously correct. I am grateful to him also for other help in preparing this paper.

[*Eds.*:– The papers of Lukasiewicz and Popper referred to were presented to the same Symposium as Professor Anscombe's, and can be found in *Proceedings of the Aristotelian Society*, Suppl. Vol. 27.]

8

I. Mueller

Aristotle on Geometrical Objects

156 From the perspective of ontology or of epistemology the question may be asked: 'What is the nature of mathematical objects?' To ask the question ontologically amounts to asking for the real subjects, the things in the world, with which mathematics deals. Epistemologically the question is more likely to be directed at mathematical reasoning: 'What is mathematical reasoning about?'

Plato seems to have given the same answer to the question from both perspectives. It is even possible that his answer to the ontological question was inferred from his epistemological analysis of mathematics in some way like the following: Mathematicians reason as if they were dealing with objects that are different from all sensible things, perfectly fulfill given conditions, and are apprehensible by pure thought; mathematics is correct; therefore, there are such objects. Argument of this kind is also characteristic of the modern mathematical Platonist. For example, K. Gödel writes: 'It seems to me that the assumption of such objects [classes and concepts] is quite as legitimate as the assumption of physical bodies, and there is quite as much reason to believe in their existence. They are in the same sense necessary to obtain a satisfactory system of mathematics as physical bodies are necessary for a satisfactory theory of our sense perceptions ...'[1] Ancient and modern mathematical Platonism rests its case largely on being a direct inference from the nature of mathematical reasoning.

Other philosophers, however, begin their inquiries either by denying or being sceptical about the entities postulated by Platonists. The intuitionist in A. Heyting's 'Disputation' is made to say, 'We have no objection against a mathematician privately admitting any metaphysical theory he likes, but Brouwer's program entails that we study mathematics as something simpler, more immediate than metaphysics.'[2] A consequence of this **157** metaphysical or ontological scepticism is the intuitionist's denial of the reality of mathematical objects; they are 'mental constructions'.

Aristotle begins his philosophising about mathematics with an ontology that excludes mathematical objects of the kind envisaged by Plato. For Aristotle the paradigms of real things are sensible substances like animals, plants, and the heavenly bodies. (I ignore the prime mover [or movers] on the ground that in the philosophy of Aristotle this is a 'special case', being both fully real and completely abstract.) On the other hand, Aristotle does

1. K. Gödel, 'Russell's Mathematical Logic', reprinted in *Philosophy of Mathematics: Selected Readings*, ed. P. Benacerraf and H. Putnam (Englewood Cliffs, N. J. 1964), p.220.

2. A. Heyting, *Intuitionism: An Introduction*, 2nd ed. (Amsterdam 1966), p.2; reprinted in *Philosophy of Mathematics*, p.56.

accept Plato's mathematical epistemology: mathematicians treat objects which are different from all sensible things, perfectly fulfill given conditions, and are apprehensible by pure thought. To resolve the discrepancy between his mathematical epistemology and his ontology, Aristotle is not willing to construe mathematical objects as merely mental constructions dependent on human thought for their existence. Aristotle, of course, does place emphasis on the role of human thinking in mathematics but he also accepts the Platonic assumption that there must be a significant correlation between the apparent objects of mathematical reasoning and the real world – the assumption, as Zeller puts it, 'that the truth of knowledge keeps pace with the actuality of its object'.[3] But for Aristotle this assumption precludes the merely mental existence of mathematical objects. In this paper I shall describe the way in which Aristotle attempts to develop an account of mathematical objects while leaving intact the beliefs just described.

I begin with a quotation from *Metaphysics* XIII 3 in which there occurs what looks like a very straightforward account:

Just as the universal branches of mathematics are not about separate things apart from magnitudes and numbers but rather about these, although not as having magnitude or being divisible; obviously there could be assertions and proofs about sensible magnitudes, not as sensible but as of some sort. And just as there are many assertions about things simply as changing separate from the being of all such things and their properties, but it is not thereby necessary that there be something changing separate from sensible things nor some distinct entity in them; so also there may be assertions and theories regarding changing things, not as changing but only as bodies, or again only as planes, or only as lengths, or only as divisible, or as indivisible and having position, or only as indivisible ... If geometry happens to be of sensibles but not as sensible, the mathematical sciences will not therefore be of sensibles nor of other things separate from these. Many properties belong essentially to things as having such and such characteristics, since there are properties peculiar to an animal as male or as female and yet there is no male or female separate from animals. Thus things may have properties just as lines or as planes ...

Each thing is investigated best if someone posits as separate what is not separate, which is what the arithmetician and the geometer do. For a man as man is one and indivisible; the arithmetician posited one indivisible thing and then inquired whether anything belonged to the man as indivisible. The geometer treats of things neither as man nor as indivisible but as solid. (1077b17-30; 1078a2-9; 21-6).

158

The geometer, then, deals with sensible substances, not as sensible substances, but as solids, planes, lines, and points. But what does this mean? The mathematician never really reasons about a man, whether as solid, indivisible, or anything else. Sensible substances, moreover, no matter how they are treated, do not fulfill the idealised conditions imposed on

3. E. Zeller, *Aristotle and the Earlier Peripatetics*, tr. B. Costelloe and J. Muirhead (London 1897), p.339.

mathematical objects. This Aristotle observes with regard to the question, 'With what sort of things must the mathematician be supposed to deal? Certainly not with the things around us. For none of these is like what the mathematical sciences investigate' (*Meta.* XI 1, 1059b10-12; cf. III 2, 997b35-998a6). A bronze sphere (even as solid) does not touch an iron bar (even as plane or line) in a point.

Formulas like 'sensible substances as solids' do not adequately represent Aristotle's account of mathematical objects. *Metaphysics* XIII 3 is designed primarily to provide an alternative to the claim that there are actually existing mathematical objects either separate from or in sensible substances. XIII 3 reaffirms Aristotle's ontology and makes it seem closer to his mathematical epistemology than it really is. Other passages widen the gap between the two. In *Physics* II 2 Aristotle undertakes to explain how the mathematician differs from the physicist:

159   Physical bodies have planes, solids, lengths, and points which the mathematician investigates ... It would be absurd if the physicist were supposed to know what the sun or moon is but nothing about their essential properties, since physicists clearly do discuss the shape of the sun and moon and whether or not the earth or the cosmos is spherical. The mathematician too is concerned with these [properties] but not as limits of physical bodies. Nor does he investigate their properties as belonging to such bodies. Therefore he separates them; for in thought they are separable from change, and it makes no difference; nor does separation produce falsehood. Those who speak of ideas do the same thing without being aware of it; they separate the objects of physics, which are less separable than mathematical objects. This would become obvious if someone tried to give definitions of these [objects] and properties. For the even, the odd, the straight, the curved, and also number, line, figure would be without change; but flesh, bone, and man would not. These latter are defined like snub nose and not like the curved. (193b24-194a7)

In this passage the idea of separation plays a much more important role than in *Metaphysics* XIII 3. The mathematician's separation of solids from the bodies which have them is something like the Platonists' separation of the forms. The solids, of course, cannot really exist separate from physical bodies, but they are somehow adapted to being considered separately. There seems to be a significant difference between separating mathematical objects from physical bodies and treating physical bodies as mathematical objects. I take the former to be essential to mathematics as Aristotle conceived it, and I shall try in what follows to make clear what separating amounts to.

Aristotle refers fairly frequently to mathematical objects as abstractions (*ex aphaireseôs, en aphairesei, di' aphaireseôs*: see Bonitz, *Index*, 126b21-6), but he does not explain what these expressions mean. The Greek verb, 'abstract', (*aphairein*) means 'take away' in a number of senses. I shall cite four passages where Aristotle uses this verb in a way relevant to mathematical **160**   abstractions.[4] In the *Posterior Analytics*, he discusses the problem of

4. For a fuller account of the relevant Aristotelian vocabulary, see Philippe, [252].

determining the proper subject of some attribute, e.g., having angles equal to two rights. The method is to take away things until one finds the primary subject to which the attribute belongs. Aristotle's example is the bronze isosceles triangle with angles equal to two rights. From this the bronze and the isosceles must be taken away (I 5, 74a33-b1). In VII 11 of the *Metaphysics* Aristotle speaks of taking away in thought the bronze from the bronze circle, disparaging the Platonists for taking away matter (1036a34-b3; b22-3). Earlier in VII, in discussing the question whether matter is substance, Aristotle speaks of taking away length, breadth, depth, and leaving matter.[5]

In all of these passages, abstracting involves eliminating something from consideration. This is not a matter of collecting particulars and somehow arriving at a general idea,[6] although abstraction is facilitated by seeing a number of different individuals. In the above-mentioned passage where Aristotle speaks of taking the bronze away from the bronze circle he says that this procedure would be hard if we never saw any non-bronze circles. Only once when he speaks of abstractions does Aristotle seem to imply that abstracting is a positive procedure and not just a matter of eliminating things from consideration. In the *Posterior Analytics* he says that abstractions are made known by induction.[7] However, the context makes it very likely that Aristotle is speaking of mathematical truths, i.e., assertions about abstractions, rather than of abstractions themselves. The commentators on this passage give propositions as examples of abstractions.[8] Aristotle's point seems to be that the student is led to believe mathematical axioms by being shown that they hold in a number of particular cases.

161

Separating seems to be a correlate of abstracting. Abstracting from an object A gives rise to an object B lacking certain things belonging to A. Considering B is separating B. In the sequel I will refer to mathematical objects as abstractions, although it would be more accurate to call them separations or, to use a literal translation, 'from-abstractions'. We have already seen that Aristotle interprets mathematics as involving the separation of what is not separate or separable. It is easy to conclude that for Aristotle mathematical objects exist only in the mind of the mathematician and not independently of him. Such a conclusion involves failure to distinguish two kinds of separating. One kind is instanced in

5. 3, 1029a16-19. Just prior to this passage at 1029a11 Aristotle uses *perihairein* in the relevant sense of take away. Compare the use of this verb in *Cat.* 7a31-b9.

6. This notion of abstraction is the one which becomes crucial in British empiricism. See, for example, Locke, *An Essay Concerning Human Understanding*, II.xi.9: 'The mind makes the particular ideas received from particular objects to become general; which is done by considering them as they are in the mind such appearances, separate from all other existences and the circumstances of real experience, as time, place, or any other concomitant *ideas*. This is called ABSTRACTION, whereby *ideas* taken from particular beings become general representatives of all of the same kind.'

7. I 18, 81b2-5. Charles Kahn has pointed out that *ta ex aphaireseôs legomena* could be rendered 'things asserted as a result of abstracting'. Such a rendering would, of course, add support to the interpretation of the passage given above.

8. Themistius, *Analyticorum Posteriorum Paraphrasis*, ed. Wallies (Berlin 1900), 31.4-32.2; Philoponus, *In Aristotelis Analytica Posteriora Commentaria*, ed. Wallies (Berlin 1899), 215.15-24.

Plato's theory of forms and involves notions corresponding to nothing in reality. The other kind is instanced in mathematics and affords access to features of reality which are inaccessible in any other way.[9] The mathematician ignores certain features of the sensible world. The result, however, is not falsification, but knowledge, of the world. Mathematics is applicable to reality whereas the study of forms advocated by Plato has no application whatsoever. In the sequel I will argue that Aristotle explains this applicability by considering mathematical objects to underlie physical reality.

In places where Aristotle uses the verb 'abstract' in the relevant sense he speaks indifferently of taking away matter – e.g., bronze – and taking away properties – e.g., isosceles. There is, of course, nothing wrong with speaking in these two ways, but each of them if emphasised gives rise to a different notion of mathematical object. If abstraction is primarily thought of as eliminating properties, one will think of mathematical objects as physical objects looked at as if they did not have certain properties. On the other hand, if one thinks of abstraction primarily as eliminating matter, one will think of mathematical objects as properties like roundness and triangularity.

It is, I think, fair to say that the second view is more commonly attributed to Aristotle than the first. Both Philoponus and Simplicius make this attribution in interpreting the passage from the *Physics* quoted above: 'The mathematician deals with figures and their properties, thinking these things to be embodied in no matter whatsoever; rather he studies the figures and their properties, separating them mentally from all matter.'[10] 'The mathematician differs from the physicist first because the physicist speaks not only about the properties of physical bodies but also about the matter; the mathematician is not concerned with matter.'[11] All the commentators, moreover, use the contrast between the snub and the curved, referred to at the end of the passage, as an illustration of the difference between the natural scientist and the mathematician. In defining the snub, one must include reference to the matter in which it inheres – namely, a nose; but the curved can be defined and understood independently of matter.

The contrast between the properties of a thing and its matter is, of course, fundamental for Aristotle. In general he seems to treat properties as universals common to a number of individual things. If properties are universals, the mathematician who studies them will be studying universals. The doctrine that mathematical objects are properties fits, therefore, with Aristotle's account of demonstrative science in the *Posterior Analytics*. For

9. Compare Philippe [252], pp.476-7: '[L'abstraction] ne crée pas [les êtres mathématiques], ne les invente pas, au sens fort, mais elle leur donne leur propre mode d'être. Elle les extrait pour ainsi dire du monde physique où ils se trouvaient comme cachés et enveloppés; elle les libère. L'abstraction joue, par rapport au monde mathématique, le rôle de l'experience par rapport au monde des autres sciences.'

10. Philoponus, *In Aristotelis Physicorum Libros Tres Priores Commentaria*, ed. Vitelli (Berlin 1887), 219.28-31.

11. Simplicius, *In Aristotelis Physicorum Libros Quattuor Priores Commentaria*, ed. Diels (Berlin 1882), 290.27-29. Compare Alexander of Aphrodisias (?), *In Aristotelis Metaphysica Commentaria*, ed. Hayduck (Berlin 1891), 739.17-18: 'For they are existent, though not as enmattered but as matterless and forms.'

underlying this account is the assumption that the basis of all scientific reasoning is the so-called categorical syllogism. But the categorical syllogism consists of sentences which, for Aristotle, are analysable into terms. And these terms stand for universals:

> Therefore there do not have to be forms or some one apart from the many if there is to be proof, but there does have to be some one truly said of many. For if there were none, there would be no universal (I 11, 77a5-7).

There are, then, good grounds for thinking Aristotle's view to have been **163** that mathematical objects are universals separated in thought from matter. However, there are also grounds for doubt. First of all, universals do not have exactitude of the kind which Aristotle attributes to mathematical objects. Circularity does not touch straightness in a point or in any other way. For Aristotle, moreover, universals are not fully real. To suppose them to be the objects of mathematics would be incompatible with the assumption 'that the truth of knowledge keeps pace with the actuality of its object'. Of course, no supposition about mathematical objects will completely satisfy this assumption, given Aristotle's beliefs about the ontological primacy, but mathematical inadequacy, of sensible substances. One would, however, expect Aristotle to make at least some attempt to construe mathematical objects in the manner of sensible substances. This expectation is only strengthened by Greek mathematics itself, which is quite different from the study of universals. Its character is thoroughly geometric. The core of its reasoning is what we now call spatial intuition. Consequently, the objects in terms of which mathematical argument proceeds are intuitively perceived or imagined spatial objects, points, lines, plane figures, solids. Even numbers (positive integers) are represented by lines or points and thought of as collections of units subject to combinatorial manipulation. Finally, if Aristotle thought of mathematical objects as universals separated from matter, it is difficult to see how he could distinguish legitimate mathematical separation from illegitimate separation of Platonic forms.

Some of the difficulties involved in treating mathematical objects as universals are eliminated or lessened by treating them as particular properties, like the 'certain white' of the *Categories* (2, 1a27). Such properties are perhaps more like sensible substances although they seem to be no more 'exact' than universals. Moreover, in the *Metaphysics* Aristotle himself mentions a question which would make no sense if the objects of mathematics were matterless properties: 'What is the matter of mathematical objects?' (XI 1, 1059b14-16). Elsewhere he says explicitly that mathematical objects have intelligible matter (*Meta.* VII 10, 1036a9-12; 11, 1037a2-5). And once he describes the process of abstraction as the elimination of sensible properties:

> The mathematician theorises about abstractions, for he theorises **164** having removed all sensibles such as weight and lightness, hardness and its opposite, heat and cold, and the other sensible opposites. He leaves only the quantitative and continuous in one, two, or three

[dimensions] and the properties of these as quantitative and continuous.[12]

If the passage from *Metaphysics* XIII 3, quoted at the beginning of this paper, is interpreted in the light of the above, more sense can be made of it. To say that the mathematician studies a man as solid is not to say that he studies a man at all. Rather, it is to say that he studies what is quantitative and continuous in three dimensions. And the mathematician comes to understand the quantitative and continuous by abstracting – i.e., ignoring – all the sensible properties of some sensible substance such as man. There is, then, at least an initial plausibility in supposing Aristotle to have entertained a conception of mathematical objects, not as matterless properties, but as substance-like individuals with a special matter – intelligible matter. I want now to explain this conception in more detail, to introduce more evidence for Aristotle's holding of it, and to show how it is related to the conception of mathematical objects as properties.

The first four categories discussed by Aristotle in the *Categories* are substance, quantity, relation, and quality. He himself gives no explanation for this order, and probably no deep significance attaches to it. However, all the commentators begin their discussion of ch. 6 of the *Categories*, the chapter on quantity, by attempting to explain why it immediately succeeds the chapter on substance. Many of the reasons advanced are trivial (e.g., 'Substance can be primary or secondary but primary and secondary belong to quantity').[13] But one reason mentioned by all the commentators is quite interesting; Philoponus states it thus:

165
>   Prime matter, which is without body, form, or figure before it is
>   filled out, receives the three dimensions and becomes three-
>   dimensional. This Aristotle calls the second substratum, since thus it
>   receives quality and produces the elements.[14]

The term 'second substratum' is not found in the extant works of Aristotle. Probably it should not be ascribed to him. Nor can one assume that Aristotle reasoned this way in organising the *Categories*. Yet the basic idea of the reasoning does seem Aristotelian; for Aristotle thinks of quantity in the way this reasoning suggests, as ch. 6 itself shows. There Aristotle does not, as one would expect,

12. *Meta.* XI 3, 1061a28-35. There seems to be general agreement that XI 1-8 is genuinely Aristotelian in content although perhaps written by a student on the basis of lectures by Aristotle. (See e.g. Ross [4] I, p. xxvi.) The greater attention paid to mathematics in XI than in the parallel III is perhaps explained by Jaeger's assumption of XI's temporal priority ([28], pp.208-21.) As Aristotle's thought evolved away from Platonism he may have considered questions of mathematical ontology less interesting. I have not found satisfactory evidence of changes in Aristotle's conception of mathematical objects.

13. Elias, *In Porphyrii Isagogen et Aristotelis Categorias Commentaria*, ed. Busse (Berlin 1900), 185.32-3.

14. Philoponus, *In Aristotelis Categorias Commentarium*, ed. Busse (Berlin 1898), 83.14-17.

list or attempt to classify quantitative properties (like the property of being a foot long) or corresponding predicates (like 'a foot long'). Instead he lists and groups owners of quantitative properties: lines, surfaces, solids, numbers (aggregates), time periods, places, utterances (Ackrill [42], p.91).

This difference between the discussion of quantity and the other non-substantial categories does not seem to be accidental. The quantitative and continuous, which Aristotle says remain after the sensible opposites have been removed, seem to be identical with these first three quantities: lines, surfaces, solids. And even in a passage where he affirms the difference between quantity and substance, the three dimensions are treated as more fundamental than properties:

> Other things are properties, actions, and powers of bodies, but length, breadth, and depth are certain quantities and not substances. For quantity is not substance, which is rather that to which these things primarily belong. But, when length, breadth, and depth are taken away, we see nothing remaining, unless what is bounded by these is something (*Meta.* VII 3, 1029a12-18).

We find, then, in Aristotle the notion that if one abstracts properties in the proper order one is left with the idea of an object having only length, breadth, and depth, the continuous and quantitative in three dimensions, **166** the solid. From this idea by abstraction one may obtain the idea of length and breadth, the continuous and quantitative in two dimensions, the plane; and by further abstraction the idea of length alone, the continuous and quantitative in one dimension, the line. The point is not a quantity for Aristotle because it cannot be measured. It is, however, a basic geometric object presupposed in many geometric constructions. Aristotle's notion of how we grasp the idea of a point is not completely clear. Sometimes he says the point is what has position and is indivisible (e.g. *Meta.* V 6, 1016b24-31); at other times he characterises it as the limit or division of a line (e.g. *Meta.* XI 2, 1060b12-17). The latter suggestion seems to fit better with the process by which we come to understand solids, planes, and lines. Perhaps the former should be thought of as the logically correct definition of point rather than the description of our ordinary conception of it (cf. Apostle [257], 100).

Regardless of how he treats points, Aristotle seems to have the idea of the purely dimensional underlying other properties. In part this is the idea of the three-dimensional underlying sensible properties in the physical world. But for Aristotle there is little if any difference between this idea and that of the one-, two-, or three-dimensional underlying geometric properties, which he calls intelligible matter. The phrase 'intelligible matter' is found in three passages in the *Metaphysics*. In two of them it is introduced in connection with the problem of explaining in what sense a semicircle is a part of a particular mathematical circle (VII 10, 1036a9-12; 11, 1037a2-5). The author of the commentary on the *Metaphysics* which is attributed to Alexander of Aphrodisias refers to the intelligible matter in these passages as extension (510. 3-5; 515. 26-8), and he is clearly right. For it is the extendedness of geometric objects, their continuity in one, two, or three dimensions, which makes them divisible. The third passage causes some difficulty, however. Aristotle says: 'Some matter is intelligible, some sensible; and part of a definition is always matter, part actuality. For example, a circle is a plane figure' (VIII 6, 1045a33-5). 'Alexander' says

167   that 'intelligible matter' here means 'genus' – genera being 'analogous' to matter. According to him, figure is an example of intelligible matter (562. 14-17). W.D. Ross accepts this interpretation; but in his view plane figure is an example of intelligible matter and Aristotle fails to give the formal element in defining circle ([4], II, p.238), namely, 'contained by one line such that all the straight lines falling upon it from one point among those lying within the figure are equal to one another'.[15]

If we look at this passage in the light of the previous discussion, it becomes clear that plane, i.e., the continuous and quantitative in two dimensions, is the element of matter in the definition of circle and that figures stands for the formal element. This interpretation is confirmed in the discussion of genus in *Metaphysics* V 28: 'The plane is genus of plane figures, the solid of solid; for each of the figures is such and such a plane or solid, and this is the substratum of the differentiae' (1024a36-b4). Thus it becomes necessary to distinguish two kinds of geometric object in Aristotle. First, there are the basic objects: points, lines, planes, solids. The last three are conceived of as indeterminate extension and, therefore, as matter on which geometric properties are imposed. The imposition of these properties produces the ordinary geometric figures, straight or curved lines, triangles, cubes, etc. The definition of such a figure will include both the form, the properties imposed, and the matter; but in the definition this matter will also play the role of genus. A circle is a plane figure.

The distinction between the quantitative substratum and the geometric properties imposed on it has an important function in Aristotle's account of the first principles or elements of a demonstrative science in the *Posterior Analytics*. Aristotle says that there are three kinds of element: (1) the common axioms; (2) the genus, the things whose existence and meaning are assumed; (3) the properties, whose meaning only is assumed (I 10, 76a31-6; b11-16). As examples of the genus he gives the unit or units, points, lines, magnitude; as examples of properties, odd, even, square, cube, straight,

168   triangle, incommensurable, inclination, deflection (76a34-6; b3-11). If allowance is made for the difficulty about points the distinction between genus and property is seen to be exactly the distinction between intelligible matter and form in the *Metaphysics*. For in Aristotle 'magnitude' is just a general term referring to lines, planes, and solids (see e.g. *Meta.* V 13, 1020a7-14; *Cael.* I 1, 268a7-8). These examples also show how different Aristotle's conception of geometry is from the one represented by Euclid's *Elements*. In both, the meaning of all terms used is supposed known, and common axioms are assumed. But the postulates of Euclid do not give the genus being discussed, rather, three simple constructions and two assumptions on the basis of which theorems and other constructions are justified. Aristotle looks at geometry quite differently. The point of departure in, say, plane geometry is extensionality in two dimensions

15. Euclid, *Elements*, Bk. I, def. 15 (Heath [255], I, p.153).

(planes) with the concomitants of extensionality in one dimension (lines) and positional dimensionlessness (points). One must not only understand what these things are; one must also suppose them to exist. For, unlike the hot and the cold, the existence of these things is not obvious and cannot be just an implicit assumption (*A.Pst.* I 10, 76b16-19). Once these things are understood and posited, geometry proceeds by examining properties like straightness or triangularity which they possess. Because the geometer is primarily concerned with properties, Aristotle often speaks of him as separating properties. However, although the geometer does consider geometric properties separate from the physical things in which they inhere, geometric objects are none the less compounds of these properties and intelligible matter.

If Aristotle held the conception of geometric objects which I have developed here, it is easy to see how their exactitude is explained. For by abstraction one eliminates all sensible characteristics and arrives at the idea of pure extension. Pure extension does not seem to be sensible in the way that triangularity is, nor is it completely undifferentiated or purely potential in the way that prime matter seems to be. We cannot see a thing as just extended but only as extended so and so much with a certain shape. Simple extendedness we must grasp rationally. Geometric properties are imposed on this intelligible matter, but these properties are not the approximate properties of sensible substances precisely because they are imposed upon intelligible matter. The resultant objects are still intelligible rather than sensible. In postulating such objects, the mathematician separates what is not separable. Intelligible matter, even when endowed with geometric properties, is no more capable of existing separately than are sensible properties. Such separation is not harmful, however, because the separated objects are rationally comprehensible and closely connected with the real world. According to Aristotle, at any rate, the idea of a man separated from flesh and bones is an incomprehensible fabrication.

In the final part of this paper I want to bring together the things I have said about Aristotle's conception of geometric objects. Aristotle starts from the Platonic notion of geometry as the study of forms and from the intuitive character of Greek geometry. The former leads him to the idea of geometry as the study of universals, an idea most fully embodied in the *Posterior Analytics*. The latter leads him to the idea of geometry as the study of objects which result from the combination of geometric properties and intelligible matter. The problem is to reconcile these two ideas.

Some of the neo-Platonists, who tried to reconcile everything in Plato and Aristotle, attribute to Aristotle a distinction between two kinds of reasoning about two kinds of objects corresponding to the upper half of the divided line in Plato's *Republic*. Proclus speaks of reasoning about forms perfectly embodied in the *phantasia* and, secondly, of reasoning about disembodied forms – forms having, therefore, no spatial properties.[16] Proclus' suggestion is that Aristotle made this distinction in terms of active and passive intellect (52. 3-4), a suggestion obviously without basis in what Aristotle says. The

169

16. Proclus, *In Primum Euclidis Elementorum Librum Commentarii*, ed. Friedlein (Leipzig 1873), 48.1-56.22. A similar doctrine is attributed to Aristotle by Simplicius in his commentary on *De Anima – In Libros Aristotelis De Anima Commentaria*, ed. Hayduck (Berlin 1882). See, for example, 233.7-35.

most significant feature of Proclus' distinction is perhaps that it makes particular geometric objects mental objects – objects having their subsistence in the *phantasia*. He invokes Aristotle on this point too by referring to an alleged Aristotelian distinction between two kinds of matter, 'one of things correlated to sense, the other of imagined things' (51. 13-17). By the latter Proclus presumably means intelligible matter, but there is no good reason to suppose that Aristotle thought of intelligible matter as mental or imagined. Indeed, although Aristotle explicitly recognises the role of imagination in geometric thinking (*De An.* III 8, 432a3-10) and although he calls the mathematician's act of separation mental, he always connects mathematical objects directly with the sensible world. 'Physical bodies have planes, solids, lengths, and points which the mathematician investigates.' 'There could be assertions and proofs about sensible magnitudes not as sensible.'

Not only does Aristotle seem unwilling to make the objects of mathematics mental but also he never espouses a division of scientific reasoning into two kinds along the lines suggested by Proclus. The mathematics described by Aristotle in the *Posterior Analytics* is for him basically that of the ordinary geometer. Nor does the discrepancy between the two kinds of geometric object seem to be a special case of the general difficulty which Aristotle mentions and tries to handle in the *Metaphysics*: How can knowledge be of universals if what is most real is the particular?[17] For Aristotle treats this difficulty only as a general problem arising from the attempt to combine the theory of knowledge of the *Posterior Analytics* with the ontology of the *Metaphysics*. He does not treat it as a problem relating to any particular mathematical or physical science.

I am inclined to think we must credit Aristotle with a much more subtle and reasonable position than the one attributed to him by Proclus. There is clearly some distinction to be made between knowledge of universals or conceptual knowledge and intuitive knowledge.[18] Both are a part of geometry, but the mistake of Proclus and others is to assume that a sharp distinction can be made between the two. In the words of P. Bernays:

> The sharp separation of intuition and concept ... does not appear on closer examination to be justified. In considering geometrical thinking in particular it is difficult to distinguish clearly the share of intuition from that of conceptuality, since we find here a formation of concepts guided so to speak by intuition, which in the sharpness of its intentions goes beyond what is in a proper sense intuitively evident, but which separated from intuition has not its proper content.[19]

The intimate connection of concept and intuition underlies, I suggest, Aristotle's account of geometry and geometric objects. It is illustrated most

17. *Meta.* III 6, 1003a5-17; XI 2, 1060b19-23; XIII 10, 1087a10-25.

18. In the last passage cited in the previous footnote Aristotle makes an analogous distinction between knowledge of the particular and knowledge of the universal in terms of a distinction between actual and potential knowledge. I have been unable to apply this distinction to geometry in a satisfactory way.

19. P. Bernays, 'Comments on Ludwig Wittgenstein's *Remarks on the Foundations of Mathematics*', reprinted in *Philosophy of Mathematics*, p.518.

clearly in Aristotle's treatment of extension as a kind of underlying stuff and as a very abstract notion, the genus of mathematical objects. A modern analogue of Aristotelian extension would be space, which is formally nothing but a class of elements (points) related in certain ways but which is also in some sense an object of perception or intuition.

Aristotle's account of geometric objects would seem, then, to be something like the following. In his reasoning the geometer deals directly with the particular geometric objects which I have been describing. These objects, though not real in the sense in which sensible substances are, are intimately connected with sensible reality and in a certain sense underlie it. However, out of ordinary geometric reasoning arises a universal knowledge, e.g., the knowledge that any triangle has interior angles equal to two rights. Universal knowledge is conceptual and can be formulated syllogistically. However, it has no object over and above the objects of ordinary geometric reasoning, and in fact conceptual syllogistic reasoning is only a reformulation of ordinary reasoning.[20] Thus there is only one kind of geometric object although there are two ways of reasoning about it, one apparently more abstract than the other.[21]

20. Aristotle was, of course, mistaken in believing geometric reasoning could be represented syllogistically, but in this context his mistake can be treated as one of detail not of principle.

21. This paper has benefited greatly from judicious criticism of an earlier draft by a number of people. I am particularly grateful to Charles Kahn, John Stevenson, Manley Thompson, and Vernon Wedin.

9

Jaakko Hintikka

Necessity, Universality, and Time in Aristotle

65   1. A perceptive student of the Aristotelian *Corpus* cannot fail to notice that the Stagirite used modal notions (such as possibility and necessity) in a way different from ours. In this paper, an attempt will be made to study certain particular kinds of such discrepancy. We shall investigate the relation of Aristotle's modal notions to certain non-modal notions. First and foremost of these is the notion of universality (generality). One can find plenty of *prima facie* evidence that there was for Aristotle a far closer connection between necessity and universality than there is for us.

2. One piece of such evidence evolves as a by-product of G.E.M. Anscombe's recent analysis of Aristotle's discussion of future particulars in the ninth chapter of *De Interpretatione*.[1] Part of her findings may perhaps be put as follows: What Aristotle is concerned with in *De Interpretatione* 9 is not to deny that 'the law of excluded middle' in our sense applies to statements about future events. It does. Rather, what he is worried about is whether such statements are *necessarily* true or necessarily false. His discussion is calculated to show that they are not necessary in *his* sense of 'necessary'. But this sense of 'necessary' is different from ours, for in Aristotle's view statements describing past or present events *are* necessarily true or necessarily false.

66   These interesting conclusions by Miss Anscombe are not concerned with the notion of universality. But they suggest a further inference. In *De Interpretatione* 9, 18a27-33, Aristotle not only says *apropos* statements referring to past or present events that 'it is necessary that affirmation, or negation, should be true or false'; he also says that the same holds for 'universals universally quantified', i.e. for universal statements in our sense. Concerning statements of the former kind, Miss Anscombe argues that what is at stake here is their *necessity*. This suggests strongly that the same is true of statements of the latter kind, too. It suggests, in other words, that for Aristotle each genuinely universal statement is either necessarily true or impossible (necessarily false).

3. Another indication of an intimate relation between necessity and universality in Aristotle is connected with his most explicit explanation of 'universality': 'I term universal an attribute which belongs to every instance of its subject, and to every instance essentially and as such; from which it

---

1. Anscombe, [100].

clearly follows that all universals inhere necessarily in their subjects' (*Analytica Posteriora* I 4, 73b26-9). Under this definition, two things are required for (strict) universality: (a) truth in every instance and (b) essentiality.

What is surprising about this notion of (strict) universality is that it implies necessity. How does this come about?

Aristotle does not say explicitly whether the necessity of truly universal attributes is due to their being true in every instance or to their essentiality. Usually, people seem to assume the latter. It seems to me, however, that we should seriously consider the possibility that the necessity of strictly universal attributes is rather due to the other component of strict universality, viz. to what Aristotle calls 'truth in every instance'.

This is suggested by the following facts: In the argument by means of which Aristotle tries to show that essential attributes inhere in their subjects by necessity (*A.Pst.* I 4, 73b16-24), essentiality plays a minor rôle. Exactly the same argument could apparently be used to show that every pair of opposite attributes one of which always applies to a given individual inhere in their subjects by necessity. The possibility of an argument like this seems strange to us. We have no way of inferring, say, from the fact that every animal is either male or female, the conclusion that all males are males necessarily.

Also, it appears from Aristotle's remarks and from his examples that the requirement of essentiality is calculated to secure the immediacy of attribution rather than its necessity. For instance, the equality to two right angles is not a strictly universal attribute of isosceles triangles, for this attribute does not belong to an isosceles triangle immediately (as such) but only *qua* triangle (*A.Pst.* I 4, 73b37-40; 74a2-3). Nevertheless the equality to two right angles is plainly a necessary attribute of isosceles triangles.

4. A third indication of a close connection between necessity and universality in Aristotle is the highly important rôle he ascribed to the assertoric syllogism as a vehicle of scientific demonstration. Since he also held that 'the truth obtained by demonstrative knowledge will be necessary' (*A.Pst.* I 4, 73a21-4) and that 'demonstrative knowledge must be knowledge of a necessary nexus, and therefore must clearly be obtained through a necessary middle term' (*A.Pst.* I 6, 75a12-14), an assertoric syllogism must clearly be capable of establishing necessity. On the other hand, Aristotle distinguished between assertoric (simple) and apodeictic (necessary) premisses and conclusions. Since even the assertoric syllogisms were seen to be capable of establishing necessary scientific truths, one may expect that they somehow are related to the apodeictic syllogisms in a closer manner than what we are accustomed to.

This hunch will be supported, I think, by an examination of the details of Aristotle's theory of modal syllogisms. One of the salient features of this theory is that, according to it, one may sometimes draw a conclusion which is stronger than one of the premisses. For instance, from a necessary and an assertoric premiss a necessary conclusion may sometimes be drawn (*A.Pr.* I 9-12). This suggests that there must somehow be an 'apodeictic element' hidden in the ordinary assertoric premisses. The fact that Aristotle used the very same terms 'animal' and 'man' in 25a25, 26a8, 26b7, and 28a32 to illustrate assertoric propositions as he used in 30a24, 30b33, 31b41, 32b6 *etc.*

to illustrate apodeictic propositions points in the same direction.[2]

This suggestion, however, is in need of a further elaboration for it is not taken up by the current interpretation of Aristotle's modal logic.[3] I shall not try to outline an alternative interpretation here, for this paper is not designed for that purpose. Rather, its purpose is to clear the ground for such an undertaking by examining the philosophical background of the notions Aristotle employed in his modal logic. I shall only indicate some of the reasons why I find the current interpretation unsatisfactory, and give a few examples to show how certain rather perplexing procedures of Aristotle's may be understood if we assume that he sometimes invested universal assertoric premisses with the same properties as the apodeictic ones. Even these scattered remarks are more readily understood if we postpone them until we have had a closer look at the background of Aristotle's notions. I shall therefore relegate them to the end of the paper (Sections 16-20).

5. The above remarks, concerned though they are with passages of some difficulty, unmistakably suggest that there was *some* connection between universality and necessity in Aristotle. Once this is perceived, it is relatively easy to see what this connection was. It was established by the notion of *time*.

In order to show that the notion of time serves to bridge the gap between the apparently disparate notions of necessity and universality we have to show that in Aristotle temporal notions are connected on one hand with the notion of universality and on the other with modal notions. The first half of this double task is straightforward. Aristotle says explicitly that the universality of the premisses of a syllogism implies universality in time and not only universality in space:

> We must understand 'that which belongs to all' with no limitation in respect of time, e.g. to the present or to a particular period, but simply without qualification. For it is by the help of such premisses that we make syllogisms, since if the premiss is understood with reference to the present moment, there cannot be a syllogism ... It is clear then, that the universal must be understood simply, without limitation in respect of time. (*A.Pr.* I 15, 34b7-18)

The context shows that Aristotle is here speaking of assertoric premisses. Similarly, the 'truth in every instance' which goes into the definition of 'strict universality' in *A.Pst.* I 4, 73b27-9 implies universality in time:

> I call 'true in every instance' what is truly predicable of all instances – not of one to the exclusion of others – and at all times, not at this or that time only. (*A.Pst.* I 4, 73a27-30)

> Thus 'to hold in every instance and always is of the nature of the universal'. (*A.Pst.* II 12, 96a14-15)

2. Aristotle, *Organon* I. Text and translation by H.P. Cooke and Hugh Tredennick. Loeb Classical Library, Cambridge, Mass. 1938 (see p.190).

3. See I.M. Bochenski, *Ancient Formal Logic* (Amsterdam 1951), pp.55-62; I.M. Bochenski, *Formale Logik* (Freiburg 1956), pp.94-101; A. Becker [108]. For a different interpretation of highly unorthodox nature, see Jan Lukasiewicz [107].

6. There is nothing strange or surprising about this part of Aristotle's doctrine. The real peculiarity of his view lies in the other half of the 'bridge' created by the notion of time between the notions of universality and necessity. It lies, in other words, in the relation of Aristotle's modal notions (necessity, possibility, and impossibility) to the idea of time. This peculiar relation may be expressed by saying that for Aristotle

(T) *each possibility must be realised at some moment of time.*

The existence of this connection between time and modality in Aristotle is the main thesis of this paper.

7. Before presenting evidence for our thesis and qualifying it in certain respects, we shall see exactly what is involved in (T). For this purpose, it is advisable to reformulate (T) in terms of other modal notions. The feasibility **70** of such reformulations is due to the inter-relations of different modal notions in Aristotle. Thus, in order to reformulate (T) we must first recall precisely what the interrelations of different modal notions were for Aristotle.[4]

These interrelations are complicated by the fact that Aristotle had more than one notion of possibility. The two main variants of this notion I shall distinguish in Sections 7-9 as 'contingency' and 'possibility' wherever the distinction is relevant. For Aristotle, contingent was 'that which is not necessary but, being assumed, results in nothing impossible' (*A.Pr.* I 13, 32a18-20; cf. *Meta.* IX 3, 1047a23-6). This notion is sometimes referred to by Aristotle as 'possibility as defined'. The notion which I shall designate by 'possibility' is distinguished from 'contingency' by the fact that 'that which is necessary is also possible' (*Int.* 13, 23a17-19). Hence 'possible' means that which does not involve any impossibility. In other words, impossibility and possibility are negations of each other. The primary meaning of 'necessary' is for Aristotle that which cannot possibly be otherwise (*Meta.* V 5, 1015a33-6). The negation of a necessary proposition therefore expresses the possibility of its contradictory: something is not necessary if and only if it is possible for it not to be. Since 'contingent' meant that which is possible but not necessary, something is contingent if and only if it is both possible for it to be and possible for it not to be.

8. By means of these interrelations, (T) is readily transformed. It follows from (T) that if it is possible for something *not* to be, there must be a moment when this something is not. Conversely if something exists (or is true) forever, then it cannot possibly not exist (or not be true). In view of the relation between necessity and possibility, however, this means that

(T)* *that which is always, is by necessity.*

Hence the attributes 'necessary', 'imperishable', 'indestructible', 'omnitemporal', and 'eternal' become virtually equivalent.

Thus if something is eternal, it must be necessary. But if something is **71** necessary, it is *per definitionem* not contingent. Hence, for Aristotle,

(T)** *nothing eternal is contingent.*

It also follows from (T) that we may draw a modal conclusion from the fact that there never are things of a certain kind, viz. the conclusion that

4. For the interrelations of different modal notions in Aristotle, see *Int.* 12-13, *passim, A.Pr.* I 12, *Meta.* IX 4 and *Meta.* V 12.

things of that kind are *impossible*. This is an instance of the principle

(T)*** *that which never is, is impossible.*

It must not be thought that the transformation of (T) into (T)* is an extrapolation from scattered remarks of Aristotle's which it may never have occurred to him to combine. On the contrary, a closely related argument is given by the Stagirite himself in *Meta*. IX 8, 1050b6-23. Similar ways of reasoning also occur in *De Caelo* I 12.

It is not difficult to see that the four principles (T)-(T)*** are equivalent provided that one makes the same assumptions concerning the interrelations of different modal notions as Aristotle does. All evidence for the acceptance of *one* of these principles by Aristotle therefore serves as evidence for the acceptance of *all* of them.

9. There is plenty of evidence for our main thesis. In *Meta*. IX 4, 1047b3-6, Aristotle writes: 'If, as we have said, that is possible which does not involve an impossibility, it cannot be true to say that a thing is possible but will never be ...' This proves that (T) is found in Aristotle. Similarly we read: '... that which is capable of not existing is not eternal' (*Meta*. XIV 2, 1088b23) and: 'It is impossible that the destructible should not at some time be destroyed' (*Cael*. I 12, 283a25-6).

There are also passages which show that Aristotle accepted (T)*: 'Anything then which always exists is absolutely imperishable' (*Cael*. I 12, 281b26); '... a thing is eternal if its "being" is necessary; and if it is eternal, its "being" is necessary. And if, therefore, the "coming-to-be" of a thing is necessary its "coming-to-be" is eternal; and if eternal, necessary' (*GC* II 11, 338a1-4).

That Aristotle accepted (T)** is shown by *Meta*. IX 8, 1050b8 and 1050b20-1: '... No eternal things exist potentially'; 'Nor does eternal movement, if there be such, exist potentially'. The context shows that the 'potentiality' here is tantamount to what we have called contingency. And the principle (T)*** is stated explicitly by Aristotle when he says (in *Meta*. IX 3, 1047a13) that 'impossible' or 'incapable' 'denotes precisely that which neither is nor will be'.

For further evidence for the main thesis of this paper, the reader is referred to the following passages: *Int*. 9, 18b11-15; *Top*. V 1, 128b16-18 and VI 6, 145b26-30; *Cael*. I 12, *passim; Meta*. V 30, 1025a33; *Phys*. III 4, 203b29-30; *Meta*. VI 2, 1026b27-37; *Meta*. IX 3, *passim*; and *Meta*. IX 8, *passim*. Many other passages show that there was an intimate connection between the notion of time and modal notions in Aristotle without letting the reader know exactly what their relation was. Among them, there are *Int*. 13, 23a20-2; *A.Pr*. I 15, 34a8-20 and 34b18; *A.Pst*. I 6, 74b26-38, and 8, 75b20-30. They give indirect support for our thesis.

10. Aristotle's reasons for assuming the connection (T) between time and modality seem to have been rather heterogeneous. Some of them appear from *Meta*. IX 3-4 and 8, and from *Cael*. I 12. The belief that every possibility must be realised at some moment of time is in Aristotle connected with certain broad metaphysical doctrines, such as the priority of actuality over potentiality. Aristotle also seems to have thought that the recognition of possibilities which have not been and never will be actualised 'would imply that there is nothing incapable of being' (*Meta*. IX 4, 1047b5-

6). He seems to have thought that if we can say in *one* case that something which never has happened and never will happen is possible, there is nothing which would prevent us from saying the same thing in *every* such case. We would then say, Aristotle thinks, e.g. that the side and the diagonal of a square 'can' have a common measure although the Euclidean algorithm never yields one.

One of the best articulated motives which Aristotle had for assuming that every possibility is or will be realised is his belief that each potential member of a species is preceded by an actual member of the same species by which it has been produced (*Meta.* IX 8, 1049b17-32). This doctrine is explained by Aristotle by means of the following example: 'What I mean is this: (a) the matter, (b) the seed, and (c) that which is capable of seeing, which are potentially but not yet actually (a) a man, (b) an ear of corn, and (c) a seeing subject, are prior in time to the latter individuals which already exist in actuality; but they are posterior in time to other actually existing things from which they were produced.' On this view, the fact that there potentially are things of a certain kind suffices to enable us to infer that at some (earlier) moment of time there were actual things of the same kind. (Cf. *Meta.* VII 8, 1033b19-1034a8.)   **73**

Perhaps the deepest reason for Aristotle's assumption is that by 'possible' he understood more than merely 'conceivable'. He seems to have thought of 'possibilities' as something not unlike 'natural tendencies'. In some cases at least, they become actualised unless there is something to prevent them from doing so. For what is there, Aristotle asks, to prevent a possibility from coming to pass, unless it is impossible? (*MA* 4, 699b29). Thus Aristotle writes of a man who potentially knows a certain subject: 'When he is in this condition, if something does not prevent him, he actively exercises his knowledge; otherwise he would be in the contradictory state of not knowing.' And he goes on to say that 'in regard to natural bodies the case is similar ... A change takes place ... unless something prevents or hinders it.' (See *Phys.* VIII 4, 255b3-8; and cf. *Meta.* IX 7, 1049a12-14). On this view, a possibility is never realised only if there is *always* something which prevents it from being realised. But saying that something is always prevented from happening seems to be the same as to say that it is *impossible* for it to happen. Hence, on Aristotle's view every genuine possibility is bound to be actualised sooner or later.

All these reasons for Aristotle's assumption are connected with his metaphysical doctrines. The connection between time and modality is therefore for him a deeper one more than a mere formal analogy between certain modal logics and the logic of the tenses. Formal analogies of this kind have been studied by the Schoolmen and recently by A.N. Prior.[5] What we have found in Aristotle is an assumption concerning a real   **74** connection between necessity and time.

This connection gives us a partial explanation why people have been misled by Aristotle's formulations in *Int.* 9 into thinking that he was there concerned with 'the law of excluded middle' instead of necessity. One of the

5. For the Schoolmen, see e.g. William Ockham, *Summa Logicae* (ed. by Ph. Boehner, St Bonaventure, N. Y. 1951 and 1954), III, 1, chapters 17-19; for Prior, see *Time and Modality* (Oxford 1957), and the literature referred to there.

ways in which Aristotle is inclined to put his problem is: Are statements about future particulars *always* true? What we have seen suggests that this question was for him tantamount to the question whether they are true *necessarily*. (Cf. *Int.* 9, 18b10-14. As Miss Anscombe points out, this is the crucial step of Aristotle's argument.)

11. From some of our quotations it may appear that there was for Aristotle no potentiality whatsoever which will not be actualised at some moment of time. Yet in a few passages, notably in *Int.* 13, 23a25, *Physica* III 6, 206a18-35, and *Meta.* IX 6, 1048b9-17, Aristotle says that there are certain things which exist potentially but which are never actualised, e.g. the void and the infinite. However, according to him, these things exist potentially in a sense different from those potentially existing things which are or will be actualised. What makes the difference between the two senses is never stated explicitly by Aristotle, and perhaps never quite clearly grasped by him. His remarks allow for an informed guess, however, about the nature of the distinction.

According to Aristotle, even the infinite 'exists fully in the sense in which we say "it is day" or "it is the games"' (Phys. III 6, 206b13-14). This sense turns on the fact that in such cases 'one thing after another is always coming into existence' (*loc. cit.* 206a22-3). This remark recalls Aristotle's discussion at the end of *De Generatione et Corruptione* (II 11, 338b7-15) about why certain things 'return upon themselves' cyclically and why certain other sequences produce constantly new members which are the same only in *species* but different from one another *numerically*. The recurrence of ever new days as well as the recurrence of ever larger and larger numbers clearly falls into the second category. This suggests that the principle according to which nothing can be potential without being actualised at some moment of time applies fully and primarily to *species* of individuals. An infinite magnitude does not exist (as it appears, not even potentially) as an *individual* (see *Phys.* III 6, 206a30-4). Although Aristotle was not consistent on this point, there is at least one passage which suggests that, in another sense, an infinity may be said to exist 'fully' (and not just potentially), viz. as a general attribute of things finite, on which it is thus dependent (*loc. cit.* 206b13-15). But in this sense the 'full' or actual existence of (say) an infinite number only seems to mean that for each number there will at some moment of time *actually* be found a larger number. Existence of this kind is in any case compatible with Aristotle's doctrine of infinity. If this is the case, the peculiarity of the Aristotelian infinity is better expressed by saying that it attaches to attributes of finite things (*versus* individual finite things) than by saying that it is an unactualised possibility.

The importance of this interpretation for our present purpose lies in showing that the existence of unactualised possibilities like infinity and the void does not necessarily entail that the connection of possibility and time is severed in so far as it pertains to kinds (e.g. species) of individuals. This squares very well with the reasons we saw Aristotle give for his view. For instance, all that follows from the actualisation of each member of a given species by the sole means of another member of the same species is that every potential *species* must be actualised in time.

Similarly, all the other unactualised potentialities recognised by Aristotle – including a coat's capacity of being cut up in *Int.* 9, 19a12-17 – seem to pertain to individual things or individual events, not to kinds of events or kinds of individuals.

Thus, in order to be completely on the safe side, we must qualify the principles (T)-(T)*** if we want to say that Aristotle always adhered to them: we must say that in them the modal notions are applied only to *kinds* of things or *kinds* of events, not to individual things or individual events. For instance, instead of (T) we must say that *each possible kind of individuals or of events must be instantiated at some moment of time.*

12. When the view we have thus reached is combined with the explicit omnitemporality of Aristotle's notion of universality, it follows that each **76** genuinely universal statement is for Aristotle necessary if it be true and impossible if it be false. For a general statement is according to this notion true only if there are not, and never will be, any counterinstances; and this was just seen to be tantamount to its necessity in Aristotle's sense. Of course, this is exactly the principle we were led to expect at the very beginning by an extension of the arguments of Miss Anscombe. Now we also see that this probably was the principle to which Aristotle was appealing in his demonstration (in *A.Pst.* I 4, 73b) that strict universality implies necessity.

13. The connection between time and modality was not a peculiarity of Aristotle's. It occurs, among other places, in the conclusion of the so-called Master Argument of Diodorus.[6] 'Our sources indicate that this argument ... was very famous in antiquity, and that the logicians of that time did not challenge its validity.'[7] According to Epictetus[8] this argument consisted in deducing from the two assumptions that (1) every true statement about the past is necessary and that (2) no impossibility follows from that which is possible, the conclusion that something is possible if and only if it is or will be actualised. The argument itself is lost. (Recently, however, A.N. Prior has offered an ingenious reconstruction of the argument.[9]) But it is interesting to observe that the only possible novelty about the Master Argument from the Aristotelian point of view was that it created a connection between different doctrines all of which are already found in Aristotle. The conclusion is the view we have been examining. The first premiss (1) is stated by him in *Int.* 9, 19a24-5. And the second premiss (2) occurs repeatedly in Aristotle's works; it is essentially tantamount to his **77** definition of possibility (see *A.Pr.* I 13, 32a18-20).

It thus appears that the connection between modality and time constitutes a rather widespread common assumption among the Greeks. There are further facts that support this suggestion. For the Greeks, there was traditionally a close connection between *anankê* and *chronos*,[10] between

6. Cf. I.M. Bochenski, *Formale Logik* (Freiburg 1956), p.132, which supplies further references.

7. Benson Mates in the *Journal of Symbolic Logic*, vol. 21 (1956), p.200.

8. *Dissertationes ab Ariano digestae* (Leipzig 1916), II, 19, 1; Bochenski, *loc. cit.*

9. *Time and Modality*, pp.86-87; 'Diodoran modalities', *Philosophical Quarterly*, July 1955, part II. Cf. also M. Kneale (Martha Hurst), 'Logical necessity and metaphysical necessity', *Proceedings of the Aristotelian Society*, vol. 38 (1937-8).

10. R.B. Onians, *The Origins of European Thought* (Cambridge 1954), pp.250-1 and 332.

moira and *aiôn*,[11] etc. The former occurs explicitly in Plato.[12]

Nor did the idea lose its hold after the Greeks. It played an important rôle in mediaeval thought, a rôle which largely remains to be investigated.[13] Perhaps the most important single application of the principle that possibility entails actuality at some moment of time occurs in the so-called third proof of God's existence in St Thomas Aquinas which has been given a particular prominence by the neo-Thomist commentators.[14] One of the steps of this proof is an inference from the assumption that everything in the world is contingent to the occurrence of a moment when there is nothing whatsoever in existence. This is but an application of the Arisotelian idea we have been studying.[15] In William of Ockham, however, the theory of temporal syllogisms is already sharply separated from that of the modal syllogisms in the proper sense of the word.[16] This is a big step toward the modern separation of modal and temporal notions. How and why the change took place remains to be investigated.

The distinction is found completed in Leibniz. For him, 'possible' meant the same as 'distinctly intelligible'.[17] Of course, the mere fact that things of a certain kind are distinctly intelligible does not suffice to guarantee that there is, has been or will be things of this kind. This is particularly obvious when Leibniz speaks of 'possible worlds' alternative to the actual one, for these 'possibilities' cannot conceivably be realised at any moment in time.

In spite of Leibniz, however, there occur lapses (real or apparent) back to the Aristotelian assumption all through the history of philosophy. Thus we read in Kant: 'Alles Zufällige ist einmal nicht gewesen (... das ist das Merkmal, woran die Zufälligkeit erkannt wird)'; 'jederzeit (das heisst notwendigerweise) ...'; 'das Schema der Notwendigkeit ist das Dasein eines Gegenstandes zu aller Zeit'; etc.[18] And even Russell writes: 'One may call a propositional function necessary, when it is always true; possible when it is sometimes true; impossible when it is never true.'[19]

11. Onians, *op. cit.*, pp.204-5.

12. *Republic*, X, 617.

13. To give only a few instances, see Moses Maimonides, *Dalatat al-Hairin*, introduction to Part II, Proposition VIII; Harry Wolfson, *Crescas' Criticism of Aristotle* (Cambridge, Mass. 1929), pp.82, 249, 551; L.G. Lévy, *Maimonides* (2nd ed., Paris 1932) p.128; Averroes' *Tahafut al Tahafut*, translated, with introduction and notes, by Simon van den Bergh (Oxford 1954), vol. I, p. xxiii and vol. II, p.36; St Thomas Aquinas, *Summa Theologiae* Ia, q. 14, art. 13, obj. 2; *Summa Contra Gentiles*, I, 83, 3.

14. Etienne Gilson, *The Christian Philosophy of St Thomas Aquinas* (New York 1956), pp.68-70 and 77-83.

15. According to Gilson (*op. cit.*, p.452), the Aristotelian origin of Aquinas' mode of inference has been pointed out by Cl. Baeumker in *Witelo, ein Philosoph und Naturforscher des XIII Jahrhunderts* (Münster 1908), p.128.

16. *Summa Logicae* (ed. Boehner), III, 1. The Aristotelian conception about the relation of time to necessity is explicitly rejected by Buridan in his *Consequentiae* (Paris *ca.* 1495) I, ch. 1 (quoted by Ernest A. Moody, *Truth and Consequence in Mediaeval Logic*, Amsterdam 1953, p.58).

17. *Nouveaux essais sur l'entendement humain*, II, *xxx*, § 4.

18. See Guido Schneeberger, 'Kants Konzeption der Modalbegriffe', *Philosophische Forschungen* n.s., vol. 1 (Basel 1952), pp.82-3, 90-3. And cf. Hobbes, *De Corpore* II, 10, §4.

19. See Russell's lectures on 'The philosophy of logical atomism', reprinted in *Logic and Knowledge* (ed. by R.C. Marsh, London 1956) p.231.

14. The long history of the Aristotelian view may lead the reader to wonder whether I have been correct in implying that the connection between time and modality is foreign to our own way of thinking. In trying to answer this question we must keep in mind on the one hand the modern distinction between *logical* possibility and *real* (natural) possibility and on the other hand the fact that this distinction was not consistently made by Aristotle. On the contrary, on one occasion at least he seems to equate syllogistic necessity with the relation of material causation. (Cf. *Phys.* II 3,   **79** 195a18-19. But see also the distinction made in *MA* 4, 699b17-22.) The answer to our question therefore depends on whether we are comparing the one Aristotelian notion of possibility to the modern notion of logical possibility or to the notion of natural possibility.

As far as the former is concerned, the Aristotelian assumption is patently wrong. There is not the slightest reason to think that every logical possibility would be realised sooner or later. For instance, since natural laws are not usually thought of as being *logically* necessary, the Aristotelian assumption would imply that every natural law will ultimately be refuted by a counterinstance.

In the case of natural possibility and necessity, the consequences of the Aristotelian assumption are not plain absurd. On this assumption, a general statement would be necessary in the sense of natural necessity, i.e. would express a natural law, if and only if it has no counterinstances. In other words, every state of affairs compatible with natural laws would be realised at one time or another. As pointed out by Prior, this would constitute a cosmic analogue to the 'ergodic hypotheses' studied in the statistical mechanics.

On the Aristotelian assumption, the problem of the appropriate logical form of natural laws would be solved. For on this assumption, saying that a general implication expresses a natural law would be tantamount to saying that it is (materially) true. For it is true only if it does not have any counterinstances; and on the Aristotelian assumption this is sufficient to show that it expresses a natural law. Using a different terminology, W. Kneale[20] has pointed out that 'philosophers who treat suggestions of law as universal material implications' are in effect making the Aristotelian assumption. He also offers plausible arguments to show that the assumption is inconsistent with our ordinary view of natural laws. If he is right – as I think he is – then the Aristotelian view is foreign also to the modern way of   **80** thinking of natural necessity and natural possibility. I don't think we have to go beyond stock examples in order to begin to expect this. There is nothing logically or physically impossible about golden mountains nor (apparently) anything biologically impossible about unicorns; and yet we certainly do not expect ever to find them actualised.

It may be worth pointing out, however, that certain problems which many moderns discuss do not arise at all on the Aristotelian view. E.g., the problem of general implications with empty antecedents would scarcely have worried the Stagirite, for the only empty antecedents were for him the

20. William Kneale, 'Natural laws and contrary-to-fact conditionals', *Analysis* vol. 10, no. 6, 1950; reprinted in *Philosophy and Analysis*, ed. by Margaret Macdonald, Oxford 1954, pp.226-31.

impossible ones. This also shows why he naturally assumed the existential import of universal premises. They could fail to have existential import only if some of their terms were impossible. And by means of impossible terms no real knowledge obviously can be gained; they play no part in science.

15. The comparison between the Aristotelian and the modern conception of the relation of necessity to universality suggests an almost paradoxical conclusion. We have seen that, for Aristotle, universality in the sense of omnitemporality implied necessity. The converse implication holds trivially: what is true necessarily is true always and everywhere at least in so far as we are concerned with general truths. The notions of necessity and universality are thus virtually equivalent for Aristotle. For us, however, natural necessity is different from universality; not every true universal sentence expresses a natural law. *Prima facie*, Aristotle and his followers therefore had much less reason to build a modal logic different from the logic of assertoric propositions. For us moderns, building a logic of modality would appear an interesting problem since one may expect it to be different from 'ordinary' logic. But if Aristotle had followed his intentions far enough, he apparently would have had to abolish the distinction between assertoric and apodeictic premises at least in so far as universal premises are concerned. The problem therefore arises: why did Aristotle nevertheless distinguish between assertoric and apodeictic, between simple and necessary propositions?

The most plausible explanation seems to me the following: Aristotle saw that there unmistakably *is* a difference between whether an individual event takes place by necessity or by chance. Hence to say that an event happens necessarily means more than simply to say that it happens. The difference, however, between statements of this kind and statements of general rules was not always clear to him. For instance, in *A.Pr.* I 15, 34a8-18 he discusses certain undetermined *A*'s and *B*'s as if they were propositions speaking of individual things. But the outcome of this discussion is immediately (*loc. cit.* 34a34-b5) applied to propositions which are, according to Aristotle's own analysis, of the form '*C* can be said of all that of which *D* is said' (cf. *A.Pr.* I 41, 49b15-32, *A.Pr.* I 13, 32b23-37 and *A.Pr.* I 1, 24b27-30), i.e. to general propositions. This confusion made him think that there must be some definite difference between assertoric and apodeictic *general* propositions, too. Apparently, the *problem* of distinguishing the two never occurred to him. In Aristotle, the problem is only shown by his occasional failures to maintain the distinction between the apodeictic and assertoric propositions. It is no accident that for Aristotle there was 'hardly any difference between syllogisms from necessary premises and from premises which merely assert' (*A.Pr.* I 8, 29b35-7).

16. I cannot here argue for this suggested explanation as fully as it deserves. I shall only call attention to a few passages in Aristotle which show how fleeting the line between necessity and simple universality was for him.

In *A.Pr.* I 15, 34b19-31, Aristotle proves (to his satisfaction) the following syllogism:

> *A* belongs to no *B*
> *B* possibly belongs to all *C*
> _____
> *A* possibly belongs to no *C*.

The argument to this effect is by *reductio ad impossibile*. Aristotle takes the negation of the conclusion and tries to show that it leads, in conjunction with the second premiss, to a violation of the first premiss. He points out that in order to do this, the 'possibility' in the conclusion must be different from what he had originally defined in 32a18-20, i.e. from what we have termed 'contingency'. Rather, it must be taken in the wider sense in which even necessary things are called possible. On this interpretation, the negation of the conclusion is

A necessarily belongs to some *C*.   Together with   **82**
B possibly belongs to all *C*,

this is supposed to lead to a violation of the first premiss. However, there is in Aristotle's syllogistic no consequence which can be drawn from these premisses and which could violate the assertoric premiss (see *A.Pr.* I 22, 40a39 ff.). Hence, Aristotle must make a further move. Expanding his argument a little by means of his own preceding explanations (cf. *loc. cit.* 34a1-33), we may render it as follows: When we say that *B* possibly belongs to all *C*, we assume that at some moment of time this actually takes place. (It does not matter which version of the notion of possibility we are using.) At such a moment, we may truly say that

B belongs to all *C*.   Since we assumed that
A necessarily belongs to some *C*,

we can conclude that

A belongs to some *B*.

In fact, Aristotle had earlier proved this mode. (Cf. *A.Pr.* I 11, 31b20-7; it is to be observed that we cannot draw a necessary conclusion.) The conclusion we have thus reached is said to contradict the first premiss of the original syllogism we set out to prove. This contradiction does not come about, however, without an extra assumption. What we said when we concluded that *A* belongs to some *B* was something that was only supposed to hold at the particular moment of time at which the premiss '*B* possibly belongs to all *C*' was supposed to be actualised. Our conclusion therefore only violates the first premiss '*A* belongs to no *B*' if this premiss is assumed to hold with no limitation in time, i.e. if it is assumed not to pertain to the present or to any other particular moment. It is obviously to justify this step of the argument that Aristotle explicitly states this assumption in the passage which immediately precedes our argument (*A.Pr.* I 15, 34b7-18). This step is the only one that is not obviously and completely correct upon Aristotle's general assumptions. If it is admitted, the syllogism is proved.

In the same way, one can analyse the argument in *A.Pr.* I 15, 34a34-34b6   **83**
which has puzzled many commentators.

17. In a similar way, we may analyse Aristotle's necessary syllogisms. It is a peculiarity of his doctrine that syllogisms with an assertoric and a necessary premiss sometimes have a necessary conclusion and sometimes don't. As a paradigm of the former case, we may choose the following syllogism:

(a)
$$\frac{\begin{array}{l}A \text{ necessarily belongs to every } B\\ B \text{ belongs to every } C\end{array}}{A \text{ necessarily belongs to } C.}$$

As a paradigm of the case in which a necessary and an assertoric premiss do not yield a necessary conclusion we may choose the (fallacious) syllogism

(b)
$$\frac{\begin{array}{l}A \text{ belongs to every } B\\ B \text{ necessarily belongs to every } C\end{array}}{A \text{ necessarily belongs to every } C.}$$

What makes the difference between the two syllogisms (a) and (b)? Ross has pointed out that, in Aristotle's mind, whenever a necessary conclusion can be established, it can be established by a *reductio ad impossibile*.[21] In accordance with this observation, the two syllogisms

(c)
$$\frac{\begin{array}{l}A \text{ possibly does not belong to some } C\\ B \text{ necessarily belongs to every } C\end{array}}{A \text{ possibly does not belong to some } B}$$

and

(d)
$$\frac{\begin{array}{l}A \text{ possibly does not belong to some } C\\ A \text{ belongs to every } B\end{array}}{B \text{ possibly does not belong to some } C}$$

84 which might be expected to carry out the *reductio* of (b) both fail. (c) has a conclusion too weak to contradict the first premiss of (b), and (d) is explicitly rejected by Aristotle. (For (c) see *A.Pr.* I 22, 40b2-3, and for (d) *A.Pr.* I 18, 37b40.)

On the other hand, it may seem as if (a) could be proved by a *reductio* which might run as follows: Suppose the contradictory of the conclusion, i.e. suppose that *A* possibly does not belong to some *C*. This means that at some moment of time we may truly say that *A* does not belong to some *C*. Since the second premiss '*B* belongs to every *C*' must not be subject to any temporal limitations, we can at this particular moment also truly say that *B* belongs to every *C*. From these two propositions we then could (by means of an assertoric syllogism) draw the conclusion that *A* does not belong to some *B*. This, however, would contradict the first premiss '*A* necessarily belongs to every *B*', and show that (a) is valid.

There is little point in criticising this argument in favour of (a) or the rejection of (b) There is no inherent absurdity in either of them. It may be pointed out, however, that they are incompatible. If the modes of reasoning which underlie the above proof of (a) as well as the syllogism quoted on page 118 are applied consistently, they would eliminate the distinction between assertoric and apodeictic premisses for all practical purposes. I shall not demonstrate this general thesis here; I shall only show, as an example, how (b) could be justified by means of reasoning similar to that by means of which (a) and the syllogism on page 118 are justified.

We can vindicate (b) simply by restoring (d) as follows: The premiss '*A* possibly does not belong to some *C*' means that at some moment of time we

21. W.D. Ross [6], pp.42-3.

can truly say that A does not belong to some C. Since universal premisses are to be understood with no limitations in respect of time, at the same moment A belongs to every B. From these two propositions, we can by an assertoric syllogism infer that B does not belong to some C, which was just the conclusion of (d). (d) is thus vindicated, and thereby (b).

There is thus an inconsistency in Aristotle's procedure. For the purpose of establishing some of the syllogisms he thinks valid he makes use of a mode of reasoning which, if strictly adhered to, would abolish the distinction between universality and necessity.

This inconsistency is strikingly shown by the fact that the syllogism (b) is **85** rejected by Aristotle (in *A.Pr.* I 9, 30a29-31) by means of an example of exactly the kind which is later dismissed by him as inappropriate (in *A.Pr.* I 15, 34b7-17) and which he has to dismiss if he is to validate syllogisms like the one quoted on page 118.

18. The current interpretation of Aristotle's modal logic takes a view different from the one we have adopted.[22] The strange inference from a necessary and an assertoric premiss to a necessary conclusion is explained in a different way by assuming a 'fine structure' of the premisses. It is assumed that, to use a convenient modern term, the operators of necessity and possibility are applied by Aristotle not to the premisses as independent wholes but rather to certain parts of them.[23] It is assumed, moreover, that Aristotle recognised two different ways of so distributing the operators of necessity and possibility to the terms of the premisses. It is finally assumed that he sometimes made use of one such way and sometimes of the other.[24]

I shall close this paper by indicating some of the reasons why I find this **86** interpretation unsatisfactory.

Far from saying anywhere explicitly that modal premisses have a 'fine structure' of the kind just explained, Aristotle on one occasion says that modal operators are applied to whole statements and not to individual

22. See p.110, n. 3 above.

23. Bochenski, *Ancient Formal Logic*, pp.57-9; Bochenski, *Formale Logik*, pp.96, 100-1; Becker [108], pp.16-20, 32-6.

24. Using 'N' and 'P' as the operators of necessity and possibility, respectively, and otherwise employing the usual notation, the two 'fine structures' of a universal necessary premiss are

(i) $(x) (A(x) \supset NB(x))$ and
(ii) $(x) (PA(x) \_ NB(x))$.

Correspondingly, a universal possible premiss may be interpreted as

(i)* $(x) (A(x) \supset PB(x))$ or as
(ii)* $(x) (PA(x) \supset PB(x))$;

and similarly for the other types of premisses. Of these two interpretations, (i) is the one usually resorted to by Becker and Bochenski.
The reading (ii) is needed mainly in *A.Pr.* I 14.

A third interpretation would be to prefix the modal operator to the whole (non-modal) premiss. In this way we obtain

(iii) $N((x) (A(x) \supset B(x)))$
as the universal necessary and
(iii)* $P((x) (A(x) \supset B(x)))$
as the universal possible premiss.

I shall suggest that we have little justification for assuming that Aristotle ever employed the structure (i) or that he made use of (ii) before *A.Pr.* I 14.

terms (see *Int.* 12, 21b27-32 and 22a8-12). That this view also underlies *Analytica Priora* is suggested by 25b18-26. (Cf. also 32b1-3) Becker's attempt to disqualify this passage is rejected by Ross.[25]

19. The main and, as far as I can see, the only passage that seems to give some *direct* evidence that Aristotle employed two different kinds of 'fine structure' is *A.Pr.* I 13, 32b25-37. The interpretation of this passage is far from easy, however. *Prima facie* it says that the premiss

(X)   *A* may apply to all *B*

is ambiguous in that it may mean either

(X₁)   *A* may be predicated of everything of which *B* is predicated

or

(X₂)   *A* may be predicated of everything of which *B* may be predicated.

This scarcely will do without qualification, however. When Aristotle later makes use of his analysis of (X) and refers back to the passage under discussion, there is no trace of *two* alternatives. Only one of the two interpretations (X₁) and (X₂), viz. the latter, verifies the syllogisms which Aristotle sets up in *A.Pr.* I 14. And he defends his syllogisms by saying that the interpretation (X₂) is what the phrase '*A* may apply to all *B*' was seen to mean (*loc. cit.* 33a1-2) and even that the interpretation (X₂) is what the phrase (X) was *defined* to mean (*loc. cit.* 33a24-5; *cf.* also *loc. cit.* 33a4-5). Furthermore, if Aristotle really had wanted to distinguish two alternative readings of the universal possible premiss (X), one would naturally expect that he should set up two alternative sets of syllogisms, one in terms of (X₁) and the other in terms of (X₂). Yet we only find syllogisms in terms of (X₂).

All this suggests that the real point of Aristotle's analysis is that the phrase (X) was *defined* to mean (*loc. cit.* 33a24-5; *cf.* also *loc. cit.* 33a4-5). case, why did he then speak of *two* different uses to which (X) may be put? What did he mean by saying that (X) means (X₁) or (X₂)? I shall suggest that by this he meant that (X) is equivalent to the *conjunction* of (X₁) and (X₂). In other words, I am suggesting that Aristotle is not here distinguishing two meanings of one and the same phrase but rather explaining its meaning by pointing out that it can be expanded into a conjunction of two more explicit propositions. This is supported by the fact that the expression (*dichôs*) used by Aristotle in the passage under discussion is not one of his usual terms for ambiguity (*homônuma* or *pollachôs legomena*). In fact, the same expression is later used by him in a context (*A.Pr.* I 17, 37a16-21) where he has in mind, according to Bochenski, a complex proposition of the form of disjunction (negation of a conjunction) rather than two meanings of one and the same proposition.

However, this interpretation of Aristotle's analysis seems self-contradictory. For how can (X) be equivalent to (X₂) and also to the *conjunction* of (X₁) and (X₂)?

In trying to find an answer to this question, it is not advisable to assume that Aristotle introduced any fundamentally new idea at this late stage of his systematic theory of modal syllogisms. One would expect that Aristotle is here only elaborating the idea he is constantly making use of. Is there, then, anything in the other passages of *Analytica Priora* which gives an answer to our question?

It is easy to see that there is. We have only to recall the fact that, throughout *Analytica Priora*, Aristotle used more than one notion of possibility. The equivalence of (X_2) to the conjunction of (X_1) and (X_2) can be understood if we assume that in the conjunction Aristotle used the variant of the notion of possibility which we have termed contingency and that in the single (X_2) he used the other notion of possibility which includes necessity. For, on this assumption the single (X_2) may be expanded into the conjunction

(X_3) *A* may be predicated of everything of which *B* is contingently **88** predicated and of everything of which *B* is necessarily predicated.

Since everything necessary is also actual, this is implied by

(X_4) *A* may be predicated of everything of which *B* is contingently predicated and of everything of which *B* is predicated.

(X_4), however, is exactly the conjunction of (X_1) and (X_2) provided that we are in them using the notion of contingency. Conversely, since everything actual is either necessary or contingent, the implication also holds in the other direction.[26]

I conclude that the real purpose of Aristotle's analysis is to show that '*A* may be predicated of all *B*' or, as we rather should read it, '*A* applies contingently to all *B*' is to be interpreted as '*A* applies contingently to everything to which *B* possibly applies'. Since he did not have a separate term for 'possibility' as distinguished from what we have called 'contingency', he only could make his point by saying that '*A* may be predicated of all *B*' can be expanded into the conjunction '*A* applies contingently to everything to which *B* is applied and to everything to which *B* applies contingently'.

20. This is not calculated to show that Aristotle never had in mind any kind of 'fine structure'. One may still use this idea in interpreting what he says in *A.Pr.* I 14. But if we are correct, the passage we have been discussing **89** does not indicate that Aristotle assumed two different 'fine structures' or that he elsewhere made use of the one structure he possibly had. This agrees pretty well with Becker's view[27] that most of *A.Pr.* I 13, 32b25-37 is made up of later additions (perhaps by Aristotle himself). Only Becker does not seem to notice that this interpretation greatly reduces the evidence for his general

26. Denoting contingency by '*E*' and possibility by '*P*', my point can be expressed in formal terms by saying that the following formulae are all equivalent:

$(x) (B(x) \supset EA(x))$ & $(x) (EB(x) \supset EA(x))$;
$(x) ((B(x) \vee EB(x)) \supset EA(x))$;   and
$(x) (PB(x) \supset EA(x))$.

The equivalence of the last two formulae is based on the simpler equivalence

$(B(x) \vee EB(x)) \equiv PB(x)$

which is valid on the Aristotelian assumptions.
27. *op. cit.*, pp.34-47.

thesis that Aristotle made use of a 'fine structure' consistently.

It seems to me that we have no valid evidence for ascribing *two* alternative 'fine structures' to Aristotle or for assuming that he made use of any fine structure before *A.Pr.* I 13. This means that we cannot explain the majority of his modal syllogisms by the sole means of the 'fine structure' interpretation. We need other insights; and the purpose of this paper has been to suggest a few new ones. I am the first to admit that Aristotle on different occasions worked on different intuitions, and that no single idea probably suffices to explain all he said on modal notions.[28] But it seems to me that the attempt to explain his whole theory of modal syllogisms in terms of a 'fine structure' omits some of the intuitions which he used and which perhaps were most characteristic to him.

The inadequacy of the 'fine structure' interpretation is further indicated by the fact that Aristotle completely fails to refer to this structure in places where, according to the proponents of the interpretation, he needs it most (in particular in *A.Pr.* I 9-12.) Even more serious is the fact that the 'fine structure' interpretation fails to verify some of the rules of conversion of which Aristotle is constantly making use (cf. *A.Pr.* I 3).[29] Becker's attempts to explain away these discrepancies are not very convincing.[30][31]

28. There is, for instance, Aristotle's habit of thinking of syllogisms in terms of class-inclusion (the relation of whole to part). This may have played a more important rôle in his syllogistic than what is usually realised, and may explain why the structure (iii) (footnote 24) does not verify all the syllogisms Aristotle recognised as valid.

Ross (*op. cit.*) says that the 'class-inclusion view' only appears in *Analytica Priora*. There is a counterinstance, however, in *A.Pst.* I 26, 87a22-4.

29. Cf. Bochenski, *Formale Logik*, p. 101.

30. *Op. cit.*, pp.83-91. In Aristotle's assertoric syllogistic, the rules of conversion are the most important methods of proof (cf. Jan Lukasiewicz [107] pp.51-4). It seems very strange to suppose that they were not cast for the same rôle also in the modal syllogistic. They are constantly used by Aristotle. And whether the 'proofs' Aristotle offered for them are correct or not, they certainly show how he thought about modal notions. Becker's objections are not accepted by Ross nor (apparently) by Bochenski.

31. I have greatly profited from the criticism to which an earlier version of this paper was subjected by Professors G.H. von Wright and Julius Moravcsik.

10

Jaakko Hintikka

Aristotelian Infinity

In an earlier paper, I have argued that Aristotle accepted and used, in some
form or other, the principle which has been called by A.O. Lovejoy 'the
principle of plenitude'.[1] That is to say, he accepted the principle that every
genuine possibility is sometimes actualised or, possibly, another form of the
same principle according to which no genuine possibility can remain
unactualised through an infinity of time.[2]

Aristotle's theory of infinity might seem to constitute a counterexample to
this interpretation. In many expositions of this theory, it is said that
according to Aristotle infinity had merely potential existence but was never
actualised. (The very terms 'actual infinity' and 'potential infinity' which
are still used hail from Aristotle's terminology.) As one author puts it, for
Aristotle infinity is 'never realised, though conceivable'. If this is all there is
to the subject, we would in fact have here a clear-cut counterinstance to the
principle of plenitude in Aristotle.

This interpretation is encouraged by certain remarks Aristotle himself
makes. For instance, in *Int.* 13, 23a23-6 he writes: 'Some things are
actualities without capability ... others with capability ... and others are
never actualities but only capabilities.'[3] Aristotle's remarks in *Meta.* IX 6,
1048b9-17 are sometimes construed in the same spirit (mistakenly, I shall
argue later).

In view of the wealth of evidence that there is for ascribing the principle of
plenitude to Aristotle, his views on infinity need a closer scrutiny.[4] I shall
argue that Aristotle did not give up this principle in his theory of infinity,

---

1. See Chapter 9. In this paper, I did not use the term 'principle of plenitude'. For
the principle, see A.O. Lovejoy, *The Great Chain of Being* (Cambridge, Mass. 1936).

2. What is here supposed to count as a 'genuine' possibility is not obvious from
Aristotle's formulations. It lies close at hand to suggest that for Aristotle each *general*
possibility (each possible *kind of* individuals or of events) was actualised sooner or
later. There are indications that Aristotle went further than this, however. The
second formulation given in the text seems to catch his intentions fairly accurately
without violating such well-known Aristotelian examples as the coat that could be cut
but is worn out before it is (*Int.* 9, 19a12-15). Just because the individual coat in
question perishes, we do not have a possibility here which would remain unactualised
through an infinity of time.

3. In quoting *De Interpretatione*, I shall use J.L. Ackrill's new translation [42]. In
quoting other works of Aristotle, I shall usually follow the familiar Oxford translation
(ed. by W.D. Ross), with changes that are not always explicitly indicated.

4. In fact, a form of the principle of plenitude is assented to by Aristotle at the
beginning of his discussion of infinity: 'in the case of eternal things what may be must
be' (203b30).

but rather assumed it in certain important parts of the theory. I shall argue that by noticing this we can understand better certain issues that come up in the course of Aristotle's discussion of infinity in his *Phys.* III 4-8.

As so often in Aristotle, we cannot take his preliminary discussion of reasons for and against the existence of infinity at its face value.[5] The arguments presented in this discussion, like the corresponding preparatory arguments in other Aristotelian discussions, primarily serve to set the stage for Aristotle's own solution of the difficulty. Usually, such preliminary arguments give rise to apparently contradictory conclusions. These contradictions are normally resolved by means of a conceptual distinction. In the case at hand, it is a distinction between the different senses in which the infinite may be asserted or denied to exist (206a12-14).

Aristotle first indicates that an infinite potentiality must be said to exist (206a14-18). He goes on to suggest, however, that in order to understand the sense in which the infinite exists potentially we have to heed the different senses of existence (206a21-23). In other words, it is not true (*pace* Evans)[6] that 'potentiality has here a special sense', different from the sense in which finite things may be potential. Rather, the infinite *is* (potentially *and* actually) in a sense different from the one in which a finite thing *is*. In the latter sense of being, the infinite does not exist even potentially: 'The infinite does not have, even potentially, the independent (*kath' hauto*) being which the finite has' (206b15-16; trans. by Wicksteed and Cornford).

In what sense, then, does the infinite exist? It exists, Aristotle says, in the sense in which a day 'is' or the Olympic Games 'are'. These are not actualised in their entirety at any given moment of time in the way an individual is. Rather, their parts come to existence successively one by one. As Aristotle says, 'one thing after another is always coming into existence' (206a22-3). In other words, infinity is not a term which applies to individual things, such as men or houses, in any sense, either actually or potentially. Rather, it is an attribute of certain sequences of individual things or individual events – 'definite if you like at each stage, yet always different' (206a32-3). This is the gist of the Aristotelian theory of infinity.

Saying that the infinite exists potentially might perhaps be used to express that it exists in this derivative sense. Occasionally Aristotle allows himself the luxury of this locution. It is a very misleading way of speaking, however, not merely because it does not fully express the mode of existence of the infinite according to Aristotle, but even more so because it muddles an important distinction. As Aristotle is well aware, the distinction between actuality and potentiality applies also to the kind of existence which is enjoyed, *inter alia*, by the infinite, by a day, and by the Olympic Games: 'For of these things too the distinction between potential and actual existence holds. We say that there are Olympic Games, both in the sense that they may occur and that they are actually occurring' (206a23-5). When this

5. The structure of Aristotle's discussion of the infinite may be compared, e.g., with the structure of his discussion of the problem of future contingents in *Int.* The latter discussion is analysed in [101], Ch. VIII, esp. pp.153-7. In reading Aristotle, it is vital to keep constantly in mind his characteristic method of approaching a problem.

6. Cf. Melbourne G. Evans, *The Physical Philosophy of Aristotle* (Albuquerque, 1964), p.47.

distinction is made clear, the principle of plenitude is seen to apply. Although there perhaps is a (rather loose and inappropriate) sense in which the infinite may be said to exist only potentially, in the exact and proper **200** sense in which, according to Aristotle, it exists potentially, it also exists actually. 'The infinite is actual in the sense in which a day or the games are said to be actual' (206b13-14); and this, we have seen, is just the proper sense in which the Aristotelian infinite exists.[7] For instance, the infinity of time does not mean for Aristotle merely that later and later moments of time are possible; it implies that there will actually be later and later moments of time.

In a way, the Aristotelian theory of infinity has thus been found to entail exactly the opposite to what it is usually said to assert. Usually it is said that for Aristotle infinity exists potentially but never actually. In the *precise* sense, however, in which the infinite was found to exist potentially for Aristotle, it also exists actually. Far from discrediting my attribution of the principle of plenitude to Aristotle, an analysis of Aristotle's theory of infinity serves to confirm it.

The fact that Aristotle abides by the principle of plenitude in developing his theory of infinity is not without <u>consequences</u> for the theory. One of these is that he cannot accept any infinite (except in a relative sense as the inverse of infinite divisibility), not even in the 'potential' sense of the infinite in which an infinite division or an infinity of numbers is possible. For the potential infinity of extension would mean that arbitrarily large extensions are possible. But if they were possible, they would have to be actual at some time or other. There cannot, however, be any actually existing extended magnitude greater than the universe itself (says Aristotle at 207b19-21), hence there are no arbitrarily large (actual) extensions; and hence there is not even a potential infinity with respect to extension. As Aristotle puts it, 'A potential extension can be only as large as the greatest possible actual extension' (207b17-18).[8] Aristotle's universe is thus finite in an especially strong sense: no extension beyond it is even possible.[9]   **201**

7. Hence Aristotle in fact assumed the existence of actually infinite sets of objects (in the modern sense of actual infinity), though not the existence of infinite sets whose members all exist simultaneously.

8. This feature of Aristotle's theory of infinity is pointed out by Harold Cherniss [124], p.34: 'That is, infinity by addition, in the sense that any given magnitude may be surpassed, does not exist even potentially [according to Aristotle]. And the reason he himself gives is that it is impossible for an infinite body to exist actually.'
What is being added to Cherniss' account here is an explanation *why* Aristotle inferred the nonexistence of arbitrarily large *potential* magnitudes from the nonexistence of arbitrarily large *actual* extensive magnitudes. This inference was clearly mediated by the principle of plenitude.
A closely related explanation is offered (without explicitly mentioning the general principle on which Aristotle is relying) by Friedrich Solmsen in [261], p.168, esp. n. 35.

9. Aristotle's way of thinking is rather amusingly illustrated by the words *exô tou asteôs* at 208a18 which were taken by Alexander, Themistius, and Philoponus (*apud* Ross [5], p.562) to mean 'outside the city'. They suggest that Aristotle was worried about too large a magnitude's 'sticking out' of the boundaries of the physical universe, in the same way too large a man would have to be 'outside the city'. If this is right, there do not seem to be good reasons for omitting *tou asteôs* and *ê* from 208a18.

Aristotle's argument would make no sense if he were not actually making use of the principle of plenitude. By possibility he could not mean here mere conceivability, for he admits at 203b23-25 that we can think of extensions extending beyond the boundaries of the physical universe.

What we have found about Aristotle's theory of spatial magnitude shows that the problem of reconciling his theory of infinity with mathematical practice is a much more serious one than commentators have usually realised. Aristotle thought that he could get away with saying merely this:

> Our account does not rob the mathematicians of their study, by disproving the actual existence of the infinite in the direction of increase, in the sense of the untraversable. In point of fact they do not need the infinite and do not use it. They postulate only that the finite straight line may be produced as far as they wish. It is possible to have divided in the same ratio as the largest quantity another magnitude of any size you like. Hence, for the purposes of proof, it will make no difference to them to have such an infinite instead, while its existence will be in the sphere of real magnitudes (*Phys.* III 7, 207b27-34).[10]

202   Aristotle is not saying here merely that a mathematician does not need an infinite magnitude all of whose parts are simultaneously actualised. If this were all that he were saying, he would have a plausible argument. The quoted passage shows him doing much more, however; he is also arguing that a geometer does not even need arbitrarily large potential extensions. He is suggesting in effect that all the geometer needs is the kind of infinite extension that exists merely as the inverse of infinite divisibility, and that a geometer therefore does not even need arbitrarily large potential extensions. All that he needs according to Aristotle is that there be *arbitrarily small* potential magnitudes.

What Aristotle's statement therefore amounts to is that for each proof of a theorem, dealing with a given figure, there is a sufficiently small similar figure for which the proof can be carried out. In short, each geometrical theorem holds in a sufficiently small neighbourhood. From this it does not follow, however, that the theorem really holds. There are in fact geometrical

10. Evans (*op. cit.*, p.49) and Sir Thomas L. Heath, in his *Manual of Greek Mathematics* (Oxford 1931), p.199, omit, when quoting this passage, the sentence 'It is possible ... any size you like'. They are thus presupposing that the infinite extension which according to Aristotle's last sentence suffices 'for the purpose of proof' is the possibility of producing lines 'as far as one wishes'. This is not, however, what the passage says; the last sentence of the quotation clearly refers to the penultimate one, saying that what suffices for the purpose of proof is the infinite extension that exists merely as the inverse of infinite divisibility. This kind of infinity Aristotle discusses at 206b3-12, a passage which is echoed by the penultimate sentence of our quotation.

The point is correctly made by Cherniss [124], p.35, n. 129, and to some extent also by Heath in his *History of Greek Mathematics* (Oxford 1921), I, 344. Heath there suggests that Aristotle's statement is incompatible with the mathematical practice of his time. This is criticised by Sir David Ross in his edition of *Aristotle's Physics*, p.52. Ross is right in the case of the particular assumption he is discussing (the so-called axiom of Archimedes), but there are other mathematical assumptions that are in fact vitiated by Aristotle's theory.

assumptions requiring arbitrarily large extensions. The best-known case in point is of course Euclid's fifth postulate, the famous 'axiom of parallels': 'If á straight line falling on two straight lines makes the interior angles on the same side less than two right angles, the two straight lines, *if produced indefinitely*, meet on that side on which are the angles less than the two right angles' (trans. by Heath). If there is a maximum to the extent to which lines can be produced, this postulate fails. What we can justify on Aristotle's principles is merely the statement that, given the situation described by Euclid (line *AB* falling on the straight lines *AC* and *BD*, angle *CAB* + angle **203** *ABD* being less than two right angles) there is a point *A'* on *AB* sufficiently near *A* such that a parallel to *BD* through *A'* meets *AC* on the side Euclid specifies. This does not, however, guarantee that the resulting geometry is Euclidean (in the present-day sense of the word); it only guarantees that it is *locally* Euclidean, as a non-Euclidean geometry can of course be.

It might be thought that this nevertheless makes no difference to the truths which we can prove about those geometrical configurations that in fact exist, that is to say, about those configurations that are 'in the sphere of real magnitudes' (207b33-4), in other words, that are wholly contained within the finite Aristotelian universe. This claim is not justified, however, for very often we can prove something about a given figure only by means of auxiliary constructions. (Aristotle was aware of this need and in fact keenly appreciated the role of these constructions.) These auxiliary constructions may require the existence of longer lines than any of the ones involved in the given figure. Hence we are back at the same difficulty.

Was Aristotle perhaps misled by his own terminology? In *Meta*. IX 9, he refers to a certain auxiliary construction as a 'division' (*diairesis*), and similar locutions occur elsewhere, too.[11] This suggests that he might have thought that our auxiliary constructions are mere 'divisions' in the sense that they never transgress the limits of the given figure. This assumption is gratuitous, however.

Thus we have to conclude that Aristotle's peculiar doctrine of the existence of a maximal spatial extension made it impossible for him to justify fully the practice of the geometers of his time. In particular, the use of Euclid's fifth postulate could not be reconciled with his doctrine. If understood according to the letter of Aristotle's statements, his physical universe is non-Euclidean: the axiom of parallels is not satisfied in it.[12]

Naturally, Aristotle could not have been himself aware of this conclusion. **204** In fact, it may be doubted whether he would have argued in the way he did if he had known that Euclid's fifth postulate is even prima facie an indispensable part of the usual system of geometrical postulates and axioms. In other words, Aristotle's theory of infinity makes us doubt whether the indispensability of this postulate was realised in Aristotle's time (or at any rate by Aristotle) as clearly as it was realised by Euclid. It may be indicative that in *Phys*. II 9, 200a16-18, Aristotle traces one of the theorems that turns on the axiom of parallels to the straight line's being 'such as it is' without specifying its nature in any more detail and without mentioning the

11. The same word is used by Aristotle at 203b17 of those 'divisions' of mathematicians which sometimes induce belief in the existence of the infinite. Here, too, mathematical *constructions* are probably meant.

12. Cf. Solmsen [261], p.173, n.57.

axiom of parallels. In the form in which it was stated by Euclid, the axiom of parallels would scarcely have been taken by Aristotle to express a part of the essence of the straight line, as the subsequent criticism of the postulate brings out. It has a form entirely different from the Aristotelian definitions that according to him expressed the essence of this or that thing.[13]

Far from containing 'a sort of prophetic idea' of a non-Euclidean geometry, as Heath suggests,[14] this passage might on the contrary indicate that the role of the axiom of parallels was not particularly clear to Aristotle. Elsewhere Heath argues himself, with reference to Aristotle, that the fifth postulate was not known before Euclid.[15]

Aristotle's compunctions about geometrical constructions were apparently shared by at least one well-known mathematician of antiquity. Heron *mechanicus* tried to dispense with the production of particular straight lines as much as possible, motivated by the idea that there might not always be enough space available to carry out such a production.[16] (It does not matter for my purposes whether Heron was himself worried about this or whether he was trying to reassure others.) In fact, Heron gave proofs of certain propositions in Euclid alternative to Euclid's own proofs. They were designed to dispense with the applications of Euclid's second postulate which justifies the production of straight lines. This line of thought is potentially very interesting, for if it had been pushed far enough, it would have led into difficulties not only in connection with Euclid's second postulate but also in connection with the fifth.

It is not impossible, however, that mathematicians' attention was unfortunately directed away from the fifth postulate by its explicitly hypothetical form: '*if* [the two straight lines are] produced indefinitely ...' This may have led Heron and others to think that the second postulate is the only one in Euclid that leads into trouble in connection with the finitude of the universe.

There are statements elsewhere in the Aristotelian corpus which seem to contradict the doctrine of the largest possible geometrical extension that we have found in *Phys.* III 7. The most important one is *Cael.* I 5, 271b28-272a7, which was in fact referred to by Proclus in his attempt to prove the fifth postulate.[17] There Aristotle says that the space between two divergent straight lines is infinite. This passage is, however, inconclusive. The principle Aristotle there seems to appeal to, if it can be accepted, suffices for Proclus' purposes. Aristotle's apparent argument for it is fallacious, however. Moreover, Aristotle is in any case conducting there a *reductio ad absurdum* argument against the alleged infinity of the world, and hence may have appealed to the principle in question merely because he thought that his opponents were committed to it. In any case, his argument is carefully couched in explicitly hypothetical terms: '*If* the revolving body be infinite, the straight lines radiating from the centre must be infinite.'

13. For one thing, typically Aristotelian definitions were equivalences, whereas the converse of the fifth postulate was demonstrable in Euclid's system.

14. T.L. Heath, [256], pp.110-1.

15. T.L. Heath, *The Thirteen Books of Euclid's Elements*, 2nd. ed. (Cambridge 1925), I, 202.

16. See Heath, *Euclid's Elements*, I, 22-3.

17. Cf. Heath, *ibid.*, p.207.

Apostle suggests that, according to Aristotle, a mathematician need not worry about problems occasioned by the finitude of the universe because 'it belongs to the physicist to investigate the shape and magnitude of the universe'.[18] The remarks of Aristotle to which he refers (*Phys.* II 2, 193b22-35) do not warrant this complacency, however. Aristotle's doctrine is that 'the geometer deals with physical lines, but not *qua* physical' (194a9-11). In other words, a geometer deals with physical lines by abstracting from certain of their attributes. (This is also suggested by *Parva Naturalia* [*Mem.*] 449b31-450a6.) Now the real problem here is that some of the lines which a geometer needs do not seem to be forthcoming at all, and of course *this* existential problem is not alleviated by the possibility of abstracting from certain attributes of lines. If the requisite lines do not exist, there is nothing to abstract from. In fact, Aristotle's words at 204a34 ff. show that he included the mathematical sense of infinity within the scope of his discussion, at least when he was arguing *logikôs*.

To return to the problems connected with the principle of plenitude, the doctrine that the infinite is in a sense actualised is apparently denied by Aristotle at 206a18-21: 'But possibility can be understood in more than one way. A statue exists possibly in that it will in fact exist. But the infinite will not exist actually.' This does not yet give us Aristotle's settled view of the matter, however, for he hastens to emphasise the peculiar sense of existence which is involved here, not the sense of potentiality that is being used. Hence the quotation does not disprove my interpretation.

In the last analysis, Aristotle's references to the 'merely potential' existence of the infinite tell us less of his notion of infinity than of his idea of genuine fully-fledged existence. This was the separate, independent (*kath' hauto*) existence of an individual substance. All the other modes of existence were viewed by him with some amount of suspicion, and were sometimes liable to be assimilated to 'merely potential' existence. The mode of being that belongs to the infinite is a case in point. Here the crucial consideration was clearly that there is no moment of time at which one can truthfully say: the infinite is *now* actualised, in the way we can say of an existing individual that it is *now* actually existent. Hence the burden of such Aristotelian remarks as the one just quoted is perhaps not so much that the infinite is not actualised but that it does not exist *as an individual* – that no infinite body exists or can exist. As Aristotle formulates his point:

> We must not regard the infinite as a 'this' (*tode ti*), like a man or a house, but must suppose it to exist in the sense in which a day or the games are said to exist – things whose being has not come to them like that of a particular substance (*ousia tis*), but consists in a process of coming to be and passing away (206a29-33).

When Aristotle says that the infinite 'will not exist actually', what he has primarily in mind is therefore merely the fact that there will not be any moment of time at which it can be said to be actualised. This does not go to show, however, that the infinite is not actualised in some other sense.

It would nevertheless be too rash to disregard contrary evidence

18. H.G. Apostle, *Aristotle's Philosophy of Mathematics* (Chicago 1952), p.79.

altogether. There are indications that Aristotle is himself hesitating between different views. It may be significant that some of the clearest statements to the effect that for Aristotle the infinite was in a sense actualised come from passages which appear somewhat parenthetical. This is clearly the case with the passage which was just quoted from 206a29-33; it is in fact considered by Ross as 'an alternative version which ... was at an early date incorporated in the text' (p. 556). The same may be the case with the words 'The infinite, then, exists in no other way' at 206b12-15 which do not contribute anything to what Aristotle is discussing there. It is also interesting to note that the passage we quoted earlier from 206a23-5 is missing from one of the manuscripts (*sc.* E). It almost looks as if we had caught Aristotle here in the process of changing his mind, or perhaps rather changing his emphasis. This assumption would also serve to explain Aristotle's reliance on the descriptions of the infinite as 'potential but not actual' which we have found to be unrepresentative of Aristotle's definitive statements on the subject.

The line of thought which these statements to some extent replace seems to turn on assimilating the mode of existence which the infinite enjoys to that of the material which, for example, may become a statue. This line of thought is seen from 206b14-16, 207a21-32, and 207b34-208a4. It is not obvious that it has to contradict the emphasis on the principle of plenitude which we found elsewhere; the two ideas seem to coexist happily in 206b14-16. The contrast between matter and form, however, is elsewhere (for example *Meta.* IX 6, 1048b1-8) assimilated by Aristotle to that between potentiality and actuality. Hence this seems to lead at least to a different emphasis in the case of infinity.

Another problem with wider implications comes up in the course of Aristotle's discussion of infinity. I quoted a statement to the effect that for Aristotle infinity is 'conceivable though never realised'. This was found to be a misleading formulation in that the infinite is in a sense realisable for Aristotle. It may now be asked whether the formulation is perhaps equally misleading in so far as the conceivability of the infinite is concerned. I shall argue that it is.

In general, there appears to have been little difference for Aristotle between actual physical realisability and realisability in thought. The difference between these two, should one make a distinction here, would be in effect a distinction between two senses of possibility, a distinction which bears some resemblance to our distinction between logical possibility and physical possibility. In most cases Aristotle completely fails to appreciate distinctions of this sort, even in cases where he would find it convenient to use it. How foreign the general trend of his thought is to such a distinction is perhaps seen by considering the equivalent distinction between two senses of necessity (the impossibility of conceiving of the contradictory to something versus the impossibility of actually realising the contradictory). The main burden of *Analytica Posteriora* is to make definitions, or truths essentially like definitions, the ultimate starting points of each science.[19] The way of coming to know the basic principles of a science is described by Aristotle as a way of coming to have the basic concepts of that science.

19. See, e.g., *A.Pst.* I 8, 75b31; II 3, 90b23; II 17, 99a22.

208

This idea has a neat counterpart in Aristotle's psychology. There we learn that thinking is an actuality and that the thinking mind is formally identical with the object of which it is thinking. 'Knowledge when actively operative is identical with its object' (*De An.* III 6, 431a1-2). In other words, in thinking of *x* the mind assumes the form of *x* and even in a sense *becomes* this form.[20] For this reason, the conceivability of a form entails that this form is in a sense actualisable. In being thought of, this form is actualised in the mind of the thinker: being conceivable is a form of being realistic.[21]

Of course, what is realisable in the mind need not for that reason be **209** realisable outside the mind, according to Aristotle. What makes the difference in such cases is apparently the material factor; what for Aristotle was realisable in one medium was not necessarily realisable in another. This is shown, for instance, by Aristotle's remarks on the Socratic paradox in *EE* I 5, 1216b6 ff. A man may know what virtue is – that is, the form of virtue may be present in his mind – but he may nevertheless fail to become virtuous. This is explained by Aristotle in terms of the material factor, which therefore is to be blamed for the failure of realisation in this case. A similar point is made in *Phys.* II 2, 194a21 ff.

When we discuss realisability without qualifications, however, we are discussing actualisation in any material whatsoever, and for this purpose actualisation in one's mind seems to serve perfectly well in Aristotle's view. In being able to bring about a certain result *x* the main thing was to have in one's mind the form of *x*. This was taken for granted by Aristotle; what he argues for in *Ethica Eudemia* is the further point that one must *also* have knowledge of the material 'out of which' *x* is to be formed.

It is not quite clear, however, exactly how Aristotle thought of the actualisation of the various forms in one's mind. In what kind of material are these forms realised? Is a bodily change involved? Is Aristotle dealing with the images which he says must accompany all thinking, or with thinking proper? What exactly is the distinction between these two? We cannot discuss these difficult and involved questions here. It may be pointed out, in any case, that the realisation in one's mind takes place in a material different from the ones in which forms are normally embodied outside us. Hence knowing an individual *x*, which involves having its form in one's mind, does not necessarily give us a capacity of realising the same (numerically the same) individual in one's mind or in any other medium, but only the capacity of reproducing the same form in some material or other.

What is also clear is that Aristotle repeatedly insists that actualisation in one's mind is in principle as good a sort of actualisation as any other. Aristotle wants to apply his principle that 'everything comes out of that which actually is' (*De An.* III 7, 431a3-4) to artificial products like houses or **210** to such results of skilful activity as the health which a doctor has brought about. In order to do so, he has to say that the process of building or of healing has as its starting point another actual instance of the form of house

20. See, e.g., *De An.* III 4-5.
21. Apostle (*op. cit.*, p.79) claims that, according to Aristotle, 'we may have thoughts of impossibilities'. In support of this view he refers to *Meta.* VI 3, 1027b25-27. But in this passage Aristotle is not discussing possibility and impossibility at all, merely truth and falsity, which are said to be 'not in things ... but in thought'.

or of the form of health – namely, the form which exists in the mind of the builder or of the healer. In *Meta*. XII 4, 1070b33-4 he writes: 'For the medical art is in some sense health, and the building art is the form of the house, and man begets man.' The analogy presented here shows that the form of a house that exists in the builder's mind is for Aristotle as good an instantiation of the form in question as the father of a son is an instance of the form of man. Essentially the same point is made more fully in *Meta*. VII 7, 1032b1-15 (cf. also *Meta*. VII 9, 1034a22-4). The obvious connection between these passages and Aristotle's discussion of the temporal priority of the actual in *Meta*. IX 8, 1049b18-29 shows that the thought (or image) which one has in one's mind when one knows *x* is for Aristotle as fully actual an instance of the form of *x* as an external object exemplifying this form.

This parity of actualisation in thought with actualisation in external reality is what leads me to say that for Aristotle conceivability implied actualisability. According to Aristotle, to conceive of a form in one's mind was *ipso facto* to actualise it.

This idea is also applied by Aristotle to mathematical entities. They exist only in thinking, but since thinking is an actuality, they are not any less real for this reason.[22]

A case in point is the existence of the auxiliary constructions or 'divisions' that are often needed in a geometrical proof. These divisions are obviously of the same kind as the divisions that are contemplated by Aristotle when he discusses infinite divisibility and are hence of immediate relevance to his theory of infinity. Of the 'divisions' or constructions needed in geometrical proofs Aristotle writes in *Meta*. IX 9, 1051a21-31:

> It is by an activity also that geometrical constructions [or theorems, *diagrammata*] are discovered, for we discover them by dividing. If the figures had been already divided, the constructions [theorems] would have been obvious; but as it is they are present only potentially. ... Obviously, therefore the potentially existing constructions are discovered by being brought to actuality: the reason is that a geometer's thinking is an actuality.[23]

Now this idea of conceivability as realisability in one's mind seems to fare very badly in Aristotle's discussion of infinity. Initially, Aristotle appeals to

22. Cf. esp. *Meta*. IX 9, 1051a21-33, to be quoted (in part) below, and *Meta*. XIII 3. There is something of a contrast between these two passages, however. At *Meta*. XIII 3, 1078a30-31 it is implied that mathematical objects exist *hulikôs* – i.e., by way of matter – whereas in the *Meta*. IX 9 passage it is stressed that 'a geometer's thinking is an actuality'. This appears to be a matter of emphasis, however. Cf. also Apostle, *op. cit.*, pp.11-17, and Anders Wedberg, *Plato's Philosophy of Mathematics* (Stockholm 1956), pp.88-9.

23. In interpreting *diagrammata* as theorems, I am following Heath (*Mathematics in Aristotle*, pp.216-17) who refers to *Cat.* 12, 14a39 and *Meta*. V 3, 1014a36 for further evidence. The context itself shows rather clearly that this is what Aristotle has in mind here. Cf. also Eckhard Niebel, 'Untersuchungen über die Bedeutung der geometrischen Konstruktionen in der Antike,' *Kant-Studien*, Ergänzungshefte, LXXVI (1959), esp. 92-5, where further references to the literature on this subject are given.

it in the way he might be expected to use it on the basis of what we have found:

> Most of all, a reason which is peculiarly appropriate and presents a difficulty that is felt by everybody – not only number but also mathematical magnitudes and what is outside the heaven are supposed to be infinite because they never give out in our thought (203b22-25).

Aristotle's words reflect the importance he attached to this argument. Nevertheless, it seems to be rejected in *Phys*. III 8, 208a14-19:

> To rely on mere thinking is absurd, for then the excess and defect is not in the thing but in thinking (*epi tês noêseôs*). One might think that one of us was bigger than he is and magnify him *ad infinitum*. But it does not follow that he is bigger than the size we are, just because someone thinks he is.

In fact, these words seem to indicate that Aristotle made a clear distinction between conceivability and actual realisability. If this were really the case, this passage would have important consequences for our interpretation of Aristotle's thought in general.

We can see, however, that Aristotle's purpose here is severely restricted, **212** and that it cannot therefore support any general conclusions concerning the relation of conceivability and realisability in Aristotle. The fact that Aristotle formulates his point in terms of 'excess or defect' shows that he has in mind only quantities, and indeed only spatial magnitudes. He hastens to point out (at 208a20-21) that his remarks do not apply to movement or time. There is no trace anywhere of an application of this idea to the other concepts which Aristotle had been considering and which he had mentioned at 203b22-25 – for example, to number or to divisibility. On the contrary, at 207b10-13 he seems to rely on the conceivability of a higher and higher number of divisions to establish infinite divisibility:

> But it is always possible to think of a larger number (*epi de to pleion aei esti noêsai*); for the number of bisections of a magnitude is infinite. Hence (*hôste*) the infinite exists potentially, although never actually, in that the number [of bisections] always surpasses any assigned number.

It is also significant that in reassuring us of the infinity of time and movement at 208a20 Aristotle adds thinking to the list. His point seems to be that in the case of time and movement, infinity in thought and infinity in fact go together. In fact, time and movement are at once contrasted by Aristotle to magnitude, which 'is not infinite either in the way of division *or of magnification in thought*' (208a21-22).

What Aristotle has in mind in 208a14-19 is his idea that although in thinking of *x* one's mind assumes the form of *x* (or, alternatively, makes use of an image having the form of *x*), it need not assume this form in the same size as the original. The replicas of outside forms that one has in one's mind are merely scale models of these forms, as it were. That this is what Aristotle had in mind is shown by *Parva Naturalia* (*Mem.*) 2, 452b13 ff.:

> How, then, when the mind thinks of bigger things, will its thinking of them differ from its thinking of smaller things? For all internal things are smaller, and as it were proportional to those outside. Perhaps, just as we may suppose that there is something in man proportional to the forms, we may assume that there is something similarly proportionate to their distances.

213

Hence Aristotle's whole point turns out to be this. Because of limitations of size ('all internal things are smaller'), a human mind can think of large things only as being large in relation to something else. Because of this, it does not follow that an imaginable size is realisable, because what is realised in one's mind is merely large in relation to something else, but not absolutely. It does follow that there is no limit to *relative* size; and this is in fact a conclusion in which Aristotle acquiesces at 206b3-9.

Thus Aristotle does not give up the general principle that conceivability (or imaginability) implies realisability, but only that this principle applies to the realisability of (absolute) sizes. It is only in the case of spatial 'excess and defect' that Aristotle can say that they lie 'not in the thing but in conceiving'. The form that is being thought of ordinarily lies *both* in the thing and in the conceiving or imagining mind.

There is even more direct evidence that for Aristotle infinity was not 'conceivable though never realised'. Properly speaking, for Aristotle infinity was inconceivable. In *Meta.* II 2, 994b20-7, Aristotle denies in so many words that we can apprehend an infinity. 'The notion of infinity is not infinite,' Aristotle says, thus emphasising that in the sense in which the infinite is not actualised in external reality it is not realised in thinking, either, for that would involve the realisation of an infinite form in one's finite mind. In the sense in which the infinite was for Aristotle unactualisable, in that sense it was also inconceivable.[24]

214

In general it may be said that Aristotle has a distinction which prima facie looks very much like a distinction between conceivability and actual realisability (or perhaps our modern distinction between logical and physical possibility) and which serves some of the same purposes but which from a theoretical point of view is entirely different. This distinction is used, *inter alia*, in *MA* 4, 699b17-22, and *De An.* II 10, 422a26-9. The corresponding (in effect, equivalent) distinction between two different kinds of necessity is even more familiar. It is often referred to as a distinction between absolute and hypothetical necessity. It is explained, *inter alia*, in *Phys.* II 9, *PA* I 1, 639b25 and 642a8, as well as in *A.Pr.* I 10, 30b31-4, 38-40.

24. By the same token, in the sense in which the infinite was in Aristotle's view conceivable, it was also actualisable. At 208a20-21 *noêsis* is accordingly said to be infinite in the same sense as time and movement, viz., 'in the sense that each part that is taken passes in succession out of existence'. It is well known that time and movement are according to Aristotle's doctrine in a perfect good sense *actually* infinite, viz., in the sense that there actually has been and will be an infinite number of moments of time and movements of bodies, although Aristotle does not usually express himself in this way.

The distinction between two senses of possibility can be characterised as a distinction between what is possible absolutely speaking (that is, in so far as we merely consider its own nature) and what is possible on certain conditions – for example, possible to us in our present circumstances. To use Aristotle's own example, if there are men on the moon, they will be visible in the ordinary unqualified sense of the word, though *we* cannot see them. It is important to realise that Aristotle is not here postulating two different irreducible senses of possibility but rather two senses, one of which is in effect definable in terms of the other. This interpretation is confirmed by Aristotle's terminology; he refers to the distinction by means of such locutions as *posachôs legetai* (204a2-3) and *legetai pleonachôs* (699b17). As I have shown elsewhere, Aristotle uses these expressions not of outright ambiguities, but rather of interrelated but different uses of one and the same word.[25]

The fact that Aristotle deals in this way with cases which we might characterise in terms of a difference between logical and physical possibility suggests that he either had no recourse to the latter distinction or else did not want to use it. In the unqualified sense of the word, conceivability implied for him realisability somewhat in the same way as it did later for Descartes.

There are in any case indications that Aristotle's distinction between intrinsic possibility and possibility under certain circumstances is different from the distinction he makes in his discussion of infinity between possibility in thought and possibility in actual physical reality. In the course of this very discussion, Aristotle also uses the former distinction, applied to a special case: **215**

> We must begin by distinguishing the various ways in which the term 'infinite' is used. (1) What is incapable of being gone through, because it is not its nature to be gone through ... (4) What naturally admits of being gone through, but is not actually gone through or does not actually reach an end (*Phys.* III 4, 204a2-6).

A comparison with Aristotle's remarks elsewhere suggests that this distinction between the different senses in which it is impossible to go through something is an instance of the distinction he makes elsewhere between different uses of possibility. Nevertheless, it is in no way related by Aristotle to the distinction between realisability in thought and realisability in actual reality which he makes later in his discussion of infinity. This strongly suggests that the two distinctions were not connected by Aristotle with each other.

Our discussion of the sense in which the infinite was conceivable for Aristotle shows that his theory of infinity does not constitute a counterexample to this relation between conceivability and realisability in Aristotle.

Our conclusions also help us to understand what Aristotle is really up to in his brief pronouncement on infinity in *Meta.* IX 6, 1048b14-17, and are confirmed by what we find there. If I am right, what Aristotle says in this

25. Jaakko Hintikka [101], Ch. I.

passage may be expressed as follows:

> The infinite does not exist potentially in the sense that it will ever
> exist actually and separately; it exists only in thinking. The potential
> existence of this activity ensures that the process of division never
> comes to an end, but not that the infinite exists separately.

This version follows Ross's translation fairly closely. Nevertheless it
requires a few explanatory comments.

(1) The first and foremost thing to be noted in this passage is Aristotle's
main conclusion. Understanding this conclusion is completely independent
of the difficulties which we may have in understanding the passage in other
respects. The conclusion is that the infinite does not exist *separately*
(Aristotle's word is *chôriston*). Now what would such a separate existence
mean for Aristotle? It is contrasted by him not with potential existence but
to the kind of nonseparate existence which, for example, qualities enjoy in
relation to the substances whose qualities they are.[26] The Platonists had
supposed that the forms exist separately, Aristotle tells us, and goes on to
argue that they were wrong and that the forms exist only in those things
whose forms they are and on whose existence their being is dependent.[27] In
the same way, Aristotle is here pointing out the peculiar way in which the
infinite exists. According to him, it depends for its existence on the finite
beings which one after another come into being.

In short, he makes here the same point we found him making in *Phys.* III
7. He is pointing out that the infinite *exists* in an unusual sense of existence,
not that it is potential in a new sense of potentiality. As he says himself in
introducing the subject of infinity, 'but also the infinite and the void and all
similar things are said to exist potentially *and actually* in a sense different
from that which applies to many other things' (1048b9-11).

(2) The second clause of the first sentence is sometimes taken to mean
that according to Aristotle the infinite exists *separately* only in thinking (or
knowledge, *gnôsei*). This is surely wrong. As we have seen, Aristotle's
doctrine is that the infinite does not exist as an individual (that is,
separately) in any sense at all.

Ross translates the clause by 'it exists *potentially* only for knowledge'. This
may quite well be right, although it does not quite square with Aristotle's
avowed purpose of showing that the infinite exists potentially *and actually* in
an unusual sense. The difference does not matter, however, since for
Aristotle each potentiality eventually actualises. For then we might equally
well render Aristotle's thought by saying 'it exists (potentially and therefore
also actually) only in thinking'. What Aristotle is bringing out here is not
any special way in which the infinite exists, but rather the way in which all
mathematical objects exist according to him.

(3) The second sentence of our quotation is very difficult to understand
and to translate. We shall not discuss here the philological details but refer

---

26. It is also contrasted with the mode of existence of mathematical objects which do
not exist apart from sensible particulars and which can be separated from them only in
thinking; see *Meta.* VI 1, 1025b27; XI 1, 1059b13; XIII 3, 1078a21-31; XIII 6,
1080b17; XIII 9, 1086a33. Cf. (2) *infra.*

27. Cf. e.g., *Meta.* VII 14-16.

the reader once and for all to Ross's comments in his edition of *Metaphysica* (II, 252-3). The main problem is whether the subject of the sentence is the phrase which may be translated 'the potential existence of this actuality' (or 'activity') or the phrase which may be translated 'the fact that the division never comes to an end'. Accordingly, we shall have a choice of two translations which run somewhat as follows: 'for the potential existence of this activity ensures that the process of division never comes to an end' and 'for the fact that the process of dividing never comes to an end ensures that this activity always exists potentially'. Ross points out that the philological evidence favours the former interpretation, but he finds in favour of the latter on topical grounds. These grounds are inconclusive, however, for they amount to taking Aristotle's statement at 203b22-5 as being accepted by him and viewed 'as a given fact'. We have already seen that Aristotle returns to the same subject in 208a14-19 and qualifies his earlier statement in certain respects. It is true that we have also seen that these qualifications are not nearly as sweeping as commentators have often taken them to be; but perhaps they should nevertheless warn us not to rely too much on 203b22-25.

The question is really this. In *Phys.* III 4, 203b18-20 Aristotle mentions as a putative proof of the actual (better: separate) existence of the infinite the idea that an endless coming-to-be (*mê hupoleipein genesin*) can only take place if there (actually) exists an infinite supply from which the things that are coming to be are coming from. In *Phys.* III 8, 208a8-11 Aristotle points out that this explanation is not needed. At 208a8-11, however, he does not give any alternative explanation, maybe because such an explanation is implicit in the rest of his discussion of infinity in *Physica*.

Now the statement at 1048b15-17 can be understood as offering just such an alternative explanation, formulated in terms of infinite division. The endless coming-to-be of further and further divisions is 'ensured' (Aristotle's verb is *apodidômi*) by the potential existence of the activity of dividing. Hence it is compatible with everything Aristotle says to follow the philological evidence and to parse Aristotle's sentence in a way different from the one Ross endorses.

It is seen, however, that something is still missing here. (This insufficiency of our interpretation so far may have been instrumental in leading Ross to the other reading.) How can the merely potential existence of the activity of dividing ensure that the actual process of dividing never comes to an end? The answer is of course that no genuine potentiality is for Aristotle a *mere* possibiltiy: if it continues to exist as a potentiality, it will ultimately be actualised. Hence the principle of plenitude supplies the link which our interpretation might prima facie seem to fail to provide.

Far from being incompatible with the principle of plenitude, the passage we have been discussing again turns out to presuppose it.[28]

218

28. In writing the present version of this paper I have profited from the friendly criticism to which Richard Sorabji and Peter Geach have subjected an earlier version of it, although I have probably failed to meet most of their criticism. I greatly regret that I could not take into account Professor Friedrich Solmsen's interesting and pertinent comments, which (through a fault of my own) reached me too late for the purpose.

11

G.E.L. Owen

Aristotle on Time

3   Aristotle's discussions of time in the *Physics*, principally in IV 10-14, remain
a classic source of argument for philosophers and historians of science. His
problems are often ours, and his solutions often enlarge our view of the
problems. Through Augustine his arguments continued to exercise later
philosophers such as Wittgenstein; through other post-Aristotelian schools
and commentators they shaped the debates on the subject in pre-Newtonian
science. Aristotle's chief concerns are the nature of the present, the reality of
time, and the relations between time, space and motion that he evidently
takes to show time both real and measurable.[1] So these are the issues in his
argument on which I shall concentrate.

The issues are directly linked, but there is a methodological interest
which may also help to draw the discussion together. I can best introduce
this by recalling, briefly and with apology, some suggestions made
elsewhere (Vol. I, pp.32-3 and nn.). It is a commonplace that Aristotle is
alert to philosophically important expressions which have more than one
sense or kind of use, and critical of philosophers who innocently build on
these without noticing the ambiguities they harbour. The fifth book of the
Metaphysics is given up to exploring thirty such sources of ambiguity. But in
a more positive mood, when he is pressing his own analysis of some key-
concept, there is often a different impulse in his treatment of such
expressions, and it does not readily mesh with the first. He is apt now to
start his explanation from some particular, favoured use of the expression
and deal in various ways with other sorts of use which do not seem to fit the
primary case though they bear some relation to it. (This notion of primacy
rightly exercised him (e.g. *Meta.* V 11, VII 1); we shall have examples to
discuss later.) One way of dealing with such recalcitrant uses seems to be to
4   argue them away; another is to extend and often to weaken his account of
the basic occasion of use to accommodate them; a third, and perhaps the
only one to deserve the name of a method, is to import a device or family of
devices, sometimes now discussed under the rubric 'focal meaning', which
enables him to marry his interest in the paradigm case with his interest in
the plurality of an expression's uses by explaining other kinds of use in
terms of one that he represents as primary.

The second of these ways does not concern us here: it can be illustrated
from many texts such as the analyses of change and finality in the first two

---

1. Since drafting these arguments I have seen a forthcoming paper on some of the
same topics by Professor Fred D. Miller, Jr., and felt able accordingly to shorten mine
at some points and push it further at others. (Professor Miller's paper has now
appeared: see [306].)

books of the *Physics*.[2] The others play substantial parts in Aristotle's analyses of time and motion; and I shall suggest that in fact the first is used where the third would be appropriate, and the third is used where the question of a primary use cannot properly arise at all. But such cavils on method are subordinate to understanding the argument. This is not primarily a study of method.

Motion at a moment

There is an important but still debated case where Aristotle seems so preoccupied with paradigm conditions of use that he rejects other uses of an expression – or, in this instance, of a family of expressions, the verbs of motion and rest. I mean his denial that there can be motion or rest at a moment, an unextended point of time.

(Some translators prefer 'instant' to 'moment'; that does not matter provided it is understood that Aristotle is talking of temporal points with no duration. What matters more is that the same Greek expression is the word for 'now' or 'the present'; but that connection, and the reason for it, will not concern us yet.)

Aristotle reasonably argues that any movement must be taken to cover some distance in some period of time; for movements differ in speed, and speed is a function of extended times and distances, one measured against the other. And an extended time is one in which different moments can be distinguished and ordered as earlier and later (*Phys.* 222b30-23a15). Not, of course, that he will allow a period to be regarded as merely a class or collection of the moments by which we can mark off subdivisions in it, any more than he will have a line built of points (231b6-10). Start, as Aristotle does, with the thought that points are produced by divisions of magnitude, and it comes to seem evident that however far such divisions proceed they will at any stage be finite in number and the points produced by them finite and separated by stretches which are the real factors of the magnitude. Still, if motion and velocity require some period of time within which different moments can be distinguished, one conclusion seemed to follow: there can be no talk of something moving, or therefore moving at any velocity, at one moment (234a24-31, recalled at 237a14, 239b1-2, 241a24-6). Nor yet can a body be said to be stationary at such a moment, as Zeno had argued;[3] for if movement entails being at different places at different moments rest surely entails being at the same place at different moments. If we consider only one moment neither description applies (239a26-b2).

Now the Greeks like ourselves could speak of a body as moving, and moving relatively fast or slowly, just when it reached a winning-post or overtook another body; and this, we may surely object, is to speak of movement as going on at a moment. Aristotle himself rejects Zeno's paradox that a slow runner pursued by a fast one 'will never be overtaken when running' (239b15-16, cf. 26-9). Our talk of a body as moving at a

5

2. Cf. 'The Platonism of Aristotle', Vol. I, 1.c.; 'Aristotle' in the *Dictionary of Scientific Biography*, ed. C.C. Gillespie, Vol. I, pp.254-5.

3. This is how Aristotle read Zeno's conclusion, and not merely as holding, as Ross suggests ([5], p.658) that the arrow is not moving (which Aristotle would accept, adding that it is not stationary either): see *Physics* 239b30.

moment is common usage, preceding any mathematical theory of limits
designed to accommodate it. No doubt it is in an important sense parasitic
on descriptions of the body as moving over distances through periods of
time, for our assessments of speed begin with these. To consider a body as
moving with some velocity at a moment is to consider it as moving at some
over-all speed or speeds during periods within which the moment falls.[4] We
can allow too that 'moving' has a different sense or use in the two contexts;
for we can ask how much ground the body moved over in a period, and we
cannot ask this of its performance at a moment. But between the two uses
there are familiar translation rules, rougher in ordinary discourse,
sharpened in post-Aristotelian theories of mechanics. When Aristotle rejects
the derivative use of such verbs he is rightly impressed, but unluckily over-
impressed, by the requirements of the paradigm case in which motion takes
so much time to cover so much ground. Hintikka has found another
instance of the same tendency in Aristotle's unwillingness 'to speak of a
possibility at an instant' ([101], p.162). His rejection of such ways of talking
of motion and velocity, force and possibility at a moment, seems to have
contributed to the final sterility of his mechanics ([321], pp.221-2). Yet the
author of the *Mechanica*, once ascribed to Aristotle and probably written not
6   much later (cf. [256], p.227), can resolve circular motion into two
rectilinear components, tangential and centripetal (848b1-849b19), and
make the remarkable suggestion that the relation between these
components must be instantaneous and not maintained for any time at all;
otherwise, so long as it was maintained, the resultant motion would be not
circular but in a straight line (848b26-7). This and other constructions in
the same author seem to be ruled out for Aristotle.[5]

But this objection to Aristotle itself faces objections. In pressing on him
one difference in the senses or uses of verbs of motion we may have given too
little weight to another. For there are two senses in which we might want to
deny motion at a moment: we might want to deny that at any moment a
1. body can *move*, carry out a journey from A to B; or we might want to deny
2. that at any moment a body can *be moving* from A to B. In English the senses
are divided between the non-continuous (perfective) and continous
(imperfective) forms of the verb; both are covered by the Greek present
tense, though in past forms the difference can be marked. Now there is good
sense in saying that a body cannot move at a moment, for this is only to say
that it takes time to make a journey. It would be a mistake to say that at a
moment a body cannot be moving, in transit between A and B. But surely, it
may be protested, it is the first point that Aristotle is making. And
considerations can be found to strengthen the protest.

First, the phrase I have rendered by 'at a moment' is more literally
translated 'in a moment'. That suggests that Aristotle is making the
legitimate point: a moment is not the sort of time within which a journey
can be carried out. On this view, he has grasped a mistake in Zeno's
paradox of the Flying Arrow, the paradox he introduces immediately after

---

4. 'Over-all', d/t, rather than 'average', which itself requires analysis in terms of
momentary velocities and is therefore doubly general.

5. Notice e.g. his refusal to assimilate circular and rectilinear motion in *Physics*
VII 4 (248a10-249a25).

denying motion or rest at a moment (*Phys*. 239a20-b9). In Aristotle's version of the argument – and we have none earlier – Zeno had held that at any moment in its path a flying arrow cannot cover more than its own length and hence (since, presumably, there is no room for movement then) is stationary (cf. n. 3 above). And what is true of it at each moment of its flight is true of it throughout, so the arrow is stationary throughout its flight. The second step of the argument, with its inference from the moments to the period, Aristotle attacks by saying that a period is not composed of moments (239b8-9, 30-3);[6] we gave some sense to this earlier and we shall meet it again. The first step he rejects by arguing that when there is no time for movement there is equally no time to be stationary (239a35-b4). In both | 7 replies he can be interpreted as locating Zeno's mistake in treating moments as cripplingly short periods of time, too small to move in and only sufficient for staying in one place. He corrects it, on this reading, by arguing that what cannot move *in* a moment cannot stand still in a moment either. *Move*, carry out a journey; not *be moving*, for the question what if anything can be contained in a moment can only be sharply discussed in terms of the first. Again, he often insists that motion is from one place to another and from one point of time to another (e.g. 224a34-b2, *EN* 1174a29-b5); and this can be taken to show that when he speaks of motion he always has in mind an X that carries out the journey from A to B, not just an X in transit between these points. A little earlier in the *Physics*, for example (237a17-28), he argues that whatever has moved must have taken some time to do so, for it could not have journeyed from A to B in an instant.

Does the issue have a disappointingly verbal air? The brunt of the protest seems to be just this, that Aristotle's rejection of motion at a moment is misrepresented in English by casting it in the continuous forms of the verb; translate it into the non-continuous forms and it is simply valid. Offer Aristotle a choice such as the past tenses in Greek allow, and (it is implied) he will choose wisely, confining his rejection to the former way of talking. But what has this issue of surface grammar to do with mapping the emergence of an exact science? Well, everything, as the protester recognises. The question is whether Aristotle does, in theory if not always in practice,[7] discard *all* talk of motion at a moment – including (and, as it will turn out, primarily) such talk as goes better into our continuous tenses. By such a rejection – and it is of course an argued rejection, not a mere confusion

6. T.M. Penner ([314], p.458) contends against some earlier arguments of mine that Aristotle 'has no *general* presumption against saying that if X was φ-ing throughout a period *p*, then at any moment *t* during *p* X was φ-ing' (or, we may add in view of Penner's argument, against the converse). 'It is just that this cannot be said with movement, or, more generally, with *kinêsis*' (the latter being Aristotle's word for all changes for which he takes movement in important respects as a model). So Penner holds that Aristotle would readily concede my point that if I am asleep at any and every moment of the afternoon I am asleep throughout the afternoon, and the converse; but this would not spoil his reply to Zeno, which is that where movement is concerned no such inferences lie between moments and periods, for sleeping is not a movement or *kinêsis* but what Aristotle calls an *energeia*. But by the tests proposed by Penner *being at rest* is also an *energeia*; and Aristotle denies that a body can be at rest at a moment.

7. The corollary for rest is ignored at *Phys.* 236a17-18.

G.E.L. Owen

drawn from an ambiguous Greek tense – he will equally debar himself from all talk of velocity and rest at a moment; and therewith debar himself from considering, as the author of the *Mechanica* can, the idea of a 'force' or 'strength' operating on a point whose resultant motion can be characterised only for that instant. So the protest deserves to be met.

First, so far from using the expression 'in a moment' to point a logical error, Aristotle takes it as an unexceptionable part of speech. He imports it earlier in his own argument in the *Physics* (234a24, 237a14), and in our context (239a35-b3) he says: 'In a moment it (sc. the moving body) is over against some static thing,[8] but it is not stationary itself ... What is true of it in a moment is that it is not in motion and is over against something ...' Translators commonly write '*at* a moment', knowing that the Greek preposition *en* has other senses than that of containment, and they are right.

Further, on the appeal to Aristotle's general account of movement it is sufficient to recall the theorems about moving bodies that he has defended just before his criticism of Zeno. One is that what moves, or is moving, must already have moved (236b32-237a17). *Moves*, or *is moving*: which? Surely the second, for it would be unreasonable to maintain that whatever makes a journey from A to B must have travelled previously (that way a pointless regress lies), but reasonable to say that something currently engaged in making that journey must have already come part of the way.[9] So too with the logic of 'coming to a halt', which Aristotle treats in parallel with that of 'moving'. He argues that, given a period in which something is coming to a halt, it must be coming to a halt in any part of that time (238b31-239a10).[10] Read 'come to a halt' instead of 'be coming to a halt', and the claim becomes nonsense. So does the connected claim that a thing is moving when it is coming to halt (238b23-9) if you substitute the non-continuous forms of the verbs. The point that 'the Greek present tense is generally imperfective' was made (and subsequently forgotten) by T.M. Penner in a recent paper.[11] For verbs of motion, at any rate, it holds good, and it explains much else in Aristotle's account of movement.[12]

8. I retain the *menon* of the mss. at 239a35-b1 against Prantl, etc.: what Aristotle says does not entail that the static body is static at that moment, and the repeated *men* is not needed.

9. The point is generally well taken by translators and commentators, together with the equally important point that the perfect tense is (of course) perfective, 'have moved' and not 'have been moving'.

10. The argument requires this, and not just that the object must come, or be coming, to rest in any arbitrarily late part of the time in which it is coming to rest. Any such time can itself be divided into others in any of which the coming to rest is proceeding quickly or slowly (238b26-30).

11. Point made, [314], p.400; neglected in the argument manufactured for Zeno, p.459 ('At a moment no distance is traversed', etc.). To speak of 'Aristotle's claim that there is moving only if there is a movement' is either misleading, if it is taken to support this rewriting in the non-continuous present, or transparently acceptable if all it says is that to be moving requires that a movement takes place from some A to some B – even though to be moving from A to C does not require the movement from A to C to be completed.

12. E.g. (i) the use of imperfect tenses as proxies for the present in *Phys*. 231b30-232a2, (ii) Aristotle's unreadiness to use the present tense in saying that A *becomes* B at a given moment rather than to say that it then has become or earlier was becoming B (e.g. *Phys*. 263b26-264a1).

In logic and in grammar, then, the defence fails. Aristotle can in theory allow no talk of motion proceeding at a moment. No doubt it might still be protested that the notion of an exact moment having no duration in time is only adumbrated, approached only asymptotically, in the common discourse from which Aristotle professes to set out in shaping the basic concepts of his physics.[13] Modern English can be more precise because it is heir to so much analytic thought on the issues, including Aristotle's. If Aristotle is refining a vaguer notion for technical use, he is surely entitled to stipulate conditions for its use. And if he discounts linguistic clues which lead to motion at a moment in order to safeguard clues which connect motion with periods, his dialectical method allows for that too.[14]

It is no reply to point to the resultant theory of mechanics, cumbrous and impoverished by comparison with the almost Newtonian insights of the *Mechanica*. Quite apart from the question whether we yet have a 'theory' on our hands, it was already a major advance in the science to insist that movement and velocity must in any final analysis be treated as functions of distances and periods. Not all advances can be expected at one time, or the papers in this volume[14A] would not have been written. But there is another reply to the protest.

Elsewhere in his analyses of time and motion Aristotle several times uses a device, or family of devices, which would have let him exploit the linguistic clues he jettisons, even while recognising that any talk of motion and speed at some moment in a period must be explained (no doubt roughly at first) in terms of motion and speed over periods. If there are two uses of 'moving' here, Aristotle knows ways of analysing a secondary use in terms of a primary without either conflating them or discounting the first. His stock examples of expressions amenable to such treatment are 'medical' and 'healthy': it is medical science that is called 'medical' in the primary sense, for medical treatment and medical instruments are so called as being a product of that science or adapted to its exercise, and the explanation could not proceed in the opposite direction (e.g. *Meta.* 1003a33, 1060b36-1061a7). These are nursery examples, but (in reply to the protester) when Aristotle puts such patterns of analysis to larger use in his philosophy, he is often trying to put a harder edge on ideas implicit in common speech. It is hard to deny that an entrée could have been found here for motion at a moment.

Yet when he does use such analyses in his treatment of time and motion we shall find other difficulties arising. Once try to mark off different uses of a key-expression and put them in some order of dependence, and it becomes a question how the primary use is picked out and what sort of primacy is being claimed for it. Let us turn to these troubles.

The primary use of 'now'

One example of the kind of analysis just sketched is his review in *Physics* III of uses of 'infinite' (which in this context signifies *infinitely divisible*, divisible

---

13. Owen, 'Tithenai ta phainomena', *Aristotle et les problèmes de méthode* (Louvain-Paris 1961), pp.83-103. Reprinted in volume I of *Articles on Aristotle*.

14. Thus *EN* 1145b2-5: if all the common conceptions on a topic cannot be vindicated, we must defend most and the most commanding.

14A. [Sc. the volume where this chapter originally appeared: see p. xi. Eds.]

into parts which are themselves always further divisible). He writes (207b21-5): 'The infinite is not one and the same sort of thing in the case of distance and of motion and of time. The term has a primary use and another dependent on it. Motion is called infinite because the distance covered by the motion is called so ... and the time is so called in virtue of the motion.' Notice the ordering, on which we shall find Aristotle putting much weight later: first the application to spatial magnitude, then derivatively to the motion which traverses it, then, by a further explanatory step, to the time taken. In his treatment of time in the next book of the *Physics* he repeats the claim (219a10-14, b15-16), substituting 'continuous' for 'infinite' (which in effect comes to the same thing); and then he argues from this[15] that the expressions 'before' and 'after' are also used primarily of spatial distinctions and only secondarily, 'by analogy', applied to movement and thence in turn to time (219a14-19).[16] At this stage of the argument I cite these only as illustrations of what Aristotle evidently regards as a valuable (though flexible, and perhaps too hospitable) form of analysis. The results must be questioned later, and that questioning is better approached by considering yet another example of the same technique.

In *Physics* IV 10-14 Aristotle gives much discussion to the character of *now* or *the present*. When he takes himself to have settled its character he says (222a20-4): 'This is one way we speak of *now*; it is another now we speak of when the time is near to that first now. We say "He is going to arrive now" because it's today that he's going to arrive, and "Now he arrives" because it's today he came; but not "Now the events in the Iliad have taken place" or "Now the end of the world" – not because the time stretching to these events (sc. from the present) is not continuous, but just because they are not near.' Not near, that is, to the primary now: but what is the primary use of 'now'?

In the set of puzzles with which Aristotle introduces his discussion of time he argues: How can time exist, except at best in some reduced and obscure sense? For part of it is past and exists no longer, part of it is to come and exists not yet; and between them this pair exhausts the whole of time and any particular stretch of it (217b32-218a3). If we object that this discounts the now, the present time lying between past and future, Aristotle counters with an argument that the now is no part of time; for (i) any part must serve to measure the whole of which it is a part, and (ii) time is not composed of nows.[17] But when a thing with parts has no part of it currently in existence, it does not exist itself (218a3-8).

The premisses (i) and (ii) should show us something of what Aristotle understands by 'now', but they are surely debatable. How is time not composed of nows? Take all the times that ever have been or are or will be present and that is surely all the time there could be: 1975 is present, 1974 was, 1976 will be, and so on, each year having its turn. So too with premiss (i): the present year can surely serve as a measure of time, inasmuch as

15. I read *dê* = 'therefore' with Ross at 219a14: cf. his synopsis of the argument, [5], p.386.

16. 'Analogy' covers but is normally wider than the asymmetrical relation of prior-posterior between different uses of an expression that is at issue here. Cf. Owen, 'Logic and metaphysics in some earlier works of Aristotle', pp. 24-6 above.

17. On the implications of this cf. n. 6 above.

(e.g.) a decade is just ten times its length. But, other objections apart,[18] it becomes clear that Aristotle will not have 1975, or any other period, as an instance of the now, the present he is trying to explain. For a few lines later (218a18-19) he says: 'Let it be taken that one now cannot be next to another, any more than one point can be next to another'. So the instances of *now* or *the present* that he is prepared to accept seem plain, and his later discussion bears this out. They answer, we may say (as he could not), to such time-references as '1200 hours 18 May 1974' *provided* this is somewhat artificially understood as fixing a point of time without duration. For on this understanding there is theoretically no *next* time-reference of the same order: however close we call our next reference, provided it has some finite value in the same system some period of time must have elapsed between the two within which a still closer reference could have been called. The spatial analogue is indeed the point.

But why should a point of time seem a satisfactory value of *now* rather than a present period such as 1975? So far from explaining this, our premisses (i) and (ii) merely presupposed it. But Aristotle's argument is not far to seek. It lies in the comment that past and future time together will be found to exhaust any period whatever (218a1-2). It is a line of reasoning that recurs in the Sceptics and perhaps most famously in the eleventh book of Augustine's *Confessions*. The present century, Augustine observes, is a long time. But is the whole century present? No, for we are living now in one year of it, and the others are past or to come. And so on down, through days and minutes, shedding whatever can be shed into the past and the future until we are left at last with the durationless present moment which has no parts to shed.

Here is trouble indeed. The present is like the point, and lines are not collections of points.[19] But we are not required to tackle the fairy-tale task of building lines out of points, for there are countless lines in the world that can be drawn and shown and used to measure other lines. When we use the edge of the ruler, it is of no use to know that the twelve-inch mark is to the right of the one-inch mark, or to wonder how many points to the right it is. Distance cannot be measured in points alone. But then how to measure times, when Aristotle's argument leaves us with no lines in time present, only present moments? And apparently all we can know of these is that one **12** is earlier or later than another, which is no more than knowing that the twelve-inch mark is to the right of the one-inch mark. Augustine was so exercised by this that he supposed that what we measure in time is a kind of proxy time-stretch held in our memory. Others such as Marcus Aurelius drew morals: each of us lives only in this instantaneous present. The morals may be excellent, but the argument is insufficient. Aristotle evidently

18. There are older arguments alleging the lacking of parallel between measurements of space and time and based on the possibility of transporting a rigid measuring-rod in space but not in time. Aristotle does not discuss this issue, and the rigid transportable measuring-rod has become an anachronism.

19. They can of course be treated as classes of points for many purposes, e.g. for the inference sketched in n. 6 above. Aristotle's principal objection relies on the Zenonian argument (p.141 above) that, on any common rule of division, no exhaustive division of a magnitude into points can be completed.

thought his paradoxes could be evaded even though he retained his account of the primary use of 'now'.[20]

The retrenchability of 'here' and 'now'

Let us start by considering a way of avoiding the first step into these paradoxes, and then look at Aristotle's way of retrieving the reality and measurability of time. Consider 'here' as the spatial counterpart of the temporal demonstrative 'now'. It is not an exact counterpart, as Dummett and others have pointed out,[21] but for the present argument it is close enough.

When Kingsley Amis entitled a book 'I like it here', it was not hard to find what he intended by 'here'. It became apparent from the disaffection he showed for those living beyond a certain perimeter – in fact, the English coast; and he might well have wanted to narrow that perimeter too. The compass of his 'here' was settled by what he took to lie outside. The same holds good of 'now'. If we are told, once more, that we live now in an Age of Anxiety or an Age of Violence we shall be clearer on our informant's meaning if we find him, for example, relegating the Boxer Rebellion to the past tense and providing for the future by saying that if certain détentes follow quickly he will retract his observation as spoken too late or too soon. Such dismissals into the past or the future are all we usually require or assume in taking ourselves to understand a claim about the present. Of course there are certain semantic rules that must not be broken except in artificial situations: I must not as a rule relegate the whole year 1975 to the past or the future tense when I am speaking in that year, for instance. But within the application of such rules it remains true that what a speaker counts as present can be seen from what he counts as past or future or both; and the Greeks were as flexible in this as we are. When Plato talks of the order of nature that obtains *now*, he shows the scope of his 'now' by contrasting the present with a pre-historic past age in which the order was reversed (*Politicus* 273E).[22] What a speaker consigns to the past or future – subject to those semantic rules – depends on his immediate purposes and subject-matter (as well as, no doubt, on his training and culture). That is why it can vary, as it familiarly does, from utterance to utterance.

This is troublesome to one like Aristotle who aims to bring uniformity into the linguistic procedures taken over by a science. But if 'here' behaves in this respect like 'now', it is tempting to find a counterpart to Aristotle's paradox about 'now'. Suppose I tell you 'It's all public land here', and you ask 'What do you mean by *here*? Just this field, or more?' Repeating 'here', with whatever emphasis and gestures, is useless. What will help will be to specify land and landmarks that lie inside and others that lie outside the

13

20. There is a question here: given that the paradoxes are not systematically and directly answered in the sequel, how and when were they prefaced to the argument? Compare the question how the paradoxes of *Metaphysics* III were given their present place.

21. M.A.E. Dummett, 'A Defense of McTaggart's Proof of the Unreality of Time', *Philosophical Review* 59 (1960), p.500.

22. *Politicus* 270D6-E1 does not say or imply that in some sense the order of time was reversed in that other age; even if it did, the point would not be affected.

borders of whatever my spatial demonstrative was meant to cover. Given an interest in a smaller stretch of land or a different interest in this one (say, the placing of a rare plant), the scope of my 'here' could have been narrowed by counting more things into the surroundings, to left or right or beyond. There is no one reason for setting the frontier closer or farther: the demonstrative carries no privileged reference to a measure of ground that could not for another purpose be narrowed. Let us say, for short, that 'here' is retrenchable.

But then it might be argued that, understood strictly, 'here' cannot be taken to pick out any stretch of ground. For if there is no stretch such that part of it could not equally be counted as *here* and the rest consigned to the surroundings, there is no reason to stop at any of these arbitrary and dwindling frontiers in trying to determine what really answers to 'here' on any occasion of using it to make a spatial reference. What really answers to it is of course something within which no relegations to left or right or beyond are possible. In its paradigm use, 'here' must on any occasion pick out a point of space. Given that use it can be allowed, derivatively and on sufferance, to indicate any stretch of land containing or (I parody Aristotle's account of 'now') near to that point.

As an account of our use of spatial demonstratives this is absurd. In settling the scope of the statement 'It's all public land here', we had no need (and probably no time or technique) to come to an agreement on the identifying of some unextended spatial point. To understand 'here', as to understand 'now', the idea of retrenchability for different purposes is essential, and that of picking out an unextended point is not.[23]

This would be a sufficient answer if the pseudo-paradox about 'here' were **14** a sufficient parallel to Aristotle's paradox about 'now'. But there is an asymmetry that seems to tell against it, and no doubt this is why Aristotle does not extend his temporal paradox to space. Past and future, we are inclined to protest, are not comparable to left and right and yonder, just because what *can* be counted on any occasion as past *is* then irretrievably past: it is not up to the speaker to retrieve it by deciding, within certain semantic conventions, what he will then count as past and hence as present. With space it is otherwise: what is counted as lying to the left for one purpose can on the same occasion be included in the central ground for another purpose, for all such options remain open in a space all of whose parts remain accessible. No doubt an observer falling ineluctably like an Epicurean atom in one direction might think of any fixed landmarks he had passed (if there were such landmarks) as irretrievably above or behind. Spatial logic might then match temporal logic. And, conversely, there have been attempts to give sense to the suggestion that progression in time could have more than one direction, like movement in space. But, as things are, the asymmetry seems undeniable so long as we stay within the confines of 'here' and 'there' and 'now' and 'then'.

There are difficulties in this argument; but I cannot pursue them here

23. Of course one can imagine, under artificial conditions, a situation in which my utterance of 'now' or 'here' will pick out a point of time or space for my hearer. Suppose the chronometer set up to start just when I start to say, 'Now I see him pass the starting-point': I could not say it without being able to say, 'Now he is running fast'.

beyond asking whether Aristotle is entitled to such a reply after some further arguments we have yet to examine about spatial and temporal order. Those arguments we shall meet when we come to consider how Aristotle tries to vindicate the reality of time in the face of his paradox. But there is another issue to be considered first.

The now and the moment

In the opening discussion of motion and rest I made much use of the notion of a moment which occupies no stretch of time. In discussing Aristotle's treatment of 'now' I have made more use of it. In the first discussion I warned that the same Greek expression which is translated 'moment' in some contexts is the normal Greek for 'now' or 'the present'. Someone impressed by the argument from retrenchability might argue: what Aristotle says of 'now' makes poor sense of that expression, but good sense of our talk about moments. Is it not, after all, the idea of a moment that Aristotle in his discussion of time is trying to explain? Perhaps by Aristotle's day the expression has acquired a conventional sense in philosophical contexts which depends on discarding the presentness and stressing the momentariness of a *now*. After all, he refuses to be upset by the paradox he retails. He does not directly confront the argument that, if all present time is momentary, all we have as materials from which to build time is a class of moments which by their nature cannot serve as building materials. In *Physics* IV 11 (219a10-b2) he sets up a parallel between the distance covered by a moving body, the movement that it performs, and the time taken by the movement. He remarks there (219a25-30, 220a14-21) that, just as between any two points on the ground there must be a distance which is not a collection of points, so between any two nows some time must elapse which is not composed of nows. Read 'moments' for 'nows', and the claim becomes recognisable and valid. In fact, we may feel, it is better served by casting it in those tenseless forms of speech which allow us to treat of moments as standing in a linear order of earlier and later without either explicitly or implicitly importing a reference to the present or its concomitants the future and the past.[24] Science needs the bedrock of the first, not the shifting sands of the second.

The suggestion would be a mistake and an anachronism. Aristotle does not discuss the nature of moments in abstraction from the idea of the present. His paradox about the unreality of time plainly has teeth only if it is understood in his terms, as contrasting a present that exists with the non-existent past and future, not as making the perverse suggestion that there are only moments and not days. Nor, and here I agree with Hintikka, is he near to grasping the idea of tenseless statements; Parmenides and Plato came closer.[25] In his other arguments on time the word for 'now' brings together what seem to us two distinct concepts, that of the moment and that of the present. When he speaks of the lapse of time as marked by different

24. *Generalized* references to future, present and past go without remainder into this form: cf. Nelson Goodman, *The Structure of Appearance* (Cambridge, Mass. 1951), pp.298-99.

25. Hintikka, [101], ch. iv; Owen, 'Plato and Parmenides on the Timeless Present', *Monist* 50 (1966), pp.317-40.

15

nows in an order of earlier and later (219a26-30), we think of moments. When he speaks of the now as progressing through time in a way comparable to that of a body progressing through a movement, collecting different descriptions according to the stage it has reached (219b22-33), we think of the present as something continuously overtaking such successive moments and leaving them in the past. When he claims to show how the now is perpetually different yet perpetually the same, since on the one hand there is a succession of nows (219b13-14, cf. 219a25-9) yet on the other there **16** is the one progressing now (219b22-8), we cannot think of him as distinguishing the two concepts but rather as conflating them.

How then are the two wedded in the one expression? And how far was the divorce managed by Aristotle's successors?

In reply to the first question we might hazard that, once Aristotle had argued himself into the belief that in its strictest use 'now' must always denote a present moment, the word became for him, by a natural extension and in default of any technical Greek equivalent, the stock expression for any moment. Such extensions of usage are common enough with him (cf. Vol. I, pp.32-3 and nn.). We might alternatively father Aristotle's 'now' on Zeno, recalling the account of the Flying Arrow in which the arrow is stationary at any *now* of its flight (239b7, 32). Neither reply is enough. Aristotle's version of the Arrow, even if we could reconstruct the text with certainty, may be a recasting in his own terms of what he takes to be Zeno's point. And there is a fuller and more secure precedent for Aristotle's usage, one in which we can see 'now' being tailored for its philosophical use, and one which must have shaped the recasting of Zeno's argument if any such recasting took place. I mean an argument in that treasury on which Aristotle drew so extensively for his own *Physics*, the second part of Plato's *Parmenides*.[26] Given the importance of Zeno in that dialogue I have no doubt that his paradox stands behind the argument, but I shall not debate the extent of the debt.

Plato is coining puzzles from the logic of growing older (*Parm.* 152A-E). Nothing will be lost for our purposes by replacing his special subject 'the one' by a neutral 'X', or by omitting arguments which offer to show that if X is becoming older it is also becoming younger.

The reasoning Plato puts into Parmenides' mouth is this:

> Whenever in this process of becoming older X is at the time that is *now*, between *was* and *will be*, then X *is* older. After all, in its journeying from the past to the future it is not going to skip the now. So whenever it coincides with the now, at that time it stops becoming older: at that time it is not becoming, but just is, older. For if it were moving on it could never be caught by the now: what characterises something moving on is that it is in touch with the future as well as the now, letting go of now and laying hold of the future and carrying out a change between the two. But then, given that nothing in process of change can by-pass the now,[27] it stops becoming on any occasion

26. For the documentation cf. n. 13 above.

27. F.M. Cornford, in *Plato and Parmenides* (London, 1939), p.187, translates the 'by-pass' (*parelthein*, 152B7) by 'it can never *pass beyond* the present', suggesting that

17   when it is at the now, and then is whatever it may be becoming.[28] So
it is with X: whenever in the process of becoming older it coincides
with the now, forthwith it stops becoming: then it *is* older.

Then (152E1 ff.) Plato generalises this to cover X's whole career.
'Moreover the now always accompanies X throughout its existence, for
whenever X is it is *now*. So X always *is* older, not just becoming so.'

Generally it is poor practice to isolate any argument in the *Parmenides*
from the network of paradox that it serves, but this has a special interest for
us. It shows 'now' being groomed for its Aristotelian part. First Plato
maintains that *now* X cannot be becoming so-and-so, and only is so-and-so:
if it is getting older, or moving to the left, it cannot be engaged in the
business now; now it can only be older or further to the left. And then he
argues that this conclusion can be generalised for the whole of X's career:
whatever holds good of X must hold good at some time that is then present,
a time that is then properly called 'now'.

The second arm of the argument seems innocuous. It generalises on the
uses of one temporal demonstrative, at the price of one kind of referential
opacity; but the possibility of such generalisation is already assumed in the
first arm. Plato does not go on to say that sooner or later every time becomes
a present time, or that a time only exists when it is present. Otherwise he
might have been vulnerable not only to some of McTaggart's paradoxes but
to a dilemma of Aristotle's (*Phys.* 218a14-18). For when does a moment
cease to be present? Not at the time of its own occurrence, nor at any later
time; for the first requires it to stop when it is still present, and the second
requires it to linger to a later moment and so stretch into a period of time.
The dilemma is artificial, depending on treating a moment as something
with a career in time and not as itself an element of time. But Plato does not
court this difficulty. Nor does he pursue, what this second arm of his
argument suggests, the Aristotelian image of the present as progressing
through time. He avoids the language which presents Aristotle with another
paradox (218b13-18). For Plato the nonsense-question, how quickly the
present proceeds on its path, does not arise.[29]

It is the first arm of the argument, then, that carries the load. Why cannot
we say that X is growing older, or the arrow is flying, now? Because, Plato
argues, such descriptions make tacit reference to the future as well as the
18   present. It could not be the case that X is becoming older unless at some
later time X will be older than it now is; it could not be the case that the
arrow is moving unless it will later be in some place other than where it is

---

Plato means that it cannot break out of the present. What Plato means is that it
cannot avoid or side-step the present.

28. Cornford (*loc. cit.*) translates here as 'whatever it may be that it was
becoming', a possible imperfectival past sense of the participle but not relevant to the
argument, which is to show that for a chosen X ('older') if *a* is becoming X, then at
any given present time *a* just is X.

29. C. Strang ('Plato and the Instant', *Proc. Arist. Soc.*, Supp. Vol. 48 (1974), pp.63-
79) draws other inferences from the text translated, together with an earlier reference
to time as moving on (152A 3-4) – a reference at once replaced by an innocuous
description of the subject as 'proceeding temporally' (not, *pace* Mr. Strang, as
'keeping pace with time'). His interpretation is not adopted here.

now. Otherwise the flight is at an end, the business of growing older is finished. So if we are to say only what is true of the subject now, we have to eliminate this future component from our description. The arrow is now in just the place it occupies, X just is older. The second is Plato's example, and it seems ill-chosen; for if X is now older, it is older than it was, and this implicit reference to the past should be excluded together with references to the future. *Now* X is just whatever in time it happens to be. But Plato uses the Greek idiom 'X is (or becomes) older *than itself*', and this obscures the point as well as furnishing him with other paradoxes.[30]

What more is there in Plato's argument than we found summarised (surely because it was now too familiar to spell out) in Aristotle's? Nothing, so far as I can see. But here is Aristotle's 'now' in the making. Its retrenchability is discounted by shedding from its scope whatever can be relegated to the future (and, Aristotle adds, to the past). So 'now' becomes a paradigm way of referring to a moment, and the way is open for Aristotle to extend it to all moments. But only by considering them all as becoming sooner or later present, in the sequence future-present-past. The word never came to signify the 'moment' of the translators or of our detensed text-books in physics. It kept its connotation of time present, the sense on which the arguments of Plato and Aristotle were built.

So the two senses, that of the moment and that of the present, stay wedded in the one expression, and we have to turn to our second question: was the appropriate divorce arranged later in Greek philosophy? I think it was, but the evidence has been sometimes misread.

Consider what Chrysippus the Stoic is reported to have maintained about time present. According to Plutarch (*Comm. Not.* 1081c-82a), his contribution to the topic consisted chiefly in three theses. First, there is no such thing as a shortest time (1081c); secondly, the now is not something indivisible (*ibid.*); thirdly, any part of present time can equally be taken to be past or future (1081d-82a). Here, surely, is our retrenchable present. Elsewhere in their physics the Stoics were ready enough to admit indivisibles: they insisted, as Aristotle had before them (and to the scandal of Plutarch), that contact between bodies is not the juxtaposition of some smallest possible parts or volumes of those bodies, for there are no such volumes; contact is a function of surfaces without depth or of points without magnitude (1080e-81b). But they were clear that such indivisibles were not the model on which to explain our use of 'now'.

Although I cannot be sure that the Stoics have our point clearly in view, I am sure that they once had less than justice from one of their most persuasive sponsors, Samuel Sambursky. In *The Physical World of the Greeks* (p. 151) he had this to say concerning the third thesis credited to Chrysippus: 'This formulation, with its definition of the present as the centre of a very small, but still finite, portion of time, is clearly an attempt to comprehend the elements of time as finite "quanta" and not as extensionless points. The present thus becomes, so to speak, an "atom of time", or, to use the language of the calculus, a differential of time.' A little later he said: 'So great was the desire of the Stoics to give a clear answer to the paradox of the

19

arrow, that these bitter opponents of the atomic hypothesis and ardent champions of continuum and no compromise had to have recourse to an "atomic" solution.'

But not only is atomism in general just as repugnant to Stoic physics as Sambursky recognises, the suggestion that 'now' is always or primarily used to identify some time-atom is incompatible with the first two of Chrysippus' propositions and, as soon as it is reconsidered, with the third. Sambursky's belief that even for Chrysippus the use of our temporal demonstratives must ultimately reduce to a reference to just one sort of time-element – if not moments, then atomic times or real infinitesimals of time – seems to be one more sign of the spell that Zeno's Arrow or its interpreters cast on philosophy. It is this spell that Chrysippus seems anxious to break.

Priorities and parallels between space and time

We left Aristotle in the grip of his paradoxes. Only the present is real, yet the present is never a stretch of time and time must consist of successive stretches, not of unextended moments. Moreover time is a function of change (218b21-219a10), but nothing can be changing at a present moment. How can time be real? Yet later Aristotle claims to have said of time both that it is and what it is (222b27-9). How does he break free?

His reply is that there could not be a present moment *without* time, any more than there could be time without a now (219b33-220a1). He argues it by developing a detailed analogy between temporal and spatial structure. Just as there cannot be points without lengths that they divide and join, so there cannot be temporal points – 'nows' – without periods that terminate in such points, and specifically the stretches of time past and time future that meet in them (220a9-11, 222a10-12). The idea of a now that is not the boundary of a period is vacuous, and the idea of a period that is merely a collection of boundaries is absurd. Indeed, to notice that some time has elapsed is just to notice such a temporal boundary, and remark that something is true now that was not true at another moment once called 'now'. Both nows are limits of a period housing a change, and the change has taken time (219a22-b2). And if the change is of a certain sort, a regular and continuously repeated motion, time can be measured. Aristotle's ideal chronometer is of course the cycling of the astronomical system (223b12-224a2).

He is anxious to allow that the analogy between points and present moments is not complete. When we pick out a spatial point that divides a line, we can say, 'This point is the end of segment AB' and then, indicating the same point, 'This point is the beginning of segment BC'; but temporal points do not loiter to be picked out twice in this way (220a12-18, cf. 222a13).[31] It is not the most questionable element in his analogy, as we shall see.

The outcome is that, so far from shedding the past and future as unreal, the present cannot do without them (222a10-12). It might seem indeed that without his spatial analogy Aristotle already had sufficient grounds for this

31. This seems the most direct interpretation of his argument and appears to agree with Ross's 'we must in thought pause over the point, as it were' ([5] p.602).

conclusion, for his arguments and those of the paradox-mongers he wants to disarm are in an important sense general: they are meant to apply to *any* present time, and so assume an inexhaustible range of different values for the variable. Hence his question whether the now of which we speak is always one thing (our inescapable fellow-traveller, as he seems to represent it later, collecting different descriptions from one stage of its progress to another) or always different. From this he might even have come to recognise those detensed forms of statements we desiderated earlier (cf. nn. 24 and 25 above). But he did not; and the generality in question was not his reason for reclaiming the past and future as co-adjutants to the present. His reason was the parallel he worked out between the logics of space and of time.

Before looking harder at that parallel one point seems worth making. With the past and future restored, there seems to be no reason to shy at uses **2 ¹** of the present tense (or therewith of the hospitable 'now') to describe occurrences or states of affairs that take time, even if the present is finally a mere point of time. To the extent that the analysis of such descriptions imports a reference to periods or points of time lying beyond the present moment, the reference can be divided between the past and the future. That is the option left open by Plato's argument in the *Parmenides*, where the reality of past and future is not called in question, and it seems to be the option Aristotle would adopt. Yet it generates a curious regress of analysis. Suppose we analyse 'X is walking to Tring this afternoon' as 'X is *now* at some place *p*, and until now X has been walking to *p* this afternoon, and after now X will be walking this afternoon from *p* to Tring'. Then we must provide some comparable analysis for the components relegated to the past and future tenses, for they go proxy for some present-tense statements that are true at some time before or after our now. More nows (in Aristotle's sense) must accordingly be introduced, and once more the time-stretches and their contents that we want to provide for are dismissed into the before and after, perpetually eluding us like Alice's jam. The readiest way of avoiding the regress is of course to reject at the start the analysis in terms of a *now* without duration. But is the regress noxious? Yes, if it is made an epistemological argument. If the identification of some now is the prerequisite of understanding any talk about a period containing that now, our understanding cannot get started. And just that requirement on our understanding of nows and periods seems to be maintained by Aristotle (219b28-33).

Let us come to the spatial parallel by which Aristotle assures himself of the reality of stretches of time and thereby of past and future. He introduces it near to the start of his positive account of time (219a10-21), after arguing that a lapse of time can neither be any sort of change nor yet occur independently of any change. It cannot be the first, for any change is a change in this thing or at that place, and time cannot be localised in this way: it is common to all things and places that share it (218b10-13). Moreover time does not go, as changes go, quicker or slower, for 'quick' and 'slow' are determined by, and not properties of, the passage of time (218b13-18). But neither can there be time without change. Here his first reasons are questionable: he argues (218b21-9a10) that we do not *notice* that time has passed unless we notice at least some mental change in ourselves; **22** and later (223a21-9) he even suggests that there could not be time if there were not a mind capable of counting off and measuring time, even if there were some change going on which would otherwise supply material for the counting and measuring. It is no comfort that he prefaces this last suggestion with an argument that any change entails time, since it can proceed more or less quickly (222b30-223a4). What we need is an argument that any time entails change. For that conclusion his reason seems to be that we do not recognise time if we do not recognise a change we can measure by it. The reason is not enough, and later mechanics dispensed with it.

Still, grant that though time is not change it can always be plotted against change. Aristotle asks us to think of three lines and evidently draws them on his blackboard (an anachronism: it would have been a whiteboard). One represents the distance covered by a movement, the next represents the movement over that distance, and the third represents the time taken by the movement. Call them 'D', 'M' and 'T', as he does not. About these lines he

a   b   c   D   argues two things. First, they are parallel in structure,
a'   b'   c'   M   all three being continua having parts which can be
a"   b"   c"   T   correlated, so that each of them can be measured by its

neighbour: time by motion and vice versa, motion by distance and vice versa (220b14-32). Moreover we can take a particular point on M (b') as representing the moving body at that stage of its movement and correlate it with the appropriate spatial and temporal points (b, b") on D and T (219b12-220a21).[32]

Secondly (and this is the stronger claim, though it comes first in his analysis), spatial order is somehow basic to the others: the structure of D prior to that of M, and that in turn prior to the structure of T. 'Since the moving object is moving from something to something' (e.g. from a to c in our diagram), 'and since every magnitude is a continuum, the movement answers to[33] the magnitude: movement is a continuum because magnitude is a continuum. And time is so because movement is so, for we always take the amount of time that has elapsed to correspond to the amount of the movement. Thus (cf. n. 15 above) *before* and *after* are found primarily in location, where they depend on position; and since they are found in the magnitu. D) 'necessarily they are found in movement too, by analogy with those there' (sc. the before and after in D). 'But in turn *before* and *after* are found in time, because the one always answers to the other' (sc. time to movement).[34] This claim of priority (219a10-19) he recalls later (220b24-8, cf. 219b15-16, 220a9-11). It is the last example we shall meet here of the pattern of analysis we desiderated in his treatment of motion at a moment, and found present but questionable in his account of 'now'. Here too its use is questionable.

As a preliminary question, what sort of priority or basicness has he in

32. At 219b19 I read a comma after *auto*, and *hê* for *ê* before *stigmê*: Aristotle says 'the point (on my diagram) is (to be taken as) either a stone or something of the kind'.
33. The verb is *akolouthein*; Hintikka ([101], pp.43-7) makes a case for reading it in some contexts as expressing either compatibility or equivalence, but here as usually it does not stand for a symmetrical relation.
34. *Physics* 219a19, *thâterôi thâteron*: 'the one to the other', not 'each to each'; Simplicius and the Loeb version have it right here, the Oxford and Budé, wrong.

mind? Elsewhere, and notably in *Metaphysics* V 11, he distinguishes some main uses of 'prior' and 'posterior' (cf. pp.18-19 above). It is worth notice that he gives spatial order an earlier place in his account than temporal order (1018b12-19): that suits his analysis in the *Physics*, but it reverses the explanation in the post-predicaments of the *Categories*, if these are his work (14a26-9). But, more important, he distinguishes between what came to be called ontological and epistemological priority. Sometimes, as here, he brings 'priority in definition' under the second head (1018b32-3), sometimes he distinguishes the two more sharply (1028a34-b2); once (in our context, 1019a11-14) he implies that the epistemological is a kind of extrapolation from the ontological, the priority 'by nature and substance'. But the distinction holds firm. If A is prior to B 'by nature', then A can exist without B but not B without A. If A is prior 'for knowledge', the understanding or explanation of B requires that of A, and not the converse. There are different ways of understanding and explaining, and this priority can accordingly go different ways (1018b30-1019a1); what matters for present purposes is that the epistemological priority does not entail the ontological, nor vice versa (cf. pp.18-19 above).

Aristotle might have believed that there could be space but no movement over it; but then it could not be measured (220b28-32), and this he rejects. He might even have believed, for the brief span of one argument we noticed earlier (223a21-9), that there could be movement without time; but this too he consistently rejects elsewhere (e.g. 222b30-223a4, 232b20-3). Ontological priority is not what interests him here. He wants to show that spatial order is conceptually basic to the rest, that by starting from this we   **24** can explain the order of movement, and at another step the order of time, without circularity – i.e. without importing into our explanations the things they were meant to explain. The enterprise fails. But enough remains of his parallel between space and time to make an argument for time's reality.

He argues first that, since the distance D is a continuum, so is the movement M over D; and since M is, so is T, for the time taken varies with the extent of the movement (219a12-14). Already we feel a qualm. The parallel between D and T relied, for a first step, on the parallel between D and M: the size and divisions of the movement corresponded directly to the size and divisions of the ground covered. But the time taken does not correspond equally directly to the ground covered, for speed can change. To bring the M/T parallel into line with the D/M parallel, we shall have to say that *at a given speed* the greater distance requires both a greater movement and, in the same ratio, a greater time; but this is to reimport the notion of speed, which employs the idea of time as well as of distance. The qualm can be met by giving up the requirement of a direct ratio between M and T or between D and M, and therewith the simple model of measuring one by its neighbour. Perhaps all we need to retain of the argument is the suggestion that (to put it roughly) further on in space is further on in the movement, and so further on in the time. But this is just the claim that spatial order is basic to the rest, and that claim seems untenable.

Spatial before-and-after is relative to some more or less arbitrarily chosen position on a line (cf. *Meta.* 1018b12-14). Thus on D, b is before c relatively to a if and only if ac contains ab but ab does not contain ac. Similarly b is before a relatively to c, because ac contains bc but bc does not contain ac.

Now if temporal order is to be explained by the order of motion on such a line as D, evidently the motion must have a direction: for instance, on M, b′ must precede c′. But can this direction be derived from the spatial before-and-after we have just defined, without importing just the temporal priority we meant to explain? Evidently not. We might define a direction *abc for D, by saying that ac contains ab but ab does not contain ac; but of course we could on the same terms define the direction *cba. It is of no use to think we have given the movement a temporal direction by saying that it is on a line for which the spatial direction *abc can be defined, for the opposite direction can equally be defined for that line. It is just as useless to suppose we have given it such a direction by saying that the body moving on abc may move over ab without moving over ac but not vice versa – hoping thereby to indicate that by moving from a towards c it may reach b but not c. For this is compatible with its moving from b to a. And if we try to sharpen the condition by specifying where on the line the movement begins or ends, our explanation of temporal order becomes immediately circular. Spatially the movement can take either direction, temporally it can take only one. Just this was what prompted the earlier qualm about our appeal to retrenchability.

If Aristotle hopes to show spatial order conceptually prior to temporal order, the attempt fails. But does this spoil the general parallel between space and time by which Aristotle hopes to meet the paradox of time's unreality? Surely not, for the gist of that was that in both cases there cannot be points without the stretches they join and bound. The moment 5.30 and the period from 5.30 to 6 are interdependent. Time is left with periods which are, in Aristotle's sense, 'measures' of time. What he says of this goes admirably, as we can put it now, into a tenseless language of moments and durations. But it does not meet the paradox that at any real present the measurable stretches of time are behind or in front of us; that, as Marcus Aurelius holds, 'each of us lives only this momentary present' – with the possible comfort he derives from this, that dying is no loss since we cannot lose a past or future that is not real now.[35]

---

35. *Meditations* vii 27, ii 14; both references I owe to Professor Miller's paper (n. 1 above).

12

Richard Sorabji

Aristotle on the Instant of Change

The problem

'The train leaves at noon', says the announcer. But can it? If so, when is the last instant of rest, and when the first instant of motion? If these are the same instant, or if the first instant of motion precedes the last instant of rest, the train seems to be both in motion and at rest at the same time, and is not this a contradiction? On the other hand, if the last instant of rest precedes the first instant of motion, the train seems to be in neither state during the intervening period, and how can this be? Finally, to say there is a last instant of rest, but not a first instant of motion, or *vice-versa*, appears arbitrary. What are we to do?

This is not only an intriguing puzzle. It has some further importance, because I think we must decide how to handle it *before* we can decide how best to define motion or rest at an instant. Aristotle's answer also has some historical significance. One of his solutions, a denial of motion or rest at an instant, has been picked on for impeding the progress of science. Here I want to suggest a solution to the puzzle, which turns on treating motion differently from rest. I want then to argue that Aristotle was attracted by a second solution very close to the one I shall advocate, and that his treatment of dynamics can to this extent be reassessed. In an appendix, I shall suggest that some versions of the puzzle also bear on recently revived problems about vague concepts. The puzzle has had a long history. It is to be found already in Plato's *Parmenides* (156C-157A), and it had a great revival in mediaeval times.[1]

Does it apply to the real world?

First we need to consider whether the problem could apply to the real world. It may be doubted whether it could, for the statement of the problem involved a number of assumptions. First, I assumed (what Aristotle argues in the *Physics*)[2] that time is continuous. This has many implications. It

1. This revival has been discussed by Curtis Wilson in *William Heytesbury*, Madison, Wisconsin 1956, and now in an illuminating paper by Norman Kretzmann, 'Incipit/Desinit', in Machamer and Turnbull (eds), *Motion and Time, Space and Matter*, Columbus, Ohio 1976, pp.101-36. This should be read by anyone interested in the continuing history of the subject. Professor and Mrs Kretzmann plan further publication on the mediaeval treatments.

2. Aristotle argues in the *Physics* that time and space are both continuous. The point in space is like the instant in time, in not being a very short line, or having any size. It is the boundary of a line, and (*Phys.* VI 1, 232a6-11) it cannot be next to

70   means that time will be infinitely divisible, and there will be no such thing
as a time-atom, that is, an indivisible period with an indivisible duration.
An instant will be not a time-atom, nor any kind of period, but rather the
boundary of a period, itself having no duration. Instants, unlike time-atoms,
cannot be next to each other. Rather, between any two instants, there will
be another, indeed, an infinity of others. This is what is involved in time
being continuous, and our problem will apply to the real world only if time
is so. If there were time-atoms, so that time was not continuous, the train
would be in its old position at one time-atom, and in a new position at the
next. The earlier time-atom would be the last time-atom in the period of the
train's resting; the later time-atom would be the first time-atom in the
period of the train's moving,[3] and our problem would not arise. The
problem does arise, however, if Adolf Grünbaum is right[4] that neither
quantum theory, nor anything else in modern physics, has given us reason
to deny that time is continuous.

Another reason why someone might question whether our problem
applies to the real world is that a train consists of a mass of moving atoms,
and so does the railway track. Can the train have any *first* instant of motion,
or last of rest, if its atoms are moving all the time, and how would these
instants be defined? Yet another doubt concerns the fact that a train is not
perfectly rigid. When some parts of the train, or of the engine, have started
to move, other parts will be lagging behind, so that there is not a single first
instant of motion or last of rest for the train as a whole. Both these doubts
can be met by raising our problem not about the train as a whole but about
some point within the train, such as the centre of mass, and its first instant
of motion and last of rest, in relation to some point on the railway track.[5] In
talking of points, rather than of trains, we will be moving beyond the range
of observable entities.

So far as I can see, then, our problem does apply to the real world, in as
much as it applies to unobservable points on a real train. But two further
things need to be said. First, the problem would still be of interest, even if it
applied only to a world different from ours. Second, we have so far

---

another point. Aristotle is well aware that other views had been taken. Some people
had believed in atomic spatial magnitudes, and Aristotle spends a lot of time
attacking them (*Phys.* VI 1, 2, 4, 10, VIII 8).

3. Its motion would be discontinuous; for continuity of motion involves occupying
intervening positions between any two; and even if we imagine space to be
continuous, so that there are intervening positions between any two, we are
imagining time to be discontinuous, so that between adjacent times there will not be
intervening times at which intervening positions can be occupied. Aristotle makes
related points in his attack on atomism. Discontinuous motion would result, he
argues, if there were atomic motions or distances (*Phys.* VI 1, 232a6-11), or if the
moving object were of an atomic length (*Phys.* VI 10, 240b31-241a6).

4. Adolf Grünbaum, *Modern Science and Zeno's Paradoxes*, Middletown, Connecticut
1967.

5. It may be objected that if the atoms of a body are forever joggling, and if their
motions are not equal and opposite so that they cancel each other out, then the centre
of mass will also be for ever moving, so that it will have no *first* instant of motion. We
may reply that, even if this is so, we can still ask about the first instant of motion (and
last of non-motion) of the centre of mass in a *given* direction, or in response to a *given*
force. I shall neglect this complication in what follows.

considered only one version of the problem, and if this version were   **71**
inapplicable to the real world, it might still be the case that other versions
were applicable. Thus far I have considered only the transition between rest
and motion. But our problem can be raised, and was raised by Aristotle, in
connexion with other kinds of transition. He discusses the transition from
being one colour to being another colour, from being non-existent to being
existent, and from being invisible to being visible. (The last will be
discussed in the appendix). In each case, the question can be asked: when is
the last instant of the old state, and when the first instant of the new? Or
moving from time to space, we may be able to ask where is the last point of
the one state, and the first point of the other? In some of these new forms,
the question may well apply to our world.

Proposed solution for cases of continuous change

With the problem now stated and generalised to apply to all kinds of
transition, we can start making some suggestions about how to handle it.
But first we should be clear how much we need to ask of a solution. The
original question was about when the last instant of the old state occurs,
and when the first instant of the new. One of the difficulties about
answering was that if we said that one of these instants existed, but not the
other, we seemed to be being arbitrary. It would be a sufficient solution, if
we could show that it would not be arbitrary to prefer one instant to the
other. For this purpose, we need only show that there is a reason for
preferring one to the other; we need not show that it is mandatory to do so.
On this basis, I would suggest that there is a solution available for those
cases where the earlier state, or the later state, or both, consists in a
continuous change. We can illustrate by considering a transition from rest   *why?*
to motion and back again to rest, provided that the motion is construed as
continuous, not jerky. By this I mean that the motion involves passing
through an infinity of points, between any two of which there are other
points, which are also passed through. Ordinary usage is not precise, but
leaves it indeterminate whether we should regard the instant of transition
between rest and continuous motion as an instant of motion or not. We   **72**
must therefore make a recommendation about how to regard it, if we want
to solve our problem. Fortunately, there are at least two considerations
which would justify the decision to call it an instant of rest.

First, there is an asymmetry between the series of positions away from the
position of rest and the position of rest itself. There can be no first *position*
away from the starting point, or last *position* away from the finishing point in
a continuous motion, or in any other continuous change. Hence there can
be no first *instant* of being away from the starting point or last *instant* of being
away from the finishing point. No such considerations apply to being at the
position of rest. This already supplies us with a solution to our paradox, in
some of its applications. For if someone were to ask, 'when is the last instant
of being at the position of rest, and when the first of being away from it?', we
could safely reply that the latter instant does not exist. But we can go
further. The asymmetry between the position of rest and the positions *away*
from it can provide us with the excuse we want for treating rest differently
from *motion*. It would be perfectly reasonable to mark the asymmetry by

saying that just as there is no first or last instant of being *away* from the position of rest, so equally there is no first or last instant of *motion*. It would be reasonable, but not mandatory. Reasonableness is all we need in order to escape the charge of arbitrariness.

In more detail, my idea is this. If we are going to introduce an asymmetry between motion and rest, it is not arbitrary to introduce it by denying first and last instants of motion, rather than the other way about. This is not arbitrary because we must in any case admit that there can be no first or last instants of being away from the position of rest. And the period of motion is in *other* respects a period of being away from the position of rest, if we ignore for a moment the problematic instant of transition.[6] Thus if we introduce the asymmetry between motion and rest in the direction I recommend, we will be aligning the asymmetry between motion and rest with an already existing asymmetry, and this is not arbitrary. Contrast the opposite decision, according to which it is rest that lacks first and last instants. Certainly, that decision is theoretically possible, but it would be an arbitrary one, because the asymmetry introduced would not be aligned with an already existing asymmetry. Indeed, it would fly in the face of one, for when something started moving, the state of motion on which it was embarking would be assigned a first instant, while the state of being away, on which it was also embarking, would not be. In other words, of the two theoretically possible ways of introducing an asymmetry, one is not arbitrary because it has the backing of an asymmetry which is always there, while the other does not.

My second consideration is this. Let us suppose that not only change of place is continuous, but also change of velocity. In other words, in passing from one velocity to another, an object passes through all the infinitely many intervening velocities. Once again, quantum theory has nothing to say against this assumption. If it is made, then there cannot be a first or last instant of having a velocity greater than zero, for there is no first or last velocity above zero. There is, however, no corresponding objection to there being a first or last instant of having velocity zero. Now it seems more natural, though again it is not mandatory, to connect zero velocity with rest, and velocities above zero with motion. If we do, we get the result that there is no first or last instant of motion, but that there may be first or last instants of rest.

These two arguments are based on slightly different strategies. The argument about an already existing asymmetry is only meant to show that it would be *permissible*, not that it would be *desirable*, to deny first and last instants of motion. It shows that *if* we deny this, we shall not be open to the threatened objection of arbitrariness in preferring this asymmetry to the opposite one. This is not yet to say that the decision is positively *desirable*. To show that, in the absence of obstacles, the decision is *desirable*, I appeal to the existence of the paradox I begin with, the paradox about whether the train can start. The asymmetry I recommend would solve the paradox; that

6. We must also ignore the special case in which the object moves back through its position of rest, as Norman Kretzmann has pointed out to me. Even so, for each instant of moving back through the position of rest, there will be an infinity of instants of being away from it. So this exception seems too minor to upset my claim that the asymmetry I recommend is aligned with an already existing asymmetry.

is what makes it *desirable*. It would be in line with an already existing
asymmetry; that is what makes it *permissible*. The status of the second
argument, the one about velocity, is different. For I there try to show that
the asymmetry I advocate is not merely permissible, but positively
desirable, on the basis of considerations *other* than the existence of our
paradox. I appeal instead to the naturalness of associating motion with
velocities above zero.

In arguing for the non-arbitrariness of the decision to deny first and last
instants of continuous motion, I am not saying that the period of motion has
no boundary. It will have an instant bounding it on either side, and my only
question has been whether that instant should be regarded as one at which
there is motion, or rest.

I do not deny that there are considerations which point to the opposite
decision, that the instant of transition is after all one of motion, and it will
be as well to bring one of them into the open. A doubt which might be raised
is whether change of acceleration always behaves in the same way as change
of velocity. We have supposed that velocity always changes continuously.
But does acceleration, the rate of change of velocity, always in its turn
change continuously, or can it jump discontinuously from zero to, say, one
foot per second per second? A similar question could be raised about yet
higher derivatives, such as the rate of change of acceleration. Nonetheless, I
do not think our solution is seriously threatened. On the one hand, if
acceleration does change continuously, there will be no first instant of
acceleration above zero, and so we will have yet further incentive to deny a
first instant of motion. On the other hand, if acceleration were sometimes to
jump discontinuously from zero to something higher, we should admittedly
have no obvious general reason for choosing between talk of a last instant
when acceleration is zero and a first instant when acceleration is above zero.
But even if on some of these occasions we were to talk of a first instant of
acceleration above zero, the considerations we rehearsed earlier would still
be strong enough to make us hesitate before calling that first instant of
positive acceleration an instant of motion.

74

In spite of this defence, our proposal must be understood in a flexible
spirit. We should recognise that for everyday purposes, and for many
scientific purposes, it simply does not matter which way one talks. One's
choice can legitimately be based on the most transient of reasons, or on no
reason at all, while the reasons we have given can without penalty be
ignored. The point of our reasons is simply that they are available to rebut
the charge of arbitrariness in case of need. If a discontinuous jump from
zero acceleration were to occur, and if in the context our whole interest were
in the acceleration to the exclusion of position and velocity, and in the
positive acceleration, rather than in the zero acceleration, then our reasons
for denying a first instant of motion might be overridden in that particular
context; and this would not matter. The point is that we would still not be
forced to be arbitrary.

The solution suggested does not in any way preclude physicists' talk of
initial velocity. For the initial velocity of a projectile is not a first velocity in
its entire motion, but merely the first velocity which it is convenient to
consider for the purposes of a given calculation. We should also recognise
that the last instant of rest in relation to one point may, of course, be an

instant of motion in relation to a different point. Throughout we must be understood as talking of rest or motion in relation to a *given* point.

75   The solution will apply not only to continuous motion, but to all changes which are continuous in the same sort of way. It will apply to changes of size, of temperature, or of colour, if these involve a continuous progress through a series of points between any two of which others are traversed. It will not apply to *discontinuous* changes, or to other processes or states which lack this kind of continuity. If, for example, we considered the transition from not singing to singing, we should not have the same reasons to deny a first instant of singing. Clearly, arguments based on direction or velocity would be inapplicable. It might be thought that something like our first argument would still be applicable, for the singing lasts through a continuous series of instants, and there can be no first instant after the instant of transition. But our first argument cannot in fact be applied, for it depended on the *asymmetry* between the single position occupied during a period of rest and the continuous series of positions occupied during a period of motion. In the case of singing, there is no asymmetry, for there is a continuous series of instants traversed during the period of non-singing, just as much as during the period of singing.

One might expect the proposed solution to appeal to Aristotle, for in his attack on the atomists he is at great pains to insist that motion, time and space are all alike continuous.[7] He argues hard against the atomists that what has moved must previously have been moving (*Phys.* VI 1, 232a6-18; VI 6, 237a17-b22; VI 10, 240b31-241a6); it cannot simply have *jerked* into its new position (232a6-11; 240b31-241a6). It was his successors Diodorus Cronus and Epicurus (or his followers)[8] who were willing to accept jerky motion. Nonetheless, we shall later see that Aristotle's solution is somewhat more complicated.

Treatment of other cases

Our solution leaves a very large range of cases unsolved. For often neither the earlier state nor the later state is a process of continuous change, as we have remarked. The transition may be from one colour to a different colour,

76   from non-existence to existence, or from invisibility to visibility. In these cases, what considerations are there, to help us to a decision? If we are watching a receding aeroplane, or looking for an approaching one, we cannot normally tell at the time what will prove to be the last instant of visibility as it recedes, or the last instant of invisibility as it approaches. If we want to register this instant as it arrives, we shall normally have to wait until the new state is upon us, before we can do so, and it may then reasonably be held that we are not registering the end of the old state, but, at best, the beginning of the new. This means that, in many contexts, we have a good reason for not talking of the last instant of the old state, but (if it has one) of the first instant of the new. This solution seems to have appealed

7. For the continuity of motion in *Phys.* VI, see VI 1, 231b18-232a18; VI 4, 235a9-37; VI 5, 236a7-27; VI 6 throughout; VI 10, 240b31-241a6.

8. Diodorus Cronus, according to Sextus Empiricus *Adv. Math.* X.48; 85-6; 91-2; 97, 102, 143, cf. 120. Epicurus or his followers, according to Themistius, *Phys.* 184.9, and Simplicius, *Phys.* 934.24.

to Peter of Spain, for certain kinds of case.[9] But it needs to be noticed that our interest is not always in registering the instant as it arrives. We may instead want to discuss the instant of transition prospectively or retrospectively. So the present consideration does not provide a solution for all cases, or even for all the cases Peter of Spain applies it to.

Aristotle himself may have another consideration relevant to the particular example of visibility. For he classifies seeing as an *energeia*, and on one interpretation, an *energeia* has no first instant. This is how J.L. Ackrill[10] interprets Aristotle's idea (e.g. *Sens.* 446b2) that 'he is seeing' entails 'he has seen'. Ackrill treats the perfect tense 'he has seen', like 'he has *been* seeing', as implying an earlier period of seeing. This interpretation has been disputed,[11] but if it is correct, it implies that there will not be a first instant of seeing, and therefore not a first instant of seeing the approaching object in Aristotle's problematic example, to be discussed in the appendix below.

The various considerations we have mentioned do not begin to cover all the cases there are. There may well be unique considerations attaching to particular occasions of discussion. And we must add that there may well be cases in which there are no adequate considerations to guide us. In these last cases, we shall not be able to answer the question, 'what is the last **77** instant (or point) of the one state and the first of the other?' The most we shall then be able to do is this. If our questioner happens to assume (without reason) that one of the instants (or points) exists, we shall always be able to tell him that in that case the other does not exist.

Two rival solutions

An entirely different way of trying to cope with our problem has been advocated by Brian Medlin in his paper 'The origin of motion' (*Mind* 1963). Medlin says, in effect, that a thing can be both in motion and at rest at an instant, and equally neither in motion nor at rest at that instant. The first may sound as if it violates the law of contradiction, the second as if it violates the law of excluded middle. But Medlin avoids this, by simply defining motion at an instant, and rest at an instant, in such a way that they are neither contradictories nor contraries of each other.[12] Given his definitions, all four statements can be true together, namely, that a thing is in motion at an instant, not at rest at that instant, and that it is at rest at

---

9. According to Kretzmann, *op. cit.* It looks as if Peter of Spain failed to see that whether one's interest is in identifying the instant as it arrives is quite independent of whether one is discussing what he calls 'permanent' states, or 'successive' states, or the beginnings or endings of either.

10. J.L. Ackrill, 'Aristotle's distinction between *energeia* and *kinesis*', in *New Essays on Plato and Aristotle*, ed. R. Bambrough, London 1965, esp. pp. 126-7.

11. Disputed by L.A. Kosman, 'Aristotle's definition of motion', *Phronesis* 1969, and Terry Penner, 'Verbs and identity of actions', in *Ryle*, ed. Oscar Wood and George Pitcher, New York 1970.

12. In effect, he defines 'it was in motion (not at rest) at instant t' by saying something like 't was either followed, or preceded, or both, by a period throughout which it moved'. And he defines 'it was at rest (not in motion) at instant t' roughly as 't was either followed, or preceded, or both, by a period throughout which it did not move'.

that instant, not in motion at it.

My objection to this is not so much that it runs the risk of causing confusion, but that it is not sufficient to solve the problem that interests us. Medlin is free to define motion at an instant and rest at an instant in such a way that they are not contradictories or contraries of each other. But he cannot, and does not, deny that there *is* a contradictory of the claim that something is in motion at an instant. He himself suggests a way in which we might formulate the contradictory. We could talk of its *being the case that* something is in motion at that instant. Once we have found a formula for picking out the contradictory, we can pose our original problem all over again in terms of the new formula. We shall simply ask what is the last instant when it is *not* the case that our object is in motion, and what the first instant when it *is* the case that it is in motion. To this question Medlin himself would agree that we cannot say it is the same instant. When the problem is posed this way, we see that we shall have to fall back on a different solution from Medlin's, such as the one, we have advocated, according to which there can be a last instant when it is *not* the case that our object is in motion, but not a first instant when it *is* the case that it is in motion.

A second rival solution has been called by Norman Kretzmann the neutral-instant analysis, and ascribed to Aristotle. I do not find it in Aristotle myself,[13] although there is something more like it in Plato, *Parmenides* (156C-157A). It differs from the two solutions I shall ascribe to Aristotle, even from the first one, because that first one will deny that there is motion or rest at *any* instant, and will thereby fall foul of modern dynamics. The neutral-instant analysis avoids this; it allows that there can be rest or motion at an instant, and denies rest or motion only at the instant of transition between motion and rest. In thus avoiding Aristotle's difficulties, however, it pays a price. For it assumes that at most instants a body *must* be in motion or at rest. The question then arises how it can *avoid* being in motion or at rest at the instant of transition. It would not be enough simply to *stipulate* that it avoids this, on the grounds that in this way we can

---

13. The first difficulty about finding the neutral-instant analysis in Aristotle is that he seems in his first solution to deny motion or rest at *any* instant. It might be replied that he only means that an instant has no duration within which a thing could get any distance – and indeed some of his arguments do seem to suggest only this. This would leave him free to go on to say (a) that at an instant a thing can nonetheless be *in course of* moving or resting, and (b) that it is so at all instants, except the instant of transition between motion and rest. This would amount to the neutral-instant analysis. But, first, I do not find statements (a) and (b) spelled out by Aristotle. And, second, there are three places at which Aristotle's argument would actually suffer if he allowed (a), without more ado. These three passages are VI 3, 234a34-b5; VI 6, 237a11-17; VI 8, 239a3-6. In the first passage, Aristotle cites our paradox in order to show that nothing can move at an instant. If it could, then at the instant of transition it would both move and rest. If, in spite of this denial, Aristotle were prepared to allow (a), then his remark here would leave us wondering how he escapes saying that at the instant of transition a body is both in course of moving and in course of resting. This would surely be the place for him to add, if he really held (a) and (b), that although he concedes (a), that a body can at an instant be in course of moving or resting, he still escapes the paradox, because (b) withholds this concession from the instant of transition.

win free of the paradox. It needs to be shown *how* it can avoid this, given that at *other* instants a thing has to be either in motion or at rest. To show this, we need some consideration, independent of the existence of the paradox, to show us that it is right, or at least permissible, to say that it avoids being in motion or at rest at the instant of transition. I do not rule out such a consideration being found, and if it is, the neutral-instant solution might either replace mine, or be put alongside it, depending on the nature of the consideration. But I think the consideration has yet to be given. And it would not do simply to define motion or rest at an instant, so as to make the instant of transition neutral. This would only raise the question what consideration made it right or permissible to define motion or rest at an instant in this way rather than in one of the other ways.

There is one special instant for which the neutral-instant analysis may well be a good one, and that is the instant of reversing direction. We can imagine the centre of mass of a ball travelling vertically upwards and slowing down until it reverses direction at an instant, without pausing for any period of time at the apex of its journey. We will now have an extra incentive for denying that the centre of mass is in motion at the instant at which it is at the end of its upward journey. For not only will its velocity be zero at that instant, but we could not say that its motion had one direction rather than the opposite direction at that instant.[14] This favours our saying that at the instant of reversal the centre of mass is not in motion. But there is a consideration, which I acknowledged in my original paper, but whose import I perhaps failed to consider sufficiently, which could make it reasonable to say that the centre of mass is not at rest either. This is that at the instant of reversing direction, the centre of mass is (as in all cases of coming to a halt) at a different position from that occupied at preceding instants, and also (differently from ordinary cases of coming to a halt) at a different position from those occupied at succeeding instants. There is thus no sameness of position at all, and since sameness of position is important to the concept of rest, this may make it reasonable to say that the instant of reversing direction is not one of rest. In that case, since it is not an instant of motion either, it will be a neutral instant, an instant of non-motion.[15]

It would take a further argument, however, to show that the neutral-instant analysis is viable for ordinary cases of coming to a halt or starting off.[16] In case a suitable argument is found, I would simply make two points.

14. Someone may object that we are in any case committed to motion without any particular direction. For imagine that the centre of mass of a ball is deflected only slightly, so that it does not stop moving, but at the same time is deflected at an angle rather than in a curve. In that case, we shall be unable to assign the earlier direction rather than the later at the instant of deflection, in spite of wanting to describe the ball as moving. It can be replied, however, that if deflection, in cases where there is no stopping, is always in a curve (since otherwise there would be discontinuity in the velocity in some direction), it will be possible to assign a direction to the motion at any instant, by taking a tangent to the curve. And in that case, we are not committed to motion without a particular direction.

15. I am grateful to Colin Strang for pointing out to me the implications of my acknowledgement.

16. One argument that might be urged is that even if, on starting off, a thing is at the same position as it occupied at arbitrarily close *preceding* instants, it is at a *different* position from those occupied at arbitrarily close *succeeding* instants. This *difference* of

First, the neutral-instant analysis shares my view that the instant of starting is not one of motion, and should therefore welcome my argument that the velocity is zero. Second, if the paradox were put in terms of a choice not between motion and rest, but between motion and non-motion, then the neutral-instant analysis would make an asymmetrical choice parallel to my own, and reject motion.

Aristotle's treatment. Preliminaries (i): The four main kinds of change and the thesis that they all involve a gradual transition

I shall now turn to Aristotle's solutions of the problem. He is well aware that different kinds of case need different solutions, but, not surprisingly, he looks for solutions of some generality, and does not acknowledge that the matter might ever be decided by the unique interests of a particular context. We shall suggest that in the case we are going to discuss, Aristotle is attracted by two solutions. Sometimes, like us, he denies that certain continuous changes can have a *first* or *last* instant, without, however, making it very clear that it is the continuity which precludes this. At other times, he goes further, and denies that there can be change or stability at *any* instant.

Before expounding his two solutions, we shall have to make some preliminary points clear. A first thing to notice is that Aristotle recognises only four kinds of change as being changes in the full sense of the word. There is change of quality (as when something changes colour), change of place (in other words, motion), change of size (in growth and diminution), and finally the creation or destruction of substances (*Phys.* III 1, 200b32-201a16; cf. V 2; *Meta.* XI 12).

A second point is that in all four kinds of change, he thinks there is a gradual process of transition (*Phys.* VI 6, 237a17-b3; b9-21). Qualitative change, such as change of colour, is said to take time. Change to a new place or size involves passing through intervening points. The creation of something like a house takes time, and occurs part by part, the foundation before the whole.

Aristotle does not by any means think that changes other than the four genuine ones must all involve a gradual process of transition. Indeed, he sees that an infinite regress would be involved, if the gradual process by which something came into being had itself to come into being by a gradual process (*Phys.* V 2, 225b33-226a6). In the very passage where he explains that a house comes into being only part by part, he points out that this cannot be true of things that have no parts (VI 6, 237b11; b15), points and instants, for example.

position might be thought to make it, if not desirable, at least permissible to avoid talk of rest, while the *sameness* of position made it permissible to avoid talk of motion. In that case, calling the instant of starting a *neutral* instant would be at least *as* allowable as my decision of calling it an instant of rest. I think the argument is weak, however. Certainly, if there is *no sameness* of position, this makes a case for avoiding talk of rest, but it is less clear that *some difference* of position gives us much pretext for avoiding it, when there is also some sameness. Admittedly, the difference of position makes it less than a paradigmatic case of rest; but does that prove enough? Ordinary thought connects rest with sameness of position, and hence with the absence of difference, so long as difference *excludes* sameness. But in the present case, difference of position is *combined* with sameness.

Preliminaries (ii): How can change of colour be gradual?   **79**

It may be wondered how change of colour can be gradual, given the view
stated in the *De Sensu* (6, 445b21-9; 446a16-20) that there is only a finite
number of discriminable shades. In that case, a change to a new colour
would be gradual when it involved passing through a number of intervening
shades. But within this process, how could the change from one shade to the
next be treated as gradual?

Aristotle seems to have two incompatible answers. One answer is implied
in *Physics* V 6 (230b32-231a1), VI 4 (234b10-20), VI 9 (240a19-29), VI 10
(240b21-31), when he says that certain changes occur part by part.[17] While
a surface is changing from white to the next shade, grey, he says, part of the
surface must still be white, and part already grey. The greyness spreads
gradually over the surface. This claim, that certain changes occur part by
part, is used in combating the view that a partless atom could undergo
change or motion. In its turn, the claim has as its ground that, while a thing
is actually changing or moving, it cannot yet be in its terminal state, nor can
it still be in its initial state. It must therefore be partly in one state, partly in
the other, and so must have parts. In the case of motion, it must move part
by part into the adjacent area. Diodorus Cronus and certain Epicureans
were later to get round this objection to the motion of partless atoms, by
denying that an atom actually *is* moving at any time; rather, at any given
time it *has* moved with a jerk.[18]

But Aristotle seems not always to keep in mind the view that these
changes occur part by part. For in the *De Sensu* (6, 447a1-3) he actually
denies that qualitative change has to occur part by part, and illustrates how
it can happen with the case of a whole pond freezing over at once. In one of
the *Physics* passages where he says that qualitative change (*en tois enantiois*,
237b1) is gradual, he speaks as if he must prove this on the basis of time
taken, but cannot prove it on the basis of space covered (237a19-28; a29; b2;
b21). Why not, if he remembers his view that a surface changes colour part
by part? He seems to be forgetting that view, and he probably forgets it
again in VIII 8, where he declares that while something is becoming white,
it is not yet white (263b27; b30). This way of putting things seems to neglect   **80**
the idea that there will be a stage of being partly white. How then can the
transition from one shade to the next be represented as gradual?

A second way of arguing that the transition is gradual serves to refute the
idea that part by part changing is indispensible for this purpose. The second
way is suggested by what Aristotle says in *De Sensu* 6. Admittedly, there is
only a finite number of discriminable shades, so that discriminable colours
form a discontinuous series (445b1-9; 446a16-20). But nonetheless colours,
musical pitches, and other ranges of sensible qualities have a kind of
derivative continuity (445b28; b30, *to mê kath' hauto suneches*). The sort of thing
Aristotle seems to have in mind is that a change to the next discriminable

17. Aristotle probably has this answer in mind also in VI 5, 236b5-8, where he
stresses that, even if colour is not in itself divisible, the surface to which it attaches is
divisible.

18. References in note 8 above. See esp. Sextus *Adv. Math.* X 143 where the idea
that bodies can only *have* moved is connected with the idea that bodies and places are
indivisible.

pitch, in the *discontinuous* series of discriminable pitches, may be produced by a *continuous* movement of a stopper along a vibrating string. Or in the case of colour, a change to the next discriminable shade, in the *discontinuous* series of discriminable shades, may be produced by a *continuous* change in the proportions of earth, air, fire and water in a body. As the stopper moves along the vibrating string, we hear the sound all the time, but do not hear a change of pitch, until the stopper has moved the distance that corresponds to a quarter tone (446a1-4). Variations of pitch less than a quarter tone are not perceptible except by being part of the whole variation (446a18, *hoti en tôi holôi*), by which Aristotle probably means that they only *contribute* to the perceptibility of the whole variation. This suggests a way in which Aristotle can maintain that a change to the next discriminable colour or pitch can be continuous. A body is changing to the next discriminable shade all the time that the continuous change in its elemental ingredients is going on, which will eventually lead to its displaying that next discriminable shade.

In what follows, we shall only consider Aristotle's treatment of the four genuine kinds of change. This will leave open how he might have treated the many other cases of (non-genuine) change.[19] In connexion with the four genuine kinds, and the transitions involved in them, we find two rather different kinds of treatment.

81 *Aristotle's first solution*

The better known one is less satisfactory. It is most fully expressed in connexion with rest and motion in *Phys.* VI 3 (234a24-b9) and 8 (239a10-b4). Here Aristotle says that there can be neither rest nor motion at an instant. He explicitly cites our problem as one ground for his conclusion (VI 3, 234a34-b5), saying that if something stops moving, the instant of transition between motion and rest is an instant neither of motion nor of rest, since otherwise we could not avoid the contradiction of saying that it is an instant of both motion and rest. At VI 6, 237a14-15, Aristotle extends his treatment of motion to all change, saying that a thing cannot be changing (*metaballein*) at an instant. An extension is also attempted in VI 8, 239a3-6, where Aristotle denies that there is a first instant of slowing to a halt, by arguing that slowing to a halt implies moving, and that there is no moving at an instant. (To make the argument valid, he ought to show that slowing to a halt at an instant would imply not just moving, but moving at an instant).

Aristotle gives several grounds for denying rest or motion at an instant, besides the need to avoid difficulties about the instant of transition between rest and motion. In VI 3 (234a24-b9), one argument is that to rest is to be in the same state now as then, but an instant does not contain a then. Another argument is that differences of speed would be impossible at an instant, because such differences would imply that the faster body had traversed in *less* than an instant what the slower body traversed in an instant. Finally, if we cannot speak of motion at an instant, we cannot speak of rest at an

19. We earlier made a suggestion about one of the non-genuine cases, the transition from not seeing to seeing, when we pointed out that, on one interpretation, Aristotle is committed to denying a first instant of any *energeia* such as seeing.

instant, since we can only talk of rest where there would have been the possibility of motion.

Aristotle allows that, when something stops moving, there is a single instant which is both the last of the period during which the object is moving, and the first of the period during which it is resting (VI 3, 234a34-b5). And something parallel is true when a thing *starts* moving. But this does not in the least commit him, as he makes very clear, to saying that this is an instant at which the object is moving or resting.

Since Aristotle thinks his view holds not only for motion and rest, but for change and stability in general, we can apply his remarks, for example, to a change of colour, in which a surface starts off wholly of one shade, and by a gradual process of transition, finishes up wholly of another shade. If we raise problems about the first and last instants of its changing colour, Aristotle will say, for reasons similar to those already quoted from VI 3, that there is no first or last instant, nor indeed any instant, at which it is *changing* colour, or *remaining* the same colour.

Aristotle sees, however, that this solution is not a complete one. For although he denies that things can *change* or *remain* in the same state at an instant, he concedes that there are many other things that can be true of them at an instant. He is quite prepared to allow that what is moving can be at a point (VIII 8, 262a30; b20), or level with something (VI 8, 239a35-b3) at an instant. As regards other kinds of change, the object that is changing colour can be white at an instant (VIII 8, 263b20; 23), or the white have perished and non-white have come into being at an instant (263b22). In general, a change can have been completed, and the new state of affairs can have come into being at an instant (VI 5, 235b32-236a7; VI 6, 237a14-15). In allowing something to *be* white at an instant, he is not allowing that it could *remain* white, or *rest* in the white state, at an instant.[20] Since he allows something to *be* of a certain colour at an instant, he cannot finally dispose of our problem by ruling out of order questions about a first or last instant at which a surface is *changing* colour. For this still leaves us free to ask about a first instant at which the surface is no longer grey, or wholly grey, and a last instant at which it is not yet white, or wholly white. Aristotle recognises the need to deal separately with this further question, and this brings us on to the second kind of treatment that we find in his work.

Aristotle's second solution

In *Phys.* VIII 8, 263b15-264a6, Aristotle discusses a change from not-white to white (or *vice versa*), and a change from not existing to existing. He thinks of the final state (e.g. white) as being reached by a gradual process of transition, but this is one of the passages where he does not construe the process as one of white spreading part by part over the surface. Instead, he implies that throughout the process of transition the surface will remain non-white (263b27; b30). He distinguishes an earlier state, by which he means the state when the surface is still not-white but is changing to white, from a later state, by which he means the final state of being white. Or rather, since he switches his example in mid-discussion, the earlier state is

20. All he is committed to is the view expressed elsewhere (*Phys.* VIII 8, 264b1), that what is white must remain white *over a period*.

one of being white while changing to not-white, and the later state is one of being not-white, but for simplicity I shall stick to the one example. He then says that there is no last instant of being in the earlier state, but there is a first instant of being in the later. I take it that it is crucial to understanding the passage to notice that the earlier state, of which there is no last instant, is one which involves changing[21] while the later state does not. His view is generalised in an earlier chapter (VI 5, 235b6-32),[22] where it is said in connexion with all genuine change that there is a first instant of being in the terminal state after a process of transition. One ground Aristotle gives for his verdict is again the existence of the very problem that interests us. He says that the verdict provides a way (he fails to consider whether it is the only way) of avoiding the contradiction of something being in its old state and in its new state at the same instant (263b11; b17-21). He concedes that there is an instant which is equally the end of the period during which white was coming into being and the beginning of the period during which the surface is white, but he insists that at that instant the surface is already in its later state, white (263b9-15; 264a2-3).

Aristotle's treatment of the problem here is by and large very much in line with the solution which we have advocated. For we should agree with him that there is no last instant of being not yet white, *if* changing to white is a continuous process. However, we must to some extent qualify our claim to be in agreement. For when Aristotle gives his reasons for denying a last instant of the earlier state, he does not give our reason, the *continuity* of the process of becoming white. This continuity may well be what influenced him, but if so, he has not managed to identify it explicitly as the reason.[23]

There are further passages, besides the pair we have mentioned, where Aristotle is attracted to a view close to our own. We have so far considered his denial of a *last* instant at which something is non-white while becoming

21. That he thinks the process of change is going on is clear e.g. from 263b21-2, 'non-white *was coming into* being, and white *was ceasing to be*'. 263b26-7, 'If what exists now, having been previously non-existent, *must have been coming into being*, and did not exist *while it was coming into being* ...'. 264a2, 'The time in which *it was coming to be*'. 264a5, '*It was coming to be*'.

22. There is such a thing as the time 'when first a thing has changed' (VI 5, 235b7-8; b31; b32), i.e. has completed its change. This is an indivisible time (235b32-236a7). And at that instant the thing is already in its new state (235b8; b31-2).

23. Aristotle's solution is only appropriate, given his two assumptions that the discriminable shades form a discontinuous series, and that nonetheless the change from one discriminable shade to the next is a continuous one. A quite different treatment of colour changes would be called for, if he took the view (i) that colours form a continuous series. In that case, the possibility would arise of producing a continuous alternation of shade along the spectrum. In a continuous change of shade such as this, there could not be a last instant of one shade, nor a first of another. The situation would be different again, if (ii) he took colours as forming a discontinuous series, and also took the change from one colour to the next as being discontinuous. In that case, nothing we have so far said would enable us to decide which colour to speak of at the instant of transition from one colour to the next. As for (iii) a discontinuous transition through several intervening shades to a distant one, such a transition might be thought of (though it need not be) as having a first instant (namely, the first instant at which a colour other than the original one existed), and a last instant (namely, the last instant at which the penultimate colour was in existence).

white. But he also discusses whether there can be a *first* instant at which
something is changing. At VI 5, 236a7-27, he wants to show that there is no
earliest time at which something was changing (236a15, reading:
meteballen), whether that earliest time is construed as a divisible period, or as
indivisible. If indivisible, it might be construed either as an instant, i.e. as a
boundary with no duration, or as an atom of time with an indivisible
duration. In 236a17-20 (whatever may be true of a16-17), he is construing
the putative earliest time as a durationless instant. And he takes the view
which we have advocated in connexion with continuous changes, that there
is not a first instant at which something is changing. Moreover, for the first
time he actually contradicts his other solution by saying that there is a last
instant at which something is resting (contrary to the doctrine of VI 3 and 8,
which denies rest at an instant). His ground for denying a first instant at
which it is changing is yet again the existence of the kind of problem we are
discussing. Once we assume that there is a last instant at which it is resting,
there cannot be a first instant[24] at which it is changing. For at such an
instant, the object would already have changed to some extent,[25] and it
cannot have changed to any extent at the very instant at which it is still
resting. Aristotle does not give as his ground for denying a first instant at
which something is changing the view he takes in VI 3 and 8 that there are
no instants at which something is changing. He may instead be influenced
by our kind of consideration; for just as we associated moving with being
away from the starting point, so he associates changing with having
changed to some extent. And he may be influenced by the fact that in a
continuous change there is no first instant of having changed to some extent.
But if this is what has influenced him, he has again not articulated the
reason.

There is one more place where Aristotle comes close to our view. The
theme of *Physics* VI 6 is that what has changed must have been changing
earlier (237a17-b22), and what was changing earlier must before that have
accomplished some change (236b32-237a17), so that it has already changed
an infinite (237a11; a16) number of times, and you will never get a first in
the series of changing and having changed (237b6-7). This implies that
there cannot be a first *instant* of having to some extent changed, not, for
example, a first instant of having ceased to be wholly grey, or of having
started to be partly white. This implication, which is admittedly not
explicitly spelled out by Aristotle in so many words, is precisely what we
considered to be true of continuous changes.[26]

24. It is confusing that this putative instant is referred to by *two* letters, *AΔ*, and not
just one. The reason is that *AΔ* stands for the putative earliest time of changing, which
is later treated as a period with *A* and *Δ* as its terminal instants. Here, however, it is
treated as a durationless instant, so that *Δ* is not separate from *A*.

25. Or 'have begun to change'. At 236a7-10 'has changed' (*metabebléke*) is said to be
ambiguous between 'has completed its change' and 'has begun to change'. The latter
sense is relevant in the present lines (236a19-20); the former is not.

26. There is another way in which this passage diverges from Aristotle's first
solution. Though there is no first instant of having to some extent changed, there is an
instant which divides the period of stability from the period of change. This instant is
the last instant of the period during which the object is not changing, and Aristotle's
view elsewhere (234a34-b5; 263b9-15) suggests that it can also be called the first

There are then two strands of thought in Aristotle about the process of transition involved in the four genuine kinds of change. Sometimes he argues or implies, in conformity with our view about continuous changes, that there cannot be a first instant at which a thing is changing, nor a first instant at which it has left its initial state, nor a last instant of not having reached its terminal state. Unfortunately, he does not seem to have a firm grasp of the latter point of view. For in *Phys.* VIII 8, 262a31-b3; b21-263a3, he appears to contradict it, by assuming that when a moving object reverses direction, there is a first instant of having left the point of reversal. At least, this is the assumption which he seems to require for his conclusion, which is that the reversing object must spend a period of time at the point of reversal. The assumptions seem to be that there is a first instant of having reached the point of reversal, and a first instant of having left it, and that these cannot be adjacent or identical instants, so must be separated by a pause during which the reversing body rests.

Assessment of Aristotle's first solution

Let us return briefly to the first strand of thought, according to which a thing cannot be changing or resting at an instant. This view may have appealed to recent philosophers,[27] and is not to be lightly dismissed, but it does have severe disadvantages. For it ignores that it is possible, and very useful, to give sense to the idea of changing at an instant. It is possible, so long as we acknowledge that change at an instant is a *function* of change over a period. It is useful because the velocity of a body in a given direction at an instant is one of several factors from which we can calculate in detail its future behaviour. Much of modern dynamics depends on the possibility of talking of acceleration at an instant, whereas Aristotle would rob us of this possibility.

Relevance of our problem to the definition of motion at an instant

Nonetheless, the task of defining motion at an instant is by no means easy. And the kind of problem we have been discussing, about last and first instants of rest or motion, gains importance from the fact that it needs to be resolved, if we are to obtain a satisfactory definition of motion at an instant. What definition will be satisfactory depends in part on our purposes. But if motion is continuous, then at least for some purposes, our discussion suggests that motion at an instant ought to be defined so as to exclude a first or last instant of motion. For a start, we may suggest that an instant of motion will be one that falls *within* a period of motion, while an instant of

---

instant of the period during which the object is changing. But at one point in the present chapter, VI 6, wittingly or not, he casts doubt on the latter description. For he says (237a15) that at any instant of the period during which a thing is changing, it has already changed. This would seem to rule out not only a first instant of having to some extent changed, but also the applicability of the description 'first instant of the period during which a thing is changing'. Aristotle thereby contradicts for a second time an aspect of his other solution.

27. I am not sure whether this is the intention of Vere Chappell in 'Time and Zeno's arrow', *Journal of Philosophy* 1962.

rest will be one that falls within *or bounds* a period of rest. But this definition may need revision in the light of other difficult examples, such as that of the ball thrown vertically upwards, and slowing down until it changes direction at an instant. We found reason to regard this instant either as an instant of rest or as a neutral instant, whereas the definition just proposed would make it an instant of motion, and may need to be revised, for this and other reasons. But however the definition may eventually be formulated, our discussion suggests that for some purposes it should be formulated so as to exclude first and last instants of continuous motion, and so as to avoid, if possible, our problems about the relation to first and last instants of rest. The necessity of getting clear about these things may not always be appreciated. Bertrand Russell gives a definition of motion at a moment in § 446 of *The Principles of Mathematics* (London 1903, 2nd edition 1937) and denies, unlike us, that the instant of transition between rest and motion can be an instant of rest. He does not, however, make it so clear whether or not it can be an instant of motion.

General assessment of Aristotle's position

I should like to finish with a general assessment of Aristotle's treatment of our problem. He has earned notoriety for his refusal to allow motion at an instant. G.E.L. Owen remarks that this refusal not only 'spoilt his reply to Zeno' on the paradox of the flying arrow, but also 'bedevilled the course of dynamics'.[28] In more detail, Owen explains: 'Unable to talk of speed at an instant, Aristotle has no room in his system for any such concept as that of initial velocity or, what is equally important, of the force required to start a body moving. Since he cannot recognise a moment in which the body first moves, his idea of force is restricted to the causing of motions that are completed in a given period of time. And, since he cannot consider any motion as caused by an initial application of force, he does not entertain the Newtonian corollary of this, that if some force F is sufficient to start a motion, the continued application of F must produce not just the continuance of the motion but a constant change in it, namely acceleration. It is the clumsy tools of Aristotelian dynamics, if I am right, that mark Zeno's major influence on the mathematics of science.'[29]

With the first part of this I entirely agree. Aristotle cannot accommodate the useful concept of initial velocity, by which is meant, of course, not some first velocity in the entire motion, but the first velocity which it is convenient to consider in a given calculation. But what about the second part? A reader might take 'a moment in which the body first moves' to be a first instant at which the body is moving. We have argued that it is precisely Aristotle's merit that he denies that there is such an instant; I would not regard this denial as a defect.

28. 'The Platonism of Aristotle', *Proceedings of the British Academy* 1965, p.148. Similarly 'Aristotle' pp.225-6 in vol. I of *The Dictionary of Scientific Biography*, ed. C.C. Gillespie, New York. Owen's papers on the continuum are required reading for students of this subject.

29. 'Zeno and the mathematicians', *Proceedings of the Aristotelian Society* 1957-8, pp.220-2.

I would accept, then, some charges against Aristotle, but not others, and at the same time I would draw attention to two merits of his discussion. First, it is a merit that he recognises that not all cases call for the same treatment. The treatments we have been discussing apply only to those processes of gradual transition which he believes to be involved in the four genuine kinds of change. Second, Aristotle does express the view which we believe to be reasonable for continuous change, namely that there is no first instant at which a thing is changing, or at which it has begun to abandon its original state, and no last instant at which it has not yet achieved its final state.

Appendix: another version of the problem

By way of appendix, I will draw attention to an interesting version in *De Sensu* 7 (449a21-31) of the problem with which we began. Here Aristotle has an unsatisfactory argument, which is intended to prove that an indivisible thing is not perceptible. If it were perceptible, he says, then we could imagine some particular occasion on which an indivisible point approached a particular observer, until it came into view. But there are difficulties about imagining this. For there would have to be a last point at which it was still invisible, and a first point at which it was visible. Now where would these points be? Points cannot be adjacent, he maintains. If the points are the same, or if the last point of invisibility is closer than the first point of visibility, the approaching object will be still invisible, but already visible, at the same time. On the other hand, if the first point of visibility is closer than the last point of invisibility, the approaching object will be in neither state when at the intervening distance. The moral that Aristotle draws is that we were wrong to suppose an indivisible point would ever become visible.

This inference is unwarranted, because the problem which Aristotle has raised will apply not only to an approaching point, but also to something which he admits to be in principle visible, namely an extended surface that is approaching an observer on some particular occasion, until it comes into view. We can ask, as before: what is the nearest distance at which the surface is still invisible, and what the furthest at which it is visible? If we were to copy the solution that Aristotle proffers for the case of the approaching point, we should have to say (absurdly) that it is wrong to suppose that a surface which started off invisible would ever become visible. Aristotle is not entitled to his inference; the problem he seeks to raise merely for the case of an approaching point has wider implications than he bargains for.

It may be thought (wrongly) that there is a very easy solution for this version of the problem along the following lines. Aristotle has made a false assumption, it may be said, in supposing that there is no third state between being invisible and being visible. Why should there not be an intermediate distance at which there is no straightforward answer to the question whether the approaching object is visible or invisible? For one thing, it is not entirely clear what conditions must be met in order for an object to count as visible. Must it, for example, stand out from its surroundings? For another thing, it may be difficult to be sure with regard to some conditions whether they have been met, or not. Does the object really stand out from its surroundings? What conditions must be met may vary according to one's purposes in different contexts. Is one being asked to identify the approaching object by vision, or simply to shoot at it regardless of its identity? One may be uncertain what one's task is supposed to be, so that one is also uncertain what it is reasonable to count as visible. The intended conclusion is that we should not join Aristotle in expecting a sudden switch from invisible to visible. There will be an intermediate distance at which neither predicate is straightforwardly applicable.

This suggestion does not dispose of the problem, however. Even if we do not revise our terms, so as to provide a clear-cut test of visibility, the problem can still be stated. We are talking about a *particular* observer on a *particular* occasion. Of course, there is no *general* rule about the distance at which things are visible, any more than there is a general rule about how many grains make a heap, or how many hairs are needed to save a man from baldness. But on a particular occasion, given a particular context, and a particular observer, there may be a first time at which he ceases to be confident whether an object is invisible. Now we can state the problem not as one about the transition from invisibility to visibility, but as one about the transition from being indisputably invisible to being problematic. The question will be about the nearest distance at which an approaching object on some particular occasion is *indisputably* invisible, and the first position at which there is *not a straightforward answer* to the question whether it is invisible. Thus formulated, the problem cannot be so quickly brushed aside.[30]

Some of these remarks should help in solving the ancient Megarian paradox of the heap or bald man, which has been revived in recent discussions of vague predicates.[31] The Megarian paradox starts with no grains or hairs, and declares that you can never obtain a heap or a non-bald man. As each grain or hair is added, it is argued that the addition of *one* could never make a difference. If we take a *particular* occasion, however, and supply some context and point to the discussion, it could well be that for a particular man the addition of one hair did make a difference at some stage. He might for the first time *hesitate* as to whether he was still bald.[32]

30. There is a somewhat similar version of it in the 3rd century A.D. commentary by Alexander of Aphrodisias on Aristotle's *De Sensu* (p. 122 in the Berlin edition). Referring to the claim that Aristotle makes in an earlier chapter (ch.6), that some magnitudes are too small to be perceptible on their own, Alexander argues that nonetheless we cannot have both a largest imperceptible magnitude and a smallest perceptible one. Without further argument, he concludes that we have neither.

31. Max Black, 'Reasoning with loose concepts', *Dialogue* 2, 1963, pp.1-12; Crispin Wright, 'Language mastery and the Sorites paradox' in *Truth and Meaning*, ed. G. Evans and J. McDowell, Oxford 1976; Hans Kamp, 'Two theories about adjectives', in *Formal Semantics of Natural Languages*, ed. E. Keenan, Cambridge 1975.

32. I have had many helpful discussions on this topic, but I am particularly indebted to Geoffrey Lloyd for a thorough correspondence about some of the texts, to my student Marcus Cohen and to Malcolm Schofield for some very helpful discussions on the philosophical issues, and to Professor Clive Kilmister for patient advice on Newtonian mechanics. The present version has been revised not only by the addition of an appendix, but also in light of the excellent comments I received, especially from Norman Kretzmann and Colin Strang, when the first version was delivered at the Joint Session of the Aristotelian Society and Mind Association in 1976.

BIBLIOGRAPHY

1. TEXTS

The classic edition of the Greek text of Aristotle was prepared by Immanuel Bekker for the Berlin Academy, and published in 1831; references to Aristotle's works are standardly given by page, column and line of this edition. As a text, however, it has been largely superseded; most of Aristotle's works can be found in the OCT, Teubner, Budé and Loeb series.

The standard English version of Aristotle is the 'Oxford Translation':
[1] J.A. Smith and W.D. Ross (eds.), *The Works of Aristotle translated into English* (Oxford, 1910-52).
There is an extremely useful abridgment of this in
[2] R. McKeon (ed.), *The Basic Works of Aristotle* (New York, 1941).
The volumes in
[3] J.L. Ackrill (ed.), *The Clarendon Aristotle* (Oxford, 1961-) contain translations and commentaries tailored to the needs of the Greekless philosophical reader. The commentaries by W.D. Ross are invaluable, not least on account of the comprehensive and accurate English analyses of the texts which they contain
[4] W.D. Ross (ed.), *Aristotle's Metaphysics* (Oxford, 1924),
[5] *id., Aristotle's Physics* (Oxford, 1936),
[6] *id., Aristotle's Prior and Posterior Analytics* (Oxford, 1949),
[7] *id., Aristotle's Parva Naturalia* (Oxford, 1955),
[8] *id., Aristotle's De Anima* (Oxford, 1961).
Many of the ancient Greek commentaries were published by the Prussian Academy in the series
[9] *Commentaria in Aristotelem Graeca* (Berlin, 1882-1909).
Several of Aquinas' Latin commentaries are now available in English. An indispensable aid to the study of Aristotle is
[10] H. Bonitz, *Index Aristotelicus* (Berlin, 1870);
there is an English concordance, based on the Oxford translation,
[11] T.W. Organ, *An Index to Aristotle in English Translation* (Princeton, 1949).

A comprehensive bibliography of writings on Aristotle up to 1896 can be found in
[12] M. Schwab, *Bibliographie d'Aristote* (Paris, 1896),
and a selective one in
[13] M.D. Philippe, *Aristoteles*, Bibliographische Einführungen in das Studium der Philosophie, 8 (Berne, 1948).

Our bibliography can be supplemented by
[14] *Isis Cumulative Bibliography 1913-65.*
Many of the books mentioned in this list contain their own bibliographies;
Düring's *Aristoteles* [15] has a particularly good one. The Archivum
Aristotelicum of Berlin is eventually to produce a comprehensive
continuation of Schwab.

2. GENERAL

There is a magisterial guide to all aspects of Aristotle's life and thought:
[15] I. Düring, *Aristoteles* (Heidelberg, 1966).
Of several shorter studies in English that give a general account of
Aristotle's thought, the following are especially good:
[16] W.D. Ross, *Aristotle* (London, 1923),
[17] D.J. Allan, *The Philosophy of Aristotle* (Oxford, 1952),
[18] J.H. Randall, *Aristotle* (New York, 1960),
[19] M. Grene, *A Portrait of Aristotle* (Chicago, 1963),
[20] G.E.R. Lloyd, *Aristotle* (Cambridge, 1968).
It is still worth consulting
[21] G. Grote, *Aristotle* (3rd edition, London, 1883).
The surviving evidence about the life of Aristotle is collected in
[22] I. Düring, *Aristotle in the Ancient Biographical Tradition*, Studia Graeca et
      Latina Gothoburgensia 5 (Göteborg, 1957).
See also Volume I of
[23] A.H. Chroust, *Aristotle* (London, 1973).
All questions about Aristotle's writing are exhaustively discussed in
[24] P. Moraux, *Les Listes anciennes des ouvrages d'Aristote* (Louvain, 1951).
There is an amusing reconstruction of Aristotle's lecture-room in
[25] H. Jackson, 'Aristotle's lecture-room and lectures', *Journal of Philology*
      35 (1920), pp.191-200.
On the history of Aristotelianism, see
[26] P. Moraux, *Der Aristotelismus bei den Griechen*, Peripatoi 5 (Berlin, 1973);
      and on the history of the Lyceum,
[27] J.P. Lynch, *Aristotle's School* (Berkeley and Los Angeles, 1972).

A major part of the scholarly work done on Aristotle during the last fifty
years has taken its start from the hypothesis of
[28] W.W. Jaeger, *Aristotle* (English translation by R. Robinson, 2nd
      edition Oxford, 1948; first German edition Berlin, 1923).
Two of the most ambitious contributions to this line of scholarship are
[29] F. Solmsen, *Die Entwicklung der aristotelischen Logik und Rhetorik*, Neue
      Philologische Untersuchungen 4 (Berlin, 1929)
and
[30] F.J. Nuyens, *L'Evolution de la psychologie d'Aristote* (Louvain, 1948;
      originally published in Flemish, 1939).
Solmsen's views are conveniently expounded in
[31] J.L. Stocks, 'The composition of Aristotle's logical works', *Classical
      Quarterly* 27 (1933), pp.114-24,
and Nuyens's in the introduction to Ross's edition of the *Parva Naturalia*.
The scholarly squabbles which these works have excited can be enjoyed at
second-hand in

[32] A.H. Chroust, 'The first thirty years of modern Aristotelian scholarship', *Classica et Mediaevalia* 24 (1963/4), pp.27-57.
Two papers by Ross and Owen (chapters 1 and 2 of our Volume 1) offer two views of the present state of play in this field:
[33] W.D. Ross, 'The development of Aristotle's thought', *Proceedings of the British Academy* 43 (1957), pp.63-78,
[34] G.E.L. Owen, 'The Platonism of Aristotle', *Proceedings of the British Academy* 50 (1965), pp.125-50.

Since 1957 triennial Symposia Aristotelica have been held in Europe; their published proceedings provide excellent examples of modern Aristotelian scholarship. See:
[35] I. Düring and G.E.L. Owen (eds.), *Aristotle and Plato in the mid-Fourth Century*, Studia Graeca et Latina Gothoburgensia 11 (Göteborg, 1960),
[36] S. Mansion (ed.), *Aristote et les problèmes de méthode* (Louvain, 1961),
[37] G.E.L. Owen (ed.), *Aristotle on Dialectic* (Oxford, 1968),
[38] I. Düring (ed.), *Naturforschung bei Aristoteles und Theophrast* (Heidelberg, 1969),
[39] P. Moraux (ed.), *Untersuchungen zur Eudemischen Ethik*, Peripatoi I (Berlin, 1970),
[40] P. Aubenque (ed.), *Etudes sur la Métaphysique d'Aristote* (Paris, 1978),
[41] G.E.R. Lloyd and G.E.L. Owens (eds.), *Aristotle on Mind and the Senses* (Cambridge, 1978).

3. METAPHYSICS

As the Introduction indicates, the topics discussed by our authors count as metaphysical upon a modern view of metaphysics, not on any Aristotelian definition. Partly for this reason, and partly because Aristotle does not rigorously adhere to his own formal divisions of theoretical philosophy, the reader has to consult several Aristotelian treatises in investigating his treatment of metaphysical questions. For convenience, but with inevitable artificiality, items in this bibliography are listed in connexion with the treatise which provides the principal textual evidence for their subject matter.

(a) *Editions and commentaries*

For *Categories* and *De Interpretatione* the English reader is best served by the translation with notes published in the Clarendon Aristotle series [3]:
[42] J.L. Ackrill, *Aristotle's Categories and De Interpretatione* (Oxford, 1963).
Two much older works contain valuable commentary:
[43] J. Pacius, *In Porphyrii Isagogen et Aristotelis Organum commentarius* (Frankfurt, 1597),
[44] T. Waitz, *Aristotelis Organon*, 2 volumes (Leipzig, 1844-6).
These cover the *Topics* also, whose first four books are available in an excellent French edition in the Budé series:
[45] J. Brunschwig, *Aristote: Topiques* (livres I-IV) (Paris, 1967).
Of the *Metaphysics* there is a magisterial edition by Ross [4], and an older edition with commentary well worth consulting:

[46] H. Bonitz, *Aristotelis Metaphysica*, 2 volumes (Bonn, 1848-9).

Perhaps the best of all ancient Greek commentaries on Aristotle is available in the Berlin Academy series [9]:

[47] Alexander of Aphrodisias, *In Aristotelis Metaphysica Commentaria*, ed. M. Hayduck (Berlin, 1891).

There is a translation of Books IV-VI, with valuable notes, in the Clarendon Aristotle series [3]:

[48] C. Kirwan, *Aristotle's Metaphysics Books Gamma, Delta, Epsilon* (Oxford, 1971).

Another volume in the same series is devoted to Books XIII-XIV:

[49] J. Annas, *Aristotle's Metaphysics Books Mu and Nu* (Oxford, 1976).

Ross has also given us a fine edition of the *Physics* [5]; in [3] there has appeared a translation and commentary on Books I and II:

[50] W. Charlton, *Aristotle's Physics Books I and II* (Oxford, 1970).

Some of Aristotle's early lost works were devoted to metaphysical topics. See the Teubner edition of Aristotle's fragments:

[51] V. Rose, *Aristotelis qui ferebantur Librorum Fragmenta* (Leipzig, 1886³).

A translation of many of the more important fragments was published by Ross in Volume XII of [1]; he later edited a Greek text of this selection in the OCT series:

[52] *Aristotelis Fragmenta Selecta*, ed. W.D. Ross (Oxford, 1955).

An ambitious attempt to reconstruct the *Protrepticus*, with full edition, translation and commentary, was made in:

[53] I. Düring, *Aristotle's Protrepticus*, Studia Graeca et Latina Gothoburgensia 12 (Göteborg, 1961).

The fragments of *De Philosophia* have been edited with commentary in:

[54] M. Untersteiner, *Aristotele Della Filosofia* (Rome, 1963).

For a general discussion of the lost early works see

[55] E. Berti, *La filosofia del primo Aristotele* (Padua, 1962).

And on *De Ideis* in particular

[56] W. Leszl, *Il 'De Ideis' di Aristotele e la Teoria Platonica delle Idee* (Florence, 1975).

(b) *Categories, De Interpretatione and Topics*

The authenticity of the *Categories*, in particular of its second part (the so-called *Postpraedicamenta*), has been much debated. Doubts have been silenced by the powerful defence of both parts of the treatise made by

[57] I. Husik, 'The *Categories* of Aristotle', in his *Philosophical Essays* (Oxford, 1952), and

[58] L.M. de Rijk, 'The authenticity of Aristotle's *Categories*', *Mnemosyne* Ser.IV. 4 (1951), pp.129-59.

See also

[59] *id.*, *The Place of the Categories of Being in Aristotle's Philosophy* (Assen, 1952).

General treatments of the three works are to be found in

[60] H.W.B. Joseph, *An Introduction to Logic* (Oxford, 1916²),

[61] E. Kapp, *Greek Foundations of Traditional Logic* (New York, 1942),

[62] W. and M. Kneale, *The Development of Logic* (Oxford, 1962),

[63] A.N. Prior, *The Doctrine of Propositions and Terms* (London, 1976).

The origin and general character of Aristotle's doctrine of categories have long been debated. Two notable contributions in the nineteenth century were

[64] F.A. Trendelenburg, *Geschichte der Kategorienlehre* (Hildesheim, 1846, repr. 1963), and

[65] H. Bonitz, *Uber die Kategorien des Aristoteles* (Vienna, 1853, repr. 1967).

Gillespie's article (our chapter 1) is one of many more recent discussions which pay particular attention to the question of origins; others are usefully collected with his in

[66] F.-P. Hager (ed.), *Logik und Erkenntnislehre des Aristoteles* (Darmstadt, 1972).

But none brings out so helpfully as Gillespie's the dialectical context of the doctrine, which is also stressed by Owen [34] (cf. on dialectic our Volume I, especially chapters 3, 6, 7, 8). Among essays which study in particular the relation of the theory of predication in the *Categories* to ideas in Plato or current in the Academy, see besides [34] [72]below and

[67] P. Merlan, 'Zur Erklärung der dem Aristoteles zugeschriebenen Kategorienschrift', *Philologus* 89 (1934), pp.35-53, and

[68] R.G. Turnbull, 'Aristotle's debt to the "natural philosophy" of the *Phaedo*', *Philosophical Quarterly* 8 (1958), pp.131-43.

The theory of categories inspired the influential thesis of

[69] G. Ryle, 'Categories', in *Collected Papers*, Volume 2 (London, 1971).

For a recent survey of some of the philosophical issues see

[70] J.M.E. Moravcsik, 'Aristotle's theory of categories', in *Aristotle: A Collection of Critical Essays*, ed. Moravcsik (New York, 1967).

On the treatment of categories in the *Topics* see

[71] S. Mansion, 'Notes sur la doctrine des Catégories dans les *Topiques*' in [37].

The character of individuals in categories other than substance was explored in a controversial essay by

[72] G.E.L. Owen, 'Inherence', *Phronesis* 10 (1965), pp.97-105,

which has provoked a good deal of discussion of many aspects of Aristotle's theory of predication, including

[73] J.M.E. Moravcsik, 'Aristotle on predication', *Philosophical Review* 76 (1967), pp.80-96,

[74] G.B. Matthews and S.M. Cohen, 'The one and the many', *Review of Metaphysics* 21 (1967-8), pp.630-55,

[75] R.E. Allen, 'Individual properties in Aristotle's Categories', *Phronesis* 14 (1969), pp.31-9,

[76] B. Jones, 'Individuals in Aristotle's Categories', *Phronesis* 17 (1972), pp.104-23, with the reply

[77] J. Annas, 'Individuals in Aristotle's Categories: two queries', *Phronesis* 19 (1974), pp.146-52.

This discussion is now wending its way to fuller consideration of the notion of substance in the *Categories*, as in

[78] C.L. Stough, 'Language and ontology in Aristotle's *Categories*', *Journal of the History of Philosophy* 10 (1972), pp.261-72,

[79] R.E. Allen, 'Substance and predication in Aristotle's *Categories*', in *Exegesis and Argument* (ed. E.N. Lee *et al.*), *Phronesis* Suppl. Vol.1, 1973,

[80] R.M. Dancy, 'On some of Aristotle's first thoughts about substances',
      Philosophical Review 84 (1975), pp.338-73.
See also the entries on substance in the section on the *Metaphysics* below,
particularly [209]. A more comprehensive essay is
[81] B. Jones, 'An introduction to the first five chapters of Aristotle's
      Categories', *Phronesis* 20 (1975), pp.146-72.

In the *Topics* Aristotle develops a classification of types of predication
known as the theory of predicables. Every proposition is said to indicate
either a property or a definition or the genus or an accident of the subject.
The last three predicables will be covered in the section on *Metaphysics*; on
property (the subject of Book V) see
[82] G. Verbeke, 'La notion de propriété dans les *Topiques*', in [37],
[83] J. Barnes, 'Property in Aristotle's *Topics*', *Archiv für Geschichte der
      Philosophie* 52 (1970), pp.136-55,
which has provoked
[84] V.E. Wedin, 'A remark on *Per Se* accidents and properties', *ibid.* 55
      (1973), pp.30-35,
[85] W. Graham, 'Counterpredicability and *Per Se* accidents', *ibid.* 57
      (1975), pp.182-7, and
[86] D.J. Hadgopoulos, 'The Definition of the "Predicables" in Aristotle',
      Phronesis 21 (1976), pp.59-63.
A fundamental notion of the *Categories*, the idea of homonymy (developed
also in *Topics* I and IX, and used by Aristotle pervasively), has been much
discussed. See the important papers of Owen ([134], [161] and our chapter
2) and Hintikka ([101], ch. 1); also
[87] J.P. Anton, 'The Aristotelian doctrine of *homonyma* in the *Categories* and
      its Platonic antecedents', *Journal of the History of Philosophy* 6 (1968),
      pp.315-26,
[88] *id.*, 'Ancient interpretations of Aristotle's doctrine of *homonyma*', *ibid.* 7
      (1969), pp.1-18,
[89] *id.*, 'The meaning of *ho logos tês ousias* in Aristotle's *Categories* 1a', *Monist*
      52 (1968), pp.252-67,
[90] J. Barnes, 'Homonymy in Aristotle and Speusippus', *Classical Quarterly*
      n.s. 21 (1971), pp.65-80.
See also the readings on 'focal meaning' and on *Metaphysics* Book V given
below.

On Aristotle's treatment of language in *De Interpretatione* see the
monumental work
[91] H. Steinthal, *Geschichte der Sprachwissenschaft bei den Griechen und Römern*,
      2 volumes (Berlin, 1890², repr. 1961).
A recent treatise is
[92] R. Brandt, *Die aristotelische Urteilslehre* (Marburg, 1965).
Aristotle's view of the conventional nature of language has been discussed
by
[93] N. Kretzmann, 'Aristotle on Spoken Sound Significant by
      Convention', in *Ancient Logic and its Modern Interpretations*, ed. J. Corcoran
      (Dordrecht, 1974).
See also

[94] G. Nuchelmans, *Theories of the Proposition* (Amsterdam and London, 1973), ch. 3,
and for a linguist's view
[95] R.H. Robins, *A Short History of Linguistics* (London, 1967), ch. 2.

Chapter 9 of *De Interpretatione* is devoted to a celebrated argument against fatalism, which takes as its example the sea-battle which will or will not occur tomorrow. According to one line of interpretation, Aristotle answers the fatalist by saying that predictions about future contingents are not, or not yet, true. This interpretation was developed by Jan Lukasiewicz, who was led by it to introduce values other than 'true' and 'false' into modern formal logic. His papers of 1920, 1922 and 1930, the last containing an excellent historical appendix, can be read in English translation in
[96] S. McCall (ed.), *Polish Logic 1920-39* (Oxford, 1967), chs. 1-3,
or in
[97] L. Borkowski (ed.), *Jan Lukasiewicz, Selected Works* (Amsterdam, 1970).
This kind of view is well expounded by
[98] A.N. Prior, 'Three-valued logic and future contingents', *Philosophical Quarterly* 3 (1953), 317-26,
and more scholarly discussions which incline to the same interpretation are given by J.L. Ackrill in [42], M. Kneale in [62] and R. Sorabji in [284]. Prior later took a less favourable attitude to Aristotle's argument, as in
[99] *id., Past, Present and Future* (Oxford, 1967).
From antiquity on, there have been rival interpretations of Aristotle's reply, some ancients declaring that Aristotle denies not truth, but only 'definite' truth to predictions, and some later writers declaring that he is making a point about not truth, but necessity. The best known modern statement of this last view is
[100] G.E.M. Anscombe, 'Aristotle and the sea-battle', *Mind* 65 (1956) 1-15 (revised version in Moravcsik, *Aristotle*, see [70] above).
A quite different version of it is supplied by
[101] J. Hintikka, *Time and Necessity* (Oxford, 1973), ch. VIII.
For mediaeval versions of this kind of interpretation see
[102] N. Rescher, 'An interpretation of Aristotle's doctrine of future contingency and excluded middle', in his *Studies in the History of Arabic Logic* (Pittsburgh, 1963).
Further information about mediaeval discussions of the problem is to be found in
[103] L. Baudry, *La Querelle des futurs contingents* (Paris, 1950).
A recent monograph, with select bibliography, is
[104] D. Frede, *Aristoteles und die 'Seeschlacht', Hypomnemata* 27, Göttingen, 1970.
A fuller bibliography is supplied by
[105] R. Gale (ed.), *The Philosophy of Time: A Collection of Essays* (London, 1968), pp.506-9; also by Hintikka [101], who in addition discusses the treatment of possibility and necessity in chapters 12 and 13 of *De Interpretatione* in chs. II and III. With this topic we approach both Aristotle's syllogistic and his metaphysics: for readings on his metaphysical explorations of possibility and necessity see chapters 9 and 10 and items on *Metaphysics* IX and on *Physics* below; for the logic we

must refer in general to the bibliography in our Volume 1, save only to
mention four classic works

[106] H. Maier, *Die Syllogistik des Aristoteles*, 3 volumes (Tübingen, 1896-
1900),

[107] J. Lukasiewicz, *Aristotle's Syllogistic* (Oxford, 1957²),

[108] A. Becker, *Die aristotelische Theorie der Möglichkeitsschlüsse* (Berlin,
1933),

[108A] G. Patzig, *Aristotle's Theory of the Syllogism* (Dordrecht, 1969³).

This is also a convenient place to mention two treatments of the 'square
of opposition' expounded in *De Interpretatione* (see chapters 7, 8, 10, 14
especially):

[109] H.L.A. Hart, 'A logician's fairy tale', *Philosophical Review* 60 (1951),
pp.198-212,

[110] M. Thompson, 'On Aristotle's square of opposition', *ibid.* 62 (1953),
pp. 251-62 (reprinted in Moravcsik, *Aristotle*; see [70] above).

(c) *Metaphysics*

General works on the *Metaphysics* include

[111] J. Owens, *The Doctrine of Being in the Aristotelian Metaphysics* (Toronto,
1963²), with excellent bibliography, and

[112] P. Aubenque, *Le Problème de l'être chez Aristote* (Paris, 1966²).

Jaeger's work on the development of Aristotle's thought began with a
monograph on the *Metaphysics*:

[113] W. Jaeger, *Studien zur Entstehungsgeschichte der Metaphysik des Aristoteles*
(Berlin, 1912)

(and see [28], chs. VII and VIII); a useful collection, bringing together
much of the best work inspired by his approach, is

[114] F.-P. Hager (ed.), *Metaphysik und Theologie des Aristoteles* (Darmstadt
1969).

An older treatment of the structure of the *Metaphysics* was

[115] P. Natorp, 'Thema und Disposition der aristotelischen Metaphysik',
Philosophische Monatshefte 24 (1887), pp.37-65, 540-74.

See also the proceedings of the sixth Symposium Aristotelicum ([40]
above).

An extended essay on Aristotle, devoted principally to his views on
substance but touching on other topics in the *Metaphysics*, is published by
G.E.M. Anscombe in

[116] G.E.M. Anscombe and P.T. Geach, *Three Philosophers* (Oxford, 1961).

On the name 'metaphysics' in its application to Aristotle's treatise see

[117] H. Reiner, 'Die Entstehung und ursprüngliche Bedeutung des
Namens Metaphysik', *Zeitschrift für Philosophische Forschung* 9 (1955),
pp.77-99,

[118] P. Merlan, 'Metaphysik: Name und Gegenstand', *Journal of Hellenic
Studies* 77 (1957), pp. 87-92 (both reprinted in [114]),

[119] *id.*, 'On the terms "Metaphysics" and "Being-qua-Being"', *Monist*
52 (1968), pp.174-94.

On Aristotle's method in the *Metaphysics* see

[120] J.M. Le Blond, *Logique et méthode chez Aristote* (Paris, 1939),

[121] G. Verbeke, 'Démarches de la réflexion métaphysique chez Aristote',
in [36],

[122] J. Brunschwig, 'Dialectique et ontologie chez Aristote', *Revue Philosophique* 89 (1964), pp.179-200.

In Book I Aristotle explores the views of his predecessors on the principles of being. His procedure is discussed by

[123] S. Mansion, 'Le rôle de l'exposé et de la critique des philosophies antérieures chez Aristote', in [36].

Massive attacks on Aristotle's credentials as a historian and historical critic of philosophy were mounted by

[124] H. Cherniss, *Aristotle's Criticism of Presocratic Philosophy* (Baltimore, 1935),

[125] *id.*, *Aristotle's Criticism of Plato and the Academy* (Baltimore, 1944),

[126] *id.*, *The Riddle of theAcademy* (Berkeley, 1945).

Aristotle has been defended by

[127] W.K.C. Guthrie, 'Aristotle as a historian of philosophy', *Journal of Hellenic Studies* 77 (1957), pp.35-41,

but the defence has itself been attacked by

[128] J.G. Stevenson, 'Aristotle as historian of philosophy', *ibid*. 94 (1974), pp.138-43.

Aristotle's general posture towards Platonism is discussed in chapters 1 and 2 of our Volume I, nos [33] and [34] above, and in

[129] H. Flashar, 'Die Kritik der platonischen Ideenlehre in der Ethik des Aristoteles', in *Synusia*, ed. H. Flashar and K. Gaiser (Pfüllingen, 1965),

translated as chapter 1 of our Volume 2. See also

[130] L. Robin, *La Théorie platonicienne des idées et des nombres d'après Aristote* (Paris, 1908),

[131] P. Wilpert, *Zwei aristotelische Frühschriften über die Ideenlehre* (Regensburg, 1949),

[132] E. de Stryker, 'Aristote, critique de Platon', *L'Antiquité Classique* 18 (1949), pp.95-107,

[133] S. Mansion, 'La critique de la théorie des idées dans le *Peri Ideôn* d'Aristote', *Revue Philosophique de Louvain* 47 (1949), pp.169-202,

[134] G.E.L. Owen, 'A proof in the *Peri Ideôn*', *Journal of Hellenic Studies* 77 (1957), pp.103-11,

[135] *id.*, 'Dialectic and eristic in the treatment of the forms', in [37].

Two recent contributions to the discussion are

[136] J. Annas, 'Forms and first principles', *Phronesis* 19 (1974), pp.257-83, and

[137] R. Barford, 'A proof from the Peri Ideôn revisited', *ibid*. 21 (1976), pp.198-218.

See also the classic discussion by

[138] J. Cook Wilson, 'On the Platonist doctrine of the *asumblêtoi arithmoi*', *CR* 18 (1904), pp.247-60.

Book III of the *Metaphysics* is a dialectical exposition of the problems of philosophy, conceived largely in Platonist terms. It has prompted little discussion in recent years; but see

[139] S. Mansion, 'Les apories de la métaphysique aristotélicienne', in *Autour d'Aristote* (Louvain, 1955).

The idea of 'first philosophy' expounded in Book IV has given rise to exhaustive discussion. Besides the articles of Owen (chapter 2) and Patzig (chapter 3), see

[140] P. Merlan, *From Platonism to Neoplatonism* (The Hague, 1960²),

[141] A. Mansion, 'Philosophie première, philosophie seconde et métaphysique chez Aristote', *Revue Philosophique de Louvain* 56 (1958), pp.165-221,

[142] H. Wagner, 'Zum Problem des aristotelischen Metaphysiksbegriff', *Philosophische Rundschau* 7 (1959), pp.129-48,

together with Merlan's reply (cf. also [117], [118], [119] above),

[143] P. Merlan, '*on hêi on* und *prôtê ousia*: Postskript zu einer Besprechung', *ibid.*, pp.148-53,

[144] V. Décarie, *L'Object de la métaphysique chez Aristote* (Montreal/Paris, 1961),

[145] G. Reale, *Il concetto di filosofia prima e l'unitá della metafisica di Aristotele* (Milan, 1965²).

See also Part 2 of

[146] H.J. Krämer, 'Zur geschichtlichen Stellung der aristotelischen Metaphysik', *Kant-Studien* 58 (1967), pp.313-54.

Philosophy is contrasted by Aristotle with dialectic, the subject of the *Topics* and of

[147] J.D.G. Evans, *Aristotle's Concept of Dialectic* (Cambridge, 1977).

Owen's work (ch.2) has illuminated another much debated topic, known since he wrote as 'focal meaning', the notion by which Aristotle ties together the concept of being. His views have met with some opposition: see e.g. Flashar (above [129]) and

[148] W. Leszl, *Logic and Metaphysics in Aristotle* (Padua, 1970), a book severely criticised by

[149] D. Frede, review of [148], *Gnomon* 47 (1975), pp.340-9,

[150] E. de Stryker, 'Prédicats univoques et prédicats analogiques dans le "Protreptique" d'Aristote', *Revue Philosophique de Louvain* 66 (1968), pp.597-618,

[151] E. Berti, 'Multiplicité et unité du bien selon EEI8', in [39], whose opinion has in turn been controverted by

[152] J. Barnes, review of [39], *Archiv für Geschichte der Philosophie* 55 (1973), pp.335-6.

An older work is

[153] F. Brentano, *Von der mannigfachen Bedeutung des Seiendes nach Aristoteles* (Freiburg im Breisgau, 1862), now translated into English as *On the Several Senses of Being in Aristotle*.

Much of Book IV is given over to a discussion of the most notable axiom of first philosophy, the Law of Non-contradiction, discussed by Lukasiewicz in chapter 4. The Law is also discussed by Anscombe [116] and Kirwan [48], and by

[154] I. Husik, 'Aristotle on the law of contradiction and the basis of the syllogism', in his *Philosophical Essays* (Oxford, 1952),

[155] J. Barnes, 'The law of contradiction', *Philosophical Quarterly* 19 (1969), pp.302-9.

Aristotle's arguments in this context against relativism are examined by

[156] A.J.P. Kenny, 'The argument from illusion in Aristotle's Metaphysics', *Mind* 76 (1967), pp.184-97,

to whom a reply was made by

[157] M.C. Scholar, 'Aristotle *Metaphysics* IV 1010b1-3', *Mind* 80 (1971), pp.266-8,

and

[158] J.D.G. Evans, 'Aristotle on relativism', *Philosophical Quarterly* 24 (1974), pp.193-203,

who was answered by

[159] F.C.T. Moore, 'Evans off target', *ibid.* 25 (1975), pp.58-9.

Book V, sometimes called Aristotle's philosophical dictionary, was presumably included in that position within the *Metaphysics* by Aristotle's ancient editors because it gives definitions or accounts of many of the basic notions studied by first philosophy (although these accounts prove later to have been only preliminary). One of its fundamental ideas is that most metaphysical concepts are 'said in many ways', an idea which has important links with Aristotle's theory of categories and his notion of homonymy. Most recent discussion has centred on his treatment of being and the verb 'to be' along these lines. See the relevant section of

[160] S. Mansion, *Le Jugement d'éxistence chez Aristote* (Louvain/Paris, 1976²).

Besides our chapter 2 see also

[161] G.E.L. Owen, 'Aristotle on the snares of ontology', in *New Essays on Plato and Aristotle*, ed. R. Bambrough (London, 1965).

Of general interest, and including remarks specifically on Aristotle, is

[162] C.H. Kahn, 'The Greek verb "to be" and the concept of being', *Foundations of Language* 2 (1966), pp.245-65.

Detailed studies of Book V 7 (on being) are offered by

[163] R.A. Cobb, 'The present progressive periphrasis and the Metaphysics of Aristotle', *Phronesis* 18 (1973), pp.80-90,

which has elicited a reply,

[164] R.K. Sprague, 'Aristotelian periphrasis: a reply to Mr Cobb', *Phronesis* 20 (1975), pp.75-6,

[165] J.W. Thorp, 'Aristotle's use of categories', *Phronesis* 19 (1974), pp.238-56.

Aristotle's doctrine that being is not a genus and its relation to his view that 'be' is homonymous are discussed by

[166] J. Cook Wilson, *Statement and Inference*, Volume II (Oxford, 1926), pp.696-706,

[167] M.J. Loux, 'Aristotle on the transcendentals', *Phronesis* 18 (1973), pp.225-39.

There is a fine treatment of one of the other 'transcendentals' by

[168] J.L. Ackrill, 'Aristotle on "good" and the categories', in *Islamic Philosophy and the Classical Tradition*, ed. S.M. Stern *et al.* (Oxford, 1972), reprinted in our Volume 2.

Aristotle's views on unity and sameness in Books V and X are explored in

[169] N.P. White, 'Aristotle on sameness and oneness', *Philosophical Review* 80 (1971), pp.177-97, which provoked a reply,

[170] F.D. Miller, 'Did Aristotle have the concept of identity?', *ibid.* 82 (1973), pp.483-90,

[171] M.C. Stokes, *One and Many in Presocratic Philosophy* (Washington, D.C., 1971), ch. 1,

[172] K.T. Barnes, 'Aristotle on identity and its problems', *Phronesis* 22 (1977), pp.48-62.

Books VII-VIII, in which Aristotle searches for an understanding of substance and in so doing elaborates the fundamental ideas of form, matter, essence and definition, continue to fascinate contemporary scholars and philosophers more than any other part of the work. Our chapters 6 and 7 are devoted to these books, and chapter 5 has a good deal to say about them. Besides the general works on the *Metaphysics* listed above (especially [111], [112], and [116]), recent monographs include

[173] E. Tugendhat, *Ti kata tinos* (Freiburg/Munich, 1958),

[174] E. Buchanan, *Aristotle's Theory of Being* (Cambridge, Mass., 1962),

[175] R. Boehm, *Das Grundlegende und das Wesentliche* (s'Gravenhage, 1965).

Substance, according to Aristotle, is preeminently what can be defined: see Books VII 4, 10-12 and VIII 6, together with our chapter 5, which surveys Aristotle's treatment of definition throughout the treatises (the main texts are *Topics* VI, *Posterior Analytics* II, and *De Partibus Animalium* I). For further discussion see Cherniss [125], ch. 1, Evans [147], ch. 4, and the commentaries in [3]:

[176] J. Barnes, *Aristotle's Posterior Analytics* (Oxford, 1975),

[177] D.M. Balme, *Aristotle's De Partibus Animalium I and De Generatione Animalium I* (Oxford, 1972).

See also the relevant portions of LeBlond [120], S. Mansion [160] and Sorabji [284].

Among articles may be mentioned

[178] M.S. Roland-Gosselin, 'Les méthodes de définition d'Aristote', *Revue des sciences philosophiques et théologiques* 6 (1912), pp. 236-52, 661-75,

[179] A.J. Festugière, 'Les méthodes de la definition de l'âme', *ibid.* 20 (1931), pp.83-90,

[180] S. Mansion, '*To simon* et la définition physique', in [38],

[181] R.R.K. Sorabji, 'Aristotle and Oxford philosophy', *American Philosophical Quarterly* 6 (1969), pp.127-35,

[182] R. Bolton, 'Essentialism and semantic theory in Aristotle', *Philosophical Review* 85 (1976) pp.514-44.

A contemporary essay on definition by a notable student of Plato and Aristotle is

[183] R. Robinson, *Definition* (Oxford, 1950).

According to Book VII 12, definition is to be given by genus and differentia (cf. *Topics* Book IV, *Categories* 5). On the way this requirement is worked out in Books VII and VIII see

[184] R. Rorty, 'Genus as matter: a reading of Metaphysics Z-H', in *Exegesis and Argument* (see [79] above), and

[185] M. Grene, 'Is genus to species as matter to form?', *Synthese* 28 (1974), pp.51-69, with comments by Rorty, *ibid.*, pp.71-7.

On its logical implications see besides [42], [125] and [147] above

[186] A.C. Lloyd, 'Genus, species and ordered series in Aristotle', *Phronesis* 7 (1962), pp.67-90,

and on the difficult question of its application to biology see

[187] D.M. Balme, 'Aristotle's use of differentiae in zoology', in [36], 195-212 (of which a revised version appears in our Volume 1), together with

relevant items in the bibliography to Volume 1.

Aristotle works out his conception of essence (which is what is expressed in a definition) in Book VII 4-6, 10-12. It has provoked a number of recent discussions:

[188] I.M. Copi, 'Essence and accident', *Journal of Philosophy* 51 (1954), pp.706-19,

[189] W.C. Kneale, 'Modality de dicto and de re', in *Logic, Methodology and Philosophy of Science*, ed. E. Nagel *et al.* (Stanford, 1962),

[190] C.A. Kirwan, 'How strong are the objections to essence?', *Proceedings of the Aristotelian Society* 71 (1970-71), pp.43-59,

[191] M.J. Cresswell, 'Essence and existence in Plato and Aristotle', *Theoria* 37 (1971), pp.91-113,

[192] N.P. White, 'Origins of Aristotle's essentialism', *Review of Metaphysics* 26 (1972-73), pp.57-85,

[193] M.J.Woods, 'Substance and essence in Aristotle', *Proceedings of the Aristotelian Society* 75 (1974-75), pp.167-80.

A useful philological monograph is

[194] C. Arpe, *Das ti ên einai bei Aristoteles* (Hamburg, 1938).

In chapter 6 Mansion shows in what sense Aristotle meant his doctrine that substance is form. See also her conspectus of Book VII,

[195] S. Mansion, 'La première doctrine de la substance', *Revue Philosophique de Louvain* 44 (1946), pp.349-69.

Other articles of a general character on this theme are

[196] K. Oehler, 'Das aristotelische Argument: Ein mensch zeugt einen Menschen', in his *Antike Philosophie und byzantinisches Mittelalter* (Munich, 1969),

[197] G. Patzig, 'Bemerkungen über den Begriff der Form', *Archiv für Philosophie* 9 (1959), pp.93-111,

[198] E.S. Haring, 'Substantial form in Aristotle's Metaphysics Z1', *Review of Metaphysics* 10 (1956-57), pp.308-32, 482-501, 698-713,

[199] D.C. Williams, 'Form and matter', *Philosophical Review* 67 (1958), pp.291-312, 449-521.

The relation of form to matter is considered specifically with respect to Aristotle's conception of soul by

[200] J.L. Ackrill, 'Aristotle's definitions of *psuche*', *Proceedings of the Aristotelian Society* 73 (1972-3), pp.119-133 (reprinted in our Volume 4).

The question whether it is matter or form which constitutes Aristotle's principle of individuation, raised in our chapter 7, has been much discussed. See

[201] W. Sellars, 'Substance and form in Aristotle', *Journal of Philosophy* 54 (1957), pp.688-99,

[202] R. Albritton, 'Forms of particular substances in Aristotle's Metaphysics', *ibid.*, pp.699-708,

[203] A.C. Lloyd, 'Aristotle's principle of individuation', *Mind* 69 (1970), pp. 519-29,

[204] W. Charlton, 'Aristotle and the principle of individuation', *Phronesis* 17 (1972), pp.239-49.

The following concentrate on the relations of the ideas of form and substance to that of universal:

[205] J.A. Smith, '*Tode ti* in Aristotle', *Classical Review* 35 (1921), p.19,

[206] A.R. Lacey, '*Ousia* and form in Aristotle', *Phronesis* 10 (1965), pp.54-69,

[207] M.J. Woods, 'Problems in *Metaphysics* Z, chapter 13', in *Aristotle*, ed. Moravcsik (see [70] above),

[208] J.H. Lesher, 'Aristotle on form, substance and universals: a dilemma', *Phronesis* 16 (1971), pp.169-78,

[209] E.D. Harter, 'Aristotle on primary *ousia*', *Archiv für Geschichte der Philosophie* 57 (1975), pp.1-20,

[210] R.D. Sykes, 'Form in Aristotle', *Philosophy* 50 (1975), pp.311-31.

On a related issue see

[211] W. Leszl, 'Knowledge of the universal and knowledge of the particular in Aristotle', *Review of Metaphysics* 26 (1972-73), pp.278-313.

The question whether Aristotle believed in substances which were pure forms, separate from any matter, can conveniently be studied by reference to

[212] J. Moreau, 'L'être et l'essence chez Aristote', in *Autour d'Aristote* (Louvain, 1955),

[213] E.E. Ryan, 'Pure form in Aristotle', *Phronesis* 18 (1973), pp.209-24.

Our chapter 8 also pursues the theme of abstraction from another starting point (and see [252] and [253] below).

On matter, the subject of our chapter 7, most of our readings are given in the section on the *Physics* below. But some more philosophical discussions may be mentioned here:

[214] M. Macdonald, 'The philosopher's use of analogy', in *Logic and Language* (1st series), ed. A.G.N. Flew (Oxford, 1952),

[215] V. Chappell, 'Stuff and things', *Proceedings of the Aristotelian Society* 71 (1970-71), pp.61-76,

[216] H.M. Cartwright, 'Chappell on stuff and things', *Nous* 6 (1972), pp.369-77,

[217] V. Chappell, 'Aristotle's conception of matter', *Journal of Philosophy* 70 (1973), pp.679-96, with comments by J.M. Cooper and R.M. Dancy (*ibid.*, pp.696-9).

An unorthodox discussion of the treatment of matter in Book VII 3 is given by

[218] M. Schofield, '*Metaph.* Z3: some suggestions', *Phronesis* 17 (1972), pp.97-101.

A study which considers the connection of the notion of substance in Books VII and VIII and that of actuality in Book IX is

[219] C.H. Chen, *Ousia and Energeia: Two Fundamental Concepts in the Philosophy of Aristotle* (Taipei, 1958).

Our chapters 9 (an ancestor of [101], ch. V) and 10 (reprinted in [101], ch. VI) explore the notions of possibility and actuality introduced by Aristotle in Book IX. On the arguments against the Megarians in this book see Hintikka's discussion in ch. IX of [101], 'Aristotle and the "Master Argument" of Diodorus', and

[220] N. Hartmann, 'Der megarische und der aristotelische Möglichkeitsbegriff', in *Kleinere Schriften* Volume II (Berlin, 1957).

On the Megarians see further the edition and commentary of

[221] K. Döring, *Die Megariker* (Amsterdam, 1972),
and on Diodorus, a later member of the school, consult the bibliography in
[222] N. Rescher, 'A version of the "Master Argument" of Diodorus',
Journal of Philosophy 63 (1966), pp.438-45.
Hintikka's ideas are taken up in a study of *De Caelo* I 12 by
[223] C.J.F. Williams, 'Aristotle and Corruptibility', *Religious Studies* 1
(1965), pp.95-107, 203-15.
Aristotle's notion of power, as presented in Metaphysics IX and elsewhere,
is discussed by
[224] A.P.D. Mourelatos, 'Aristotle's "powers" and modern empiricism',
Ratio 9 (1967), pp.97-104.
The idea of activity which Aristotle associates with *energeia* is discussed by
[225] A.J.P. Kenny, *Action, Emotion and Will* (London, 1963), ch. 8,
[226] J.L. Ackrill, 'Aristotle's distinction·between *energeia* and *kinesis*', in
New Essays on Plato and Aristotle, ed. R. Bambrough (London, 1965),
[227] T.C. Potts, 'States, activities and performances', *Proceedings of the
Aristotelian Society* (suppl. vol.) 39 (1965), pp.65-84,
[228] C.C.W. Taylor, 'States, activities and performances', *ibid.*, pp.85-102,
[229] F.R. Pickering, 'Aristotle on Walking', *Archiv für Geschichte des
Philosophie* 59 (1977), pp.37-43.
See further nos. [311] to [314] below.

Book IX of the *Metaphysics* ends with a chapter on truth (see also *De
Interpretatione* 1, *Metaphysics* VI 4, *De Anima* III 6). Aristotle's views on truth,
touched on in our chapter 9, are expounded and discussed in the relevant
volumes of [3] and in
[230] F. Brentano, *The True and the Evident*, ed. O. Kraus (English edition
by R.M. Chisholm, translation by Chisholm *et al.*) (London, 1966),
[231] P. Wilpert, 'Zum aristotelischen Wahrheitsbegriff' in [66],
[232] J.G. Dehninger, *'Wahres sein'* in *der Philosophie des Aristoteles*
(Meisenheim, 1961),
[233] K. Oehler, *Die Lehre vom noetischen und dianoetischen Denken bei Platon und
Aristoteles* (*Zetemata* 29, Munich, 1962),
[234] J. Hintikka, 'Time, truth, and knowledge in ancient Greek
philosophy', *American Philosophical Quarterly* 4 (1967), 1-4 (reprinted in an
expanded version in [101]).

Book XII of the *Metaphysics*, which culminates in a proof of the existence
of Aristotle's god and an exploration of his nature, is naturally read as the
culmination of Aristotle's analysis of substance. This is made clear by our
chapter 3, and is also argued by
[235] K. Oehler, 'Die systematische Integration der aristotelischen
Metaphysik', in [38].
Jaeger's investigations of the *Metaphysics* prompted accounts of the theology
much concerned with Aristotle's development from Platonism, as by
[236] H. von Arnim, 'Die Entwicklung der aristotelischen Gotteslehre', in
[114],
[237] W.K.C. Guthrie, 'The development of Aristotle's theology', *Classical
Quarterly* 27 (1933), pp.162-71; 28 (1934), pp.90-8, and now
[238] H.J. Easterling, 'The unmoved mover in early Aristotle', *Phronesis* 21
(1976), pp.252-65.

More recently scholars have paid more attention to the metaphysics of Aristotle's theology, without losing interest in its relation to Platonism. See most notably

[239] P. Merlan, 'Aristotle's unmoved movers', *Traditio* 4 (1946), pp.1-30,

[240] *id.*, *Studies in Epicurus and Aristotle* (Wiesbaden, 1960), ch. 3,

[241] H.J. Krämer, *Der Ursprung der Geistmetaphysik* (Amsterdam, 1967²), with the comments of

[242] K. Oehler, review of [241], *Gnomon* 40 (1968), pp.641-53;

and Krämer's articles [146] (Part 1) and

[243] H.J. Krämer, 'Grundfragen der aristotelischen Theologie', *Theologie und Philosophie* 44 (1969), pp.363-82, 481-505,

[244] J. Vuillemin, *De la logique à la théologie* (Paris, 1967),

reviewed by

[245] J. Brunschwig, 'Le dieu d'Aristote au tribunal de la logique', *L'Age de la Science* 3 (1972), pp.323-43,

[246] S.R.L. Clark, *Aristotle's Man* (Oxford, 1975), chs. 5 and 6.

A careful analysis of Aristotle's actual proof of an unmoved mover is by

[247] K. Oehler, 'Der Beweis für den unbewegten Beweger bei Aristoteles', *Philologus* 99 (1955), pp.70-92 (reprinted in his collected essays, see [196]).

Aristotle's theological thought impinges at crucial points on his ethics and psychology: see in our Volume 2 a translation of

[248] P. Defourny, 'L'activité de contemplation dans les morales d'Aristote', *Bulletin de l'Institut Historique Belge de Rome* 18 (1937), pp.89-101,

with which compare

[249] W.J. Verdenius, 'Human reason and God in the Eudemian Ethics' in [39];

and in Volume 4

[250] R. Norman, 'Aristotle's philosopher-god', *Phronesis* 14 (1969), pp.63-74,

together with Clark [246].

See also

[251] W.J. Verdenius, 'Traditional and personal elements in Aristotle's religion', *Phronesis* 5 (1960), pp.56-70.

Books XIII and XIV are taken up with critiques of Platonism, particularly with respect to mathematical philosophy, on which Aristotle gives his own views in Book XIII 1-3. Besides the notes in [49] see further on Aristotle's conception of geometry chapters 8 and 10. The important notion of abstraction, explored in chapter 8, is the subject of

[252] M.-D. Philippe, 'Abstraction, addition, séparation chez Aristote', *Revue Thomiste* 48 (1948), pp.461-79,

[253] E. de Stryker, 'La notion aristotélicienne de séparation dans son application aux idées de Platon', in *Autour d'Aristote* (see [139] above).

We may mention the indispensable works of Sir Thomas Heath:

[254] T.L. Heath, *A History of Greek Mathematics*, 2 volumes (Oxford, 1921),

[255] *id.*, *The Thirteen Books of Euclid's Elements*, 3 volumes (Cambridge, 1908),

and his useful collection of Aristotelian material,

[256] *id.*, *Mathematics in Aristotle* (Oxford, 1949).

See further items in the bibliography to our Volume 1, together with
[257] H.G. Apostle, *Aristotle's Philosophy of Mathematics* (Chicago, 1952),
[258] E.A. Maziarz and T. Greenwood, *Greek Mathematical Philosophy* (New York, 1968) and the old work of
[259] G. Milhaud, *Les philosophes-géomètres de la Grèce* (Paris, 1900).

(d) *Physics*

The classic general study of the *Physics* is
[260] A. Mansion, *Introduction à la physique aristotélicienne* (Louvain, 1945²).
See also
[261] F. Solmsen, *Aristotle's System of the Physical World* (Ithaca, 1960) and
[262] W. Wieland, *Die aristotelische Physik* (Gottingen, 1970²), from which chapter 9 of our Volume 1 is taken.
There is an extensive bibliography of the *Physics* in
[263] H. Wagner (ed.), *Aristoteles: Physikvorlesung* (Berlin, 1967).
General discussions of the relation of physics and metaphysics in Aristotle are given by
[264] A. Mansion, 'La physique aristotélicienne et la philosophie', *Revue néoscolastique de philosophie* 39 (1936), pp.5-26,
[265] E. Berti, 'Physique et métaphysique selon Aristote', in [38].

Aristotle's fundamental physical idea of matter is touched on in chapters 5 and 6 of our volume, and explored more fully in chapters 7 and 8. A massive discussion of his development of the concept both in the *Metaphysics* and elsewhere (see particularly *Physics* I and *De Generatione et Corruptione* I) is offered by
[266] H. Kapp, *Hyle: Studien zum aristotelischen Materie-Begriff* (Berlin, 1971).
An older, classic discussion is by
[267] C. Baeumker, *Das Problem der Materie in der griechischen Philosophie* (Münster, 1890).
On the word *hulê*, see
[268] F. Solmsen, 'Aristotle's word for "matter"', in his *Kleine Schriften* Vol. I (Hildesheim, 1968).
A useful collection of essays is
[269] E. McMullin (ed.), *The Concept of Matter in Greek and Medieval Philosophy* (Notre Dame, 1963).
The question whether Aristotle believed in 'prime matter', a single ultimate substratum of all change, has been debated in recent years by
[270] H.R. King, 'Aristotle without *prima materia*', *Journal of the History of Ideas* 17 (1956), pp.370-89,
[271] F. Solmsen, 'Aristotle and prime matter', *ibid.* 19 (1958), pp.243-52 (reprinted in his *Kleine Schriften* Vol. I).
A second round of controversy was opened by W. Charlton in an appendix to [50] entitled 'Did Aristotle believe in prime matter?', and continued by
[272] H.M. Robinson, 'Prime matter in Aristotle', *Phronesis* 19 (1974), pp.168-88.
Two treatments of Aristotle's introduction of the notion of matter in *Physics* I are by Wieland in [262], chs. 4-9 (and see chapter 8 of our Volume 1) and
[273] B. Jones, 'Aristotle's introduction of matter', *Philosophical Review* 83 (1974), pp.474-500.

See also
[274] P. Suppes, 'Aristotle's concept of matter and its relation to modern concepts of matter', *Synthese* 28 (1974), pp.27-50.

The notion of *phusis* or nature introduced in Book II is discussed by
[275] A. Mansion, 'La notion de nature dans la physique aristotélicienne', *Université de Louvain: Annales de l'Institut Supérieur de Philosophie* 1 (1912), pp.471-567,
and in [224] above.
Aristotle's celebrated doctrine of the four 'causes' or modes of explanation is the subject of
[276] D.J. Allan, 'Causality ancient and modern', *Proceedings of the Aristotelian Society*, suppl. vol. 39 (1965), pp.1-18,
[277] J.M.E. Moravcsik, 'Aristotle on adequate explanations', *Synthese* 28 (1974), pp.3-17, with a comment by J. Bogen, *ibid.*, 19-25,
[278] M. Hocutt, 'Aristotle's four becauses', *Philosophy* 49 (1974), pp.385-99
For a treatment of explanation and cause in the *Posterior Analytics*, see Barnes [176],
[279] B.A. Brody, 'Towards an Aristotelian theory of scientific explanation', *Philosophy of Science* 39 (1972), pp.20-31, which takes a different view from Hocutt's,
[280] W. Wieland, 'Zeitliche Kausalstrukturen in der aristotelischen Logik', *Archiv für Geschichte der Philosophie* 54 (1972), pp.229-37, which connects with *De Interpretatione* chapter 9,
[281] L. Robin, 'La conception aristotélicienne de la causalité', *Archiv für Geschichte der Philosophie* 23 (1910), pp.1-28; 184-210.
For a particular aspect of causation, see
[282] A.C. Lloyd, 'The principle that cause is greater than effect', *Phronesis* 21 (1976), pp.146-56.
The role of necessity in natural science is given sharply contrasting treatments by
[283] T. Gomperz, *Greek Thinkers* (London, 1912), Vol. IV, ch. X,
and by Balme in [177]; see also [176] and [181] above, and now
[284] R. Sorabji, *Necessity, Cause and Blame* (London, 1978).
On teleology see (besides chapter 9 of our Volume 1 and [260] above)
[285] D.M. Balme, 'Greek science and mechanism', *Classical Quarterly* 33 (1939), pp.129-38; 35 (1941), pp.23-8,
[286] K. Gaiser, 'Das zweifache Telos bei Aristoteles', in [38],
[287] M.P. Lerner, *La notion de finalité chez Aristote* (Paris, 1969),
[288] G.E.R. Lloyd, *Polarity and Analogy* (Cambridge, 1966),
[289] A. Preus, *Aristotle's Biological Works* (Hildesheim, 1975),
[290] A. Gotthelf, 'Aristotle's conception of final causality', *Review of Metaphysics* 30 (1976-7), pp.226-54.
Both necessity and teleology are extensively discussed in
[291] W. Kullmann, *Wissenschaft und Methode* (Berlin, 1974).

The definition of *phusis* includes the concept of motion, and the major part of the *Physics* is devoted to an analysis of *kinêsis*, or motion in the broadest sense, and of the associated concepts of space and time. According to

Aristotle, space, time and matter are continuous or infinitely divisible; Aristotle's account of the continuum and his rejection of atomism are the topics of

[292] D.J. Furley, *Two Studies in the Greek Atomists* (Princeton, 1967), and of Part I, chs. 7-9 of

[293] A. van Melsen, *From Atomos to Atom* (Pittsburgh, 1952).

The related problems of infinity are dealt with by Hintikka in our chapter 10; see also

[284] K. von Fritz, 'Das *apeiron* bei Aristotles', in [38],

[295] D.J. Furley, 'Aristotle and the atomists on infinity', in [38] and Bostock's paper [322].

Place, *topos*, occupies *Physics* IV, 1-5; see

[296] M. Dehn, 'Raum, Zeit, Zahl bei Aristoteles vom mathematischen Standpunkt aus', *Scientia* (Bologna) 60 (1936), pp.12-21; 69-74,

[297] H.R. King, 'Aristotle's theory of *topos*', *Classical Quarterly* 44 (1950), pp.76-96,

[298] M. Jammer, *Concepts of Space* (Cambridge, Mass., 1954),

[299] J. Moreau, *L'Espace et le temps selon Aristote* (Padua, 1965).

On time see, besides our chapter 11, nos. [234], [280], and chapter 4.1 of Clark's book [246]; also

[300] A. Levi, 'Il concetto del tempo in Aristotele', *Athenaeum* 26 (1948), pp.3-33,

[301] J.F. Callaghan, *Four Views of Time in Ancient Philosophy* (Cambridge, Mass., 1948),

[302] P.F. Conen, *Die Zeittheorie des Aristoteles* (Munich, 1964),

[303] W. von Leyden, 'Time, number and eternity in Plato and Arisotle', *Philosophical Quarterly* 14 (1964), pp.35-52,

[304] J. Moreau, 'Le temps et l'instant selon Aristote', in [38],

[305] G. Verbeke, 'Le statut ontologique du temps selon quelques penseurs grecs', in *Zetesis: Album for E. de Stryker* (Antwerp, Utrecht, 1973), pp.188-205,

[306] Fred D. Miller, 'Aristotle on the reality of time', *Archiv für Geschichte der Philosophie* 56 (1974), pp.132-55,

[307] J. Annas, 'Aristotle, number and time', *Philosophical Quarterly* 25 (1975), pp.97-113,

[308] W. Kneale, 'Time and eternity in theology', *Proceedings of the Aristotelian Society* 61 (1960/1), pp.87-108,

[309] A. Mansion, 'La théorie aristotélicienne du temps chez les péripatéticiens médiévaux', *Revue néoscolastique de philosophie* 34 (1934), pp.275-307,

[310] D. Corish, 'Aristotle's attempted derivation of temporal order', *Phronesis* 21 (1976), pp.241-51.

Motion is discussed in *Physics* III 1-3, and again in V-VIII. On Aristotle's difficult account of *kinêsis* see nos. [225] to [229], and

[311] L.A. Kosman, 'Aristotle's definition of motion', *Phronesis* 14 (1969), pp.40-62,

[312] A.L. Peck, 'Aristotle on *kinêsis*', in J. Anton and G. Kustas (eds.),

Essays in Ancient Greek Philosophy (Albany, N.Y., 1971),

[313] G. Boas, 'Aristotle's presupposition about change', *American Journal of Philology* 68 (1947), pp.404-13,

[314] T. Penner, 'Verbs and the identity of actions', in G. Pitcher and O.P. Wood (eds.), *Ryle* (New York, 1970),

[315] D.J. Furley, 'Aristotle and the atomists on motion in a void', in *Motion and Time, Space and Matter* (see [324] below).

Aristotle's views on motion lead him to discuss Zeno's notorious paradoxes. The paradoxes have collected a vast modern literature; some excellent pieces are collected in

[316] W.C. Salmon, *Zeno's Paradoxes* (Indianapolis, 1969).

See also

[317] G. Vlastos, 'Zeno', in P. Edwards (ed.), *The Encyclopaedia of Philosophy* (London, 1967),

[318] G. Vlastos, 'Zeno's race course', *Journal of the History of Philosophy* 4 (1966), pp.95-108,

[319] G. Vlastos, 'A note on Zeno's arrow', *Phronesis* 11 (1966), pp.3-17,

[320] A. Grünbaum, *Modern Science and Zeno's Paradoxes* (Middletown, Conn., 1967).

On Aristotle's reply to Zeno see especially

[321] G.E.L. Owen, 'Zeno and the mathematicians', *Proceedings of the Aristotelian Society* 58 (1957/8), pp.199-222 (reprinted in [316]),

[322] D. Bostock, 'Aristotle, Zeno and the potential infinite', *Proceedings of the Aristotelian Society* 73 (1972/3), pp.37-51.

The related puzzles about the 'instant of change' are discussed in our chapter 12. Mediaeval continuations of Aristotle's discussion are treated by

[323] A.C. Wilson, *William Heytesbury* (Madison, Wis., 1956),

[324] N. Kretzmann, 'Incipit/Desinit', in *Motion and Time, Space and Matter*, ed. P. Machamer and R. Turnbull (Columbus, Ohio, 1975).

On *Physics* VI in general see

[325] J. Jope, 'Subordinate demonstrative science in the sixth book of Aristotle's *Physics*', *Classical Quarterly* 22 (1972), pp.279-92.

There is a recent monograph devoted to the early Book VII of the *Physics*:

[326] B. Manuwald, *Das Buch H der aristotelischen Physik* (Meisenheim, 1971).

See also

[327] G. Verbeke, 'L'argument du livre VII de la Physique', in [38],

[328] O. Becker, 'Eudoxos-Studien III: Spuren eines Stetigkeitsaxioms in der Art des Dedekind'schen zur Zeit des Eudoxos', *Quellen und Studien zur Geschichte der Mathematik, Astronomie und Physik* B3 (1936), pp.236-44.

Book VIII of the *Physics*, which contains an argument for the unmoved mover, has not excited a great deal of analysis in recent years. It is probably best to turn to Solmsen's book [261], to articles on Aristotle's theology, and to [15] and [263] above. See also D.J. Furley's paper in [41] and G. Seeck's in [38].

Further Bibliography on the *Physics* will be found in our volume I; the methodology of the *Physics* is the subject of chapters 7 and 8 of that volume.

INDEX OF ARISTOTELIAN PASSAGES

INDEX OF ARISTOTELIAN PASSAGES

Categoriae

1	1a1-6	30n52
1	1a12 ff.	38n9
2	1a27	101
4	1b27 ff.	7
5	2a13	91n9
	2a19-27	30
	2b4-6	21
	2b29-37	21
	3a33-b9	30
	3b18-21	21
	3b33-4a9	28
6		102-3
	5a38-b10	20n23, 21
7	6a36 ff.	2n4
	7a31-b9	99n5
	8b10-20	18n17
8	8b20-4	18n17
	8b24-7	18n17
	8b26	10
	9a10-11	18n17
	9a23-b1	18n17
	10a32 ff.	38n9
	11a12-13	28n46
10	11b16	6
12	14a26-9	157
	14a39	134n23

De Interpretatione

1	16a16-18	51
4	17a1-3	51
5	17a14	47n26
9		108, 113-14
	18a27-33	108
	18b10-14	114
	18b11-15	112
	19a12-15	125n2
	19a12-17	114
	19a24-5	115
12-13		111n4
12	21b27-32	122

	22a8-12	122
13	23a17-19	111
	23a20-2	112
	23a23-6	125
	23a25	114
14		52-3
	23a27-39	52
	23b17, 20	53
	23b25-7	53
	24b1-3	51

Analytica Priora

I

1	24a16	11
	24b27-30	118
2	25a25	109
3		124
	25b18-25	122
4	26a8	109
	26b7	109
6	28a32	109
8	29b35-7	118
9-12		109, 124
9	30a24	109
	30a29-31	121
10	30b31-4	136
	30b33	109
	30b38-40	136
11	31b20-7	119
	31b41	109
12		111n4
13		124
	32a18-20	111, 115, 119
	32b1-3	122
	32b6	109
	32b23-7	118
	32b25-37	122,123
14		121n24, 122, 123
	33a1-2	122
	33a4-5	122
	33a24-5	122
15	34a1-33	119

	34a8-18	118
	34a8-20	112
	34a34-b5	118, 119
	34b7-18	110, 119, 121
	34b18	112
	34b19-31	118
17	37a16-21	122
18	37b40	120
22	40a39 ff.	119
	40b2-3	120
41	49b15-32	118
46	52a32	52 nl
II		
20	66b11	55

Analytica Posteriora
I

1	71a11-17	76 n47
2	72a23	76 n47
	72a32	68 n21
4	73a21-4	109
	73a27-30	110
	73a34-7	19 n19
	73b	115
	73b5-8	14 n3
	73b16-24	109
	73b26-9	109
	73b26-8	23 n34
	73b27-9	110
	73b37-40	109
	74a2-3	109
5	74a33-b1	99
6	74b26-38	112
	75a12-14	109
7	75b12-15	23
8	75b20-30	112
	75b31	132
9	76a16-25	23
10	76a31-6	104
	76a34-6	104
	76a37-40	15 n8, 22
	76a38-9	22
	76b3-11	104
	76b11-16	104
	76b16-19	105
	76b35	76 n47
11	77a5-7	101
	77a10-22	59 and n10
	77a26-31	23
18	81b2-5	99 n7
22	83b15	1
	84a7-9	15 n8
	84b1-2	15 n8
24	85b15-22	23 n34
26	87a22-4	123

28	87a38-b4	24 n36
32	88a36-b3	22
II		72
1		78
	89b34	77 n49
2	90a6, 14, 31	42 n18
3-8		63 n2, 73
3	90b23	132
7	92a34	73 n40
	92b37	68 n21, 73 n39
8 ff.		70 n25
8		69 n24, 75 and n44
	93a30 ff.	66 n15, 67
10		66 n15, 67
12	96a14-15	110
13		63 n2, 66, 67n18, 73, 74 and n42
	96b35	74 n42
	97b7 ff.	74
16		15 n8
17	99a22	132
19		65 n8, 68 n21, 73 n36, 74

Topica
I

		63 n2
2	101a36-b4	22 n30
4-9		3 n6
9	103b20-39	20 n24
	103b39	3 n6
10	104a8	11
14	105b30-1	15 n8
15	106a1-8	15 n5, 24 n36
	106a4-8	20 n26
	106b33-7	20 nn 24 and 26
	107a5-12	20 n24
18	108b9-29	66
	108b9	69
	108b22 ff.	74
	108b28	69
II		
1		28 n48
	109a10	6 n13
2	109b17-29	24 n36
3	110b16-111a7	15 n5
	110b16-25	24 n36
9	114a29-31	20 n26
10		28 n48
III		
2	117b10-12	20 n26
IV		
1	121a10 ff.	39 n11
2	122b7-11	30

4	124a31-4	20 n26
5	128b8-9	22 n33

V

1	128b16-18	112
5	134a18-25	21
	134a32-b1	21
	134a32-6	20 n26
	134b10-13	21, 26
8		28 n48

VI

		4 n9, 63 n2, 67 n18
1		64
2	139b32-140a17	21 n27
4		64
	141b19-22	19 n19
6	145a28-30	20 n26, 21
	145b26-30	112
10	148a23-36	20

VII

3	153a6	75
4	154a15-20	30

VIII

2	158a31-b4	19 n19
11	162a26-32	28 n47
13	162b31-8	15 n8
14	163b20-1	19 n19
	164a1-2	24 n36

De Sophisticis Elenchis
(= *Topica* IX)

4	166b16	7 n14
5	166b32	5
11	172a11-13	22
	172a36-8	22 n33
33	182b13-27	14
34	183b25	4 n8

Physica

I

1		45 n23, 72 nn33 and 34
	184a10	65 n11
	184a14 ff.	65 n12
	184b2	79
2	184b15 ff.	2
3	186a25	2
	187a1	2
4	188a15	89 n3
8	191b29	47 n26
9		63 n2

II

2	193b22-35	131
	193b24-194a7	98
	194a9-11	131

	194a21 ff.	133
	194a27-8	24 n36
	194b14-15	35 n4
3	195a18-19	117
9		136
	200a16-18	129

III

1	200b32-201a16	168
4-8		125-39
4	203b17	129 n11
	203b18-20	139
	203b22-5	135, 139
	203b23-5	128
	203b29-30	112
	203b30	125 n4
	204a2-6	137
	204a2-3	137
5	204a34 ff.	131
6	206a12-14	126
	206a14-18	126
	206a18-35	114
	206a18-21	131
	206a21-3	126
	206a22-3	114, 126
	206a23-5	126, 132
	206a29-33	131, 132
	206a30-4	114
	206a32-3	126
	206b3-9	136
	206b12-15	132
	206b13-15	114
	206b13-14	114, 127
	206b14-16	132
	206b15-16	126
	207a21-32	132
7		130, 138
	207b8-10	21 n29
	207b10-13	135
	207b17-18	127
	207b19-21	127
	207b21-5	146
	207b27-34	128
	207b33-4	129
	207b34-208a4	132
8	208a8-11	139
	208a14-19	135, 139
	208a18	127 n9
	208a20-1	135, 136 n24
	208a21-2	135

IV

4		63 n2
	211a6	68 n22
10-14		140, 146-58
10	217b32-218a3	146
	218a1-2	147

	218a3-8	146	234a24	144
	218a14-18	152	234a34-b5	166 n13, 170, 171, 173 n26
	218a18-19	147		
	218b10-13	155	4	159 n2
	218b13-18	152, 155	234b10-20	169
11	218b21-219a10	154, 155	235a9-27	164 n7
	219a10-b2	150	5 235b6-32	172
	219a10-21	155	235b7-8	172 n22
	219a10-19	156	235b31-2	172 n22
	219a10-14	146	235b32-236a7	171, 172 n22
	219a12-14	157	236a7-27	164 n7, 173
	219a14-19	146	236a7-10	173 n25
	219a14	146 n15	236a15, 16-17	173
	219a19	156 n34	236a17-20	173
	219a22-b2	154	236a17-18	143 n7
	219a25-30	150, 151	236a19-20	173 n25
	219a26-30	151	236b5-8	169 n17
	219b13-14	151	6	164 n7, 173
	219b15-16	146, 156	236b32-237a17	144, 173
	219b19	156 n32	237a11-17	166 n13
	219b22-33	151	237a11	173
	219b22-8	151	237a14-15	170, 171
	219b28-33	155	237a14	141, 144
	219b33-220a1	154	237a15	173 n26
	220a9-11	154, 156	237a16	173
	220a12-18	154	237a17-b22	164, 173
	220a14-21	150	237a17-b3	168
12	220b24-8	156	237a17-28	143
	220b28-32	157	237a19-28	169
13	222a10-12	154	237a29	169
	222a13	154	237b1	169
	222a20-1	20 n22	237b2	169
	222a20-4	146	237b6-7	173
	222b27-9	154	237b9-21	168
14	222b30-223a15	141	237b11, 15	168
	222b30-223a4	156, 157	237b21	169
	223a21-9	156, 157	8	173
	223b12-224a2	154	238b23-9	144
V			238b26-30	144 n10
2		168	238b31-239a10	144
	225b33-226a6	168	239a3-6	166 n13, 170
6	230b32-231a1	169	239a10-b4	170-1
VI			239a20-b9	143
1		159 n2	239a26-b2	141
	231b6-10	141	239a35-b4	143, 144, 171
	231b18-232a18	164 n7	239a35-b1	144 n8
	231b30-232a2	144 n12	239b1-2	141
	232a6-18	164	9 239b7	151
	232a6-11	159 n2, 160 n3, 164	239b8-9	143
			239b15-16, 26-9	141
2		159 n2	239b30-3	143
	232b20-3	157	239b30	141 n3
3		173	239b32	151
	234a24-b9	170-1	240a19-29	169
	234a24-31	141		

10		159 n2
	240b21-31	169
	240b31-241a6	160 n3, 164 and n7
	241a24-6	141
VII		
4	248a10-249a25	142 n5
	249a3-8	28 n46
	249a23-5	30
VIII		
4	255b3-8	113
7	260b15 ff.	20 n22
8		159 n2, 169
	262a30	171
	262a31-b3	174
	262b20	171
	262b21-263a3	174
	263b9-15	172, 173 n26
	263b11	172
	263b15-264a16	171-2
	263b17-21	172
	263b20	171
	263b21-2	172 n21
	263b22, 23	171
	263b26-264a1	144
	263b26-7	172 n21
	263b27, 30	169, 171
	264a2-3	172
	264a2	172 n21
	264a5	172 n21
	264b1	171 n20

De Caelo

I		
1	268a7-8	104
5	271b28-272a7	130
9	279a28-30	45 n22
12		112
	281b26	112
	283a25-6	112

De Generatione et Corruptione

I		
3	319a14	7
5		94-5
	321a29	94 n20
	321a34	94 n21
	321b19	94 n22
	321b24	95 n24
6	322b29-32	20 n22, 31 n53
	322b31-2	15 n7
II		
11	338a1-4	112
	338b7-15	114

Meteorologica

IV		
	390a10-13	30 n52

De Anima

I		72
1		76
	402a1-16	77
	402a10	73 n35
	402a11	76, 78
	402a19 ff.	74
	402b10	73 n35
	402b19	75
7		63 n2
II		
1	412b10-17	83 n8
	412b20-2	30 n52
2	413a13-15	42 n18
	413a31-b10	20
3	414b25-415a1	20
4	415a23-5	20
	415a26-b2	85 n14
	415b12-15	14 n3
	415b16-17	85 n13
10	422a26-9	136
III		
4-5		133 n20
5		65 n8, 73 n37
6	431a1-2	133
7	431a3-4	133
8	431b20-1	41 n15
	432a1-2	40 n13
	432a2	41
	432a3-10	106

De Sensu

6		169-70
	445b21-9	169
	445b28, 30	169
	446a1-4	170
	446a16-20	169
	446b2	165
	447a1-3	169
7	449a21-31	176

De Memoria

1	449b31-450a6	131
	450b21, 32	30 n52
2	452b13 ff.	136

De Respiratione

	474a26	10 n16

De Partibus Animalium

I
               63 n2
  1   67 n18
    639a10   37 n7
    639b25   136
    640b29-641a6   30 n52
    642a8   136
  5 645b14-20   83 n8

IV
  10 687b2-5   41 n14

De Motu Animalium

  4 699b17-22   117, 136
    699b17   137
    699b29   113

De Incessu Animalium

    711a6   10 n16

De Generatione Animalium

I
    726b22-4   30 n52

Mechanica

I
    848b1-849b19   142
    848b26-7   142

Metaphysica

I   33, 46-7
  1   33
  2   35
    982a8-10,
    21-3   37 n6
    983a5-9   35n4
  3 983a27-8   84 n10
    983b19   89 n2
  5 986a22   7
  6 987b7-9   19
  9   24-5, 26
    990b15-17   29
    990b22-991a8   30
    991a2-8   26
    991a20-3   30
    992a10-18   19 n19
    992a21-2   19 n19
    992b18-24   14, 25
II   33, 46-7
  1 993b23-6   39
    993b23   42 n18
  2 994b20-7   136
    994b26   90 n6

III   33, 35, 46-7,
    102 n12
  2 997a2-11,
    15-25   23
    997b35-998a6   98
  3 998b14 ff.   39 n11
  6 1003a15-17   106 n17
IV   13-14, 16-25, 31,
    33-7, 46-7, 50-62
  1-2 1003a21-b19   16 n11
  1′ 1003a21   33 n1
    1003a23-4   17 n14
    1003a24   33 n1
    1003a28-32   25
    1003a31   33 n1
  2   17 n16, 45
    1003a33-b5   31
    1003a33-b1   39
    1003a33   24, 145
    1003b1-4   39, 48
    1003b12-15   39
    1003b16-19   41 n16
    1003b16   40, 44
    1003b17   45
    1004a4   39
    1004a22-31   18
    1004a29   40
    1004b27   7
    1005a10-11   19 n19
  3 1005b19-20   51
    1005b23-4   51
    1005b25-6   54
    1005b26-32   52
    1005b32-4   59
  4   22 n32, 55-7
    1006a10-11   54
    1006a11-18   23
    1006a11-13   55
    1006a15-18   55
    1006a29-31   57
    1006b11-22   56
    1006b28-34   56
    1007b16-18   57
    1007b17-18   55
    1007b18-21   56
    1007b19   57
    1007b28-9   58
    1008a8-16   57
    1008a28-30   56
    1008a34-b1   60
    1008b1-2   60
    1008b12-19   56
    1008b31-
    1009a5   57
  5 1009a22-36   58

	1009a36-8	58
	1010a1-5	58
	1010a32-5	58
6	1011b13-14	51
	1011b15-21	52
7	1011b26-7	52
V		9, 20, 33, 140
2	1013a26-7,	
	b22-3	84 n10
	1013b34 ff.	8
3	1014a36	134 n23
5	1015a33-6	111
6	1015b16 ff.	3, 8
	1016b6-9	20 n23, 25 n39
	1016b24-31	103
	1016b31-	
	1017a3	25 n39
	1016b34-5	25 n38
7	1017a7 ff.	3 (and n5), 8
	1017a13-22	20 n23
8	1017b21-6	84 n10
10	1018a20	6
	1018a31-8	18, 20 n23
11		140, 157
	1018b12-19	157
	1018b12-14	157
	1018b30-	
	1019a1	157
	1018b30-32	31 n54
	1018b32-3	157
	1018b34-7	19 n19
	1019a1-4	19
	1019a11-14	157
12		111 n4
	1019b35-	
	1020a6	20 n23
13	1020a7-14	104
	1020a14-32	20 n23
16	1022a1-3	20 n23
18	1022a14 ff.	3 n5
	1022 a26	92 n17
20	1022b4 ff.	10
22	1022b32-	
	1023a7	22 n33
23	1023a8 ff.	10
28	1024a36-b4	104
29	1024b17-	
	1025a13	20 n23
	1024b32	5, 6 n13
30	1025a33	112
VI		16-18. 24, 33-17,
		46-7
1		33-8, 41-3, 45
	1025b27	138 n26
	1026a13-16	35

	1026a18-19	36
	1026a23-32	38
	1026a29-32	16 n11
	1026a30-1	17 n14
	1026a30	38
2	1026b27-37	112
3	1027b25-7	133 n21
VII		24, 44, 46-9,
		63 n2, 80-95
1		17 n16, 140
	1028a10-b7	47
	1028a13-16	41 n16
	1028a29-31	14 n3, 17 n16
	1028a31-b2	31 n54
	1028a32-b2	19
	1028a34-b2	157
	1028a34-6	16 n11
	1028b4	80 n1
3	1028b33-6	80
	1029a11	99 n5
	1029a12-18	103
	1029a16-19	99 n5
	1029a20	70
	1029a22	90 n7
	1029a26-34	82 n6
	1029a26-30	90 n5
	1029a26-8	81
	1029a32	91 n10, 92 n11
4-6		81, 82 n7
4		22 n32, 24 n36
	1030a9	63
	1030a21-30	69, 71
	1030a21-7	22 n32
	1030a21	71 n32
	1030a25	22 n32
	1030a27-b4	15 n7
	1030a27-8	22 n32
	1030a34-b7	31 n54
	1030a34-b3	22 n32
	1030b3-4	22 n32
	1030b10	63
5	1030b26	71
	1031a1 ff.	71
	1031a12-14	81
6	1031a17-21	92 n13
	1031b1-2	84
	1031b18-20	81
	1031b31-	
	1032a11	82 n7
	1031b31-2	81
7-9		80-7
7		83-5
	1032a12-14	83
	1032a16-25	83
	1032a24-5	81 nn3 and 4

1032a32-b30	83 n9
1032b1-15	134
1032b1-2	87 n17
1032b1	85 n12
1032b2	92 n12
1032b11-14	84
1032b14	87 n17
1032b15	92 n12
1032b29-30	83 n9
8	85-6
1033a24-b19	81, 85 n15
1033b5-7	87 n17
1033b20-	
1034a5	81 n4
1033b20-1	85
1033b21-4	86
1033b24-8	86
1033b24	88 n1
1033b29-32	81 n3, 86 n16
1033b33-	
1034a2	81 n3
1034a2-8	86 n16
1034a5-8	87 n18
9	86 n16
1034a21-4	81 n3
1034a22-4	134
1034a31-2	81 n4
1034b7-19	81
1034b16-19	81 n3
10-12	80, 81, 87
10 1034b20	65 n10
1034b21	71 n30
1034b33	65 n13
1035a1	66 n15
1035b11	67
1035b20	66 n14
1035b29	70
1035b32	84 n10, 87 n17
1035b33	70 n28
1036a1	92 n15
1036a9-12	101, 103
11 1036a28	70 n29
1036a34-b3	99
1036b11	70 n27
1036b22-3	99
1036b29 ff.	65 n13
1037a2-5	101, 103
1037a10-16	87
1037a21-b7	80
1037a24	66 n14
1037a26	93 n18
1037a27	70 n29
1037a33	67
12 1037b12	67 n18
1038a1 ff.	67 n18

13-14	81
13 1038b2-6	81 n2
1039a4	68 n20
1039a14	66 n15
14-16	138 n27
15 1039b26	80
16 1040b32-4	19 n21
17	69
1041a6-9	87
1041a15	69 n23
1041b3 ff.	69
1041b8	70 n29
VIII	44, 46-9, 63 n2
1 1042a4-22	80
1042a26-31	81 n2
1042a32-b3	90 n8
2 1042b19	9
1042b25-8	14 n3
1043a8	67 n16
1043a13	66 n15, 67 n16
1043a16, 18	66 n15
3 1043b2	92 n14
1043b5	65 n13, 66 n14
1043b23-8	64 n4
1043b31	66 n15
4 1044a36	84 n10, 87 n17
1044b8-11	25
1044b8	67 n17, 69 n24
6 1045a8	66
1045a13	63, 66
1045a14	67 n19
1045a15	76
1045a33-5	104
1045b17-23	92 n16
IX	46-9
1	17 n16
1045b27-32	17 n16
1045b29-31	16 n11
1045b32	46 n25
3-4	112-13
3	112
1047a13	112
1047a23-6	111
4	111 n4
1047b3-6	112
6 1048a35-7	48
1048b1-8	132
1048b9-17	114, 125
1048b9-11	138
1048b14-17	137
1048b15-17	139
7 1049a12-14	113
8	112
1049b16-17	31 n54
1049b17-32	113

	1049b18-29	134
	1050b6-23	112
	1050b8	112
	1050b20-1	112
9		129
	1051a21-33	134 n22
	1051a21-31	134
X		
4	1055b13	10 n16
XI		16 and n10, 35
1-8		102 n12
1	1059b10-12	98
	1059b13	138
	1059b14-16	101
	1059b24 ff.	39 n11
2	1060b12-17	103
	1060b19-23	106 n17
3	1060b31-	
	1061a10	16 n11
	1060b31-5	24
	1060b36-	
	1061a7	145
	1061a28-35	102 n12
	1061b11-12	16 n11
7	1064a33-b14	35
	1064b13-14	17 n14
12		168
XII		25, 36-7, 42-7
1	1069a36-b2	25 n39, 43
4	1070b10-21	25
	1070b19-21	25
	1070b33-4	134
5	1071a33-5	25
6-7		44-5
6	1071b3-5	44
	1071b5-6	44
	1071b19-20	44
	1071b28-9	44
7	1072b7-11	44
	1072b13-15	44
	1072b14	45
	1072b20	41
8	1073b3-8	37 n8
	1074b9	45
XIII		
2-3		35
2	1077a36-b11	19 n19
	1077a36-b2	19 n19
	1077b3-4	31 n55
3		97-8, 102, 134 n22
	1077b17-30	97
	1078a2-9	97
	1078a21-31	138 n26
	1078a21-6	97
	1078a30-1	134 n22
4	1078b28	74 n41
	1079a11-13	29
	1079a12	29
	1079a33-b3	26
	1079b3-11	19 n21
	1079b6	26 n40
6	1080b17	138 n26
9	1086a33	138 n26
10	1087a10-25	106 nn17 and 18
XIV		
2	1088b18	2
	1088b23	112
	1089a7	2
6	1093b18-21	25 n38

Ethica Nicomachea

I		
2	1094a26-7	16 n12
6	1096a17-23	18 and n18
	1096a23-9	15 n6
	1096a26-9	15 n7
	1096a29-34	15 n6
	1096a30	47 n26
	1096a35-b5	19 n21
	1096b28-9	15, 25 n38
	1096b30-1	16
II		
2	1103b26-9	16 n12
3	1105a7-8	14 n4
III		
2	1111b10-12	14 n4
10	1118a32	14 n4
V		
1	1129a26-31	30
	1129a30	40 n12
VII		
1	1145b2-5	145 n14
VIII		
1	1155b14-16	28 n49
3	1156a6-b6	47 n29
	1156b19-21	17
4	1156b35-	
	1157a3	17
X		
4	1174a29-b5	143

Ethica Eudemia

I		
5	1216b6 ff.	133
	1216b20-5	16 n12
8	1217b10-16	19 n20
	1217b12-13	19
	1217b16-19	15 n8
	1217b25-35	15 nn5 and 6

	1217b35-	
	1218a1	15 n6
	1218a1-15	18
	1218a4-5	19
	1218a10-15	19 n21
	1218a33-6	15
	1218b10-25	15, 16 n12
	1218b13-14	16 n12
II		
7	1223a26-7	14 n4
	1223b22-4	14 n4
10	1225b22-4	14 n4
III		
2	1231a17	14 n4
VII		
2	1236a7-33	17
	1236a15-b3	47 n29
	1236a15-22	17
	1236a22-9	18
	1236b2	48
	1236b20-1,	
	25-6	15 n7

VIII
| 1 | 1246b9 | 16 n12 |

Politica

I
| 2 | 1253a20-5 | 30 n52 |
| 13 | 1259b36-8 | 28 n46 |

III
| 13 | 1284b9 | 30 n52 |

Rhetorica

I
| 2 | 1358a2-32 | 22 n30 |

FRAGMENTA

De Ideis
| Fr. 3 Ross | 28-9 |

Protrepticus
| Fr. 5 Ross | 27 n44 |
| Fr. 14 Ross | 27 n45 |

GENERAL INDEX

GENERAL INDEX

abstraction (*aphairesis*), and intuition, 64-5; in mathematics, 35, 98-107, 131; *see* separation

Academy, origins of categories in, 1-4; and development of 'focal meaning', Ch. 2 *passim*

acceleration, 162-3, 174-5

accident, accidental (*sumbebêkos, kata sumbebêkos*), 3, 6 n13, 56, 65, 71

Ackrill, J.L., 103, 125 n3, 165

actuality (*energeia, entelecheia*), Chs. 9 and 10 *passim*; prior to potentiality, 27, 112-13, 134; role in definition, 66 n15, 67-8, 104; connexion with conceivability, 132-7; with categories, 1; with form, 92, 132; with Law of Contradiction, 58, 62; understood by analogy, 48; role in argument for prime mover, 44; actual knowledge, 106 n18, 113

aitia, aition (cause, explanation, reason), 8, 78

akolouthein (answer to), 156 and n33

Alexander of Aphrodisias, 16 n9, 20 n25, 22 n33, 24 n36, 28-9, 43-4, 52 n3, 127 n9, 177 n30; *see* pseudo-Alexander

ambiguity, Ch. 2 *passim*, 122, 137; of verbs of motion, 140-5; *see* homonymy

Amis, K., 148

Ammonius, 64 n5

analogy, principle of unity distinct from 'focal meaning', 15 n7, 22, 24-6, 48-9; unifies sciences, 22; good, 15; in Theophrastus's ontology, 18 n7; used in defining, 69; analogy of distance, movement, time, 146, 154-8; of form in mind and in actuality, 134; of genus and matter, 70-1, 104; of matter and form in definition of substance, 75-6, 91; and similarly of causation, 75

analysis, and definition, Ch. 5 *passim*

Analytica Posteriora, conception of science, 105-6, 132; on principles and elements of science, 22-4, 104-5; on definition, Ch. 5 *passim*; on universality and necessity, 68 n21, 108, 110; on universal concepts, 65 n8; on subjects of attributes, 98-9; on abstraction, 99; on Forms, 101; on syllogism, 4, 109; and the Law of Contradiction, 59

Analytica Priora, contrasted with *Topics*, 4-6, 11, 15 n8; analysis of proposition and syllogism, 4, 5 n11, 78; of modal syllogisms, 109-10, 118-24; of modal notions, 111; on conversion, 6 n13; on figures, 46; use of *elenchos*, 55

Andronikos of Rhodes, 47

Anscombe, G.E.M., 108, 114, 115

Antiochus II, 27 n43

Antisthenes, 2, 5, 6 n13, 62, 64

Apelt, O., 1, 3 n3, 5 n11, 11 nn17, 18

aphairein, aphairesis (abstract, abstraction), 98, 99 n7

apophansis (statement), 51

apophasis (negation), 22, 51

aporia (difficulty), 23

Apostle, H.G., 103, 131, 133 n21, 134 n22

Aquinas, St Thomas, 116

archê (principle), 44

Archimedes, 128 n10

Arnim, H. von, 17, 20 n24, 48 n30
artifacts, and analysis of substance, 70-1, 75, 81, 83-6
assertoric (syllogism, premiss, proposition), 101, 109-10, 118-24
assumptions, of geometry, 104, 128 n10, 129
Assus, 8 n15
astronomy, 37 and n8
atom, Epicurean, 149, 169; of time, 153-4, 159-60, 173
atomism, 154, 164; *see* Epicurus
Augustine, 140, 147
authenticity, of *Categories*, 3 and n7; of *EE*, 14 n4, 18 n17, 48; of *Lin. Insec.*, 21 n28; of *Mechanica*, 142; of *Meta.* XI, 16 n10, 102 n12
Averroes, 116 n13
axiom, of science, 22-4, 25, 99, 104; of Archimedes, 128 n10; of parallels, 129-30; Law of Contradiction, 59, 62

Bacon, F., 22 n31
Baeumker, Cl., 116 n15
Becker, A., 110 n3, 121 nn23, 24, 122, 123, 124
becoming, topic of *Meta.* VII (ch. 7-9), 80-1, 83-6; verbs of, 144 n12; in *Parm.*, 151-3
being, *passim*
belief, and Law of Contradiction, 51-3
Bernays, P., 106
biology, use of analogy in, 48
Black, M., 177 n31
Bochenski, I.M., 110 n3, 115 nn6, 8, 121 nn23, 24, 122, 124 n29
Boehm, R., 80 n1, 82 n6
Boethus, 14 n2
Bonitz, H., 71 n31
Boole, G., 50
Bosanquet, B., 1
Brouwer, L., 96
Buridan, 116 n16

categories, Ch. 1 *passim*; primacy of first category and 'focal meaning', 14-16, 18, 21, 24-5, 39-40; 'first' in each category, 48-9

Categories, Ch. 1 *passim*; authenticity, 3 n7; 'focal meaning' in, 21; an ambiguity in, 28; on quantity, 102-3; on spatial and temporal priority, 157
causes (*aitia, aitiai*), distinctions between, 69-70, 83-5; natural and artificial, 83-6; ambiguity in meaning, 78; material, 117; efficient, 44; knowledge of, 65 n11; role in definition, 66, 67, 69-70, 71, 74-5; connexion with essence, 42; and with categories, 1, 7; and with 'focal meaning', 39-40, 42-6
chance, 83 and n9, 118
change (*kinêsis*), topic of physics, 35-6; categorial classification, 1, 7, 11, 45, 168, 170; continuous and instantaneous, 143 n6, Ch. 12 *passim*; actual and potential, 113; substantial, 90, 95; change and contradiction, 62; and predication, 88, 90; and definition, 98; and time, 154-6; Plato's views, 151-2
changeless, subject of first philosophy, 34-6, 43; and of mathematics, 35-6, 98; perhaps uniquely subject to Law of Contradiction, 58
Chappell, V., 174 n27
Charmides, topoi in, 2 nn3, 4
Cherniss, H., 22 n32, 127 n8, 128 n10
chôriston (separate, independent, self-subsistent), 34, 36, 138
Chrysippus, 153-4
classification, and categories, Ch. 1 *passim*; and definition by genus and differentia, 68-9
Cohen, M., 177 n32
colour, change of, 161, 164, 169-73
common, nature, 39; elements, 48, 68, 74; principles or axioms, 15 n8, 22-4, 104; notions, 6, 22; opinions, 36-7; universals, 100
conceivability, 125, 132-7
concepts, of science, 132; vague, 159, 177; and form, 86-7; and intuition, 106-7; contrasted with definitions, 64-5, 73; negative, 22

conjunction, and formulation of Law of Contradiction, 54, 56, 60; and concept of possibility, 122-3

consciousness, and Law of Contradiction, 51-3

constructions, in geometry, 104, 129-30, 134; in mechanics, 142; and mathematical intuitionism, 96

contingent, 111-12, 116, 119, 123

continuous, continuum, 146, 154, 156-8, Ch. 12 *passim*

contradiction, eristic abolition of, 5; Law of, 22 n32, Ch. 4 *passim*, 165; and instant of change, 159, 165-6, 170, 172

contrariety, and categories, 3; knowledge of, 23, 24 n36; Law of Contradiction, 52-3, 58; and motion/rest at an instant, 165-6; Pythagorean scheme, 7

Coriscus, 8 n15

Cornford, F.M., 151 n27, 152 n28

Couturat, L., 60 n11

Cratylus, and disentanglement of word and meaning, 7

Cynics, 62

Cyprus, 27 n43

De Anima, on definition, 63 and nn2, 3, 72-3, 75; on soul, 20, 83 n8; on intellect, 40-1, 65 n8; on thinking, 133; on imagination, 106; on goals, 85 nn13, 14

De Caelo, modal notions, 112; on infinity, 130

De Generatione et Corruptione, on growth, 94-5; on the eternal, 112; on cyclical recurrence, 114

De Ideis, on Ideas of (i) negative concepts, 22; (ii) relatives, 28-30

De Interpretatione, on statement, 51; and contrariety, 52-3; and modality, 108, 111-12, 114-15

De Memoria, on thinking, 136

de Morgan, A., 50

De Sensu, on change of colour, 169-70; on instant of change, 176-7

Dedekind, J.W.R., 61 n14

definition, 4-6, 11, Ch. 5 *passim*; principle of science, 133; in

physics and mathematics, 98; priority in, 19, 27, 157; definition and 'focal meaning', 17-18, 21, 25, 31-2; and substance, 81, 92-4; formal and material elements in, 104; Aristotelian vs. Euclidean, 130; of predicates, 26, 29-30; of synonymy, homonymy, paronymy, 40; of analogy, 49; of truth and falsehood, 54, 60-1; of soul, 20; of living creature, 40; of motion/rest at an instant, 165-7, 174-5

demonstration, 70 and n25, 73-8, 109; *see* proof

Descartes, R., 60, 72

development, of Aristotle's logic, Chs. 1 and 2 *passim*; of his metaphysics, Chs. 2 and 3 *passim*; of his ethics, 14-19, 47-8; of his conception of mathematics, 102 n12

dia ti (why?), 42, 69, 78 and n50

diagramma (construction, theorem), 134 and n23

diairesis (division), 72 and n34, 129

dialectic, Ch. 1 *passim*; contrast with philosophy, 15-16, 22; and with science, 22, 78; concerned with common ideas, 22-3; A.'s methods of definition dialectical, 76; Platonic conception of, 23-4

dichôs (two-fold), 122; *see dittôs*

differentia, 5-6, 67, 68-71, 74

Diodorus, 115, 164, 169

Dirlmeier, F., 28 n49

discursive reason, 64-6

distance, Ch. 11 *passim*

dittôs (two-fold), 27; *see dichôs*

division (*diairesis*), Platonic, 3, 67, 72 n34, 74; geometrical, 134-5, 138-9, 141; infinite, 145-6, 147 n19; temporal, 141, 157

doxa (belief), 15 n8, 51-2 (cf. 68 n22)

Dummett, M.A.E., 148

echein (possess), 10-11

eidos (form), 41-2, 45, 48

einai (be, exist), 14 n3, 51, 71, 77-8, 92

Eleatic logic, 5, 14; *see* Parmenides

elements, of being, 25, 33, 43; of definition, 65, 67-8, 74; Euclid's,

50; physical, 102; chemical, 89; of space, 107; of time, 152, 154-5
elenchos (negative proof), 55-7
Elias, 102 n13
en (in), 144 (cf. 142-3)
enantion (opposite, contrary), 52, 169
ends, 84-5; *see* means
energeia (activity, actuality), 48, 143 n6, 165, 170 n19
Epictetus, 115
Epicurus, 164, 169
epistêmê (knowledge, science), 16 n12, 33, 73
epistemology, and mathematics, Ch. 8 *passim*; and science, 132; and time, 155; epistemological priority, 157
êrtêtai (depends), 44-5
essence, 42, 56, 58, Chs. 5 and 6 *passim*, 92, 130; essential predication, 3, 55-6, 108-9; *see ti ên einai*
Ethica Eudemia, 'focal meaning' in, 13-19, 20 n24, 22, 24, 27, 29, 47-8; Socratic paradox, 133; arguments vs. Idea of Good, 1-2, 18-19
Ethica Nicomachea, later than *EE*, 14 n4, 15-16, 47-8; arguments vs. Idea of Good, 1-2, 18-19; hierarchy of goods, 18; senses of 'good', 15-16, 25 n38; on friendship, 27, 28 n49, 47-8
Euclid, 5, 50, 104 and n15, 113, 129-30
Eudemus, 2
Euthydemus, eristic character of, 5, 9
Evagoras, Evagorids, 27 n43
Evans, M.G., 126, 128 n10
events, and definition, 67, 69, 71, 75
evidence, of Law of Contradiction, 60; and intuition, 106
examples, in Aristotle's logic, 7-12, 109-10; of definition, 70; of substance, 91, 96
existence, and definition and demonstration, 69 and n23, 73, 76-8; and elements of science, 104-5; existential import, 118; full-fledged, 131; its genesis from non-existence, 161, 164, 171-4; of

substance, Chs. 2 and 3 *passim*; of God, 116; of mathematical entities, Ch. 8 *passim*, 129-31, 134-5, 138; of the infinite, 114, Ch. 10 *passim*; of time, 146-7, 150, 152, 154-8
explanation, supplied by definition, 68-9; of *suntheton*, 93; and priority, 157; *see* cause, principle
extension, 102-7, 127-31, 141

false (*pseudês*), *see* true
Festugière, A.J., 63 n1, 64 n6, 66, 75 n45
focal meaning, 15-17 and Ch. 2 *passim*; 38-49 (NB 49n); 140-1, 145 (and Ch. 11 *passim*); *see pros hen legesthai*
force, 142, 174-5
form (*eidos*), general theory of, 25, 44, Ch. 6 *passim*, 92-3, 94-5, 133-6; role in definition, 66-7, 69-71, 74-6, 92-3, 104; ontological status, 39, 138; form = shape, 88, 91; contained by matter, 10; mathematical, 35, 105; 'form of forms', 40-1; object of thought, 105, 133, 135-6
Form, Platonic, see *Idea*
Frege, G., 50, 61 n15
friendship (*philia*), 17-18, 26-7, 28 n49, 40, 47-8

Geach, P.T., 95 n24, 139 n28
generality, of first philosophy, 37-8; *see* universal
genus (*genos*), among elements of science, 104; object of first philosophy not a genus, 37-9; hypostatisation of, 76; and species, 3, 5; and differentia, 5; in definition, 65, 67, 68-71, 74; generic unity vs. analogy, 24 n36, 25 n39; candidate for substance, 80-1; connexion with privation, 52; and with matter and extension, 104, 107
geometry, 37 and n8, 50, 61, 93, Ch. 8 *passim*, 128-31, 134-5
Gercke, A., 1

Gilson, E., 116 nn14, 15
gnôsis (knowledge), 31 n54, 138
God, subject of first philosophy, 13, 35, 38, 42-5; proof of existence, 116; place in ethical hierarchy, 15 n7
Gödel, K., 96
good, Idea of, 1, 19, 45; ambiguity of 'good', 14-19, 20, 22, 27; deparonymisation of, 47; comparison of goods, 28 n48
Goodman, N., 150 n24
grammar, and categories, 5, 7; and paronymy, 21, 41; of verbs of motion, 142-5
Grelling, K., and Nelson, L., 61 n15
Grote, G., 26, 27 n41
Grünbaum, A., 160 n4

Hager, F.-P., 49 n
Hambruch, E., 14 n2
Hamelin, O., 63 n1, 64, 71, 73, 77
'healthy' (*hugieinon*), 17 n16, 20 n24, 31, 39, 145
Heath, T.L., 104 n15, 128 n10, 130, 134 n23
Hegel, G.W.F., 53 n5, 60
Heinze, M., 43
hen (one), 8, 15 n7; *see pros hen legesthai*
heneka (for the sake of), 27 and n42
Heraclitus, 14 n4, 62 (cf. 5)
'here', 148-9
Heron, 130
hexis (possession), 10
Heyting, A., 96
Hintikka, J., 38 n9, 136 n25, 142, 150, 156 n33
Hobbes, T., 116 n18
homonymy (*homônumia*), criteria of, 14, 40; relation to *pollachôs legomenon*, 15 n5; standard illustrations, 30; in proof of Law of Contradiction, 56; alternatives to (synonymy, paronymy), 20, 24, 26, 30, 38 n9, 39-40; *see* ambiguity
horismos (definition), 4, 65 n10
hoti esti ('*that* it is'), 73 n39, 78 n50
hulê (matter), 35, 47, 48, 89, 90
Husik, I., 59 n10
Husserl, E., 53 n4

Iamblichus, 27-8
Idea, general critiques of Platonic theory, 1, 19, 21, 26-32; not necessary nor sufficient for becoming, 81, 86; not necessary for proof, 101; rejected as essence, 82; separation of, 98, 99-100, 101, 105, 138
identity, principle of, 54; criteria of, 92; of form and essence, 81-2, 83-4, 86-7, 92; of generator and generated, 81, 83; and matter, 91, 94-5
idion (special), 15, 18 n17
imagination, image (*phantasia, phantasma*), 64 n5, 65 n8, 73, 105-6, 133-4, 135-6
implication, and categories, 3, 5; in *Topics*, 6; material, 117-18
impossible, Ch. 9 *passim*, 133 n21
incompatibility, and categories, 3; treatment in *Topics*, 6
independence, criterion of subject of first philosophy, 34-6; and of substance, 81-2, 131; denied to infinite, 126; *see* separation
indeterminacy, of sensible world, 58; of matter, 81
individual, substance, Ch. 6 and 7 *passim*, 131; not definable, 64-5, 70, 73, 92-3; and matter, 88, 90-5; production of, 133; 'names' of, 3; unity of, 3; Third Man, 26; mathematical entities individuals, 102-7; not subject of modal principles, 114-15; propositions about, 118; contrast with time and the infinite, 126, 131, 138
individuation, Ch. 7 *passim*
indivisibles, 153-4, 160, 169 nn17 and 18, 173, 176; *see* atom
induction, and psychological Law of Contradiction, 53; and definition, 73-4; and abstraction, 99
infinite, 114, Ch. 10 *passim*, 145-6, 160-2, 173
instant, 141-5, Ch. 12 *passim*; *see* moment
intellect (*nous*), active, 65 n8, 72, 73; active and passive, 105; *see* reason

intuition, contrasted with definition, 64-5, 72-4, 78-9; compared with concept, 106-7; spatial, 101, 105; mathematical intuitionism, 96
Isocrates, 27 n43

Jaeger, W., 8 n15, 13 n1, 16 n12, 25 n39, 26 n40, 27 nn41 and 43, 34, 36-7, 42-3, 49, 80, 102 n12
Joachim, H.H., 27 n41, 31 n53
Joseph, H.W.B., 88

Kahn, C.H., 99 n7, 107 n21
Kamp, H., 177 n31
Kant, I., 1, 7, 12, 34, 49, 90, 116
kath' hauto (*per se*), 3, 8, 14 n3, 18, 89-90, 126, 131, 169
katholou (universal), 22, 38
Kilmister, C., 177 n32
kinêsis (change, motion), 7, 143 n6, 165 n10
Kneale, M., 115 n9
Kneale, W., 117
knowledge, theory in *A.Pst.*, 65, 68 n21, 73 n39, 73-4, 76, 106; actual and potential, 113, 133; *see* epistemology, science
Kosman, L.A., 165 n11
Kretzmann, B., 159 n1
Kretzmann, N., 159 n1, 162 n6, 165 n9, 166, 177 n32
Kühn, C., 63 n1

Lachelier, J.N.E., 73
language, a quagmire, 54; limits of, 45; connexion with categories, 1; with logic, 4-6; with philosophy, 22 n32, 37
law, natural, 117-18; of contradiction, 22 n32, Ch. 4 *passim*, 165; of excluded middle, 23, 90, 108, 113, 165
Laws, logical distinctions in, 6; on 'possession', 10
Le Blond, J.M., 70 n26, 75 n45, 78 n50
Leibniz, G.W., 116
Léonard, J., 16 n12
Lévy, L.G., 116 n13
life, concept of, 20, 27-8, 40

Lloyd, G.E.R., 177 n32
Locke, J., 99 n6
logikon (dialectical), 15 n8, 22 n32, 131 (cf. 75 and n45)
logic, Chs. 1, 2, 4, 9 *passim*
logos (defining formula), 6, 19, 21, 31 and n54, 48, 65; (explanation), 93; (utterance), 51
Lovejoy, A.O., 125
Lukasiewicz, J., 88, 90-3, 110 n3, 124 n31
Lyceum, 2-3
Lycophron, 2
Lysis, and 'focal meaning', 26-7

Maier, H., 1, 5 n11, 11 n18, 52 n2, 55 n8, 58 n9, 59 n10
Maimonides, M., 116 n13
malista, mallon (most, more), 27-8, 39, 46
Mansion, A., 16 n10
Marcus Aurelius, 147, 158
Margueritte, H., 16 n12
Mates, B., 115 n7
mathematics, Ch. 8 *passim*; division of theoretical philosophy, 34-6; universal maths. and divisions of maths., 37 and n8; foundations of, 61; existence of math. entities, 134-5, 138, and Ch. 8; matter in maths., 89, 93, and Ch. 8; infinity, 127-31; Zeno's influence, 175
matter (*hulê*), Chs. 6 and 7 *passim*; contrasted with form, *ibid.*, 10, 25, 44, 132; deparonymisation, 47; connexion with definition, 66-7, 69-71, 74-6; and with change, 35, 43 n20; compared with the infinite, 132; hinders actualisation, 133; material cause, 117; intelligible matter, 93 (cf. 89), 100-7
means, 24-n36, 84-5
Mechanica, on circular motion, 142; on force, 144; 'Newtonian', 145
mechanics, 142, 145, 156, 159, 174-5
'medical', (*iatrikon*), 17, 20 n24, 31, 39, 48, 145
Medlin, B., 165-6
Megarians, 2, 60, 62, 177

Meinong, A., 4 n10, 51, 61 and n13
Meno, on definition, 5
metaphor, 20-1
method, Platonic, 3; dialectical, 145; of definition, 72-6; of focal meaning, 140-1; *see* dialectic, division, Socrates
Miller, F.D., 140 n1, 158 n35
modality, Ch. 9 *passim*
moment, 131, 136 n24, Ch. 11 *passim; see* instant
Moravcsik, J., 124 n31
more and less, in nature, 57; *topos* of, 3 n6, 28 nn48, 49
Moser, S., 33 n
motion (*kinêsis*), and categories, 7, 11; Hegel on, 53 n5; circular, 44-5, 142; infinity of, 135, 136 n24; relation to time, 140-6, 155-8; at a moment, 141-5, Ch. 12 *passim*

name, connexion with thing and essence, 4-6; with definition, 63-4, 69; proper, 7-9, 92; connotations of, 92; in definition of synonymy, homonymy, paronymy, 40 (cf. 48-9)
Natorp, P., 34-6, 37 n8, 43, 80
natural, substance, 35, 37, 42-4, 46, 48, 70-1, 75-6, 81-6; tendencies, 113; possibility and necessity, 117; priority, 19, 25, 27, 157
necessity, 55-6, 68, 72, 73 n39, 78-9, Ch. 9 *passim*, 136
negation, 54, 56, 60
Newton, I., 145, 175
Niebel, E., 134 n23
noêsis (thinking), 135, 136 n24
nous (intellect, reason), 41, 65, 85 n13
'now' (*nun*), 131, 141, 145-58
number, 'constructive', 61; infinite, 127, 135; individuation of, 93; matter of, 89

objective, 51-2, 61
Ockham, W., 113 n5, 116
Oehler, K., 44 n21
on (being, existent), 8, 13, 15, 17 and n16, 24, 28, 33, 39

one (*hen*), ambiguity of, 14; focal analysis, 18, 25 n39, 31
Onians, R.B., 115 n10, 116 n11
opposites, varieties of, 6; focal analysis of, 18; science of, 24 n36; *topoi* of, 3 n6; contrariety, 53; change, 90; necessity, 109
Organon, date, 14; employment of 'focal meaning', 19-24
ousia (essence, substance), 6, 17 n16, 19, 37 n7, 39, 40, 41, 42, 47, 48, 57, 64 n6, 71, 73, 80, 81, 82, 90, 131
Owen, G.E.L., 49 n, 145 n13, 175 and nn28 and 29
Owens, J., 21 n29, 31 n53, 33 n

Parmenides, 2, 5, 150
Parmenides, ambiguity of 'one', 14; on time, 151-3, 155; on instant of change, 159, 166
paronymy, 21, 38-49
part, relation to whole in first philosophy, 38-40; and in syllogistic, 45-6, 121, 124 n28; of *logos*, 65-72, 81; of infinite magnitude, 128; of time, 146-7, 153-4, 156; of coming into being, 168-9, 171
Parts of Animals, 63 n2
particular, properties, 101-2; reality and knowledge of, 106; geometrical objects, 107; *see* individual, substance, universal
Peano, G., 50
Peirce, C.S., 50
Penner, T.M., 143 n6, 144, 165 n11
period, of time, 126-7, 131, Ch. 11 *passim*, 161, 171 n20, 173, 175
Peter of Spain, 165
phantasia (imagination), 105-6
philia, philon (friendship, dear), 26-7, 47-8
Philippe, M.-D., 98 n4, 100 n9
Philoponus, J., 23, 77 n48, 99 n8, 100, 102, 127 n9
philosophy, divisions of, 34-6, 43; first, 2, 13-14, 16-18, 22, Ch. 3 *passim*
phusis (nature), 17, 19, 29, 37 n7, 44, 85 n13

physics, relation to other branches of philosophy, 34-6, 37 n8, 43-4, 46, 98, 100, 105, 131; 'focal meaning' in, 20; physical possibility, 132, 136; time, motion, the infinite, etc., Chs. 10-12 *passim*; Stoic, 153-4

Physics, on enquiry, 65 n12, 72 n33, 79; on definition, 63 n2; on mathematics and physics, 98, 100; on coming to be, 81, 83; on matter, 96; on nature, 113; on change, 89; on place, 68 n22; on the infinite, 114, Ch. 10 *passim*; on time and motion, Ch. 11 *passim*; on motion and the instant of change, Ch. 12 *passim*

place, 9, 11, 89, 90-1, 93, 141, 143, 153

Plato, *see* entries for individual dialogues; Ideas, Platonism

Platonism, and the development of Aristotle's logic and metaphysics, Chs. 1 and 2 *passim*, 36, 43; in mathematics, 96-7, 98-9, 105

plentitude, principle of, 125, Chs. 9 and 10 *passim*

Plutarch, 153

Pnytagoras, 27 n43

point, Aristotle's conception, 103, 104; modern view, 107; Chs. 11 and 12 *passim*

Politicus, on division, 3; on time, 148

pollachôs legomenon, pleonachôs legomenon ('said in many ways'), 15 n5, 122, 136; *see* ambiguity

Popper, K.R., 94 n19

position, category of, 9, 11, 12 (cf. 14); and concept of motion, 160-4, 167

possession, category of, 9-12

possibility, Chs. 9 and 10 *passim*, 142; and Law of Contradiction, 62

Poste, E., 22 n30

postulates, Euclidean, 104, 128-30

potentiality (*dunamis*), posterior to actuality, 27, 112-13, 134; unactualized, 114-15; understood by analogy, 48; indeterminate, 58; relation to categories, 1; to definition, 67-8; to Law of

Contradiction, 58; to contingency, 112; to knowledge, 106 n8, 113; to matter, 92, 105, 132; to the infinite, Ch. 10 *passim*

Prächter, K., 43

pragma (thing), 4, 6, 11, 64 n6

Prantl, C., 144 n8

predicables, 3-5, 12

predication, theory of, Ch. 1 *passim*, 21, 26-32; and matter, 88, 90

present, 140-1, 146-58

primary, sense of words, 16-19, 22 n32, 27, 31 n54, 40, 140-1, 145-8; subject, 81-2, 88, 99; prime matter, 92, 102, 105; *see* priority, *prôton*

prime mover, 37 and n8, 42-5, 96

principles (*archai*), of science, 22, 33, 104; and focal meaning, 39, 42-6; knowledge of, 65; definitions included among, 72, 73, 74, 77, 132; of modality, Chs. 9 and 10 *passim*; of logic, Ch. 4 *passim*; principle of individuation, Ch. 7 *passim*; form and matter principles, 81, 83, 84, 87; *see* axiom, elements

Prior, A.N., 113 and n5, 115, 117

priority, varieties distinguished, 18-19, 31 n54, 45 n23, 156-7; natural, 21, 24, 25; logical, 20, 27-9; of first philosophy, 38; of knowledge of principles, 65 n9; of whole to part, 67; of actuality to potentiality, 27, 112-13, 134; of spatial to temporal order, 146, 154-8

privation, 6, 25, 52, 90-1

Proclus, 105-6, 130

production, 81-6, 113, 133-4

proof, and explanation, 70 and n25; and universals, 101; and the infinite, 128, 139; in geometry, 128, 130, 134; none of axioms, 23-4, 54-62; *see* demonstration, *reductio*

properties, and mathematical objects, Ch. 8 *passim*; in definition of Law of Contradiction, 51-2

proposition, 1-6, 109-10, 116-18

pros hen legomenon ('said in relation to one thing'), 15 n7, 16 n9, 17, 19 n19, 20, 22 n32, 25, 31, 38, 40,

49n; *see* focal meaning
pros ti (relative), 18, 29
Protagoras, 62
proteron (prior), 19, 27, 46
prôton (primary), 26, 33, 38, 39, 45, 46 (cf. 48-9)
Protrepticus, date, 27 n43; its Platonism, 13; 'focal meaning' in, 27-8; on law, 21 n27
pseudo-Alexander, 22, 100 n11, 103-4
psychology, and Law of Contradiction, 51-4, 60; and 'focal meaning', 20; and time, 155-6; in *Lysis*, 27
Pythagoreans, 7

quality, category of, 6, 9, 10, 11
quantity, category of, 9, 11, 21, 102-3, 135
quiddity, *see* essence, *ti en einai*

Rassow, H., 63 n1
realism, in Aristotle's early logic, 4-6; Platonic, 76
reason (*nous*), 40-1; (*aition*), 69-70, 78; *see* intellect, explanation
reductio, proofs, 55-7, 119-20, 130
Reidemeister, K., 34 n3
Reiner, H., 47 n27
relatives (*pros ti*), Academic category, 18; Ideas of, 28-30; varieties of, 2; and opposites, 6; and questions, 11
Republic, attacked in *A.Pst.*, 23; style of Books 6 and 7, 45; on divided line, 105; on relatives, 2 n4; on contraries, 24 n36; on pleasure, 28 n47; on time, 116 n12
rest, and categories, 11; verbs of, 141; at a moment, 141-5, Ch. 12 *passim*
rhetoric, and dialectic, 4, 21-2
Robin, L., 20, 63 n1, 70 n26, 75 n45
Rodier, G., 25 n37
Roland Gosselin, M.S., 63 nn1 and 3, 76
Ross, W.D., 10 n16, 21 n29, 23, 26 n40, 31 nn54 and 55, 38 n9, 44, 47, 80, 81, 83 n9, 84, 86, 87 n18, 92, 102 n12, 104, 120, 122, 124 nn28 and 30, 125 n3, 127 n9, 128 n10, 132,

138-9, 141 n3, 146 n15, 154 n31
Russell, B., 50, 61 and nn13 and 15, 116, 175

Salamis, 27 n43
Sambursky, S., 153-4
Savigny, E. von, 49 n
Sceptics, 147
Schaecher, E.J., 14 n4
Schneeberger, G., 116 n18
Schofield, M., 177 n32
Schoolmen, 113 (cf. 88, 116)
Schopenhauer, A., 36
Schröder, E., 50
science, universal vs. special, Chs. 2 and 3 *passim*; and definition, Ch. 5 *passim*; and dialectic, 22; and logic, Ch. 1 *passim*; and tenses, 150; and motion at an instant, 163, 175; *see* elements, geometry, mathematics, mechanics, physics, principles, psychology, zoology
sense perception, 64, 65 n8, 68, 72, 169-70, 176-7; *see* substance
separation, of mathematical objects, Ch. 8 *passim*, 138 n26; of the infinite, 138-9; of object of first philosophy, 34-6; form and substance not separable, 85-6, 87, 90; but in another sense separability a criterion of substance, 81-2, 90, 131; *see* independence
Sextus Empiricus, 164, 169 n18
Shorey, P., 26 n40
Sigwart, C., 54 nn6 and 7, 60
Simplicius, 18 n18, 100 n11, 105 n16, 156 n34, 164 n8
Smith, J.A., 82 n5
Socratic, method, 4 n9, 5, 7, 19-20, 74 n41; definition, 67, 74 n41; induction, 74 n41; paradox, 133; treatment of contraries, 24 n36; thought in Academy, 1-2
Solmsen, F., 127 n8, 139 n28
Sophist, and Aristotle's logic, Ch. 1 *passim*; and ambiguity of 'being', 14; on division, 72 n34, 74
Sophistici Elenchi, 5, 8, 14, 22
Sorabji, R.R.K., 139 n28

soul, definition of, 20, 25 n37, 83 n8; and essence of man, 48, 70, 75 and n45, 92-3

space, continuity of, 159 n2, 164, 169; relation to time, 140, 147 n16, 148-50, 154-8, 159 n2

Specht, E.K., 38 n9

special, sciences; *see* universal

species, and genus, 3, 5, 74; and definition, 30, 74, 92-4; existence of, 64 n5; hypostatisation of, 76; and natural generation, 86 (cf. 81), 113; modal principles applicable to, 114-15

Speusippus, 14, 19 n19

Stevenson, J., 107 n21

Stewart, J.A., 28 n49

Stoics, 153-4

Strang, C., 152 n29, 167 n15, 177 n32

stuff, 88-91, 107

Stumpf, K., 51

subject (*hupokeimenon*), 3, 4, 5 n11, 6, 8, 80-1, 88, 90-1

substance (*ousia*), focus of being and object of first philosophy, 16-19, 22 n32, 24-5, 37-8, 39-45; and definition, 65-8, 69-71, 75-6; primary and secondary, 21; *kath' hauto*, 14 n3, 131; as predicate, 3, 9; and analogy, 24-6, 48-9; and Law of Contradiction, 56-7, 58; changeless, 37-8, 43-4, 58; sensible, 36, 39, 40 n13, 43-4, 47, 58, Chs, 6-8 *passim*; natural, 37, 42-4, 70-1, 75-6, 85-6

substrate (*hupokeimenon*), 81-2, 85, 102, 104

suntheton (composite), 71 and n31; cf. 93

syllogism, origins of, 4, 13; not in *Topics*, 5, 15 n8; notation, 4; figures, 46; role in *reductio* and negative proof, 55-7; demonstrative, 73, 101, 107; modal, 118-24; assertoric vs. modal, 109-10; modal and temporal, 116; of essence, 66 n15, 67, 69 n24, 70 n25, 75, 78

Symposium, on contraries, 24 n36

synonymy, criteria of, 14, 40; distinguished from homynymy, paronymy, 20, 24, 26, 30, 38 n9; and being, 16, 18, 31; and Ideas, 21

Theaetetus, distinguishes acquisition and possession, 10

Themison, 27 n43

Themistius, 99 n8, 127 n9, 164 n8

theology, and first philosophy, 13-14, 17 n14, Ch. 3 *passim*

Theophrastus, 18 n17

thinking, A. 's analysis, 41, 133-6

'this' (*tode*), 8, 88, 90-1, 95; *see* individual

Thompson, M., 107 n21

ti (something), 14 n3, 42, 89, 90

ti en einai ('what it was to be', essence), 42, 80, 82, 92

ti esti ('what is it?', 'what it is'), 22 n32, 31 n54, 69 and n23, 71, 73, 78 n50

time, category of, 9, 11; A.'s general analysis, Ch. 11 *passim*; connexion with universality and necessity, Ch. 9 *passim*; existence of, 126-7; infinity of, 135, 136 n24; continuity of, 159-60, 164, 169

Tisias, 4 n8

tode ti ('this something', individual), 90, 131

Topics, Ch. 1 *passim*; on ambiguity, 15 n5, 20-1; on 'logical' and 'dialectical', 15 n8; date, 20

topos (place), 68 n22; (commonplace), 2, 3 n6

Trendelenburg, F.A., 7, 54 n6

Tricot, J., 22, 83 n9

truth, abolished by eristics, 5; in definitions of statement and of Law of Contradiction, Ch. 4 *passim*; and necessity, 108-10, 114, 115, 116; and natural law, 117

Tugendhat, E., 82 n5

Ueberweg, F., 43

unit, a genus, 104; the matter of number, 89, 101

unity, accidental, 3; numerical, 87; of

individual, 3; of definition, 66-8, 71, 75 n45

universal (*katholou*), concept of, 11, 29-30, 37 n6; knowledge of, 106-7; connexion with essence, 64; with definition, 70-1, 73; with science, 78-9; with substance, 80-1; with necessity, Ch. 9 *passim*; universal science, 16-18, 22-6, Ch. 3 *passim*; reasoning, 22-3; mathematics, 37 and n8; matter, 91, 93; mathematical properties, 100-1, 105

vagueness, 177
van den Bergh, S., 166 n13
velocity, 141-2, 145, 157, 162-3, 168, 170, 174-5
visibility, 161, 164-5, 176-7
void, 114

Wagner, H., 33 n
Waitz, T., 15 n8, 22-3
Wedberg, A., 134 n22
Wedin, V., 107 n21
'what?', 'what is it?', 5, 11, 42, 64 n4, 69; cf. 70
whole, *see* part
Wieland, W., 45 n23
Wilson, C., 159 n1
Wittgenstein, L., 140
Wolfson, H., 116 n13
Wright, C., 177 n31
Wright, G.H. von, 124 n31

Zabarella, 23
Zeller, E., 42 n17, 48 n31, 63 n1, 97 n3
Zeno of Elea, 141, 142-3, 144, 147 n19, 151, 154, 175
zoology, 40

SHL
WITHDRAWN

SHL
WITHDRAWN
LOWELL
UNIV.